'Sink all the shipping there'

Hath made the Hollanders an invisible eel
To swim the haven at Dunkirk, and
Sink all the shipping there...

It is an automa, runs under water
With a snug nose, and has a nimble tail
Made like an auger, with which tail she wriggles
Betwixt the costs of a ship, and sinks it straight.

—Ben Johnson, *The Staple of News,* 1630

'Sink *all* *the* shipping *there'*

THE WARTIME LOSS OF CANADA'S MERCHANT SHIPS AND FISHING SCHOONERS

Fraser M. McKee

Vanwell Publishing Limited

St. Catharines, Ontario

Vanwell Publishing acknowledges the financial support of the Government of Canada through the Book Publishing Industry Development Program for our publishing activities.

Cover and Interior Design: Renée Giguère

Front cover photo: Empress of Asia in CP colours, leaving Vancouver in peacetime. (Vancouver Maritime Museum)

Vanwell Publishing Limited
1 Northrup Crescent
P.O. Box 2131
St. Catharines, Ontario L2R 7S2
sales@vanwell.com
tel: 905-937-3100
fax: 905-937-1760
Printed in Canada

National Library of Canada Cataloguing in Publication

McKee, Fraser M., 1925-
    Sink all the shipping there : the wartime loss of Canada's merchant ships and fishing schooners / Fraser M. McKee.

Includes bibliographical references and index.
ISBN 1-55125-055-1

    1. Armed merchant ships--Canada--History--20th century.
2. World War, 1939-1945--Naval operations, Canadian. I. Title.

D779.C2M268 2004   940.54'5971   C2004-902539-2

Table of Contents

To all those merchant seamen and women who went down to the sea in ships between September 1939 and August 1945, voluntarily risking their lives, too often giving their lives for our benefit.

And to my grandchildren, Rosanna, Simon, Amy, Hana, Jamie, Ian, Sean and Madeleine, who should know of their efforts, as should all Canadians.

⚓

Foreword

Sink all the shipping there is a true story of a little known part of the war at sea. It is a story of brutality and heroism, of dedication and determination, of seamanship, death and survival.

Commander McKee's research is extremely thorough, and describes the events as experienced by the crews of the merchant ships, passenger ships and schooners that were sunk, as well as information on the U-boats and battleships involved and their commanding officers.

In 2000, fifty-five years after the end of the war, the Canadian government began paying compensation to the World War II survivors of the Canadian Merchant Marine. In many cases, this compensation is really paid to the survivors of the survivors, who would have been in their seventies and eighties when they received an average of about $9,500 each for gallant service for their country. These men were all volunteers, and most sailed on small ships that were not designed for service on the North Atlantic, and certainly not for defending themselves from a very efficient enemy.

Nearly all of Canada's ships were coal burners, and submarines could usually detect them from great distances by the plume of smoke on the horizon.

Sixty-seven Canadian merchant ships and schooners and about seven hundred seamen were lost due to enemy action by U-boats, aircraft, surface ships and mines. The survivors usually signed up again within a few weeks, and many became survivors or victims of multiple sinkings.

Commander McKee has gathered photographs of nearly all the ships involved, and of some of the crews. There were few uniforms, low pay, and no medals for merchant seamen; the captain's formal dress for going ashore was usually an old suit, and a fedora. The unlicensed seamen came from all parts of the country, but primarily from the Maritimes, and they suffered more casualties and received less recognition than any other group actively fighting the enemy. They were humble, brave men whose families in many small towns will appreciate the thoroughness with which Commander McKee has carried out his research. He has done a great service to these men and their families, by recording a very important part of Canada's maritime history.

John D. Leitch
Chairman
Upper Lakes Group Inc.

Preface

Now would I give a thousand furlongs of sea for
an acre of barren ground, long heath, brown furze,
any thing. The wills above be done! But I would
fain die a dry death.

— Gonzalo, in Shakespeare's *The Tempest*

This volume is the result of research conducted for *The Canadian Naval Chronicle*, my book with Captain Bob Darlington about the losses and the successes of the ships of the Royal Canadian Navy in the Second World War. That book included brief historical notes on the losses of forty-four Canadian-owned, registered and flagged merchant ships and also mentioned Newfoundland ships, fishing vessels, and foreign owned ships which operated under Canadian registration after their home countries were overrun by Germany. All were ships sunk or captured by enemy forces. It soon became obvious that those brief tales inadequately described the valour, and the suffering, of the merchant seamen who had sailed those ships.

There was so much more to the accounts that turned up in the course of our research that I felt it worth expanding on those often tragic, nearly always heroic, stories to give the Merchant Navy an additional and comprehensive book-length history which it richly deserved. Only in recent years, often spurred on solely by the merchant seamen themselves, have those active participants in the war at sea been able to achieve not only recognition but compensation for the risks they took, their injuries and the lives that were lost. One should mention specifically the late Gordon Olmstead who lead the way in that last battle, himself a survivor of the sinking of Anglo-Saxon Petroleum's British tanker *Agnita*.

The primary official sources used for these histories were Lloyd's Registers of Merchant Shipping and, where records existed, the British Trade Division Shipping Casualty Section's interviews with appropriate survivors —usually the master— referred to as SCS Interviews. Also the US Navy's counterpart survivor interview records (although many of these are transcript copies of Canadian and British naval interview notes, not first-person interviews) were supplied by Robert C. Fisher from the Washington Naval records. For the greatest help in obtaining and transcribing the British interviews I again thank Frank Redfern of Hampstead. In the files of the Department of National Defence's Directorate of History & Heritage in Ottawa

(D Hist) there are often, but not always, forms ID SA, the official *Reports of Submarine Attacks*, giving much detail obtained from survivors. But if there were no survivors, the ending is too frequently sketchy. Toward the war's end there are few survivor interviews. Their value in assessing how and where the U-boats operated, how they attacked and what their deck equipment looked like, as well as whether the master had managed to throw overboard his confidential books, was no longer as vital to Allied intelligence as it once had been. It really no longer mattered very much— a sorry commentary in itself.

In cases where ships were in convoy, or were stragglers or rompers (pressing on ahead of the others) from a convoy, it has been possible to consult the primary convoy records and the Report of Proceedings of each convoy and Escort Group at D Hist. Their files included a few relevant ships' histories, but even there, many records of particular convoys are now inexplicably and sadly missing, after some sixty years.

Secondary sources have also been the basis of many of these tales—very valuable books produced by previous writers, often themselves ex-merchant seamen. Each such book was carefully assessed as to accuracy. I owe, as do we all, a debt to these writers who have contributed hours of research into basic records—records in the German U-boat archives in Cuxhaven and Bonn, at Kew near London, in Washington, Ottawa and elsewhere.

This book is not an academic assessment of why the ships in these stories were sunk, nor of the impact of the sinkings on world events. The ships were sunk by the German *Kriegsmarine* (except in six of the sixty-seven cases) because they were carrying cargoes. The loss of any one of these ships individually had no huge effect on world events; no one ship's survival or loss changed the outcome of the battle. They were "but warriors for the working day." And these sixty-seven Canadian losses represented less than two percent of the total losses of all Allied ships to enemy action, some 4,786 vessels. We were a small Merchant Navy, but vital to the struggle, and our people did well—the builders, the agents, the stevedores, and the merchant seamen. It is important that their exposure to the ultimate danger be recorded.

This is the story of heroism and loss, of dedication and determination, of seamanship and survival. I have not felt it necessary to footnote exact sources and their level of reliability, except for the quoted sources at the end of each entry. Such little notes in the text are distracting and provide almost no useful information to the general reader, while interrupting his concentration. Much of the detail is personal recollections taken from secondary sources. The interviews are only as accurate as the recollections of the person interviewed and their transcription.

In the year 2002, sixty-two years after the first casualties, recognition and compensation for merchant seamen equal to the Navy's was at last being seriously addressed. In certain cases decisions are still sometimes at least questionable or unfair in providing these men and women with even some benefits. These merchant seamen were for most of the war no better paid than their naval counterparts, taking into account their salaries were fully taxed, they paid for their own uniforms or clothing; if they came ashore between trips, their salaries were reduced, and for most of them a vacation meant no pay at all. The final insult was when their ships were sunk: for most of them their pay stopped that day. It appears still to be inequitable.

It was most onerous to decide which of the ships that had served Canada and been lost to the enemy should be included as "Canadian" in these chapters. Those registered in actual Canadian ports were obvious, and their losses are described here. But what about another fifty or more that were owned in Canada by Canadian companies, even by the government, but were registered offshore, in Britain (such as all of the Fort class ships and most of the CPR's ships), Bermuda, Panama, or Nassau? What about ships like the N.M. Paterson Company's *Soreldoc*, transferred to US ownership and management for the duration and then lost? What about all the ships in which seamen lost their lives but which were not sunk, or were sunk only temporarily and were salvaged—CNSS's *Lady Nelson*; *Nipiwan Park*; Paterson's *Collingdoc*? And should we omit the Newfoundland ships lost, since that colony was not part of Canada during the war? What of many ships lost due to a marine accident at least partly caused by war conditions—*Greenhill Park, Silver Star Park*, Upper Lakes Shipping's *Watkins F. Nisbet* and Atlantic Transportation's *R.J. Cullen*? Or the several schooners run down at night by convoy ships?

In order to keep the book within reasonable size I have opted to exclude all non-Canadian-registered and flagged ships except those of Newfoundland (merely anticipating history by some five to seven years), and all non enemy-caused losses. Thus, I have included the stories of six ships that were originally foreign owned but were registered in Canada. Also, some of those excluded do appear more briefly as "other losses" in Chapter 18, and are summarized in Table 1. A few vessels, like *Collingdoc*, mined and then raised but never sailed again, and *Nipiwan Park*, only half lost, have crossed the selection boundary and are included. Another two normally included in lists of vessels lost to the enemy have been excluded—*Nereus* and *Proteus*, as it is evident their loss had nothing to do with enemy sabotage, as is usually recorded. In telling the ships' stories I have added a few brief comments on the companies that owned them originally and have grouped the ships by those companies. Others are in chapters with a common thread, where it exists. The index will locate the story of any particular ship.

Note: *While some of the photographs in this book are not of ideal quality, in many cases they represent the only known photograph of the ship. Shipping company records have largely been destroyed, and private sources may not be known to the researcher.*

Acknowledgements

No book such as this could be properly prepared without the help of many interested and knowledgeable people. While a large number of persons have been of valuable assistance and their contribution is here acknowledged, these following provided continuing and extensive help.

Doug Adams in Toronto (of the *Vancouver Island*); Fred Addis, recently of the Toronto Historical Board's The Pier Waterfront Museum (now sadly closed due to city financial stringencies); Michael A. Cooper, Merseyside, England; Charles Copelin, Hunt's Point, Nova Scotia (the Markland ships); Johanne Zwicker McKee, Halifax; Murray Manson, Toronto, Ron Beaupré of Port Elgin and Jay Bascom of Toronto for many photos; Eugene Onchulenko, Thunder Bay; Frank Redfern, Hampton, England for hours in the PRO at Kew and whose father was involved with one of the ships sunk (Chapter 15); Geoff Tozer of *Empress of Asia* and George Shaker of the *A.D. Huff*; Michael Whitby, D Hist; Captains Joe Prim of St. John's and Hubert Hall of Liverpool, Nova Scotia. I appreciate too translations from the Danish by Knut Jensen of Markdale. Notes provided by Father Peter van der Linden gave many clues to the fates of the ships. Rob Fisher of Ottawa kindly provided a very complete list and a wonderful box of files on these same vessels from his earlier researches, from which many additions and corrections were garnered.

Directors of several shipping and fishermen's museums provided leads and material from their holdings. Nearly all DEMS information came from or was assessed by Captain Max Reid of Ottawa, himself a DEMS gunner during the war, whose book *DEMS At War!* covers Canadian and British DEMS.

Photographs of merchant ships, unlike naval ships' photos, have proven very hard to locate in many cases. The web pages on the internet opened doors—in the US, in Denmark, Finland and elsewhere, through a dozen marine museums and in national libraries. As ever, I thank Ken Macpherson for the loan of U-boat photos, the first source one thinks of for warship illustrations. He has now passed all his photo files to the Naval and Military Museum of Alberta in Calgary, and I appreciate their help as well. That museum also holds the valuable John Burgess Collection of convoy records, also consulted.

The useful, often uniquely valuable, books consulted are cited at the end of each ship's story as well as in the bibliography. Without them as references the stories would be incomplete. Company histories in particular are noted—some privately published—which at least briefly mention their lost ships: Canadian National and Canadian Pacific Railways; Canada Steamship Lines; Imperial Oil; Bowaters Markland;

Park Steamship ships; N.M. Paterson and the Upper Lakes Group. It is unfortunate more of the companies did not do this.

It is a sad commentary on the preservation of our own Merchant Marine's history, that it proved far easier to determine the histories of the attacking U-boats and surface ships and the commanding officers of the German *Kriegsmarine* than of our ships. Detailed reference books on the whole U-boat arm are readily available, on every individual boat and commanding officer, on the formation and movement of U-boat Groups (the notorious Wolf Packs) and on the signals intelligence that passed back and forth. In the case of the Canadian merchantmen, it has been difficult to determine even who the master was on a ship's last voyage if he did not turn in a survivor report. And if the Merchant Navy veterans are having problems gaining their deserved recognition, it can be imagined how little is accorded to the fishermen and trading schooner crews, particularly those lost.

This book attempts to rectify that misrepresentation.

And finally the story owes much to the firm editorial hand of Angela Dobler at Vanwell, who greatly improved it throughout.

Fraser M. McKee
Markdale, Ontario
March 2004

A group of obviously happy merchant seamen survivors aboard the corvette HMCS *Arvida*. (NAC)

Introduction

Now when much time was spent, and sailing
was now dangerous... Paul admonished them,
and said unto them 'Sirs, I perceive that
this voyage will be with hurt and much damage,
not only of the lading and ship, but also of our lives.'

— Acts, Ch.27

Winston Churchill once noted that the only wartime battle that truly scared him was the Battle of the Atlantic. He considered, and others felt the same, that if that battle for the convoys to supply the United Kingdom (as a base for future operations to re-occupy western Europe) was ever lost to the German enemy, then all was lost. It could never be refought at another date or location. There could not be a partial retreat, or a fall-back position. Either the sea lanes were open to commerce, even at a risk, or they were closed.

The merchant sailors faced identical risks to those who manned the warships assigned to protect them; moreso in fact, for they were the enemy's target. The potential loss of those merchant ships and experienced crews, Allied and from countries overrun in Europe, was a major peril throughout the war, from September 1939 to August 1945.

Canada's contribution—whether directly through the Canadian Government Merchant Marine and the Canadian National Steamship Company or through Canadian-based private firms—was not a major factor in wartime Allied shipping. Britain, Norway, and later the USA contributed thousands of ships to the task; Canada a few hundred. But in those desperate days a dozen ships, or their lack, were absolutely crucial. Hence the demand from the very first days for Canada to contribute ships, even ships designed only for Great Lakes service. As well, the loss of the sixty-seven Canadian and Newfoundland registered ships in these stories, while a serious blow to cargo capacity at any time, only represented about two percent of all Allied ships lost during the war. The Alfred Holt Line of Britain (the Blue Funnel Line) alone lost fifty-two ships.

Every ship and cargo lost was a catastrophe on at least a minor scale. If an individual sailing in a trans-North Atlantic SC convoy made seven crossings a year (allowing for turn-around, repairs, loading and the trips themselves), a vessel lost in early 1941 (like the *A.D. Huff*) would result in thirty lost cargoes—more than half of one complete convoy. As well it meant lost seamen one third of the time, and even more vital, the loss of experienced masters, chief engineers, bosuns and firemen.

There have been a few first-person articles on wartime shipping losses in company newsletters, and perhaps a newspaper write-up at the time. This latter was rare because of censorship. And it has been pointed out that published stories of the horrors of torpedoings and burning tankers did nothing at the time for the morale of other merchant seamen nor the peace of mind of their families at home. Such stories were not encouraged. In a very few cases there are correspondence and interviews with survivors or their families. These all have helped to ensure accurate descriptions of the sinkings. Eight companies had arranged to print company histories with at least passing references to their ships' wartime services. But even these rarely give details, and in a few cases they contain some inaccuracies.

In other instances, there is almost no record of what happened in those last awful hours. Of the losses described, in seven cases there were no survivors to tell the tale. In most of these cases (particularly the trading and fishing schooners) the ships were travelling alone so there were not even other vessels as witnesses. In many cases the owner shipping companies have since disappeared, or like the CNSS and the ULS Group, have given up their wartime records. Often these companies were not in fact actively managing the ships during the war, but had turned them over, on a "bare boat" or time charter to the Canadian Government Merchant Marine or the British Government's Wartime Shipping Authority (under various titles). These government organizations then assigned the ships to "managers" to operate and sometimes man them and to account for their movements. But the parent companies still owned the ships, they were still "Canadian." In addition to these gaps in the record, company archives now have a low priority in business plans and many firms, even the Canadian government's merchant marine section, have cut back severely on such historical record keeping and accessibility.

But there is enough in these pages to give the flavour of what it was like to sail into submarine-infested waters, or those dominated by well armed enemy aircraft— whether this was in convoy, sometimes ill-protected, or alone. Some of these ships sailed alone across thousands of miles of the dangerous Atlantic and Indian Oceans, without any naval escort, often at speeds as slow as 5 knots. Some were unarmed ships designed only for ploughing the Great Lakes, several without even a radio, some over thirty years old. Others were fishing schooners under sail. Even so, the companies and their sailors answered the call to service. Many had no armament to combat a U-boat even if it surfaced; certainly none of the fishing schooners had any protective weaponry when approached by a surfaced U-boat.

THE MEN AND WOMEN

Many Canadian men and women who served in wartime merchant ships did not serve in Canadian ships. They would be arbitrarily assigned, if signed on in a Merchant

An elderly unidentified merchantman at sea on a singularly calm North Atlantic day. Note her First World War vintage 3-inch gun right aft, but AA Oerlikons on bandstands aft of the funnel. (Lawrence Gale)

Seamen Pool, or would volunteer for service in any ships passing through their port. Usually they tried to serve in the British, Canadian or Commonwealth ships of the Merchant Navy, a term made popular by King George VI when he adopted the phrase "My Merchant Navy." Those ships sunk while operating under the Canadian flag are included here.

Other seamen and women served in "Canadian" ships that flew the British Red Ensign—such as Canadian Pacific's *Empress of Britain*, *Beaverburn* and two dozen others—or showed flags of convenience, usually Panamanian or Bahamian, such as did many of the Imperial Oil tankers assigned to them by the Canadian Government Merchant Marine. Some of these too were lost, such as Imperial Oil's *James McGee*. Those wider ranging stories can be found in several recent excellent books on the broader concept of the merchant navies worldwide, such as Bob Halford's *The Unknown Navy*; Mike Parker's first person stories in *Running The Gauntlet*; and Robert Parson's book on the schooners, *Lost At Sea*. But they did not tell of all the losses to truly Canadian ships.

Women were not accepted as crew in any Canadian ships in those days, although passenger ships such as the CNSS's *Lady Drake* and *Lady Hawkins* and the Newfoundland ferry *Caribou* did carry women as stewardesses, galley staff and as nurses. Foreign-owned ships were more broad-minded, and in particular Norwegian ships carried quite a few Canadian women as wireless officers and operators. One of these valiant ladies made over ninety crossings of the Atlantic, and survived to marry a Norwegian captain.

Manning practices were varied. A few companies such as Imperial Oil tried to retain their own crews who were familiar with the technical nature of their tankers' operation. Some, such as the CNSS's Lady boats and to some extent Markland Shipping, and Dominion Steel and Coal were essentially continuing in their peacetime roles, so many of their own crews remained aboard. Of course the fishing schooners' crews were all hired on by the owners or even the skippers, usually from their home ports or nearby. Even replacements aboard these schooners, for those who were injured or went off to war, were located through local contacts.

Most ships were requisitioned by either the Canadian or British governments on a bareboat charter basis. This implies a forced requisitioning, which was rarely the fact. Mr. N.M. Paterson volunteered his ships in a telegram to the Prime Minister, Mackenzie King. Other companies were happy to have long-term contracts offered for ships under-used because of the Depression. Thus the ship would be turned over to the government in a designated port, without crew or supplies, but in normal sea-going condition. It was then the responsibility of the new managers and agents to crew the ship—officers, seamen, engine room and mess personnel drawn from officers' lists or the Manning Pools (established in 1940-41) in various ports. Often seamen would remain with an assigned ship for voyage after voyage—or until she was sunk. But crews "signed on articles" for one voyage only, with the option to re-sign for the next one. Usually this involved the return trip as well, but not in all cases, and in particular not in foreign-owned ships. All too often crew members of such ships found themselves in a distant port, laid off at a voyage's end, and with no guarantee of any ship to return them to Canada. It was a somewhat arbitrary and imperfect system, often not fair or even to the benefit of the sailors. But it was a wartime emergency arrangement that tended to assure that no ship missed its convoy for lack of crew.

If a ship was laid up due to breakdown or damage, her seamen, firemen and other crew could be returned again to the Manning Pool for reassignment. While service in the merchant marine was in theory voluntary, and personnel were laid off from time to time, if they refused service in more than two ships, they then became subject to conscription into the Armed Services or for other "required" services. And yet if men volunteered to transfer to the Navy, it was not unknown for them to be declared too valuable to be released from their seamen's occupation. Only rarely did these brave men and women refuse to sail however, even in the oldest, most ill-equipped and ill-provisioned local or foreign ships. They might abandon their ship at a distant port on occasion for very legitimate reasons, but sail again and again they all did. The seamen provided all their own clothing and toiletries and their own kit bags; they received no leave rail passes or free postage. The only "uniform" many wore was a small lapel pin with the letters MN within a rope circlet and surmounted by the marine rostral crown. There is a curious anomaly in the independent-mindedness of these men and women who voluntarily sailed into the face of very real danger which kept them from signing on with the more autocratic Navy that would have run their lives thereafter. They benefited very little in comparison to those in the Navy, despite the popular assumption they were much better off. They were not. Even today, fifty years and more after their services, the surviving members are only now acquiring a few of the perks and benefits accorded the Navy veterans.

As Canadian yards began turning out ships in 1942, Merchant Seamen schools were set up near Halifax and on the west coast, as well as a school for engine room hands in Prescott, Ontario. Radio operators, already trained, were drawn from the Marconi and other companies, from the "ham radio" world and the broadcasting industry, and appointed directly into merchantmen. New ships' cooks were given their initial experience by cooking in the Manning Pools, then sent off to sea as "trained."

The ultimate irony in these tales is the merchant service custom of stopping all pay and allowances from the day a ship was sunk. You might be trying to survive in a crowded, partly flooded lifeboat, even on a raft, in winter in the North Atlantic, but you got no pay for that! A few companies whose own crews still manned their ships continued to pay them after a sinking for at least a month or so. Imperial Oil was one, CN another in part. But this was not required, and this custom of pay stoppage applied to officers as well as seamen.

Ships' officers came under similar regulations, and the managers or agents were responsible for drawing captains, mates and engineers from comparable pools of qualified personnel. And if shortages or illnesses occurred at distant ports, the master was authorised to hire and even train replacements or additions locally, or promote seamen such as bosuns to be acting mates. In fact it was a growing awareness in the first year of the war that the loss of masters, mates and chief engineers when ships were sunk, was felt more than the loss of the ships themselves, which lead to more attention being focussed on survival and rescue techniques and equipment.

CASUALTIES

The lists of casualties following each ship's story in this book are not assuredly complete in all cases. The names were initially obtained via the Internet from two sources: first, from the Veterans Affairs Canada listing in the Merchant Navy's *Book of Remembrance* housed in the Peace Tower in Ottawa. It is the only more-or-less complete listing of those Canadians that gave their lives while serving in merchant ships worldwide. The book includes the names of those Canadians lost while serving in non-Canadian ships, or who died of illness and accident, as well as those lost in enemy-caused sinkings. In some cases names are recorded of non-Canadian citizens who served and were lost in Canadian ships, such as some from the West Indies and British Guyana. These seamen would be recruited by the master to round out his crew when shortages occurred (quite often for the engine room stoke-hold, for shovelling and trimming coal). The names have been shown here in the presumption that the persons all used their first given names, which may not have been true.

This listing was then cross-matched to a publication of the Commonwealth War Graves Commission which lists all the names of those Canadian merchant seamen and women who died but have no known grave but the sea (which was the norm in the merchant service). They are also listed on the Sailors Memorial in Point Pleasant Park in Halifax. It is sad to note that, in a few cases, more than one member of a family in a ship gave his life when she was sunk, a terrible blow for those at home. It was not unusual for a father or a brother to arrange for another family member to join him aboard his ship. But there was a price paid by a few families for that companionship.

Some spelling as well is in conflict between sources. I have elected to presume that the Ottawa *Book of Remembrance* is the correct one, although there is at least one known error, corrected in the ship's story, and some ships' names are misspelled. This is being corrected as a result of this book's research. The Commonwealth War Graves Commission list was also checked with its website when possible, and against the names listed for the British Merchant Navy on its impressive Memorial at Tower Hill, London.

Although the bodies of most merchant seamen were not recovered, those who were, or men who died after being plucked from the ocean by their rescuers were brought ashore, in these cases their names may have been omitted from both the *Book of Remembrance* and the Halifax Memorial, for their names are recorded on their own cemetery records. These men are deserving of listing as much as their "no known grave" counterparts, but one or two may have been missed.

Also as the Bennetts point out in their very valuable recent book *Survivors*, it is almost impossible to ensure accuracy in such lists since sometimes seamen carried as passengers in a torpedoed ship became listed with the crew, as did naval DEMS gunners and convoy signalmen. Wireless officers, many of whom were employees of Marconi Wireless, might or might not be included as crew. Last minute changes in crew manning could be missed after lists were sent ashore or lost or mistyped. If a lost seaman had no relatives to advise authorities he was at least missing, his name could be omitted for all these reasons. One hopes that over the years the lists will be updated to include every seaman who gave his or her life in the cause.

DEFENSIVELY EQUIPPED MERCHANT SHIPS; DEMS

A word is necessary about the ships, and also the men noted as "DEMS." This was, at first, a group of Canadian and Royal Navy seamen gunners assigned to man the guns and other offensive and defensive equipment soon fitted aboard almost all merchant ships of any reasonable size. The ships, and thus the group and the seamen were called Defensively Equipped Merchant Ships—thus "DEMS gunners" in

RN and RCN parlance. Later in some cases convoy signalmen and wireless telegraphists were included as well as gunners within the DEMS organization. Although the gunners were always the larger number, by the war's end there were noted in Canadian records five chief yeomen of signals, seven yeomen, seventy-one leading and ordinary signalmen, and six convoy telegraphists. These latter almost always served in the convoy commodore's or vice-commodore's ships. In the American Forces these men were called the Armed Guard, and their ranks included coxswains and boatswains, occasionally pharmacists and radar operators.

In ships operating out of Britain, many of the gunners were supplied by the Royal Marines, and by the Maritime Regiments, Royal Artillery; that is, Army Gunners. But in the ships sunk and where DEMS personnel were also lost, it has often not been possible to identify all of them by name, a sad omission. For the RCNVR gunners and signalmen, presumably their names are included in the military *Books of Remembrance* in Ottawa. But there they are not identified by ship. And, correctly, these naval and army personnel are usually not included in the Merchant Navy *Book of Remembrance*. In naval parlance, "they slipped between the floorboards."

This may not be entirely accurate, for the DEMS gunners and Sigs were signed on the ship's articles as "deckhands," so if the ship was sunk and lives were lost, their names may possibly appear in the lists. But record-keeping of DEMS was very difficult and sporadic. It depended on the men getting back to their bases and reporting what changes had taken place in their assignments. It was not uncommon for DEMS gunners to be moved to another ship in a foreign port because their original ship was in for extended repairs, or was sailing into a less dangerous area, and a replacement gunner was suddenly needed in another ship. That ship, or even the initial assignment, might also be to a foreign ship—Polish, French, or Norwegian, for example. Also if the original ship was to be in port for a time, a gunner could be assigned to another for a brief coasting voyage (sometimes even carrying with him his stripped Lewis machine gun!). No records whatsoever were kept of these supplementary trips. And the senior DEMS rating in a ship in the earlier days was usually at the most a leading seaman, a lance bombardier or a corporal Royal Marines, not trained or even very interested in careful record-keeping as long as his pay turned up periodically and he received his "three squares" a day.

In those early days the DEMS system was largely controlled by the Royal Navy, because Canada had very few ships and no spare trained seamen gunners. The Royal Navy, through the British Ministry of War Shipping, provided thousands of DEMS gunners and signalmen, some "borrowed" from the RCN. In the ships themselves, the DEMS gunners only provided a core of semi-trained gun crews. The loaders, ammunition passers and extra men required were made up from the merchant seamen aboard, including cooks, stewards, and sailmakers. For those men there was even a gunnery course they could attend, in Halifax on the Canadian side, if there was time and they could be spared while their ship was loading or awaiting convoy.

In the beginning possibly only one naval gunner was provided; as the number of weapons proliferated and the trained gunners became available there could be as many as fifteen or more aboard a single ship, sometimes mixed Navy, Royal Marine and Army gunners. Then gun crews were made up more of naval, or at least military personnel, than of merchant seamen.

Some of the early DEMS gunners returned to the Navy. But later in the war (around 1943 in Canada), DEMS gunners were specifically trained in that Branch and remained as DEMS gunners throughout the war—about 1,600 in all in the RCN. The weapons they manned varied from hand-held .303 Lewis or Hotchkiss machine guns of First World War vintage to modern 20mm Oerlikons firing drums of exploding 1-inch shells, and from pre-First War lever-action 4-inch guns to more modern, quick-firing 3-inch anti-aircraft guns. Thrown in were "pillar boxes" and PACs (Parachute and Cable), "Rube Goldberg" devices to keep attacking aircraft at bay. The PAC had hundreds of yards of wire supported from a parachute carried aloft by a rocket. These latter were cordially disliked by Atlantic seamen as being both ineffective unless carefully timed and tending to bring down in a welter of wire all the merchantman's radio aerials. Around the British coast they were considerably more valuable against the German aircraft.

All of this hardware was not of much use if a U-boat fired its torpedoes when submerged or unseen in the dark; but some armament gave heart to the merchant seamen and allowed for striking back in the odd case, particularly if the ship was under aircraft attack. There are several tales of aggressively handled merchant ships driving off U-boats (although not in this book), even attempting to ram them, when the U-boat CO felt he could not risk damage so far from any friendly base. No merchant ships were fitted with asdic anti-submarine detecting equipment or depth charges largely due to their slow speeds. Depth charge dropping required a speed of at least 12 or 13 knots, well beyond most merchantmen's capability.

An interesting view of *Empress of Asia* in her First World War camouflage, a design suggested by the marine artist Sir Norman Wilkinson.
(CFB Esquimalt)

THE MERCHANT SHIPS

Merchant ships come in a staggering range of sizes, speeds, ages, and styles. There are whole books on the subject of types alone. The stories in these pages range from one of a large passenger liner (the *Empress of Asia*) of 16,909 gross register tons and four decks down to little lakers and canallers of only 1,700 tons, little larger than the U-boats attacking them. The average tramp steamer ocean freighter of 1940 was of about 5,100 grt, or gross registered tons (White, *U-Boat Tankers 1941-45*), had a normal service speed of between 8 and 12 knots at the most, less if she had been out of drydock for a year. The lakers could make little over 6 or 7 knots. These ships often carried only one radio operator who could not keep watch throughout the twenty-four hours, and had no secret code books capable of transcribing U-boat warning messages normally sent out to convoy Commodores and escorting forces. A few of the lakers had no radio at all. None of the ships had radar, almost none had D/F, (direction finding equipment). Most were driven by relatively simple, usually coal-fired, steam triple-expansion engines (even the large *Empress of Asia*), although the Imperial Oil's tankers and a few larger ships had diesel engines. But if the engines stopped or the engine room was flooded, then there was no electricity for interior lighting, for operating equipment such as radios or electric winches for boats.

All ships were provided with theoretically adequate lifeboats and lifejackets for their crews, and most with emergency liferafts. This lifesaving equipment improved in both quality and practicality as the examples of war sinkings were absorbed. However, if a ship was torpedoed, the lifeboats and their launching equipment were often damaged, and if she rolled toward one side as she sank, the boats on the high side could usually not be launched, and the ones on the low side were sometimes smashed or swamped. If the boats did reach the water and remained upright with whatever crew managed to clamber into them, the survivors often had only the most elementary ability to sail these large steel boats unless an experienced deck officer or the bosun was among their numbers. At anything from a hundred to a thousand miles from the nearest land navigation became a critical factor as well, dependant again on experience, even with a sextant and compass. The case of Chief Officer Percy Kelly of the *Lady Hawkins* and later *Lady Drake* makes this point all too clearly. G.H. and R. Bennett's book *Survivors* is an excellent description of how to survive a sinking and how this was improved throughout the war. It is heartening to record that the Ministry, the owning and managing companies and the seamen and officers' unions did take action, quickly and effectively to correct reported shortcomings in lifesaving equipment and procedures.

The larger ocean freighters, with several holds for cargo, could often withstand a single torpedo hit as long as they were not carrying very heavy or explosive cargo. The lakers rarely could survive such an explosion. Completely inadequate even for our own shipping requirements of wartime, there was little real option.

The seven schooners in these stories (Chapter 13) were owned on a variety of systems: privately, either by an owner who had purchased one from the original ship-building shareholders, or in some cases on shares, always sixty-four in total. Anyone who could raise the funds, as much as $300 to $500 a share, could own several shares. These shares gave the holders the proportionate right to any profits from each trip to sea. Some were owned by fishing companies or small trading concerns. None of these ships were requisitioned, although the French barquentine *Angelus* had been seized and was technically owned by the Canadian Government Merchant Marine as a result.

MERCHANT SHIP CONTROL AND MANAGEMENT

Just before war was declared by Britain, in anticipation of the requirement, the Admiralty arranged through the British Board of Trade to assume control of all enterprise carried in merchant ships that were British registered. In those days of Empire this included Canadian-owned ships. From 3 September 1939 all merchant voyages were as set down by various government organizations and the respective Navies. On 13 October the Board of Trade in the United Kingdom became the Ministry of Shipping; on 9 May 1941 it became the Ministry of War Transport which included shipping. Canada too passed the required legislation to follow suit—there was little option but to form an amalgamated shipping operation.

At first the ships were left under their owners, although some were promptly requisitioned for particular naval uses as armed merchant cruisers, boarding vessels, or minesweepers. Vessels that were subsequently requisitioned for mercantile service were on variable business deals, much as in peacetime: a few on charter with officers and crew; with some officers only; or bare boat charters. The Upper Lakes and St. Lawrence Company's ships for instance were requisitioned under Regulation 48, Defence of Canada Regulations, War Measures Act RSC 1927, Chapter 206, Section 3. A more detailed example of the arrangements is given for those Upper Lakes ships in Chapter 11.

The Ministry of Shipping in the UK (with a major Canadian office on St. James Street in Montreal) and the Canadian Shipping Board, in conjunction with the Department of Transport, set up the Canadian seamen manning pools to provide crews as required. The first in Canada was established in Montreal just to hold and take care of British seamen sent to Canada to man new construction and requisitioned ships for their Ministry; this was shortly followed by a Foreign Seamen Pool to take care of seamen in ships of countries overrun by German forces in Europe. Then the general Manning Pools were established in Halifax, Sydney, Montreal, Saint John, NB, and Vancouver. On 10 October 1940 the British Ministry of Shipping in theory requisitioned all Empire shipping, although this did not mean a major change in the way they were already operating. Foreign ships who fled their home countries after German occupation similarly volunteered their services, although the actual terms varied from country to country. Norway ran its own ships; Danish ships came under the foreign flags of their managers.

Meanwhile in Halifax, thanks to advance planning by Acting Commander Richard H. Oland, (RCN, Retired, recalled to duty in the summer of 1939), the creation of a huge network to control merchant shipping movement in Canadian waters had already begun. This was the NCSO organization, Naval Control of (Merchant) Shipping Office. This formation liaised with their British counterparts and supported the establishment of local seamen manning pools. As well a small group of Navy officers and seamen formed the Naval Boarding Service under Lt Fred B. Watt, RCNVR, ostensibly to check each awaiting convoy to ensure there were no signs of potential sabotage on board. This group soon became a liaison between the ships' personnel and the owners and agents and the NCSO, arbitrating and resolving a wide range of social and crew complaint problems, as well as reporting to the naval authorities on the ships' readiness to sail.

On 4 April 1941 a federal Order in Council passed the rather draconian Merchant Seaman Order, empowering authorities to remove, by force if necessary, any troublesome crew members, Canadian or foreign, from any ship in Canadian ports,

The enemy wasn't the only danger. Completely iced up Carley float and depth charge thrower in a corvette — useless like this. (NAC)

jail them if absolutely necessary, and to man all Canadian-controlled merchant ships as required. It was usually administered with considerable and admirable tact and skill, although its implications were unpopular with any seamen not satisfied with their lot. It was only rarely that men were jailed; usually ardent Communist sympathizers deliberately stirring up trouble.

The Canadian ships were administered thus, whether they were original vessels registered in Canada, were acquired by assignment, the foreign ships assigned, the two captured enemy ships, or the wartime built vessels such as the 176 Park ships. Where possible ships were continued in their pre-war roles. Even fishing schooners continued fishing, or trading to the West Indies, as they had for generations. Canada's links to the West Indies were continued with the CNR's CNSS Lady boats. All the rest went where they were ordered, loaded what they were assigned by manufacturers, agents or owners, and sailed for ports dictated by the NCS organization, in convoys or, if capable of over 13 to 15 knots, on their own. It was a tremendous, interlocking, inter-Allied and inter-Service operation that was almost entirely successful. Except for the interruptions of the U-boats, German surface raiders, and the German and Japanese Air forces.

Once ships were loaded or the local NCS office in Halifax was notified of ships arriving for onward routing, that office's work began with intensity. The list of ships was drawn up, showing their cargoes, destinations, nationalities and reputed speeds to determine whether an up-coming convoy would be classed as "fast" at about 8 to 10 knots or "slow" at 6 to 7 knots or less. Any ships capable of 15 knots were identified as probable independents but still bound to a designated port. (For seven months, November 1940 to June 1941 the independents' speed was set at only 13 knots. But the loss ratio of sinkings versus sailings of these ships rose almost three hundred percent, and the minimal speed for an independent was re-established at 15 knots). The merchantmen were noted as to armament, any extra equipment such as D/F and so on. A tentative convoy layout was organized, with ships allocated for the convoy commodore and vice-commodore leading centre columns; rescue ships allocated as rear ships in columns; and escort oilers protectively placed within rear rows to refuel the escorts on the way. Valuable tankers were assigned to the inner positions if possible, ships destined to break off for Iceland or the African coast in outside columns and so on. The Navy was advised of the probable sailing date and convoy size so suitable escorts could be provided.

A suitable escort was hardly ever possible in the early days, although many convoys throughout the war, in fact over eighty percent, passed safely across the Atlantic without serious attack or losses. But while an escort for a 40-ship convoy should ideally have comprised at least two destroyers or large US Coast Guard cutters for hunting down detected U-boats, and maybe six to eight corvettes or other escorts to patrol the fringes, many convoys had but one elderly destroyer, often an ex-American Town class of 1919 vintage, and from one to four corvettes.

The ships gathered at anchor in Bedford Basin and in Sydney harbour. When all was ready a convoy conference was held, at first in Admiralty House in Halifax, presided over by Captain Oland. In attendance were the Escort Group commander and some of his staff, the convoy commodore and vice-commodore, all the merchant captains and often their first officers and wireless officers, plus staff weather and intelligence experts. The masters were handed the secret papers giving the convoy layout and thus their ships' numbers, sailing date and times, proposed and alternate routes in case their ships lost the convoy at night or in foul weather or they had to drop astern because of problems. Radio frequencies were assigned and convoy duties such as column leaders which then became sound- and flag-repeating ships for those astern; zigzag diagrams and timings were distributed, also wireless frequencies to monitor. Many masters of non-British ships had only passable English and the staff tried to ensure they too could follow the proposed plan. The escort group commander cautioned masters about not attracting U-boats by straggling, making too much smoke or throwing garbage overboard. Likely weather and the known potential U-boat threat to be encountered along their route was discussed. Opportunity was given for the masters to ask questions or make suggestions. The best and most entertaining description of one of these conferences is contained in Canadian poet E.J. Pratt's *Behind The Log*.

If the conference was held in the morning, the convoy usually began leaving by mid-afternoon and might take two to five hours to start forming up in the outer Halifax approaches, with the escort corvettes hustling about trying to shepherd them into the assigned columns and ensure there were no lurking U-boats as the whole mass moved slowly northeastward, often in half a gale of wind and in the dark. The same

A convoy leaving Halifax, with the gate vessels to either side of a departing merchantman.
(Lawrence Gale)

procedure occurred at Sydney for the slower ships. Close calls were frequent, collisions amazingly rare—a tribute to the skills of the masters and deck officers.

CONVOY

The first North American eastbound convoy, HX-1 consisting of fifteen ships sailed from Halifax on 16 September 1939, protected initially by two RCN destroyers, HMCS *St. Laurent* and *Saguenay*. It is to the great credit of Canada's modest naval preparedness that just after war was formally declared on the 10th, in reply to a telegram from the Admiralty asking when the RCN would be prepared to start convoying, Rear Admiral Percy Nelles, the Chief of the Naval Staff was able to reply: "IMMEDIATELY."

In convoy, the ships were organized into a broad-fronted rectangle, of about thirty to a hundred ships. Because the U-boats tended to attack from the leading corners or the beam, it was better to present a small target than a long and straggling one. Also a broad front convoy passed a point of optimum danger more quickly than a long one. For Atlantic convoys (as different from English Channel or Mediterranean convoys) the spacing varied as the war and experience dictated, but was supposed to be two cables, 400 yards, between ships in the same column. This was later increased as more inexperienced officers and helmsmen manned the new construction ships in 1943. Between adjacent columns the spacing was at first three cables by day and five at night, but was increased to five cables at all times when operational research proved that wider spacing made target selection by the U-boats more difficult, as well as again allowing for vagaries in steering due to inexperience. Thus a ten-column convoy of up to six ships per column, say fifty-five ships, occupied a rectangle of ocean five and a quarter by one and a quarter miles in area, not including the outer escorts, with a ten to fifteen mile perimeter to be covered.

Although this was laid down in convoy orders, newly qualified helmsmen and bridge officers, irregular or uneven stoking of coal-fired boilers, and the problems of elderly ships lead to a continual juggling of the convoy's supposedly orderly formation. Many convoys, in fact by far the largest number, crossed not only with no losses but were not even attacked, especially in the 1939-1940 and 1944-1945 periods. Others suffered continuous and major attacks. For instance of the 377 HX eastbound North Atlantic convoys, 322 crossed with no ships lost or damaged—over eighty-five percent. But the other 55 convoys lost 110 ships; and another 96 ships were lost from HX convoys while stragglers or after dispersal—about 2 million tons of cargoes utterly lost. No wonder Churchill became very worried.

In the slower SC eastbound convoys, which became the RCN's primary responsibility later in the war, there were 177 convoys, of which 29 lost 145 ships, with another 66 lost as stragglers or when dispersed, almost exactly the same loss ratio as the fast convoys. Comparisons are invidious, but as an example SC-7 which sailed from Sydney, Cape Breton for Liverpool on 5 October 1940 lost 15 ships to U-boats of the 34 that sailed, or forty-four percent—60,800 gross registered tons of

Deep laden ships awaiting convoy in Halifax's Bedford Basin, viewed from the shoreline.
(MARCOM Museum)

shipping and all their cargoes lost, plus 96 seamen killed in 8 of the ships. Against this may be set, for instance, convoys HX-301 (130 ships) and HX-302 (the war's largest Atlantic convoy with 166 ships) that sailed from New York via Halifax on 17 and 25 July 1944. Both crossed without a single ship, pound of cargo, merchant seaman, DEMS gunner or passenger lost.

The command arrangement at sea was a delicate one between the officer appointed as convoy commodore and the naval officer in charge of the protective escort group. Later in the war command was divided between the senior officer of the close escort, often corvettes, and the SO of the support group, usually made up of frigates, sloops or destroyers sent to help a hard-pressed convoy. The convoy commodore always travelled in one of the merchantmen leading a central column and was usually provided with a staff of up to five signalmen and telegraphists. Many of the commodores were retired senior admirals or company fleet commodores brought out of retirement. The escort group commander, often a commander or even a lieutenant commander, sometimes even a volunteer reservist, was in charge of the defence of the convoy. In theory he could order changes in its route, although he usually "suggested" or "recommended" these changes diplomatically. As the war progressed each of these gentlemen came to trust and rely on the other, although it was not always so,

A pale grey convoy passes out of Halifax, through the antisubmarine gate, between the dark and light grey smaller ships. The nearer is repairing some problem.
(MARCOM Museum)

especially in the early days of 1940-1941. Often there was no completely "right answer" and frustrations arose when the commodore did not agree with the SO escort, or when U-boats attacked anyway. Compromise was usually reached, but even this did not necessarily mean the convoy avoided the dangers.

A matter of frequent disagreement and post-operational criticism was the saving of survivors from sunken ships by escorts, even saving the ships themselves if they didn't promptly sink. In theory it was the naval escort vessels' duty to hunt submarines that had attacked, and sinking or damaging a U-boat prevented future casualties. But then merchant ships were in very short supply, and a damaged escorted or towed safely to harbour was "worth its weight in gold" for the future. Pulling men from the sea boosted morale and saved valuable trained seamen, especially if they were skilled officers. As many of the corvettes were soon commanded by naval reservists, not necessarily imbued with the Regular Force's dictum of duty before all else, it would have taken a singularly cold-hearted CO to steam away from men struggling in a heaving, freezing, oil-covered sea on the off chance of locating a U-boat—which experience told him was highly likely to evade him anyway. But these rescue operations risked the danger of attack to the stopped warship while men were fished from the sea or a tow was connected to a wallowing, damaged freighter. While this was going on, sometimes taking hours while the convoy steamed on, the defensive escort ring was reduced, often significantly and at a vital time, by the rescuer's absence.

Again, the assessment of whether the CO had acted correctly depended on who was asked and the resultant success or failure of such rescues. The rescued seaman agreed one hundred percent with the decision to stop and effect a rescue; the escort group commander, left with a reduced effective force, was likely to disagree. And all these efforts, of attack and or rescue, were then assessed by the distant, impersonal and detached Admiralty's director of the Anti-U-boat Division, who congratulated the successful ship and told other escort COs they "had incurred the Admiralty's displeasure," even "extreme displeasure," with reasons given. There are stories told of escort group commanders imparting this official "displeasure" message to a less than contrite corvette CO, then suggesting that they both go and have a gin together.

Toward the rear of most later convoys was an escort oiler which could be used to refuel escorts, although in stormy North Atlantic winter weather and at night this all too often proved impossible. A picking-up line would be streamed astern of the tanker, then grappled and hauled aboard the corvette awaiting feeding, followed by the fuelling hose. There were occasions when escort corvettes simply ran out of fuel and had to be towed, even sailed, into ports such as Iceland and the Azores. The early corvettes barely carried enough fuel to reach the United Kingdom from Halifax, not counting extra steaming about in defence of their convoy or hours steamed at their top speed of about 16 knots which devoured fuel at an unacceptable rate. Thus, sometimes in the midst of a battle, corvettes and "short-legged" destroyers simply had to steam off to Iceland to refuel, rejoining the convoy if time allowed.

By mid-1943 the convoy could also include a MAC ship, a merchant aircraft carrier, a contributing reason for records showing merchant losses falling off rapidly in mid 1943. These ships were all bulk freighters carrying grain or other foodstuffs, or tankers decked over and supplied with half a dozen anti-submarine aircraft, Swordfish or fighters. Also in this category there could be a true but small escort carrier in the central rear ranks of the convoy. A precursor to these carriers was the temporarily adopted expedient of CAM ships, the Catapult Aircraft Merchantman, with a Hurricane fighter perched on an extended catapult framework over her bows. When catapulted off to attack a shadowing German Kondor long range aircraft the pilot hoped he could later ditch in the cold ocean near an escort and be rescued, or if near Iceland or the UK land on a friendly aerodrome—a highly unlikely chance.

If the threat of U-boats was considered minimal (and intelligence was remarkable in assessing this likelihood), the convoy steamed on a straight course toward its destination, through pre-set way-points. But if U-boats were suspected along the route daytime manoeuvring of the convoy—zigzagging on a fixed time schedule to make aiming by U-boats more difficult—was signalled by flags and the commodore blowing his whistle or siren. Radios were never to be used except in emergencies. Leading ships of columns repeated the signal flags and sounds which were in theory watched for by the following freighters. No lights were ever allowed after dusk except a dim blue stern light cluster, so any movements of the convoy were organized in advance at set times, and their execution signalled by whistle. On a windy, rough sea night, too often in rain or snow, this was problematical in operation, and collisions were not uncommon, sometimes fatal; near misses were frequent.

The ships were usually supposed to be at least 600 yards abeam of each other and 200 yards astern of their next ahead. This was subject to wild variations depending on weather; different steaming and steering capabilities of the ships; inexperienced helmsmen, engine room firemen and stokers; masters and mates who did not understand the system or ignored the timing of changes; even bridge clocks not keeping accurate time to the second. Most ships were fitted in the wheelhouse with a "zigzag clock" which gave off a ping at set intervals, usually twenty minutes, when the helmsman would alter to a new course listed on a blackboard in front of him.

However, all this depended on every ship taking the same action at the identical moment. Again, it was not unknown for a ship in one of the middle columns to alter twenty degrees in the wrong direction and careen past his startled neighbours, or to lose engine steam pressure and suddenly slow to a stop with no warning to his next astern who then had to hurriedly alter course around the casualty. The U-boats were not the only danger. In fog and thick weather a "fog buoy" could be trailed astern, a wooden box-like device that threw up a spray of sea water as it was towed along and could be positioned near the next astern to indicate to her where the next ahead might be.

There were, in addition to the large freighter convoys, special convoys. There were fast convoys of troop ships which required destroyer escorts due to their much higher speeds of 14 to 20 knots. There were tanker convoys entailing extra protection when it was available, running up the east coast or direct from the West Indies to the United Kingdom, the Mediterranean or the West African coast. The trooping convoys nearly always got through safely due to their speed; the slower tanker convoys were more vulnerable. There were, in 1942-1943, before D-Day, even convoys of landing craft destined for the invasion armadas. For them the weather was as much a serious threat as were the *Kriegsmarine* and the *Luftwaffe*.

A CAM with its Hurricane fighter, in convoy. (Lawrence Gale)

What a U-boat would see in daylight. (Lawrence Gale)

Individual ships capable of over 13 knots were usually not expected to join convoys, as it was calculated that their speed and employment of random zigzagging gave them sufficient protection from U-boat torpedoes. While this applied throughout the war, these ships did not necessarily go unscathed. One of their problems was a lack of new intelligence about U-boats along their paths. Such highly secret notices were sent to convoys, but were not directed to individual ships once they had sailed.

A mention can be made here of convoys in the River and Gulf of St. Lawrence west of Cape Breton. After the depredations of only a few U-boats into the area in 1942 and the failure of the escorts to even locate most of them, let alone effectively attack them, sailings in the Gulf ceased for all but the most vital supplies from late in 1942 until 1944. This resulted in almost a twenty-five percent reduction in Canadian sailings from Montreal—a German victory apart from the sixteen merchantmen sunk. These sinkings were clearly visible to people living along the St. Lawrence shore, who then cared for the survivors and who were well aware of the enemy on their doorstep. The government irrationally tried to hide these attacks from the public through censorship, which only served to aggravate the Québec populace along the St. Lawrence, who tended to blame the Navy for not protecting them properly. The Navy did what they could in the Gulf with small ships, but kept their concentration on the wider sphere, the Battle of the Atlantic raging offshore.

The main success of the shipping battle is in the statistic that between September 1939 and May 1945, 25,343 merchant ships sailed from North American ports to Britain, or almost 138 ships a week in two convoys. In these ships, or at least the Canadian-registered ships, 1,629 men and women were lost of the approximately 12,000 who served in them. And another rare statistic is that the RCAF lost 752 men in aircraft on maritime support operations.

THE THREAT AND THE OPPONENTS

Most of the stories in this volume describe losses caused by the German U-boats, either in the North and South Atlantic, in the Gulf of St. Lawrence, in the Mediterranean (*Princess Marguerite*), or the Indian Ocean (*Jasper Park*). A few ships were lost around the United Kingdom to air attack (four ships), and three to German surface attacks. The *Robert W. Pomeroy* and *Collingdoc* were mined. Two Canadian merchantmen were lost to the Japanese: *Empress of Asia* was sunk by air power near Singapore, and *Shinai* was captured in northwest Borneo-Sarawak.

But U-boats were responsible for seventy-nine percent of these merchant losses, from early in 1940 to the last British ship sunk in the war, the Canadian-owned *Avondale Park*. For five and a half years the U-boats were the major threat. Sixty-nine percent of all British Merchant Navy casualties, amounting to about 30,246 men and women, were due to the U-boats alone, according to Kaplan and Currie in *Wolf Pack: U-Boats at War*.

While statistics vary widely on what is meant by "Allied merchant ships lost" and in the description of the war's theatres, the figures are generally in agreement: 4,786 merchant ships lost (plus another 175 naval warships) to submarine attack,

KL Otto Kretschmer's Type VII U-boat, *U 99*.
These formed by far the largest number of the U-boat fleet.
(K.R. Macpherson)

enemy aircraft, surface ships and mines. According to the 1976 reprint of the official 1947 *British Vessels Lost At Sea 1939-45*, this includes total Allied, neutral and fishing vessels lost due to enemy action. That is more than two vessels a day, every day throughout the war, with a total displacement tonnage of about 14.5 million tons. Over 37,600 merchant seamen and women lost their lives in the British, American and Canadian ships alone. Additionally some 2,000 Greek sailors were also killed and nearly the same number of Norwegians.

But, according to Gröner in *German Warships, Vol.2*, of the 1,172 German U-boats that were available for operational patrols, 754 were eventually lost, a sixty-four percent loss, including the German *Milch* cows refuelling submarines and training boats that undertook at least one operational patrol. And if one thinks of all those U-boats prowling the oceans and sinking Allied ships, it is interesting to note that of the 1,172 U-boats that were commissioned before or during the war, 550, or forty-seven percent, never sank a single ship of any size.

Initially, all the merchant shipping losses occurred around the British Isles, until about May 1940. As the war at sea developed, until June 1941 by far the majority of sinkings still took place near those waters, although there were a scattering of sinkings out as far as mid-Atlantic southeast of Iceland, and a flurry off the West African coast. The commander of U-boats, Admiral Karl Dönitz knew, as the Allied A/S forces soon learned, that the place to sink merchantmen was where they concentrated. Hunting for them in the vast open ocean was almost fruitless. The Allies also appreciated in the Second World War, unlike in the First, that the best location to hunt submarines was around the bait—the convoys on which they were concentrating. It was throughout a seesaw battle, thrust and counter-thrust, parry and attack. One shipbuilder in Britain described his firm as "Builders of targets!"

As the Allied anti-submarine forces grew and became more adept, and the U-boat attacks were thwarted in those waters, the sinkings occurred out in the mid-Atlantic between April and December 1941, a few as far afield as off Newfoundland. Admiral Dönitz had moved his boats, and the thirty-two or so Italian submarines that came under his orders from time to time, to avoid the strengthening anti-submarine efforts of the Allied navies. Further out to sea the targets were somewhat easier to attack without too much worry about anti-submarine escorts or the developing threat of air attack. By 1941 the newly commissioned 900-ton corvettes were becoming available, often with very green crews supplemented by a few "experts" who had gained perhaps six months' experience.

Then, with the United States' official entry into the war in the Atlantic (and Pacific) battles in December 1941–January 1942, there were very few sinkings around the UK or in the mid-Atlantic. In fact, in a reversal of fortunes to some extent, twelve U-boats were sunk there for twenty-four merchantmen lost between January and June. However, the US Navy was utterly unprepared for an anti-U-boat battle. From Nova Scotia down the US coast into the Caribbean and the Gulf of Mexico to the waters off South America hundreds of ships were sunk between mid-January and the end of June 1942. It was, for the U-boats, a "Happy Time," *Operation Paukenschlag* ("Drumbeat"). By July and August, the lessons had at last been absorbed, warships allocated, skills developed, convoys organized; the sinkings dropped dramatically. But it had been a very heavy price to pay for unpreparedness.

One sometimes gets the impression that there were hundreds of U-boats facing some convoys. Yet Hughes and Costello in their *The Battle of The Atlantic* (1977), give the following table to illustrate that, on average, tremendous damage was accomplished by relatively few U-boats actually operational in that Atlantic area.

DATES (JULY-SEP)	U-BOAT FLEET	AT SEA & OPERATIONAL	IN THE ATLANTIC*	PERCENT OF FLEET
1940	56	10†	8	14 %
1941	182	30	17	9 %
1942	352	95	25	7 %
1943	408	60	20	5 %
1944	396	40	15	4 %

* The Mediterranean and the Indian Ocean drew off many boats between 1940 and 1944.

† Others were on training, under repair, re-positioning, etc.

Thus the majority of the damage in the primary battle at sea was accomplished by only six percent of the operational U-boats at any one moment in time. Many others were employed in other parts of the world in the expanding conflict, on passage to and from their assigned area, were unable to find the convoy they were ordered to attack, or were under repair. At least half the operational boats at sea were going to or returning from operations. A few of these boats, even those bringing supplies to or from Germany's ally, Japan, managed to sink a distant merchantman. But then two of them contrived to sink their own German returning supply ships known as blockade-runners: *U 43* sank the *Doggerbank* and *U 333* the *Spreewald*. And two of them rammed and sank each other. But for the entire five and a half years of the war, their targets were the Allies' merchantmen.

THE U-BOATS

The main U-boat enemy right to the end was the Type VII, designed in 1934. While there were improvements in armament weapons, in torpedoes used, in fuel capacity (slightly) and in endurance, it was these Type VIIs, the "ocean boats," that carried the load. They were known by number only, although often a flotilla would adopt a device such as the laughing cow, the edelweiss flower or a hand of cards. The individual boats' numbers held no significance, ranging from *U 27* to *U 1804*, with the larger Type IX and Type XIV numbers interspersed. Construction continued to the last days of the war, despite the depredation caused by massive bombing throughout Germany. Until the very end the bombing only had the effect of slowing total production; it never halted the program.

The typical Type VIIC of mid-war was being built in sixteen yards, and was 221 ft (67.1 m) long by 20 ft (6.2 m) in diameter, with a surface displacement weight of about 759 tons and 1,070 tons in total weight. It could dive to 330 feet, about 100 metres, but with an actual "crush depth" of twice that. The later models were capable of withstanding pressures to a depth of 800 feet, although no captain would choose to try it if it could be avoided. A well handled U-boat with an experienced crew could dive and be beneath the surface in less than thirty seconds. Its crew numbers varied, growing with additional weapons, radar and other equipment, from about forty-five to fifty-six men. Usually there were only three or four officers, and senior petty officers had considerable responsibility for operations and were even in charge of watches in addition to the captain, watch officers (WOs) and the engineer. The boats had a speed of over 17 knots on the surface on their excellent twin diesel engines, supercharged in most boats, faster than the corvettes that hunted them. But submerged and running on batteries they could achieve at the most 8 knots, and that only for a few minutes. Normally they would operate at only 4 or 5 knots when submerged. Otherwise they made too much noise, attracted the Allies' asdic (sonar in USN terms), and depleted their two huge electric battery systems of 62 cells each, under the floor plates forward and aft.

Their range was up to 8,700 nautical miles on the surface on about 100 tons of diesel fuel, or about five weeks. In fact by conserving fuel and running at about 8 knots on the surface while searching for convoys, the Type VII could easily stay at sea for two months or more. For much of the middle years of the war as well they were replenished by large supply U-boats or even merchant raiders or supply ships in lonely and empty parts of the ocean. From these could be obtained additional fuel, food and fresh water, even more torpedoes and shells for their deck and anti-aircraft guns and seamen to replace those sick or injured. Despite the rumours, no U-boats were supplied in secret harbour rendezvous by sympathetic supporters in the United States or the West Indies.

The Type VII's armament consisted of five torpedo tubes, four forward, one right aft, and the U-boats carried nine reloads in later models. They also could be fitted to carry mines in lieu of torpedoes, although this was usually a special assignment. All boats initially had an 88mm (3.75-inch) deck gun forward and two or more anti-aircraft 20mm guns initially. As the war progressed and A/S aircraft became more numerous, the anti-aircraft firepower increased dramatically, with some boats carrying up to five AA guns. At one stage in 1944 the BdU policy was that if a U-boat was located by enemy aircraft and no surface vessels were in the immediate area, they were to stay surfaced and fight it out. Canada's only coastal command Victoria Cross winner, F/L David Hornell, died when the U-boat he attacked, although eventually sunk, shot down his Catalina flying boat. These Type VII boats were very difficult to sink. Time and again Allied claims of a "kill" from depth charges or acoustic torpedoes dropped and exploded near the U-boat proved unfounded and their target reached home safely, although sometimes quite severely damaged.

The Type IX which feature in some of these stories were simply larger versions of the same boat: 33 feet longer, 1 knot faster, and with their added fuel they had 2,000 miles more range. They could usually be identified by their larger deck area than the Type VIIs.

The torpedoes the U-boats fired were weapons systems in their own right. They were 23 ft. long, run initially on an alcohol and air engine, the G7A. But because this left a too visible bubble wake these were soon replaced with an electric battery-driven wakeless model, the G7E. Although the amount of actual explosive varied with different models, the usual was about 160 kg, or 350 lbs. although this was later increased to over 400 lbs. At first they were contact exploded, that is the torpedo had to hit the target to detonate the explosive charge. Later magnetic pistols were fitted that fired the charge if the torpedo passed under or near the target. This was in fact more effective as the explosion tended to break the back of the ships, whereas a torpedo hitting the mid-water hull quite often only caused a large but not fatal hole.

A somewhat larger Type IX U-boat, *U 109*. Under her three COs she sank thirteen ships.
(K.R. Macpherson)

By 1943 the boats also carried the GNAT (in Allied terms, "German Naval Acoustic Torpedo") or *Zaunkönig*, which could be attracted by the sound of engines or propellers and explode when close by. All these torpedoes were fitted with depth and course-keeping gyroscopes, and they could be set to run straight, or straight for a set distance and then circle or zigzag through a group of convoy ships. As well they could be fired in any direction and an attack course set for up to ninety degrees from the U-boat's course. The speed of the torpedoes varied with the different models, but was usually around 27 knots, and they could maintain this for up to eight kilometres, about five miles, in under six minutes. For safety reasons they did not arm themselves until they were about 300 metres away from the U-boat. The normal or most effective distance for firing at a target was around 1,000 metres, which meant it would take about thirty-six seconds for the torpedo to reach the target. All of these numbers varied as development progressed. Earlier and experimental models were notorious for their failures, incorrect depth keeping or premature firing, to the fury of the great early U-boat aces who encountered a failure rate of up to sixty percent. Throughout the war the front line crews had difficulty convincing BdU and the torpedo research group in Berlin that problems with the torpedoes were from faulty designs, not poor maintenance or firing set-ups on board. But then the same problems arose with the Allied submariners' torpedoes, in particular the USN's early models.

Often German claims for a hit or a kill of a merchantman were based only on what was heard, as U-boats frequently had to dive as soon as they had fired. And German torpedoes were set to explode at the end of their runs. This, added to premature explosions of the magnetic pistol-equipped torpedoes, often lead to wildly exaggerated claims for kills, although the assessments of the experienced aces of the U-boat arm were inclined to be close to their actual successes.

Although many Italian *sommergibili* came under German operational control, and even operated out of the German-controlled French ports, none of them sank any of the Canadian merchantmen, so will not be described. They tended to be good large boats, but were designed for considerably more crew comfort, and often were not handled as aggressively as the German aces' boats.

As an attack strategy, certainly for the first half of the war, U-boats mostly attacked on the surface, whenever possible at night. They tracked a convoy either by knowing its location through the German B-Dienst intelligence service; its discovery by far-ranging Kondor patrol aircraft; even by the trail of smoke given off by elderly and labouring merchantmen. Often patrol lines of ten or more U-boats were established by the controlling BdU of Dönitz's U-boat headquarters in France. The line of boats, spaced up to twenty-five miles apart and thus over 250 miles long, would be ordered across the probable line of advance of the convoys, outbound or homebound for Britain. But they were always on the surface unless detected by warships or Allied aircraft.

A U-boat or a Wolf Pack of them would try to get ahead of the convoy during the day, then as it approached, submerge, or if it was already dusk, lurk quietly on the outer fringe. With darkness the boats would approach the leading or wing ships trimmed down, with their decks partly awash and almost indistinguishable from the waves, firing into the collection of ships, always aiming at particular vessels. They even entered the "lanes" between ships in the convoy, firing torpedoes as they went, and then submerging to drop astern, reload torpedoes and try again. Until the advent of radar for the A/S escorts, a well handled U-boat was most difficult for even observant look-outs to see under these circumstances, and modestly trained naval asdic crews had trouble holding contact with a submerged and weaving boat in difficult water conditions.

The one major weakness in this highly trained and regimented U-boat force was their headquarters' requirement to signal frequently back and forth between U-boats and their BdU. Sightings, or even non-sightings of convoys had to be reported, as well as each attack when completed or when the U-boat knew she had been discovered. Orders went out repositioning them, recalling those short of fuel or setting up refuelling rendezvous with Milch cows or raiders. U-boats sent in reports on weather, fuel remaining, other U-boats met and a multitude of operational and administrative details. Even if the Allies could not exactly determine the content of a signal plucked from the air waves, in many cases the exact location of the U-boat transmitting it could be established by shore or ship-based D/F. Periodically the signals themselves, although transmitted in special cyphers and encoded by the notorious Enigma machine, were broken by the Allied code-breakers at Bletchley Park in England or, later, in Washington, and this happened almost continually from early 1944 on. In the years toward the end of the war the Allies were sometimes reading the German messages before the intended recipient. While the German Kriegsmarine staff and certainly the U-boat COs themselves became suspicious that their coding system had been broken, the Berlin Wehrmacht signals intelligence staff assured them this was impossible right to the end of the war. The only solution was to curtail signalling, and although it could be reduced, and was, the result was to the Allies' benefit right to the end.

And from about 1942 on, convoy escorts and some ships in the convoys had HF/DF on board and could locate with reasonable accuracy the sending U-boat's general direction and distance. Then a destroyer or other warship would be sent off on the bearing, if a spare was available, to attack or at least put down the U-boat, making it much harder for her to catch up the convoy, or causing the submerged boat to miss an emergency evasive turn ordered by the convoy commodore, which was often given about half an hour after darkness set in. Later, when aircraft were available in MAC ships, they too could scout out a line of bearing for any transmitting U-boat. It was a serious game of cat-and-mouse on both sides. And both protagonists paid a terrible price, as these stories relate.

TIMES

The times of day quoted in these narratives are often open to considerable doubt. Technically the convoys and some larger ships kept Greenwich Mean Time—GMT, often referred to as Z or "Zulu" time, named after its time zone. This could be up to five hours in advance of real or "local" time in the Western Atlantic. But the smaller ships often kept local time for where they were, and ships in port and NOICs kept local time—for instance Halifax was in the "Papa" time zone. The U-boats normally kept Central European Time, two hours in advance of Greenwich, no matter where they were, but not always. This resulted in a highly confusing and often suspect record. Men reporting on their torpedoing might quote a time for the chronicle without saying what time they were using. The times recorded in these stories are simply those appearing in reports, although when possible, to make it realistic, local time has been used when this could reasonably be determined.

Quidquid delirant reges plectuntur Achivi

—Horace, *Epistles I*, circa 15 B.C.
(For every folly of their princes the Greeks feel the scourge.)

CHAPTER 1

Canada Steamship Lines Loses Five Little Lakers

There is a tide in the affairs of men,
Which, taken at the flood, leads on to fortune;
Omitted, all the voyage of their life is
bound in shallows and in miseries.
On such a full sea are we now afloat,
And we must take the current when it serves,
or lose our ventures.

—Brutus, in Shakespeare, *Julius Caesar*

Canada Steamship Lines is still one of the country's best known owners, at least on the Great Lakes. They have owned and operated more than 330 ships under their company colours. It is possible to trace the firm's origins back to 1845 when a group of farmers and merchants in the little village of St. Charles on the Richelieu River in western Quebec, south of the St. Lawrence, launched La Société de Navigation de la Rivière Richelieu as a practical method of transporting their goods to the Montreal market. In 1847 this group merged with another similar local shipping company to become La Compagnie de Richelieu.

This larger firm became incorporated in 1857, extending its services to other local communities and servicing both Montreal and Quebec. It acquired more ships and other small shipping companies, amalgamated with the Canadian Navigation Company to become in 1875 the Richelieu & Ontario Navigation Company, with eighteen ships operating between Toronto and Quebec City, further down the St. Lawrence and up the Saguenay River.

In 1913 the Canada Transportation Company was formed, soon re-named Canada Steamship Lines Ltd. (CSL), a name retained until this day. During the First World War the Company sent a significant number of ships to the United Kingdom for war service, and lost sixteen of them.

By 1915 the company also had sixteen deep sea vessels engaged in Atlantic freight traffic. But with the acquisition of yet more St. Lawrence River shipping companies, CSL in 1925 withdrew completely from ocean-going trade to concentrate on inland shipping. In the fall of 1926 the company bought a large group of lakers from the George Hall Company (later well known in the Lakes as HALCO). In the 1920s, despite financial ups and downs, CSL acquired Davie Shipbuilding & Repairing Company Ltd. at Quebec, giving the company the capacity to build and repair its own ships as well as undertaking construction for others. By 1927 CSL owned twenty-three passenger vessels, twenty-three upper lakes bulk freighters, forty-nine smaller canallers and twenty Great Lakes package freighters.

Despite the Depression, CSL's growth continued over the next decades, and the company pioneered the development of the Great Lakes self-unloaders, ships that did not require extensive unloading equipment at dockside. In 1941 the company expanded into land transportation with the purchase of what was to become the truck fleet Kingsway Transport. Post-war it acquired more shipyards, seaside hotels (the Manoir Richelieu at Murray Bay is probably the most famous, acquired with the Richelieu and Ontario Transportation purchase), a tug company, Voyageur Bus lines and other enterprises, several of which have since been sold again. The best known symbol on the lakes since 1927 is the ships' stack colours in bands of orange, white and black. Since then CSL has branched out once again into overseas ocean services, largely in the bulk self-unloaders trade.

At the start of the Second World War, CSL had a somewhat reduced fleet of eighty-five ships, all plying the Great Lakes and St. Lawrence, mainly in the bulk grain, ore and coal trade. The war's outbreak caused a sudden and urgent change in the company's operations. The Canadian government took up many of the smaller canallers for either controlled local transport to and from Newfoundland in the iron ore shipping trade, or for moving bauxite from mine loading depots up the shallow rivers of the Guyanas and Dutch Surinam on the northeast shoulder of South America to an ocean freighter transshipment point in the Caribbean islands. Sixteen Canadian ex-lakers from several companies were to be employed in this trade, of which nine were sunk by German U-boats and two more lost to marine hazards. Eight more of these lakers were chartered to the British Ministry of Shipping for service around the British Isles, largely in the coal trade.

CSL was to lose five of these little vessels, all of about 252 feet, between July 1940 and September 1943. Before the war thirty-nine of them had been employed in inland trade between Port Arthur/Fort William at the lakehead to Port Colborne and Montreal. Those that went through to Montreal often went on downriver to load pulpwood for the return passage.

CSL's SS *Magog*. (Jay Bascom/George Deno)

MAGOG

SHIP: 2,053 grt, 259 ft. bulk lakes freighter. Built in 1923 by Fraser Brace Ltd., Trois Rivières, Que. as the *John Howard* for George Hall Coal & Shipping Company, Montreal.

FATE: Shelled and then torpedoed and sunk by *U 99* on 5 July 1940, about sixty miles southwest of Ireland. No casualties.

The small laker *Magog* was bought by CSL from the George Hall Company in September 1926, her name changed from *John Howard*, and put to bulk cargo carrying on the lakes and down to Montreal. In 1940, as her file records, she and several of her sister ships of the same size were requisitioned "on behalf of the British Ministry of War Shipping" through Canadian authorities. In mid June 1940 on her delivery trip overseas she loaded 512 standards of timber and at 10:30 on 21 June set sail in the twenty-nine-convoy HX-52 from Halifax for Blyth on the northeast coast of England. Her Master was Captain T. Swales Doughty, who had a crew of twenty-two, most of them Newfoundlanders. Contrary to popular perceptions these men were not seafarers but bush workers from the pulp and paper industry and, in Captain Doughty's words, "needed everything explained to them in detail." By the time they reached the Western Approaches south of Ireland, and although she had crossed much of the way under the protection of Convoy HX-52, *Magog* was travelling alone toward her final destination at a modest 8 knots. The was unarmed despite Doughty's request at Halifax for a defensive gun, which could not be provided due to universal shortages of such items for merchantmen.

At about 10:25 am local time on Friday July 5th, in a heavy swell and moderate sea, as the Master was giving instruction to one of his lookouts on the bridge and with no warning of the presence of any enemy vessel, a shell passed over the ship and threw up a tall splash about forty yards ahead and to starboard. Doughty without hesitation ordered the course altered toward the splash of the shell as another now fell about the same distance to port. Again he altered in that direction, on the astute assumption that the gunner would correct his point-of-aim toward the ship he had missed. This cat and mouse game went on for a few more shots, and Doughty then went onto the port bridge wing and saw a submarine firing at him from about a mile and a quarter away on his port quarter.

He at once told his wireless operator to send out an SOS (actually the letters S-S-S, the code for a submarine attack), give their position and indicate that they were being attacked. Within minutes the operator told him the message had been passed to Land's End wireless station. Meanwhile Doughty dodged about following each shell splash causing the next one to miss as the submarine worked her way closer at about twice *Magog*'s speed.

Eventually, after half an hour of this with some dozen shots fired, at about 10:55 a hit was scored on the ship's port quarter, destroying a lifeboat. The next shot, no doubt fired at the bridge, hit her foremast which brought down the wireless aerial. The valiant but unequal struggle was obviously trending in favour of the submarine, so Doughty ordered the ship's engines stopped and sent his Second Mate aft to get the crew away in the remaining lifeboat.

The submarine, now known to have been *U 99* commanded by the later famous KK Otto Kretschmer, continued firing at the little freighter, hitting her with each shot. One smashed several liferafts right aft, another two or three hit forward to ensure the wireless was silenced, one went into the Master's cabin, another hit right on the bow.

The crew all managed to get away in one lifeboat and a raft right at the stern, with the Master being the last to leave, sliding down the braided log line. They rowed away about half a mile, with one man seriously injured and two less so, as the submarine continued to try to sink the freighter with its cargo of wood. Eventually Kretschmer gave up and fired one torpedo at *Magog*, the explosion just forward of her engine room in the stern blowing away the ship's funnel and after mast. She sank by the stern, although fifty feet of her bow remained above the surface, at which Kretschmer fired another four or five rounds to little effect.

He then motored over to the lifeboat with the crew in it and waved the boat alongside for questioning. He asked the name of the ship, and Doughty at first replied "Can't say."

"Silent Otto" Kretschmer circled the lifeboat in the submarine and noted the name faintly painted out on the boat.

"The name looks like *Magog*. Is that right?"

Pause, then "Yes."

"That's better! What port of registry?"

"Canada."

"What port of destination?"

"None." Doughty was not for giving out any information that might be of any use.

In Doughty's words, "He then spoke to me about using the W/T [his wireless], saying I had no right to do so, but I replied 'There's a war on!' He then said he could treat me very harshly for doing this and I said 'It's up to you.' The officer then asked me what was my cargo and when I told him it was timber, he was rather disappointed!"

While this questioning was going on, a petty officer from the U-boat appeared on the conning tower and trained a machine gun on the lifeboat. Three or four of *Magog*'s crew jumped over the side, fearing they were to be fired at, memories from the First World War still being prevalent. But Kretschmer told them to get back into the boat and sent the petty officer and his gun below, telling him he was never to do that again!

In his report six days later Doughty noted that the U-boat looked in good condition, remarked on its camouflage paint and gun armament, as well as on the men he could see on the conning tower, dressed in leather coats and with six or seven day's growth of beard. Terence Robertson in his biography of Otto Kretschmer says that he asked if anyone was hurt, receiving a "No" reply, and passed down a bottle of brandy, for which Captain Doughty thanked him, but didn't feel this warranted a comment in his later report.

Kretschmer told Doughty, "steer east northeast; the Irish coast is about fifty-eight miles. Don't let the wind take you too far south or you'll end up in France, and you know what that means!" Doughty drew his finger across his throat.

"No, not as bad as that," Kretschmer called down. The submarine moved away westward, Doughty called out "Thanks!" and Kretschmer waved his arm in response. When about five miles off the U-boat submerged.

At 12:45 a Sunderland flying boat located the survivors and signalled that help was coming. The pilot maintained contact and at 2:45 signalled for the lifeboat to steer north, and within an hour the elderly little Finnish steamer *Fidra* picked them up and took the crew into Queenstown in neutral Ireland the next afternoon. From there they all made their way to England and home.

Doughty's final comments in his report were that he was sure if he had been armed he could have hit the submarine; "She made a good target." Also that, although he received coded messages (possibly warning of U-boats in the area) he did not have coding or decoding tables, so couldn't read them.

This was on *U 99*'s second patrol, her first having been aborted after she was damaged by a German aircraft from the pocket battle cruiser *Scharnhorst* which attacked her in error off Norway. She was part of the 7th U-Flottille, and had left Wilhelmshaven on 27 June 1940. *Magog* was Kretschmer's very first wartime success. He sank another two, possibly three ships the next day, and went on to complete seven patrols, sink fifty-six ships of over 313,000 tons (of which three were Canadian and Newfoundland vessels) and was awarded the Knight's Cross with Swords. His U-boat was sunk by the RN destroyers *Walker* and *Vanoc* in March, 1941 on his eighth patrol, and Kretschmer and all but three of his crew were taken prisoner. He spent the rest of the war in Canadian and British camps, returned to Germany in the summer of 1947 and eventually reached senior ranks in the new post-war *Bundesmarine*. He had joined the fledgling *Kriegsmarine* as a cadet in 1930 and had been one of the first new trainees for U-boats in 1936.

During the later years of the war, near an Alberta village where some German *Kriegsmarine* POWs were helping farmers with crops, Chief Radio Operator Jupp Kassel of *U 99* encountered one of *Magog's* surviving seamen who had been injured and released from the Merchant Navy, now driving an army jeep. Both treated the encounter just as interesting history.

Those lost: None.

Sources: Robertson, *Night Raider of the Atlantic* (*The Golden Horseshoe*); PRO SCS Interview with Captain Doughty; Greenwood, *Namesakes*; CSL historical brochure; Cuthbertson, *Freshwater*; Wynn, *U-Boat Operations*; Kurowski, *Knight's Cross Holders*; McCormick, *The Wishbone Fleet*; Collard, *Passage To The Sea*.

WATERLOO

SHIP: 1,905 grt, 252 ft. bulk canaller freighter. Built in 1923 by Barclay, Curle & Company, Glasgow, Scotland, as *Glenburnie* for Great Lakes Transportation Company Ltd.

FATE: Sunk by German aircraft bombs on 10 July 1940 in North Sea opposite East Anglia. No casualties.

Waterloo changed hands twice shortly after building and delivery, Playfair's Great Lakes Transportation selling her to the George Hall Company in 1926 and that firm transferring her to CSL in 1927. Like *Magog*, she served their requirements, with occasional Depression-era layoffs, on the Lakes and St. Lawrence until requisitioned in 1940.

Waterloo's loss was one of those rarities in these stories in that she was sunk by German aircraft bombing. Only two others were sunk this way, the Q & O's *Thorold* sunk by aircraft just over a month after *Waterloo*, and *Empress of Asia* sunk by Japanese aircraft in early 1942. Another two losses are attributable to aircraft: *Europa* was destroyed when in dock in Liverpool during air raids, and the Upper Lakes' *Albert C. Field* was sunk by an aerial torpedo. Almost all the rest succumbed to U-boats, to surface warships, or mines.

Waterloo was requisitioned in 1940 for overseas service, to replace larger or more ocean capable British ships in their coastal coal and bulk commodity trades. There are reports in secondary published sources that *Waterloo* and her sister *Winona* were involved in the rescue of the British and French forces during the Dunkirk

SS *Waterloo*, unloading coal. (J.N. Bascom)

evacuation in May and June 1940, but no official record of this has been found in the carefully researched lists of Dunkirk ships. While Admiral Ramsay dragooned every local ship he could lay his hands on that was of shallow enough draft in those hectic days to approach the shore and evacuate the British Expeditionary Force, *Waterloo* seems not to have actually participated, nor did *Winona*.

In early July 1940, shortly after her arrival in the United Kingdom, *Waterloo* left London bound north for the Tyne in ballast. Her Master, W.R. Jackson, had a crew of nineteen and, unusually for such a small and recently arrived freighter, she was armed with a 3-inch 12-pounder gun and a .303 Lewis machine gun. She was ordered into Yarmouth, in East Anglia south of The Wash for one day, then proceeded alone well out into the North Sea at 5:30 am on 10 July, and into the northbound route. Jackson passed across the front of a southbound convoy which he could see was already being attacked by aircraft. *Waterloo* turned north at her very modest 6 knots.

At about 11:35, about two miles north of the Smith's Knoll buoy, Jackson sighted an aircraft at a considerable height to their north and noting its changed engine pitch became suspicious. He took up his binoculars and identified the German crosses on her wings. He ordered his gun crew to stand by and load with shrapnel. The plane flew over them and disappeared to the south, but in five minutes returned, now at about 2,000 feet. This was still too high for their elderly 12-pounder which could not be trained at high angles to fire at aircraft. Without dropping lower, the aircraft passed over and dropped a salvo of bombs, later estimated by Jackson to have been six. In an unusually skilful or lucky chance she hit the with two of them, right behind the bridge, into No. 1 hold. The bridge personnel had taken what shelter they could, and when Captain Jackson looked over the after bridge railing he saw that the hatch covers had been blown off and the hold, within those few minutes, was practically filled with water. The aircraft then flew off, assured by the rising smoke it had at least scored a hit.

The ship was by now down by the head, the propeller out of water, so Jackson went aft to see to the launching of the ship's boats. He went forward again to the bridge to collect the ship's papers and dump his weighted bags of confidential books overboard. He then appreciated that the bulkhead between No.1 and 2 holds was also badly damaged and no doubt allowing flooding into No.2 hold. So Jackson himself went into a lifeboat and they rowed around to the bow, where the vessel was now submerged up to her housed anchor. The crew hoped that if the bulkhead held, or the one between No.2 and 3 holds held they might be able to re-board the ship and save some of their personal gear, if not the ship. But fifteen minutes after the bombing, the hatches blew off No.3 hold, indicating the bulkhead forward had given way. The vessel then slowly sank by the bow, hit bottom, rose again a bit, then settled to the bed of the North Sea in about 150 feet of water. No one had been injured seriously, and all reached the coast safely in their lifeboats.

In the case of ships not lost to U-boats, there is sadly very little secondary source information available to tell their story, including in recent books on the Merchant Navy. And the German *Luftwaffe* has much less documented and published material than their naval *Kriegsmarine*, so the attacker has not been identified.

Those lost: None.

Sources: PRO SCS Interview with Master; Greenwood, *Namesakes*; extract pages, *The Wishbone Fleet* (Hall Corp.); notes from Fr. van der Linden.

LENNOX

SHIP: 1,904 grt, 252 ft. bulk lakes freighter. Built in 1923 by Swan, Hunter & Wigham Richardson Ltd. of Wallsend-on-Tyne, England, as *Glenlinnie* for Great Lakes Transportation Company Ltd. Sold to George Hall Company in 1926 and to CSL in 1927.

FATE: Torpedoed and sunk by *U 129* on 23 February 1942, halfway between British Guyana and Trinidad. Two men lost.

The little laker *Lennox* is one whose loss, despite almost all of her crew surviving, has gone almost completely unrecorded in other books. Like several other CSL lakers she was built in the UK in 1923, served briefly under another name and two

CSL's *Lennox* with a deckload of cars. (Ron Beaupré/Alf King)

owners, becoming CSL's *Lennox* in 1927. In error she was registered as *Lenox* for a brief period, then the spelling was corrected to *Lennox*.

She, like others of CSL's ships, was requisitioned by the British MWT for ocean service in 1940. Unlike the two whose stories are told above, she was allocated to the bauxite trade out of the Guyanas on South America's northeast coast. Many of the little Canadian lakers were in this trade just because of their shallow draft, enabling them to go up rivers such as the *Mackenzie* up to sixty-five miles to the bauxite mine loading ports. The larger ships in that trade had to be served by barges and small steamers that brought the ore down river and their cargoes were laboriously transferred at the mouths of the rivers. Bauxite in bulk makes for a heavy cargo, and the lakers were loaded "down to their marks"—sometimes, if the weather was forecast fair, a bit more than that.

Under Captain Daniel Nolan and with a crew of nineteen she sailed on 22 February 1942 from Paramaribo, Dutch Surinam loaded with bauxite for Port-of-Spain, Trinidad, and to call in at Tobago, travelling at 7 knots. At just before 1 p.m. local time on the 23rd, in fair weather and a modest swell in good visibility, *Lennox* was struck with no warning at all by a single torpedo almost amidships on the starboard side at No.3 hold. Within a couple of minutes the ship began to break in two and was hurriedly abandoned into a lifeboat by eleven crew, with another seven leaping into the sea. One of her crew was killed by falling debris, and the other, the ship's cook, was never seen, presumably killed in the torpedo's explosion. The U-boat surfaced and motored over to the lifeboat and someone called down from the conning tower for the ship's name, registry, cargo and destination. He asked if they had enough food, indicated the course to reach land not far away, and told the boat, under the Chief Engineer, to pick up the men swimming in the water around the sinking ship.

The boat passed under the rising ship's stern as it sank, steam water still escaping from her evaporators scalding several in the boat, and went on to rescue the men in the water. Although they set off for the Guyana shoreline, they were picked up somewhat later by the little (399 grt) Georgetown-based molasses tank coaster *Athelrill*. She had been specifically sent looking for two lots of boats sighted by patrolling US Army bombers early in the morning off the Guyana coast. The aircraft had been sent out at dawn due to information reaching Georgetown about several torpedoings in the area, including the Canadian *George L. Torian* the day before. *Athelrill* found *Lennox*'s boat about two hours after their ship's loss. She brought the crew in to Georgetown where medical treatment was provided, and arrangements made to send the Canadians home.

It is significant that more is recorded in available texts about the U-boat, *U 129* and her commander, Kapitänleutnant A. Nicolai Clausen, than about the *Lennox*. Operating out of Lorient in France with 2 U-Flottille, *U 129* made ten war patrols under three commanders. She was on her fourth, having left Lorient on 25 January 1942, when *Lennox* became Nick Clausen's fourth victim. He had already sunk one Norwegian freighter when approaching his boat's patrol area off the Guyanas on 20 February. Then he scored more successes by sinking the Canadian Upper Lakes & St. Lawrence Shipping's *George L. Torian*, also in the bauxite trade; an American ship, the *West Zeda*, late in the afternoon of the 22nd, and *Lennox* the next afternoon. In the *Torian*'s case there was a violent explosion, presumably from bauxite dust, and only four survivors. So in that way the *Lennox*'s crew was relatively lucky.

U 129 under Clausen participated in the rescue of about 225 German seamen from sunken supply ships and raiders, getting them home safely. The U-boat is credited with twenty-nine ships sunk in her ten patrols, and even survived the war, being surrendered at Lorient to the French when she could not put to sea to escape the advancing Allies in late 1944. Nicolai Clausen is credited with twenty-two ships sunk including a French submarine while commanding three U-boats in the Atlantic and Indian Oceans. He was lost off Madeira in May 1943 when his *U 182* was sunk by USS *Mackenzie* with no survivors.

Those lost: Raphael Lupien and Francis R. Murphy

Sources: Notes from Fr van der Linden and DND; USN Survivor Interview transcript; SA form in D HIST file; Greenwood, *Namesakes*; Wynn, *U-Boat Operations*, Vol.1; Kurowski, *Knight's Cross Holders*.

DONALD STEWART

SHIP: 1,781 grt, 250 ft. bulk laker. Built 1923 by Smith's Dock Company,
          South Bank-on-Tees, Middlesbrough, England, for J.F.M. Stewart of Toronto.

FATE: Torpedoed and sunk by *U 517* on 3 September 1942 in Convoy LN-7
          in the Strait of Belle Isle, between Newfoundland and Labrador.
          Three men lost.

Apart from the Quebec & Ontario Transportation Company's *Thorold*, the *Donald Stewart* was about the smallest of the lakers and canallers from any fleet lost to enemy action. Like many of the CSL ships, she too had been built in England, in this case as the *Donald Stewart* for Mr. J.F.M. Stewart of Toronto, and named after his son, in 1923 an accountant with Ford Motor Company. The ship came from the shipyard that was later to become famous in naval circles as the designers of the doughty little Second World War corvette.

The *Donald Stewart* was bought by CSL in 1929 and used in the bulk cargo freight trade down through the St. Lawrence River canals. There is no reason given in CSL's history why her name was retained instead of being changed to a Canadian county name like most of her predecessors. She also was requisitioned for government control in 1941 and put to local use from the St. Lawrence River to Newfoundland. In fact, although listed +100A1 in Lloyd's Register at the time, this unusual note is added: "For Service on the Great Lakes, River & Gulf of St. Lawrence & to St. John's NFL April to 21st November." The insurers were not prepared to risk

SS *Donald Stewart*, one of the very few CSL ships to retain her previous name in their service.
(Jay Bascom)

her in those outer waters in winter months. Rear Admiral Leonard Murray noted in another context that "The Gulf of St. Lawrence is a very unfriendly part of the ocean." She had no armament fitted.

In August, 1942 the *Donald Stewart* left Toronto via Montreal for Goose Bay, Labrador with a cargo of bulk concrete, above which on deck were hundreds of forty-five gallon drums of high octane aviation fuel, on top of which was a layer of lumber supporting nine large dump trucks and an airport fire engine. All this was urgently required for the extension of runways at Goose Bay where the US Army Air Force was feverishly building up facilities. Although located in central Labrador and a hundred and fifty miles inland, its airport facilities were vital in order to provide additional air cover for the badly pressed convoys fighting the mid-ocean wolf packs in the fall of 1942, and for staging bombers being flown over to England. *Donald Stewart* put in to Gaspé overnight on 1 September, where, maybe fortunately for them, two crew deserted her and disappeared.

Early on 3 September the *Donald Stewart*, with a crew of eighteen under Captain Dan P. Nolan (who had already had the CSL *Lennox* sunk under him only seven months before), plus one passenger, was northeast-bound in the upper Gulf of St. Lawrence, at the narrow Strait of Belle Isle between Newfoundland's Great Northern Peninsula and the Labrador coast. She was in a small slow convoy of three little freighters, LN-7, following about a hundred miles astern of a US convoy, SG-6F bound for Greenland. On August 27th/28th that convoy had been attacked by two U-boats working their way southward down the Strait. These were *U 165* (KK Eberhard Hoffmann) and *U 517* (KL Paul Hartwig), heading for the Gulf of St. Lawrence, having left Kiel on 8 August. The US troop transport *Chatham* was sunk by Hartwig just before dawn, as she was running ahead of the other five ships of her convoy, escorted by a USCG cutter. Although carrying 562 troops and crew, only thirteen (or possibly twenty-three, depending on various reports) lives were lost initially, Hartwig appreciating he had sunk a troop when he saw the mass of lifeboats. A large number of crew and soldiers then perished in the frigid waters before the survivors were rescued by a USN escort and HMCS *Trail*, which Hartwig saw but forbade attacking in their humanitarian efforts. Then Hoffmann encountered the rest of the SG-6 convoy, sank one and damaged another tanker which Hartwig sank some hours later, alerted by Hoffmann's radio report to BdU. Buoyed by this success and lack of any observable opposition the two U-boats signalled back to BdU asking permission to continue down into the Gulf. Admiral Dönitz's staff replied "Go ahead" so the two boats continued down to the Gulf of St. Lawrence.

There, on the night of 2/3 September, running with decks awash on the surface the U-boats encountered two convoys just as they were passing each other. *Donald Stewart*'s LN-7 was moving northeast, escorted by the corvettes *Shawinigan* and *Trail*. In the midnight dark, no radar and of course no lights, all these ships in two convoys in the same area has produced much confusion in other histories as to who was where and who saw and did what. Convoy LN-7, consisting of three ships in line abreast was travelling at a modest 7 knots: *Trail* to port, then *Ericus, Canatco* and *Stewart*. Other small ships had joined and departed since they first passed Father Point reporting station at 1100 on 31 August, HMCS *Trail* and *Donald Stewart* coming out from Gaspé on 2 September to join. The other small convoy, NL-5, was moving southwest upriver, escorted by the corvette *Weyburn* and the Bangor escort *Clayoquot*. Convoy NL-5 was just beyond *Trail* to port.

With the escorts' bridge staff intent on watching through their binoculars the faintly seen shadows of the ships in the two passing convoys and wishing to avoid any contact between them, it was not difficult for Hartwig in *U 517* to move into position up-moon by about 1:30 am. He fired first at *Donald Stewart*. As he was lining up his shot, he saw a corvette (*Weyburn*, commanded by LCdr Tom Golby, from the other convoy) suddenly alter toward him, but got his single torpedo away. Hartwig altered away himself, increased speed and started weaving, making an attack by *Weyburn* difficult. *Weyburn* now fired two illuminating 2-inch rockets and her relatively inexperienced gun crew were firing the corvette's 4-inch gun at *U 517* without hitting her. The U-boat submerged, *Weyburn* crossed the swirl and Golby dropped two depth charges somewhat wide of the mark. The depth charge throwers had jammed and failed to release the rest of the planned pattern of six or seven charges. In the mix of fresh and salt water, the noises from the *Donald Stewart* sinking, and the disturbance caused by the two charges that did detonate, "*Weyburn* didn't get a sniff of him" as author Tony German says, who was a junior sub lieutenant in the corvette on that occasion.

U 517's torpedo hit *Donald Stewart* two thirds of the way aft on the starboard side, exploding the gasoline in the drums into a huge funeral pyre, blowing at least the fire truck into the sea, and setting the lumber on fire in turn. A couple of small boats were lowered, one a 14-foot sailing dinghy, and an emergency raft or two. It was difficult to organize, as the flames consumed the whole centre section of the little laker between the bridge right forward and the engine room aft. The ship broke her back in a few moments, rolled onto her side and sank in about seven minutes. Almost miraculously only three of *Donald Stewart*'s complement of twenty were lost, and the boats and rafts managed to avoid the burning fuel oil that surrounded the sinking vessel. The survivors in their precarious craft were rescued by *Shawinigan* and *Trail* and subsequently landed in Quebec City.

The loss of the *Donald Stewart*'s cargo reportedly delayed the completion of the Goose Bay airport's runway extension by six months, according to a news article written later.

U 165 and *U 517* prowled the waters of the Gulf and St. Lawrence River for another two weeks, sinking another nine ships including the armed yacht HMCS *Raccoon* and the corvette *Charlottetown*, as well as damaging two freighters. It was no wonder that this foray became known as the Battle of the St. Lawrence, and forced a closure of the river to almost all traffic for some time. *U 517* was hit later by an aircraft bomb off Gaspé but it failed to explode, and the U-boat reached home safely. Hartwig, who had joined the *Kriegsmarine* in 1935, survived the war to become a senior officer in the post-war *Bundesmarine*. Hoffmann, on the other hand never even reached his home base from this foray. He was lost with all his crew on the way home from his successes in the St. Lawrence when *U 165* probably hit a mine just off Lorient on 27 September 1942.

Weyburn herself was lost to a mine off Gibraltar in February 1943 with eight casualties, including LCdr Golby.

Those lost: Romeo Gaudet, Harry Kaminsky and Harvey Sutherland

Sources: Hadley, *U-boats Against Canada*; German, *The Sea Is At Our Gates*; Rohwer, *Axis Submarine Successes*; Essex, *Victory in the St. Lawrence*; Wynn, *U-Boat Operations*, Vol.1; Greenwood, *Namesakes*; Readers Digest, *Canadians At War 1939-45*, Vol.1; D Hist, LN Convoy records and Form SA; USN Survivor Interview transcript; Collard, *Passage To The Sea*.

NORFOLK

SHIP: 1,901 grt, 252 ft. laker. Built in 1923 by Swan, Hunter & Wigham Richardson Ltd., Newcastle-upon-Tyne, England, as *Glenbuckie* for Great Lakes & St. Lawrence Shipping Company

FATE: Torpedoed by *U 175* on 18 September 1942, off Georgetown, British Guyana. Six men lost.

This little laker was built in 1923 in England, as the *Glenbuckie*, bought by CSL in 1926 and renamed after Norfolk County, Ontario on the north shore of Lake Erie. She too was recorded in some records as sold for war service in 1941 (although technically she would have been requisitioned and was still owned by CSL). In fact she was on charter to The Aluminum Company of America, although this would have been arranged by the government, not CSL. Like the *Lennox*, she was put in the bauxite trade, carrying ore from the rivers of the Guyanas to a transshipment point in Trinidad. She was not armed in any way, nor, like many of these lakers, fitted with wireless. Her Master was Thomas A. Edge, whose crew of eighteen were all shown as British, although they were mostly in fact Canadians, with some Trinidadians as well.

On 15 September 1942 *Norfolk* departed Paramaribo, Dutch Surinam with a full cargo of 3,055 tons of bauxite destined for Port-of-Spain, where it would be off-loaded for ocean-going freighters. The ship was in fact loaded over her marks, given the fair weather expected, the urgency of her cargo (used to make aircraft aluminum), and the relatively short passage. It is interesting that a small ship of some 1,900 tons carried a cargo of a hundred and sixty percent of her own weight.

SS *Norfolk*. (Ron Beaupré/Alf King)

At about 7:00 a.m. local time on the 18th she was steaming northwest at 6 knots off the coast with no other ships in sight, in almost calm seas. Then with no warning of any kind the *Norfolk* was hit by two torpedoes on her starboard side. One hit between No.6 and 7 holds, flooding them, blowing up the hatches and ship's deck and evidently breaking her back. The second hit the bow and "blew up the bridge." In these two monstrous explosions the Master, a deckhand, a watchman, the cook and two firemen were killed. The survivors had no option but to leap into the water. They later estimated that *Norfolk* sank within a minute. They were fortunate that the sea was reasonably warm and they were able to climb onto rafts also blown over by the explosion. The survivors reported seeing nothing of their attacker whatsoever.

After about four hours these castaways, clinging to bits of debris, were discovered by the Spanish freighter *Indauchu*. They were taken aboard and carried to Port-of-Spain by the next day. The number killed seems to be generally agreed upon in records, although the total crew and thus the number saved varies between Canadian, British and USN reports. Also some publications and the records of the Commonwealth War Graves Commission and Veterans Affairs record the men as killed on 19 September, but *Norfolk* was assuredly sunk early on the 18th local time, or just after noon on the U-boat's Central European Time.

Norfolk had been sunk by the larger Type IXC U-boat *U 175* (KL Heinrich Bruns) on her first but very successful patrol. The U-boat had commissioned in December of 1941, transferred from 4 U-Flottille after training in the Baltic to the 10th, and left Kiel on 15 August 1942 for action in the Western Atlantic off the West Indies and South American shoulder. She encountered *Norfolk* almost on arrival, then went on to sink eight more freighters in the same general area before heading home in mid-October. Her second target had been the Norwegian freighter *Sörvagen* that Bruns, electing to save his irreplaceable torpedoes, tried to sink by gunfire. That ship ran herself aground on the coast of British Guyana and was later salvaged. Thereafter Bruns dispatched his victims by torpedo. Bruns sank only one off the African coast on his second patrol. He was sunk himself on 17 April 1943 by two USCG cutters in mid-Atlantic while shadowing Convoy HX-233 as the "contact keeper" to draw in other U-boats. Bruns and twelve of his crew were lost, and forty-one became prisoners of war.

Those lost: Thomas A. Edge, Master, Mortimer F. Bourne, Joseph Goodwill, Edwin Hughes, S. Miller and Conrad Rodney

Sources: PRO SCS Interview; Rohwer, *Axis Submarine Successes*; Wynn, *U-Boat Operations*, Vol. 1; *Lloyd's Register 1941-42*.

CHAPTER 2

Four Early Losses

In Spirit Splendour: a memory of
the history that was.

—Mary MacCarl sculpture, "Spirit Piano"

Not all ships described in these pages were from groups that were lost to companies which provided vessels for war service. The companies and Canada as a whole depended on the continuation of normal enterprise as much as was possible in wartime. Shipping was still essential in many operations, for raw materials such as coal, grain, pulpwood and sand; for finished bulk products such as newsprint and sawn lumber; and for packaged freight and oil products. Thus some companies were only asked to release a few ships. Sometimes, as in the case of the elderly *Maplecourt* of United Towing & Salvage, the company may have been relieved to be rid of an elderly and unprofitable vessel in return for generous government charter money.

But the ships' wartime stories are the same, the same losses, the same sturdy heroics, as with the ships of the larger lines. These four early losses occurred in 1940 and 1941.

THOROLD

SHIP: 1,689 grt, 250 ft dry cargo and paper carrier laker. Owned by Quebec &
        Ontario Transportation Ltd. Built in 1922 by Swan Hunter & Wigham
        Richardson of Newcastle-upon-Tyne, England, as the *Chicago Tribune*.

FATE: Sunk by German dive bombers on 22 August 1940, 2 miles south of the
        Smalls lighthouse off Wales. Nine crew lost.

The little laker *Thorold* was specifically built for Colonel Bertie McCormack's Chicago Tribune Corporation, to transport pulpwood from his distant cutting limits to his paper mills, and newsprint from those mills in Ontario and Quebec to his papers in Chicago and New York. The Colonel did not believe in being dependent on anyone for his supplies or their assured transportation, if his firm could do it better or at less cost. Thus during the early 1920s he acquired outright considerable tracts of spruce pulpwood lands in northern Ontario and in Quebec, as well as leased

The Quebec & Ontario Transportation's *Thorold* in *Chicago Tribune* stack markings. (GLHS)

lands on the huge St. Lawrence island of Anticosti. He constructed some of the largest newsprint mills in Canada to supply his papers in Chicago, New York and elsewhere with paper more cheaply than he could buy it on the open market.

McCormack also formed his own shipping company in Canada, the Ontario Transportation and Pulp Company, incorporated in January 1914. It was re-named Quebec & Ontario Transportation in 1932, and based in Montreal. It was a direct subsidiary of the Ontario Paper Company of Thorold, Ontario, a firm owned outright by the Chicago Tribune Corporation. As late as 1953 the author worked as a forester for the Quebec North Shore Paper Company at Baie Comeau, Quebec, and saw the corporation build massive power dams to supply electricity for their pulpwood plants there.

The *Thorold*, specially designed for efficiency in pulpwood loading and transport, was the colonel's first post First World War new ship. This newest vessel was at first given the primary fleet name of *Chicago Tribune*. When a new diesel-powered vessel was ordered in 1932, the original *Chicago Tribune*'s name was changed to *Thorold* in 1933. At the war's outbreak, Q & O owned one large upper laker and six canallers, and had a few more ships on long term charter.

As soon as regulations allowed when the war began, Q & O's canaller *Thorold* was taken over by the British government's Ministry of Shipping. At first only the *Thorold* was requisitioned. In 1942 two further ships of the company were requisitioned by the Canadian government, but returned to the company in 1943.

Thorold, manned by a British Master and crew, loaded a full cargo of saw logs and safely crossed the Atlantic in convoy. She was put to the coal-carrying trade around the British coast, managed by R.G. Dalgleish. This allowed larger vessels to be released for wider use. One reference (Reader's Digest, *Canadians At War*) says she helped rescue the army at Dunkirk at the end of May 1940, but this is not confirmed in records of all those valiant ships. The same applies to CSL's two ships, *Waterloo* and *Winona*, also not found on any Dunkirk lists. All of these ships were carrying bulk cargoes such as coal to and from ports around the United Kingdom

On 21 August 1940 *Thorold* left Cardiff in south Wales at 7:30 a.m. local time under Captain Henry I. Jackson, a Yorkshireman. She carried a cargo of 2,133 tons of Welsh coal, bound up the Irish Sea, north-about Scotland and down to the Thames and London's power stations. She had a crew of twenty-four including the Master, all British, and two Royal Artillery gunners (although in reports they are incorrectly referred to as RE, Royal Engineers). Their total armament was one hand-held .303 Lewis machine gun. They proceeded at a slow pace down the Bristol Channel, rounded the tip of the Dyfed peninsula during the night and steamed out into St. George's Channel. Although the sky was clear, there was a heavy Atlantic sea running from the southwest which caused the little heavily laden laker to wallow uncomfortably.

At about 11:30 a.m. on the 22nd when the was three miles off a series of rocks just west of Milford Haven called The Smalls, three German aircraft approached from the south. The Master ordered the gun manned, but DEMS Gunner Joseph J. Ducham, RA, had it disassembled for cleaning in preparation for their voyage down the North Sea and into the English Channel. He ran below to get the trigger which had been left in his mess, but he stumbled coming out of the door and this vital part fell out of his grip and was lost overboard. Chief Officer W.G. Goebel and Ducham tried to improvise with a nail, but this did not work. One aircraft flew over at about 2,000 feet, spraying the ship's decks with machine gun fire. When their target did not return fire, it circled and crossed the at lower altitude, firing at it again. Another aircraft flew over and dropped a salvo of bombs which landed about fifteen feet off the ship's side and evidently broke some of the engine bed castings. *Thorold* continued but more slowly, now circling through the waters off the coast.

With nothing now to drive them off, one aircraft referred to as a fighter "flew straight at us again at a height of about fifty feet, continuing machine gunning" noted Mr. Goebel in his subsequent report. The other two aircraft, Dornier 17s, now dropped four large bombs. One hit the bridge right forward, killing seven instantly and seriously injuring the Master, and blowing Goebel out of the wheelhouse. Another bomb dropped somewhere between the forward hatches, smashing all six and ripping up the decks, bringing down the wireless aerials (although the alarm "A-A-A" had already been transmitted, indicating an aircraft attack). The bomb evidently opened up the hull forward as well. A third bomb that landed on the deck forward was a dud, and despite its 200 pounds, was rolled over the side by Gunner Ducham. The aircraft continued to circle and strafe the ship, also dropping fifty incendiaries, all of which landed on and about the ship. Some did not ignite and again the valiant Ducham threw them overboard. He was even able to seize and toss over some that did ignite, including several brought up from the ship's stokehold. This unequal target practice went on for about one and a half hours without respite or any sign of help arriving.

With the Master badly injured and the ship well ablaze, battered and down by the bow, the Chief Officer took over command, and turned the vessel beam-on to the wind and sea to control the fires, even zigzagging, albeit at slow speed, to avoid further bombs, which did not seem to put off the aircrafts' aim. When the four aircraft at last made off, the Master told Goebel to make for Milford Haven, some thirty miles to the southeast. With the ship so damaged and still on fire, and while the seas breaking over her tended to put out most of the fires, Goebel felt later they should have just abandoned her, that pressing on tended to flood the forward hold spaces even more. But a Chief Officer argued with a ship's Master at some peril under any circumstances, so they continued slowly to the east and south, the bows sinking lower and lower in the water. All survivors, even the injured, were told to put on life belts, and the rafts in the rigging were cut adrift and towed behind the ship. One AB's nerve failed, not unreasonably, and he took the Master's life belt from his cabin and was subsequently found hiding in one of the lifeboats.

Realising the ship was now undoubtedly sinking, Goebel ordered the lifeboats lowered even if damaged, and got the remainder of the crew into them or onto the rafts. He also had two men, Second Engineer James B. Bell and AB Nicholas Keily go to the bridge and rescue the Master and the Second Mate whose legs were broken. This they eventually accomplished with quite a struggle, getting them down ladders and over the side onto a raft. They then returned to get the injured Chief Engineer from the ship's saloon. Just then the ship began to settle quickly, and there was a tremendous explosion, either from a delayed bomb or the boilers. This destroyed the lifeboats still close alongside. All the crew were now in the rough and cold water or on rafts, with the fit helping the swimmers and the injured, until there were nineteen in and about the wallowing rafts. The AB who had been in the lifeboat now was found with three life belts on.

These survivors had been in the water and on the rafts for about three hours before they were rescued by a lifeboat sent out, presumably a Royal National Lifeboat Institute rescue boat from St Anne's Head. The Master died from his injuries about fifteen minutes before the boat reached shore, as did the second officer while he was being lifted from the lifeboat onto a stretcher. The two DEMS Gunners RA survived, although one of them, Gunner Grieve, was injured. In all, nine had died in the attack and seventeen survived, crew and DEMS. And the little laker *Thorold* turned out to be the smallest Canadian merchant ship sunk during the war, excluding lost fishing schooners.

Gunner Joseph John Ducham quite properly received an official Order of the British Empire Commendation for his efforts, Engineer Bell an MBE and AB Keily a BEM as well as both of them receiving the Lloyd's Bravery Medal for their efforts that day. One suspects that it was only because, as senior survivor, Chief Officer Goebel probably wrote up the recommendations himself and so received no award for getting the surviving crew away in relative safety. The name *Thorold* was perpetuated in new Q & O lakers after the war.

Those lost: There is only one name for *Thorold* seamen in the Canadian Merchant Navy *Book of Remembrance*. These names all are taken from the Memorial on Tower Hill in London, although Timothy Gosse's name has been recently added to the Canadian *Book of Remembrance*, as he was from Newfoundland.

H I Jackson, Master	E T Baker	G L Botsford
Robert A Emery	J Freeman	H S Glass
Timothy Gosse	C Muscat	J Pace

Sources: SCS interview with the Chief Officer; notes of Fr. van der Linden; *Lloyd's Register, 1938-39*; notes from Mike Collins, England; *The London Gazette*, as amended, 19 Nov. 1940; author's notes.

TREVISA

SHIP: 1,813 grt, 250 ft. dry cargo laker. Built in 1915, at first by Swan, Hunter & Wigham Richardson, and completed by Northern Ireland Shipbuilding Company, Londonderry, who initially owned her, with Stamp & Mann as Managers. When requisitioned she was owned by Canadian Lake Carriers Ltd. of Montreal.

FATE: Torpedoed when in convoy SC-7 by *U 124*, on 16 October 1940, about 200 miles south of Iceland. Seven crew lost.

Trevisa, an elderly small laker, had had seven recorded owners, although some were just company name changes. Her building was slowed by the pressures of First World War construction, she remained in England until 1922, owned by Tawe Steamship Company of Cardiff. She was then sold to Canadian owners, which became the Canadian Lake Carriers Ltd., with Keystone Transport Ltd. as *Trevisa*'s managers.

She was requisitioned and taken over by the British Ministry of Shipping in early 1940, and since no names of those killed in her loss are listed in the Canadian Merchant Navy *Book of Remembrance*, it can be assumed she was manned from British manning pools, the men and officers sent out to pick up the ship at Montreal. In her wartime first, and fatal trip in early fall 1940, under Captain E.M. Walsh with a crew of twenty she had left Montreal, after her engines had been adapted for salt

The Montreal-registered *Trevisa* in a Welland Canal lock under Canadian Lake Carriers stack markings.
(Ron Beaupré/Al Sykes)

The inscription for *Trevisa*'s lost British seamen on the Merchant Navy Memorial at Thames Bank, London. On this memorial are listed the merchant seamen and women for whom there is no known grave but the sea.

(F. Redfern)

water, for Parrsboro in the Bay of Fundy for a full load of spruce lumber destined for Aberdeen, Scotland. The ship joined a slow Sydney group of ships the night of 5 October in what was to become the notorious Convoy SC-7. Notorious because it was to suffer one of the largest percent losses of any wartime convoy. It was routed to pass about 100 miles south of Iceland, planning to reach England in some sixteen days, depending on the weather. After the first day the convoy's only protection was the single RN sloop HMS *Scarborough*. The Convoy Commodore, retired Vice Admiral Lauchlan D.I. Mackinnon, RNR was in the small freighter *Assyrian*. He had originally joined the Royal Navy about 1896!

The thirty-four ships crawled along at no more than 5 or 6 knots in stormy weather, bearing northeasterly, in nine columns of ships, three or four in each column. The front of the convoy extended across more than a mile and a half, its depth half a mile or more, depending how much the ships straggled and had difficulty keeping up in the heavy weather. At least one CSL ship, the little laker *Winona*, turned back the first night out because of dynamo failure which had left her without electricity. She was replaced in the convoy's columns by *Shekatika* which had dropped back from a faster HX convoy ahead, unable to keep up. By the morning of the sixth day out, Thursday 10 October, the heavy seas and force 7 gale had caused the slower ships to lag considerably behind their assigned positions. By dawn on Friday the 11th the convoy had lost four more ships out of sight astern due to the weather alone, two Greek steamers and the remaining two little lakers. To the concern of the meagre escort force's Commander (*Scarborough* by the 16th had been augmented by an RN sloop and a corvette—three warships for the whole convoy), his charges appeared to be spread irregularly all over the ocean. With his escort's lack of any margin of speed, he could do nothing to help the stragglers catch up, and yet could hardly recommend holding back the convoy and thus further endangering all the remaining ships.

The two lakers, *Trevisa* and Hall Shipping's *Eaglescliffe Hall* lost contact with the convoy before it was subsequently attacked by U-boats, dropping farther and farther behind due to the heavy seas, just struggling along on their own in the dark, with no protection whatsoever. But unlike most stragglers that were soon caught by prowling U-boats and sunk, *Eaglescliff Hall*, under her Master Captain Madsen, not only reached Scotland safely but brought in twenty-five survivors from the Greek *Aenos*. That ship had also dropped back, but had paid the penalty on 17 October when sunk by *U 38*. The other Greek ship that straggled from the convoy rejoined it on the 17th, only to be sunk the next day.

Trevisa was not so fortunate. Her Master was inclined to drink, even when at sea, to the considerable concern of his deck officers. When convoy instructions were issued provision was wisely made for stragglers, with a series of courses laid down through way-points, arranged to cut some corners of the planned course to allow them to catch up. These courses were to be adopted depending on when the ship straggled from her convoy. Now the fuddled Master elected to pass through all the way-points, thus steering a series of considerably longer detour legs, rather than hustling eastward and in general trying to catch his convoy further along. Again, tradition and custom dictated that the Chief Officer dared not argue with the ship's Master. By 16 October she was almost 120 miles south and a bit west of SC-7, albeit in much calmer weather.

Fortunately *Trevisa*'s Radio Officer became concerned at this wandering about the hostile ocean, and with the Chief Officer's encouragement, plotted the ship's position ahead for twenty-four hours every half hour and taped the paper beside his morse key. He also rigged up an emergency power supply in case the ship's power failed, and put on his partly inflated life jacket.

Then at about 0140 local time, KL Georg-Wilhelm Schulz on the conning tower of the large Type IXB *U 124*, despite the black night but with faint moonlight, saw *Trevisa* coming out of a rain squall and crossing ahead of him. He submerged to periscope depth and fired a single torpedo at the ship at 0145. It hit, and the ship seemed to disappear in a welter of foam. He noted it in his log as "Sunk" and continued off on his assigned patrol. His radio operator identified the ship just as the boat dived when he heard her signal her radio identity letters.

Aboard *Trevisa* the torpedo had hit near the stern, demolishing the engine room and killing all those on duty including three Engineer officers. The explosion also destroyed the ship's lifeboats, in davits over the engine room. The Radio Officer, Charles Littleboy, leapt from his couch in the radio room, flicked on his emergency light and at once transmitted the fateful "S-S-S" submarine attack signal, the ship's call letters, her assumed position given the time taken from his piece of paper by the key, and the words "SINKING," without waiting for orders from the Master which under normal circumstances was required. He got an immediate response from both sides of the Atlantic, although he still repeated the message several times.

With her stern almost blown off, the little laker was quickly sinking by the stern and rolling partly onto her side. The Second Mate and Littleboy went to launch the remaining liferafts, elemental affairs of four 40-gallon drums in a wooden framework, only to find them inexplicably chained to ringbolts on the deck. Some of the fourteen survivors had wanted to sit on them, let the ship sink and float clear, which would have been disastrous under the circumstances.

The Master had to be roused from his cabin, sobering up rather quickly when told his ship was foundering. One raft's securing cables were soon cut and it dropped over the side. The first seaman to leap after it climbed on and started to drift away. It took considerable cajoling from those yet along the ship's rail to persuade him to paddle back alongside. Another seven men jumped into the sea and clambered onto that raft and it drifted clear. The Second Mate reappeared with two suitcases of personal items, which the Master in fury threw into the sea. Another raft was released and the survivors now jumped overboard and clambered onto it, the Master, Chief Officer and Second Mate, Littleboy and two seamen. They too drifted away as *Trevisa* rolled completely over, bottom up. The two rafts bobbed on the rolling swells, awaiting the day. Several crew anxiously asked the Radio Officer if he had got away a distress message.

Just as dawn was breaking they saw a form approaching, fearful that it might be the U-boat again coming back to finish them off as well. (In 1940 the Germans were still the hated and feared Boches of the First World War.) But it turned out to be a British destroyer, HMS *Kepple*. Although Littleboy flashed with his torch "SUB NEAR", the ship coasted alongside, and spurred by calls to hurry, the merchant seamen all managed to clamber up scramble nets onto the destroyer. Aboard *Kepple* the survivors were found to be uninjured, had a hot meal and went to bed. They were now unemployed, for as soon as their ship was sunk, their pay stopped—the conditions of their service.

Other destroyers also arrived, including HMCS *Ottawa*. The two British ships left, and *Ottawa* proposed to the Commander-in-Chief Western Approaches that she sink the little laker, twenty-five feet still showing about five feet above the surface and thus a danger to other ships. Permission was given, whereupon a few rounds of her 4-inch gun soon allowed *Trevisa* to slide toward the bottom of the Atlantic.

In Convoy SC-7 to the north all was quiet until just after midnight on 16 October, just when *Trevisa* was hit. The German submarine service had ordered twelve or more of its boats to concentrate against not only SC-7 but several other convoys in the general area between Iceland and northern Scotland. There was a faster convoy, HX-77 ahead of SC-7 and HX-78 a day behind, as well as two outbound convoys, OB-227 and 228. The U-boats were manned by some of the most experienced, deadly commanders, all but one to eventually be holders of the Knight's Cross. Names that became famous—or infamous—in the U-boat war against the convoys: Bleichrodt, Kretschmer, Endrass, Frauenheim, Schepke, Prien among them. On the 11th and 12th HX-77 was attacked, losing six ships; on the 15th and 16th the OB convoys off Scotland lost three, with more to come. SC-7 knew there was trouble ahead. Although the escort was joined by another sloop, and then two more corvettes, the convoy suffered almost a massacre over the next three days. Apart from *Trevisa*, fifteen ships were sunk in the forty-seven hours between 0353 on 17 October and 0304 on the 19th, plus the two stragglers, and three more were badly damaged but towed into port. Convoy HX-79 behind SC-7 lost ten ships. And these HX convoy figures do not count stragglers and rompers no longer under the convoys' protection. In that week in that North Atlantic area alone forty-four ships were sunk, with more damaged and out of service. The U-boat arm called it "The Night of the Long Knives."

Trevisa's attacker, *U 124*, had commissioned four months earlier under Wilhelm Schulz. Part of 2 U-Flotille she was operating out of Lorient which she left on 5 October, this being her second patrol. She sank another four ships before returning on 13 November. Schulz had a successful career in this boat for a year, although he had survived the sinking of an earlier U-boat from air attack. He turned over *U 124* to KK Johann Mohr who went on to great success in her, until she was sunk with no survivors west of Portugal on 3 April 1943. Schulz survived the war as CO of several U-boat flotillas.

Those lost: There were no Canadians among those lost from this ship. Seven are listed in the British Merchant Navy Memorial.

Charles Burdon	Jack Cook	John Evans
Samuel Mair	Cecil A. Roach	Ernest Rodger
Crighton B.J. Tait		

Sources: Winton, *Convoy*; Macintyre, *The Battle of the Atlantic*; Showell, *U-Boat Command and the Battle of the Atlantic*; Rohwer, *Axis Submarine Successes*; Wynn, *U-Boat Operations, Vol.1*; notes from Fr. van der Linden; Hay, *War Under The Red Ensign*; Kaplan and Currie, *Wolf Pack*; Lund and Ludlam, *Night of the U-Boats*; *Lloyd's Register, 1919*; Gannon, *Operation Drumbeat*.

MAPLECOURT

SHIP: 3,388 grt, 365 ft. freighter. Built in 1893/94 by Globe Iron Works, Cleveland, O. as *North West* for Great Northern Railways. When sunk she was owned by United Towing & Salvage Company Ltd., Montreal.

FATE: Torpedoed by *U 107* on 6 February 1941, 200 miles west of Northern Ireland. Thirty-five crew lost, two DEMS gunners.

The desperate situation for shipping caused by U-boat depredations in the first year and a half of war is illustrated in the loss of this forty-seven-year-old ship. The *North West* had originally been ordered in 1894 to supplement the rail service of American James J. Hill's Great Northern Railways by providing passenger travel

The *Maplecourt* in one of her mid-life reconstructions at Davie Shipbuilding & Repairing Co., Levis Quebec. Only the part of the ship aft of her foremast is original.
(Author's collection/Davie Shipbuilding)

between Buffalo, New York and the railhead at Duluth on Lake Superior. Hill also had built a similar vessel, the *North Land*. The *North West* was also designed to carry grain, because Hill considered elevator rates for grain storage at the lakehead were unnecessarily high. In her day she was described as palatial, with a single long deck of cabins, three funnels, two tall masts and steam engines that could drive her at up to 27 knots, although 20 was her usual speed. However, with competition from the Detroit and Cleveland Navigation Company's ships, Hill's two sister ships were soon "white elephants." Their Belleville-style twenty-eight boilers were known for their minor explosions, and thus there was always trouble recruiting the large number of firemen and coal-passers they required.

But *North West*'s life even before her wartime adventures was wildly improbable. She was rebuilt with two funnels and improved engine room operations in 1902. Badly damaged by fire in June 1911, *North West* sank at her dock in Buffalo. Although she was raised shortly after, she was left alongside her dock until 1918. Her boilers and engines were removed for wartime-built ships. Even then, the bow portion was lost in a storm while being towed down Lake Ontario in November 1918. Then she was cut in half to enable her passage down the Lachine Canal to Levis, Quebec for re-building in 1920. After new engines, boilers and a new bow were fitted, she was rebuilt to be strictly a cargo vessel and sold to Canada Steamship Lines in 1921, renamed *Maplecourt* and planned for ocean service. But they soon transferred her back up to the Great Lakes, again cut in two for the passage. She stranded in Lake Huron in 1929, and although salvaged again after spending the winter on the rocks, was sold to new owners, at first the Sin-Mac Lines and then United Towing and Salvage, who employed her as a salvage support vessel. That firm had connections with the Simard's Marine Industries Ltd. in Quebec. When the war started, she was requisitioned under the control of the Canadian Government Merchant Marine, sent to Montreal where once again she was rebuilt, and employed on cargo trips to the United Kingdom until sunk in February 1941.

With all this background, it would seem appropriate to have more on this elderly ship's demise, but there is almost no information available on her end. En route from Montreal for Preston, England with general cargo and a crew of thirty-seven under Captain E.H. Humphries, almost all Canadians, *Maplecourt* sailed in convoy SC-20 out of Sydney, Cape Breton on 22 January 1941. While forty-two ships had planned to sail, several were forced to turn back for various reasons: a collision with another ship, deck cargo shifting, engine troubles and other necessary repairs, and only thirty-eight kept on across the Atlantic. By 6 February, in the cold northern reaches between Iceland and Rockall, about 250 miles west of northern Ireland, *Maplecourt* had become a straggler from the convoy although it was still in sight on the horizon ahead. Just before noon she was overflown by an RAF Sunderland, aircraft Y of G flight, 15 Group, that had been sent out to cover the convoy ahead. At that time she was in no trouble, labouring along on her own.

There was later an administrative fuss over the Sunderland low-flying just a few feet above the triatic stays between the masts of several ships, including *Maplecourt*.

But the ship paid the price that stragglers often paid, being sunk by *U 107* about two hours later. One record only refers to there being "no survivors from the terrible explosion and sinking." One could therefore presume she was carrying ammunition or explosives at least in part, although her cargo is recorded as "general." Of the forty-two ships planned for SC-20, only twenty-five reached the North Channel, although only three were sunk by U-boats, all stragglers.

U 107, a Type IXB boat had commissioned into 2 U-Flotille on 8 October 1940. She was commanded by KK Günther Hessler, Admiral Dönitz's son-in-law, who had served in various surface ships and commanded another two U-boats before *U 107*. Despite his connections in high places, he was a very skilled U-boat commander, eventually to be awarded the Knight's Cross for his second patrol (following this one involving *Maplecourt*) in which he sank 86,700 tons of shipping—fourteen ships. This was the largest total sunk in one patrol by any U-boat commander during the war.

In *U 107*'s first operational patrol Hessler had sailed from Kiel on 24 January. He was ordered to patrol off Iceland where he sank a British freighter south of Reykjavik and the ocean boarding vessel SS *Crispin* to the east near Rockall on 3 February. Then he encountered *Maplecourt* south-southwest of there, sank her with one torpedo, and went on to sink one more in operations against another convoy. He had no particular notes recorded about *Maplecourt*'s sinking. Hessler was back in Lorient by 1 March. After his memorable patrol off the African coast near Freetown and one other briefer one, Hessler was transferred to the BdU staff, interviewing returning COs after their patrols. He was a witness at Grand Admiral Dönitz's Nüremburg trials in 1945, and died in 1968 at age fifty-eight.

U 107 went on to many more patrols, her two later COs being responsible for twenty more ships sunk. She herself was destroyed on 18 August 1944 in the Bay of Biscay off La Rochelle by six depth charges of an RAF Sunderland aircraft. There were no survivors of her crew of fifty-nine.

Those lost:	Enrys H. Humphries, Master		Arvo Aho
	Dedier Aucoin	James Bennett	Raymond Berry
	Edison Bowes	Claude Brent	Garfield Campbell
	Herbert R. Clements	Roy Davis	Edward Dewhurst
	Joseph E. Doucette	Andrew Dubé	Frank J. Esson
	Clarence Gallant	J.B. Kelly	Harold Langille
	C.Cornelius H. Luyten	Ray MacGougan	Elmer C. MacLeod
	James Malloy	William Matheson	Michael Morrissey
	James Mount	Albert O'Hanley	Earl O'Hanley
	Adrian Poitras	Roland Potvin	Clarence Richards

William Robertson	Joseph Shaw	Albert Shea
William Small	Ernest F. Trefry	George Young

OS John A. Lockhart, RCNVR, the single DEMS gunner recorded.

There was likely at least one more DEMS, not identified.

Sources: Stanton, *Great Lakes Steam Vessels*; notes from Fr. van der Linden; Barry, *Ships of the Great Lakes*; Bowen, *Lore of the Lakes*; *Lloyd's Register, 1919*; Wynn, *U-Boat Operations, Vol.1*; Rohwer, *Axis Submarine Successes*; McKee & Darlington, *Canadian Naval Chronicle*; Hague, *The Allied Convoy System*.

J.B. WHITE

SHIP: 6,869 grt, 411 ft. freighter. Built in 1919 by Skinner & Eddy Corp., Seattle, for the US Maritime Commission as the tanker *Jadden*.

FATE: Torpedoed in Convoy HX-112 by *U 99* on 17 March 1941 in the North Atlantic 300 miles west-northwest of Scotland. Two men lost.

Like the *A.D. Huff* in Chapter 6, the *J.B. White* was owned by the Atlantic Transportation Company of Montreal. This company had owned only one or two ships over the years, and of the three more it acquired early in the war, it lost them all. *Huff* and *White* were lost to the enemy, and *R.J. Cullen* ran aground in 1942 on the Isle of Barra in the Western Hebrides after a convoy collision. One of their pre-war fleet survived, the elderly *Philip T. Dodge*.

J.B. White's story was somewhat difficult to establish as this vessel had only been bought by Atlantic Transportation at the beginning of 1941 from the US Maritime Commission as *Jadden*. In fact she never appears in any Lloyd's Register as *J.B. White*,

SS *J.B. White* when sailing as SS *Jadden*, in Boston in January, 1922. (W.A. Schell)

as she was sunk before the change could be registered. Although built as a small tanker and used occasionally in the interwar period on short term charters, she had largely been laid up at Hog Island, N.J. during the Depression. When bought by Atlantic, she was converted in Canada to a freighter for their general services.

In March 1941 this rather elderly two-deck freighter was bound from Halifax to Belfast with a cargo of 2,500 tons of steel and 4,500 tons of newsprint. *J.B. White* had a crew of forty under her Master, Captain J.W.R. Woodward, and for defence only had one .303 Lewis gun and five Tommy guns. She left Halifax at 1500 on 1 March in Convoy HX-112.

Part of this convoy, sixteen ships in BHX-112, had come north from Bermuda to be joined off Halifax by another twenty-six ships. One returned to Halifax due to mechanical problems, leaving forty-one to plough northeast across the Atlantic at a very modest average speed of advance over the next thirteen days of only 6 knots, although the actual speed of the ships was around 8 knots. It would take them almost three weeks to reach the UK, in part due to the variable courses steered. The convoy extended across nine columns with four or five ships per column, *J.B. White* leading the ninth or starboard column. Quite a few of its ships were very valuable tankers. Part of their protection against the danger of German surface raiders was the ex-Peninsular & Orient large liner turned armed merchant cruiser HMS *Ranpurna*. The convoy was escorted by the well respected British 5th Escort Group under Commander Donald MacIntyre in the somewhat elderly W class destroyer HMS *Walker*, with four other destroyers and two corvettes. For those early days it was a quite respectable escort force. The Convoy Commodore was Cmdre. F.B. Watson, RNR in the Elder & Fyffes 5,300-ton freighter *Tortuguero*, leading one of the centre columns.

As the *J.B. White* was fitted with HF/DF direction finding equipment, she pressed on ahead of the convoy the first night out so it could be calibrated properly, then dropped back into her assigned station the morning of the 2nd at 1100. Things remained quiet for fourteen long days, until the evening of 15 March when the plodding group was southeast of Iceland. The visibility was good, although it was a pitch dark night, with moderate seas, and winds from the east at 10 to 15 mph. There they were discovered by KL Fritz-Julius Lemp in *U 110*. He promptly advised BdU of the convoy and its course, and BdU ordered up a group of U-boats commanded by the best in the fleet. These included Lemp himself, Joachim Schepke commanding *U 100*, Otto Kretschmer in *U 99*, Nicolai Clausen in *U 37* and Eitel-Friedrich Kentrat in *U 74*. All but Kentrat of this group of highly experienced submariners had already sunk some ninety-four ships between them, including Lemp's sinking of the *Athenia* on the day after war was declared and the aircraft carrier HMS *Ark Royal*.

At about 2222 convoy time on the night of the 15th, Fritz Lemp opened the attack by torpedoing the tanker *Erodona* which exploded in a mass of flames and with a thunderous crash, shocking the rest of the convoy and MacIntyre's escort group. Miraculously the ship survived, and although she dropped astern while the fires were extinguished, even made port. Meanwhile MacIntyre's group by aggressive searching and depth charging drove off Lemp and Clausen who had also joined the hunt. Daylight on the 16th passed with only feints by the U-boats against the convoy.

Meanwhile, just before the next night's attacks were to begin, *J.B. White* had been in a minor collision with the Swedish motorship *Korsholm* in the dark of the night, although neither seemed to be much damaged. Captain Woodward slowed his ship and dropped back to see if she was still seaworthy. Then against the blackness of the sea he saw a surfaced U-boat about 400 yards on his starboard side. Woodward promptly reported this by R/T, fired a white rocket which was a standard action and then quickly altered toward it in a remarkably aggressive action for a twenty-two-year-old unarmed merchantman! The U-boat seemed to dive out of harm's way, and Woodward then resumed course to catch up to the convoy which was moving on, aware of the possibility of attacks.

But during that evening Otto Kretschmer was able to enter the convoy lanes on the port side by slipping unnoticed between two escorts. There, with *U 99*'s decks just awash, he torpedoed two Norwegian tankers, *Ferm* and *Bedouin* and the British tankers *Venetia* and *France Comte* (which survived). Despite being, as he thought, brightly illuminated by the flames of burning tankers, Kretschmer ducked into the huge clouds of black smoke blowing downwind from the ships. He crossed over to the convoy's starboard side, passed down between the two starboard columns where he found and then torpedoed *J.B. White* at 0130 on the 17th just after she had regained her place in the column, as well as her earlier protagonist, the *Korsholm*, almost simultaneously. The *Korsholm* sank very quickly, but the *J.B. White* remained afloat, lying stopped and settling lower in the water as the ships astern swerved around her. Kretschmer, still surfaced, realized the ship wasn't sinking, and despite all the vessels passing, lying almost stopped he fired another torpedo at the vessel which missed and then a third which assured her destruction. Then, all torpedoes spent, *U 99* slipped down the lanes between ships and dropped astern.

The first torpedo struck the *J.B. White* on the starboard side amidships at No. 3 hatch. While there was no particular flash of the explosion and only some water thrown up, with her heavy cargo the *J.B. White* soon began to settle, obviously in danger of sinking. The starboard lifeboat had been thrown out of its davit by the explosion, but the port boat got away with thirty-four men, some in the water hanging onto the grab-ropes around the gunwale. Six crew remained on board including the Master, plus two men who were found later to have been killed in the torpedoing, a Canadian seaman and the English bosun. Woodward chopped away the falls of the starboard boat which then fell overboard into the sea right side up, so the remaining members of the crew dropped into it via the falls and pushed clear.

While the ship had not yet sunk, and the Master hoped she might be re-boarded and possibly saved, fifteen minutes later a U-boat (Kretschmer with his tubes re-loaded), put another torpedo into her port quarter and in fifteen minutes the ship sank by the stern. The survivors were quickly rescued by *Walker*, which Woodward notes, "received them with the utmost kindness and attention." No doubt they were heartened after their shocking experience when half an hour later MacIntyre sank their attacker.

MacIntyre, almost in despair he recalled later at not being able to do anything to stop the destruction, finally saw the faint white wake of a surfaced U-boat near the rear ships of the convoy. He attacked at once with depth charges, then withdrew to rescue survivors of the *J.B. White*. In fact he had severely damaged Schepke's *U 100*, which another destroyer, HMS *Vanoc* then discovered moving slowly on the surface astern of the convoy. *Vanoc* at once dashed at the surfaced boat, rammed and sank her, killing all but six men, including Schepke, pinned in the debris of the shattered conning tower. *Walker* then returned to screen the now damaged and slowly moving *Vanoc*.

MacIntyre was suddenly told by his asdic staff that there was a firm contact just astern of *Vanoc*. He made a quick "by eye" attack with only six depth charges, all that could be got ready in time. Running out and preparing for a more careful attack, he was thrilled by a light signal from *Vanoc* "U-BOAT SURFACED ASTERN OF ME." Kretschmer had been betrayed by his bridge staff, for after his convoy attacks, still on the surface astern and barely awash, his boat probably would not have been sighted when she encountered *Vanoc* by chance. In a purely reflex action, the watch officer gave the order to dive, and *U 99* was immediately picked up by *Walker*'s alert asdic team. The destroyer's charges drove *U 99* down to 700 feet, badly damaging her. Kretschmer ordered the boat surfaced, found that his engines were so damaged he could not move and opened flooding valves, signalling MacIntyre "WE ARE SUNKING. [sic]" All of *U 99*'s crew were rescued from the water as the U-boat sank, except for the Engineer officer who had ducked below to ensure the main vents were indeed open and flooding.

Considering the opposition, the convoy got away comparatively lightly, and two of the *Kreigsmarine's* aces had been killed or captured in the night's battle. (Gunther Prien, another ace, in *U 47* had also been sunk eight days before.)

Kretschmer and *U 99* had departed Lorient on this his eighth war patrol on 22 February 1941. He chased several convoys reported at the end of the month and opened his final round of sinkings on 6/7 March by sinking two large damaged ships that had been hit initially by Prien in *U 47* and left behind their convoy. Kretschmer was then directed to convoy HX-112 and sank five ships and damaged another before being himself sunk by Captain MacIntyre. The *J.B. White* was Kretschmer's third Canadian victim, for he had already dispatched CSL's *Magog* (Chapter 1) and the Newfoundlander *Humber Arm* (Chapter 17) on his second patrol. In fact he also had sunk the RN armed merchant cruiser HMS *Forfar* (the ex-CPR large freighter *Montrose*), requisitioned by the Admiralty in 1940.

He spent the war as a POW in Canada and England, rejoined the *Bundesmarine* in the 1950s and rose to rear admiral. He returned to Canada on one occasion to be a speaker at a well attended Naval Officers Association dinner in the 1960s in Toronto. The event was enthusiastically attended by a large number of those of the Navy who had been trying to defend their convoys against his attacks some twenty years before.

Those Lost: Charles Goodwin and Jack Henry Visser (English)

Sources: SCS Interview with Captain Woodward; correspondence with *Lloyd's Register, April 1966*; D Hist convoy folder *HX-112*; Winton, *Convoy*; Rohwer, *Axis Submarine Successes*; Wynn, *U-Boat Operations, Vol.1*; Robertson, *Night Raider of the Atlantic* and *The Golden Horseshoe.*

CHAPTER 3

Three Varied Losses

I sat back in my chair and soliloquised over what
had happened to all those pestilent attackers of
mine; and I said to myself in those immortal words
of Jonah, "Doest thou well to be angry?...
A worm has smote them all" and they have withered
into obscurity.

–Admiral Sir John "Jackie" Fisher, *Records*

MONT LOUIS

SHIP: 1,905 grt, 253 ft. bulk laker. Built in 1927 by Smith's Dock Company Ltd.,
          Middlesbrough, England for George Hall Corporation Ltd. of Montreal.

FATE: Torpedoed by *U 162* on 8 May 1942, sixty miles off Georgetown, British
          Guyana. Thirteen crew lost.

Bauxite was an increasingly valuable mineral to the war effort, being the primary
ingredient in aluminum. So the product of the large inland mines in British Guyana and
Dutch Surinam (and in French Guyana as well, although for political reasons its
bauxite was not available for shipment in British ships) was vital to the war effort. The
navigable rivers leading in to those mines were not suitable for ocean freighters' deeper
drafts when loaded. But the little shallow-draft lakers and canallers of the Great Lakes
were ideal for moving up the rivers as much as seventy-five to a hundred miles
to the mines, loading with the ore, and returning to a safer and more convenient
transshipment point in the West Indies. It was on this ocean portion of the voyage that
so many of the lakers were sunk when the U-boats were rampaging down the US coast
and into the Caribbean in the winter and spring of 1942 in *Operation Paukenschlag*.

Hall Corporation of Canada or Halco Inc., the firm that ordered *Mont Louis*,
originated as an American firm of 1875, when Hall and Gardner of Ogdensburg New
York purchased their first ship. In 1880 the George Hall Company was established,
often buying older ships for Great Lakes service as bulk carriers of coal and grain.
Then in 1918 the president, Frank Augsbury Sr., set up the subsidiary George Hall
Coal Company of Canada Ltd., based in Montreal. The Hall company began

This delightful photo of *Mont Louis* was evidently taken when on her travels up the rivers of the Guyanas, before May, 1942. Note the pith helmets on some crew, but also the armour plate over the aft bridge windows. Why her bows are buried deep in the shrubbery no one can say! (Mrs. Walter Bowen)

ordering its own new ships from England in 1922, and sold most of its now elderly fleet to Canada Steamship Lines in October 1925. One of these, *Eaglescliff Hall*, was featured previously in the loss of *Trevisa*, another was *Mont Louis*, a new ship ordered from Smith's Dock Company in England.

Mont Louis was named for the village and timber limits on the north shore of the Gaspé Peninsula where Augsbury had pulpwood logging interests. The ship sailed on her delivery voyage from England on 26 May 1927. She carried cargoes of coal, pulp and other bulk freight up and down the lakes until requisitioned by the government in 1940. She was put to the bauxite trade to the transshipment point at Port-of-Spain, Trinidad. Unlike many of these ships, she was to remain under Hall Corporation's Captain Walter Bowen with a mostly Canadian crew of twenty, her contract being "with crew" rather than bareboat charter. *Mont Louis* had no armament or radio aboard.

She left the mine loading port of Moengo on the upper Cottica River in Dutch Surinam on 6 May 1942, and Paramaribo on the coast the next morning, heading the 700 miles north for Port-of-Spain. In a later carefully worded and sworn statement after his ship's loss, Captain Bowen included the exonerating note required of him so that blame could not be attributed to the authorities: "She [the *Mont Louis*] being then staunch, strong, well-manned, victualled and in every respect fit to perform her said intended voyage." This, despite having no armament or escort for her defence against the known presence of U-boats along the American and Caribbean coasts.

She was at sea about 250 miles north off British Guyana, the sea calm and with only a slight swell, on a clear moonless early evening local time on the 8th when she was detected by *U 162*, FK Jürgen Wattenberg. Remaining submerged, Wattenberg tracked the little vessel northward (she would have had a midships freeboard of not much more than six feet) until able to fire a torpedo at the loaded ship, hitting her between No. 5 and 6 hatches at about 9:20 p.m. local time. The Master reported that there was a crash and a cloud of smoke over the bridge, "and at the same time the steamship went down." The *Mont Louis* sank within a minute. With no time for properly launching any lifesaving appliances, the surviving crew were forced to leap overboard into the warm water. The U-boat was never even seen, nor did it contact survivors.

Captain Bowen clung to some floating wreckage, then swam to a liferaft where he joined four other dazed survivors, his second officer, a fireman and two seamen. At dawn the next day this little group saw three more survivors clinging to the wreckage of a small lifeboat and waving, about a mile off. Those on the raft made little headway on their ungainly refuge in their attempts to join up with this other group. There had, of course, been no opportunity to send off an SOS message of any kind. They could do little except hope for a passing vessel to find them purely by chance.

Fortunately, at 8:20 a.m. the next morning, the 9th, they were encountered by the Canadian sailing schooner *Mona Marie*, registered in Nova Scotia but now owned in Barbados and trading in the West Indies and to British Guyana. This schooner picked the four from the raft and then sailed over to rescue the other three: the Chief Engineer Warren Covey, another fireman and a watchman.

Although the schooner searched the area, no more survivors were seen. Thus thirteen of *Mont Louis*'s crew perished in the explosion and sinking. The *Mona Marie* put in to Georgetown, British Guyana with her rescued survivors. They were then transported up to Port-of-Spain, Trinidad, where Captain Bowen, staying at the Queen's Park Hotel, made a statement to a local notary public about the loss of his ship before the crew were sent home to Canada. He ends his report, having barely escaped with his life in his country's service, with again a note: "I am aware that if there is any statement in this declaration which is false in fact, which I know or believe to be false or do not believe to be true, I am liable to fine and imprisonment." Again one gets the distinct impression that if any problems were to arise about the loss of the ship, the authorities certainly were not to be blamed, and maybe Captain Bowen should "carry the can."

Walter Bowen, after a brief rest at his home in Canada, went straight back to sea again and ultimately survived the war. Sadly, the little schooner *Mona Marie* was herself victim of another U-boat, *U 126*, being sunk by gunfire six weeks later just north of the same area, off the Grenadines. (See Chapter 13.)

Mont Louis's attacker, *U 162*, a Type IXC boat, was part of the 2 U-Flottille operating out of Lorient under KL Wattenburg. This was her first war patrol after moving down to those French U-boat bases from Germany. This time she left port on 7 April 1942 for the Caribbean-West Indies-South American operational area. She sank *Athelempress* off Barbados on 30 April and four more ships off Trinidad, British Guyana and off Paramaribo, so there had been plenty of advance notice to naval authorities of the dangers in those waters. Still, no escorts were available for the little solitary lakers, or the priorities for making one available were too low. *Mont Louis* was her next and easy victim. Wattenberg then moved northward to sink three more ships near Barbados, reaching Lorient with all torpedoes expended on 8 June. He was eventually to sink fourteen ships, all while CO of *U 162*.

On his second patrol, leaving Lorient on 7 July for the same area, he attacked tanker convoys in company with another U-boat, near Barbados again. Then on 3 September he fired at the destroyer HMS *Pathfinder* which he missed. Hunted by *Pathfinder* and other escort destroyers his U-boat was located by asdic, depth charged to the surface, illuminated by HMS *Vimy* and sunk. Two of the U-boat's crew died and the balance, including the CO, were taken prisoner and transferred to camps in the US.

The resourceful Wattenberg escaped from his POW camp on two occasions. He was one of only 1,036 military prisoners who actually escaped, of the eventual 288,300 POWs in American camps. Three of these ex-U-boat men, including Wattenberg, had already escaped once from the camp, travelled 130 miles and crossed into Mexico before being caught there. They were returned to the same camp, now with valuable journey details to aid in the later far larger escape. He and twenty-five others, mostly ex-submariners, again escaped through a 200-foot tunnel from the Papago Park Camp near Phoenix, Arizona, on 24 December 1944. Five were recaptured shortly after, but twenty-one remained at large, some like Jürgen Wattenberg for over a month (less than two percent of the total escapees were at large for that length of time), all trying to reach Mexico. In the end, all were recaptured and finished the war as POWs.

Those lost:	Camille Arcand	Pierre Arcand	Harold W. Bagnell
	Maurice Caya	Jean-Paul Charest	J.R. Romeo Dionne
	Charles S Gaumond	Andre LaRochelle	John A MacIntyre
	Delphis Morency	Alcide Pagé	Walter E Tierney
	Roger Vincent		

(The Arcands were not related; at least not brothers)

Sources: Correspondence with Mrs. Walter Bowen; McCormick, *The Wishbone Fleet*; *Lloyd's Register, 1938-39*; Rohwer, *Axis Submarine Successes*; Wynn, *U-Boat Operations, Vol.1*; File in Marine Rail Museum, Owen Sound, Ontario; Krammer, *Nazi Prisoners of War In America*; USN Survivor Interview transcript.

Oakton. (NAC PA 157227)

OAKTON

SHIP: 1,727 grt, 261 ft. laker. Built in 1923 for Mathews Steamship Company of Toronto by A. McMillan & Sons, Ltd., Dumbarton, Scotland. Owned by Gulf & Lake Navigation Company, Montreal.

FATE: Torpedoed by *U 517* on 7 September 1942 about twenty-five miles southeast of Gaspé, Quebec. No casualties.

This little coal and pulpwood-carrying laker had been owned by three firms since its construction in Scotland. Her initial owner, A.E. Mathews & Company of Toronto, fell on financial hard times during the Depression and its three ships were bought by Captain James B. Foote of the Lake Steamship Company in 1931. Then in 1934 R.A. Carter of Montreal purchased all three, *Oakton, Birchton* and *Cedarton,* forming the Gulf and Lake Navigation Company, continuing to employ all three under their original names in the grain, coal and pulpwood trade on the Great Lakes and canals.

Oakton and the others remained in essentially the same trade during the war, although she came under the control of the shipping authorities and was employed in carrying cargoes, usually coal, to Newfoundland. And it was while so employed that she was sunk during the rampage of KK Hoffmann and KL Hartwig in the Gulf of St. Lawrence during August and September 1942.

In late August *Oakton* had loaded 2,285 tons of coal in Sandusky, Ohio, had come down through the St. Lawrence canals and the river, stopping briefly at Quebec. Commanded by Captain Alfred E. Brown with a crew of eighteen, she carried no gun or radio equipment. One report indicates there was at least one DEMS gunner aboard, so she may have had a defensive machine gun. In a local QS convoy, Quebec to Sydney, on her way to Corner Brook, Newfoundland she and two Greek freighters had reached Gaspé on 6 September, where they turned up the Bay to lie in safety overnight, awaiting onward escort protection. Authorities already knew that U-boats had sunk two ships, the Canadian *Donald Stewart* and the Greek *Aeas*, on the 3rd and the 6th in the area just off the Gaspé Peninsula. Just before those sinkings, other ships had also been attacked far to the northeast in the Strait of Belle Isle between Labrador and Newfoundland, and even within Newfoundland's Conception Bay. There was no doubt that the *Kriegsmarine* was bringing the war once again to Canada's very shoreline, as it had in May and July.

Then at 1700 local time on the 7th *Oakton*, *Mount Pindus* and *Mount Taygetus* sailed from Gaspé harbour to join Convoy QS-33 coming downriver, bound for Sydney and Corner Brook. The convoy was composed of five ships protected by the corvettes *Arrowhead* and *Charlottetown*, the armed yacht *Raccoon* and Fairmile motor launches Q-064 and Q-083. That moonless, very dark and somewhat hazy night, just after midnight *Raccoon* was hit by two torpedoes which demolished her, leaving no survivors of her crew of thirty-seven men, although this was not discovered until the following morning when she was found to be missing. Others had heard muffled bangs, but presumed *Raccoon* or one of the Fairmiles was dropping depth charges on some possible target. The convoy had not much option but to press on at its modest 7 knots. The 7th proved to be misty and rainy, with fog making for poor visibility most of the day. A few minutes after 1700 local time, in full daylight, three more ships were hit within seconds of each other, and all sank—*Mount Pindus*, *Oakton* and *Mount Taygetus*.

Oakton was hit amidships on the port side, and with her load of coal soon flooded, folded almost in two, settled by the stern, and sank in 100 fathoms of water. However all her crew of nineteen survived, able to launch boats or jump into the sea and clamber into them. All that was lost was the ship and her large mascot, a St. Bernard dog. The Fairmile Q-083, seeing nothing to attack, hurried about and rescued the survivors from all three ships, nineteen from *Oakton*, seventy-eight in all packed aboard the little 108-foot motor launch. She took them in to Gaspé, where they later caught a train to Montreal. They were cautioned not to say anything to anyone about the attacks, a ridiculous suggestion given that all the locals, and their newspaper reporters, knew exactly what had happened. The U-boat was not seen, either before or immediately after the attacks. Asdic conditions in the lower St. Lawrence were always atrocious due to the mix of fresh water flowing downriver and the salt water welling in with the tides. U-boats had little difficulty remaining undetected under the almost impenetrable layers, then slipping away after a successful attack.

These three sinkings were the work of KL Paul Hartwig's newly worked-up *U 517*. She, *U 165* (KK Eberhard Hoffmann) and *U 513* (KK Rolf Rüggeberg) all of 4 U-Flotille at Kiel, had been sent to operate in Canadian waters, leaving Kiel on 7 and 8 August 1942, and passing north about Newfoundland. In the Strait of Belle Isle the three attacked Sydney-Greenland Convoy SG-6 sinking the American troop transport *Chatham* and damaging and then sinking another freighter. *U 513* then operated around Newfoundland, sinking three ships including the Canadian ore carrier *Lord Strathcona* at anchor in Conception Bay (see Chapter 4) before returning to Lorient. *U 517* and *U 165* moved together down into the Gulf of St. Lawrence, where *U 165* sank *Aeas* on 6 September to open that phase of the battle. Still in the Gulf, she sank another and damaged two more, before turning toward the open Atlantic and home, harassed but not damaged by aircraft as she left.

Previously Hartwig in *U 517* had sunk the *Donald Stewart* on the 3rd, being briefly attacked by the RCN corvette *Weyburn* without damage (see Chapter 1). During the afternoon of the 7th he encountered the remainder of Convoy QS-33, and even signalled Hoffmann that he was shadowing its ships. He moved ahead of the convoy, submerged just to periscope depth and avoiding the escorts, entered the lanes of the convoy itself. He fired two forward torpedoes at the two Greek merchantmen, hitting both, and turned to fire his stern tube at *Oakton*, hitting her as well. While moving off later, on the surface to gain a speed advantage, Hartwig was sighted by a Hudson aircraft of RCAF's 113 Squadron which machine gunned him, but he dove to safety before the aircraft could turn and drop depth charges. He continued upriver and on 11 September torpedoed the corvette *Charlottetown* which was returning to Gaspé from an escort job to Rimouski with the minesweeper *Clayoquot*. The corvette sank with the loss of ten of her crew. Then Hartwig attacked the same convoy harried by *U 165*, also sinking two merchantmen. Because Hartwig suffered a series of air and escort attacks, in addition to his expenditure of torpedoes and fuel, he elected to leave the Gulf on 2 October. He reached Lorient safely on 19 October.

This had been Paul Hartwig's first war patrol as a CO, and turned out to be his only one. He went on his next patrol on 17 November, was attacked by an Albacore aircraft from the aircraft carrier HMS *Victorious* just northwest of Cape Finisterre and sunk. He was taken prisoner with fifty-one of his crew. Hartwig spent most of the war in Canadian POW camps. He rejoined the new Germany's *Bundesmarine* when it was reformed in 1956, rising to rear admiral commanding the fleet in the 1970s. Hoffmann and *U 165*, the other Gulf duo, never did reach home base. While suffering from an aircraft attack on 15 September that may have damaged her, Hoffmann left for his new base at Lorient the next day, but was mined on 27 September in the approaches to that city. All of the crew of fifty were lost.

Those lost: While three men are noted in some reports as lost in *Oakton*, the official Submarine Attack form (SA Form) in file says there were no casualties. If there was a DEMS gunner he would be listed in the Naval *Book of Remembrance*, but not identified as to his ship.

Sources: Hadley, *U-Boats Against Canada*; Essex, *Victory in the St. Lawrence*; McKee & Darlington, *Canadian Naval Chronicle*; Lamb, *On The Triangle Run*; notes from Fr. van der Linden; unidentified 1972 magazine article by Peter

Moon; Wynn, *U-Boat Operations, Vols.1 & 2*; Rohwer, *Axis Submarine Successes*; Greenwood, *Ships' Names*; files from Owen Sound Marine-Rail Museum; USN Survivor Interview transcript; D Hist files, SA Report.

WATUKA

SHIP: 1,621 grt, 249 ft., single deck freighter. Built in 1918 by Nova Scotia Steel & Coal Company, New Glasgow, N.S., engines by builder, owned by Nova Scotia Steel & Coal.

FATE: Torpedoed by *U 802* on 22 March 1944, fifteen miles southeast of the Halifax light vessel. One casualty.

This little collier spent her whole life with the same company in the same trade, and even the advent of war did not change her employment. She is of particular interest to the author, as his grandfather and great uncles were involved in the founding of the Nova Scotia Steel and Coal Company in New Glasgow; and his great-grandfather, Thomas "Foreman" Fraser had been involved in the operation of the shipyards there all his life. In fact the ship would really have been built in what is now Trenton, a town that was simply an extension westward of New Glasgow. To quote James Cameron in *Ships and Seamen of New Glasgow*: "The industry and commerce of Nova Scotia in the 19th century was as solidly predicated on ships and shipping as it was later on coal and steel."

Registered in Pictou, *Watuka* was well known along the Nova Scotia coast, for she had hauled coal from mines in Nova Scotia and Cape Breton around the Maritimes, as far south as New Jersey and east to Newfoundland for twenty-six years. Then, on 18 March 1944, she was filled through her four hatches with her usual load at Louisbourg, Cape Breton with 1,998 tons of "non-gaseous screen coal" and at

Nova Scotia Steel's little collier *Watuka*, carrying on in wartime as she had in peace.
(Murray Manson)

0100 on the 19th hauled out into the stream to await escort. There she sat until the morning of 21 March when she sailed, in Convoy SH-125, Sydney to Halifax, where she was to discharge her cargo. She was commanded by Captain Bennie Pope with a crew of twenty-four and two DEMS gunners.

There were expected to be six ships in the convoy, all destined to various ports such as Halifax, St. John New Brunswick and St. John's, all laden with coal. But one of the six, the little Yugoslav collier *Vis*, was unable to sail due to some unidentified problem. They were to be protected by the small RN Western Isles class trawler HMS *Anticosti*, with the Canadian Bangor escort *Red Deer* to join the next day from Halifax. The little group was formed into three columns, with the convoy commodore accommodated in *Watuka*, leading the centre column. Although ice was encountered off Cape Canso as they approached Nova Scotia's Eastern Shore, the trip was uneventful, until early on the morning of the 22nd. Although it was known that there were U-boats in the general vicinity (hence the dispatch of *Red Deer*), the naval authorities thought they were further out to sea. This assumption was based on nothing having been seen by frequent RCAF air patrols of the area and anti-submarine sweeps by miscellaneous collections of warships available to the Port captain. This concept of "sanitized lanes," had proven impossible to guarantee during the First World War, but was still frequently employed during the Second when escort forces were scarce.

At 0545 local time, as *Watuka* was leading the centre column, still in the dark, an explosion occurred on her port side aft. While the crew later reported that they were sure it was a torpedo, and even identified it as a GNAT acoustic homing torpedo that was attracted toward the ship's propellers, those in the naval staff at Halifax, in assessing the sinking later considered it could have been an explosion caused by coal gas, or of *Watuka*'s magazine for her stern-mounted 4-inch gun—even a time bomb placed by subversives at Louisbourg—since neither submarine nor torpedo track had been seen.

Whatever the cause, the heavily laden little ship sank by the stern in a mere five minutes, all but one of her crew getting clear. Fortunately her boats were swung out, and all the crew lived forward, the officers in the midships section, so they were able to scramble into boats. Her rafts affixed to the rigging were still iced up and could not be released, and the elderly wooden boats leaked badly until they were largely flooded. But *Anticosti* was nearby and everyone was rescued within three-quarters of an hour. *Anticosti* saw and heard nothing of any U-boat, hence the wild surmises later as to what had sunk *Watuka*. In the files there is considerable back and forth correspondence re the possibility of a bomb being added to the cargo in No.4 hold. At this distance in time undetected German sympathizing subversives in clannish Cape Breton seems rather ludicrous.

Some of her crew were injured, and Captain Pope was unconscious when rescued, but only one AB, Murray MacDonald was lost. He had been seen in the doorway to the crew's quarters as the vessel settled, but must have been either struck by something or sucked down when she sank. One young seaman, Gordon Troke, was the son of the ship's third officer, both of whom were saved. There were no further losses in the convoy, or even reports of attacks, and the remaining ships entered Halifax at 0810 local time. The survivors brought in by *Anticosti* were landed in the city, where the Navy League provided them with dry clothing, and saw them on their way home to Sydney.

Red Deer was off the approaches by noon, and the C-in-C CNA sent out a mixed bag of available ships, the corvettes *Battleford, Kenogami, The Pas* and *Alberni* that afternoon. They found no sign of any U-boat. A newly reconstituted W-10 Western Local Escort Group was sent out as well to hunt for the attacker, but also found nothing. In early 1944 there was still an acknowledged communications problem with inter-Service coordination between the Navy and RCAF coastal command aircraft. A quick appearance of a searching aircraft might have found something. But the radio organization to ensure this quick reaction to local submarine reports was not really resolved until after May 1944. The loss of *Watuka* only a few miles offshore at least helped concentrate attention on the problem.

The attacker had in fact been the Type IXC *U 802*, KL Helmut Schmoeckle. He had departed Kiel on 19 January for a task of weather reporting in mid-ocean. Then he was assigned to search the Newfoundland and Nova Scotia coasts for targets of opportunity. He was the U-boat's only operational CO, and *Watuka* was his and *U 802's* only success. He claimed hits on three steamers during the *Watuka* attack, having fired three or four torpedoes, but no other ships were hit, reported seeing torpedo tracks or even any end-of-run torpedo explosions, although those could have been as much as three and a half miles away. Schmoeckle had no further successes in this patrol although he reported attacks and at least one sunk from Convoy HX-286 in an attack off Sable Island on 9 April. Records show no ships were hit. He returned to Lorient 2 May. Schmoeckle went on another war patrol in July 1944, one of the last boats to depart from French bases after the invasion of that country. He was attacked twice by USN aircraft on the way to the Canadian coast again, entered the Gulf of St. Lawrence, reported attacks on shipping there but in fact hit nothing. After his return several abortive sorties were made from Germany to Norway, and Schmoeckle was at sea in *U 802* when the war ended, putting in to Loch Eriboll and surrendering. The submarine foundered on her way out to post-war scuttling off Northern Ireland in Operation Deadlight.

Those lost: Dan A. Murray MacDonald

Sources: DND D Hist Convoy Records & DTD Report; Hadley, *U-boats Against Canada; Lloyd's Register, 1941-42;* Parker, *Running The Gauntlet;* Milner, *The U-Boat Hunters;* Rohwer, *Axis Submarine Successes;* Busch & Röll, *German U-Boat Commanders;* Wynn, *U-Boat Operations, Vol. 2;* USN Survivor Interview transcript.

CHAPTER 4

Two Ships Sunk in the Iron Ore Trade

My coals is spent, my iron gone
My nails are drove, my work is done,
My mortal part rests nigh this stone,
My soul to heaven I hope is gone.

—Epitaph in Shotley Chapel, London, to blacksmith John Hunter, 1792

Iron ore was a vital product, war or no war, and a good many Canadian and foreign ships were in that coastal trade throughout. Although they were directed by the Naval Control of Shipping offices, and when at sea given convoy when warships could be found, these ships essentially continued on their peacetime rounds. However, they faced the same dangers at times as did the merchantmen on the wider oceans bound for the United Kingdom or the Caribbean with wartime cargoes.

The large steel mills at Sydney, Cape Breton in 1939 produced almost one third of Canada's steel output. The mills used local Cape Breton coal for firing their furnaces, but the iron ore came from offshore. Much of it was brought down from Bell Island mines in Conception Bay, Newfoundland. The ore, easily accessible, abundant and of high grade, was brought up by conveyor to loading docks at the Scotia and Dominion piers, on the island's southeast side. Although it cuts deep into the northwest Avalon Peninsula the whole of Conception Bay is not deep, in the order of twenty to fifty fathoms, and when ships were loaded and awaiting convoy, or waiting for space alongside the pier, they anchored about a mile south and east off the port's loading piers.

When the war broke out, material for construction of protective anti-submarine and anti-torpedo nets was not available for other than the major ports, Halifax and Sydney, the latter only in July 1940. Indicator electric loops to detect intruding submarines and defensive mine fields were not laid until May 1942 even at Halifax. There were thus no A/S defenses at Bell Island whatsoever because of perceived more urgent commitments elsewhere, material shortages and the idea that the risk was minimal in a back-water bay. Ashore on the island the seaward defence consisted of two 4.7-inch guns on the top of the high banks above the ore and coal loading piers. A nearby searchlight battery covered the anchorage if necessary. But this was only protection if some hostile vessel were to appear on the surface. It provided no defence against submarine attack if one were to enter submerged or just awash on a dark night.

Then, in early September of 1942, the war arrived deep in Conception Bay. Two ore carriers were sunk by a U-boat in what should have been a safe haven just off Bell Island. And less than two months later, before any practical anti-submarine steps could be taken, two more ships were torpedoed under almost identical circumstances. Two of these four were Canadian registered ships, *Lord Strathcona* and *Rose Castle*. Shortages of available protective anti-submarine vessels left them exposed; static defences to detect or hopefully prevent U-boat incursions came too late. The lesson of vital A/S defences was learned in the hardest way.

LORD STRATHCONA

SHIP: 7,335 grt, 455 ft. Built in 1915 by William Doxford & Sons of Sunderland, England, for the Dominion Steel and Coal Company. Operated at time of sinking by the Dominion Shipping Company of Montreal, a subsidiary.

FATE: Torpedoed and sunk by *U 513* on 5 September 1942, off Bell Island, Conception Bay, Newfoundland. No casualties.

On Saturday 5 September 1942 there were six ships either at the loading piers on the east side of Bell Island, anchored in the bay, or just coming around Bell Island's northeast cape into the anchorage. Many reports of the sinkings refer to Wabana, but that village was more to the west side of the island, opposite the loading docks. Two of the ships at the docks or anchored were British: *Saganaga*, owned by the Scottish firm of Christian Salvesen & Company, and *Drakepool*; two were Canadians, *Rose Castle* alongside and *Lord Strathcona* at anchor. The Free French *PLM 27* (whose unusual name stood for her owners in France, the Paris-Lyon-Marseilles Shipping Company) was at anchor as well. Another Halifax-registered ship, owned by the same company as the *Strathcona* and fifty-three years old

The iron ore and coal carrier *Lord Strathcona* early in the war. (Murray Manson/RCAF)

although still classed as 100.A1 by Lloyd's insurance, was the *Evelyn B.*, under Captain Clayton Guy of Burgeo, Newfoundland. She was just coming into the bay with a load of coal to unload for the mines' lifting engines before taking on a cargo of ore. There was not the slightest sign of anti-submarine defence, no warships. Some ships' personnel commented later that they were concerned at the possibilities of attack in the huge bay, open to the wide Atlantic to the north and east.

Lord Strathcona, by now twenty-seven years old, registered in Halifax, was still in her peacetime role of carrying iron ore in bulk from Bell Island mines to the mills at Sydney, with a crew of forty-two under Captain Charles Stewart, a fifty-four-year-old Scot. She also carried three naval DEMS gunners for her poop-mounted 3-inch gun. The captains of *Saganaga* and *Strathcona* were over in St. John's at a pre-convoy conference, leaving their First Officers in charge, although traditionally these men did not really dare assume the Masters' full authority. At 4:00 a.m. local time on 5 September, *Strathcona* finished loading her full cargo of ore at the dockside at the Dominion pier, left the dock at 6:30, and anchored about one mile off to the southeast at 7:15, near Little Bell Island. There the hands were put to hosing down the ore dust from her loading while she awaited instructions and, hopefully, a convoy escort. Steam pressure in her boilers was allowed to die down to save fuel. All her crew except the Master were aboard. The British ore carrier *Saganaga*, also laden with 8,800 tons of hematite iron ore, was already anchored about 300 yards to the west of *Strathcona*. All was relatively serene on both ships, the crews going about their normal day maintenance duties, steam on no more than one boiler for lighting, water pressure and ship's supply. The Free French *PLM 27* then moved onto the ore loading Scotia pier, where the *Rose Castle* was already alongside loading; *Drakepool* was alongside another pier, the *Dominion*, just astern of these two, discharging general freight before loading ore herself. The weather was clear but with a low cloud cover, the water of Conception Bay quite cold and still.

Suddenly, with no warning or even implication of danger, at 11:07 according to the *Lord Strathcona's* Chief Engineer William Henderson, the *Saganaga* was hit by two torpedoes in rapid succession which exploded with enormous crashes. Some reports tell of her sinking in about fifteen seconds, although it was evidently more like two minutes. It certainly must have seemed like seconds to those involved. At any rate, with her ore cargo and large hatches blasted off, the ship foundered almost at once. Those of her crew of forty-five men and three DEMS gunners who survived the initial explosions were left swimming, struggling dazedly in the cold water of the Bay, covered in wet ore and coal dust, while those aboard the *Strathcona* stared in horror and then dashed to their rescue.

Aboard *Lord Strathcona* it was all too apparent that the attack could only have come from a U-boat despite no one as yet even sighting a periscope. The ships were not moving, so mines were ruled out. Almost at once the thoughtful appreciated that with no naval vessels about, their turn was very likely to be next. There was no hope of raising the anchor in time, or getting sufficient steam up again to avoid being the next target. So without further ado and with the agreement of the Chief Engineer and Third Mate M.B. Glasgow, aged twenty, the crew began to lower boats to save *Saganaga* survivors and probably themselves. The Chief Officer, Ross Creaser, aged twenty-two, who had supervised the loading during the night and had been asleep, now arrived on deck and agreed with the action already under way. He and Second Officer J. Green manned the lifeboats and rowed over to rescue the *Saganaga* men floundering and shouting in the water.

About eight minutes later, as the *Strathcona* was being abandoned, Henderson reported the underwater thud of a hit, assumed to be a torpedo that did not explode, right aft by the rudder. This was followed, at 11:30, only about twenty minutes after *Saganaga*'s spectacular disappearance, by two torpedoes into the *Strathcona* which worked to perfection. One struck at No. 2 hold forward, and the second at No. 7 hold aft. That ship as well sank in about a minute and a half, broken in two. The last crew member off was the valiant radio operator who nonetheless had managed to send out "SUBMARINE ATTACK. WABANA. *LORD STRATHCONA* TORPEDOED" three times.

While no lives were lost in *Lord Strathcona* due to the hasty abandoning of that vessel, it was later learned that thirty-three of *Saganaga*'s crew and her three DEMS gunners perished. Quite a bit of glass was broken ashore in the miners' houses in the nearest little community of Lance Cove and other nearby villages. Now well awakened, their inhabitants prepared to help the dazed survivors as they reached the shore. Also a group of small local boats put out from Lance Cove to help with the rescue efforts.

The surviving ships' gunners, in *PLM 27*, *Rose Castle*, *Drakepool* and *Evelyn B.*, managed to fire a significant number of rounds from their DEMS guns, all at shadows and imagined targets. As one report comments "They opened fire in the probable direction where they thought the submarine might be, at 1,200 yards." Nothing of the U-boat was seen whatsoever. Both *PLM 27* and *Evelyn B.* got twenty-seven rounds away from their 3-inch guns, *Drakepool* four rounds. It was just fortunate that no one else was killed in the fusillade.

An impressive anti-submarine effort was then belatedly mounted. RCAF's Coastal Command aircraft arrived about three quarters of an hour after the attacks, and four naval Fairmile motor launches some two hours later, followed by a corvette and three Bangor minesweeper-escorts. These had to come around from St. John's and steamed into the Bay about 1545, four and a half hours after the first attack. All to no avail, except to help with the survivors and recover a few dead *Saganaga* crew from the water. Infantry regiments were placed on stand-by and coastal watching posts established for the day, but all were withdrawn that evening.

The cargoes in the two sunken ships were valued at some $80,000 and the two ships at a million dollars each, probably an over-statement by their owners for twenty-seven-year-old ships, although in 1942 every ship could again be said "to be worth its weight in gold." The Navy, in the person of Captain Richard Schwerdt, RN, NOIC Dockyard in Sydney, did not take kindly to the findings of an inquiry into the two ships' losses which suggested the Navy should have had some form of protection in place for the anchorage. The Navy's response was that at least *Lord Strathcona* should have veered her cable and then with steam up have charged on it, parted the cable and got away. But it would have taken at least twenty minutes to get steam up enough to move the ship. Obviously there was insufficient time to get under way in the ten minutes between *Saganaga*'s sinking and her own. However the official naval report form SA notes "The crew behaved very badly, considering they abandoned the vessel before being torpedoed."

A Board of Inquiry was held, with the companies and merchant Masters criticising the Navy for lack of any provisions for protection, and the Navy criticising particularly those aboard *Lord Strathcona* for abandoning their too soon, and suggesting this in itself should be the subject of an investigation. But more urgent matters in the Atlantic battle raging offshore prevailed and the inquiry was soon ended and filed. Little real defensive action to prevent or even cope with U-boat intrusions was in fact taken.

Their attacker had been *U 513*, a large Type IXC boat commanded by KK Rolf Rüggeberg. He had left Kiel on this U-boat's first war patrol on 7 August, planning to join the St. Lawrence River invasion by Eberhard Hoffmann in *U 165* and Paul Hartwig in *U 517* which later caused such havoc. Rüggeberg however elected to patrol around Newfoundland when the others went down the Strait of Belle Isle into the Gulf. He was off Conception Bay the night of 4/5 September, watching the traffic entering and considering his options.

Thus before dawn on the 5th he entered the anchorage by following in the wake of the *Evelyn B*. down the western side of Bell Island. His boat was trimmed down but on the surface, as Rüggeberg presumed that the merchant ship would lead him in past whatever anti-submarine nets or defences existed, of which, not too surprisingly, he had no information. Rüggeberg submerged at first light, easing slowly and cautiously toward the Wabana anchorage. He took quick glimpses through his periscope, only raised a foot or so above the surface. There he discovered the peacefully anchored ships under a low cloud cover which made it unlikely he would be sighted by patrolling aircraft. In an unusual attack for U-boats of the time, he fired at *Saganaga* while still submerged, taking only the briefest aiming glances through his smaller attack periscope. The first two torpedoes from his bow tubes failed to even run, let alone hit. So Rüggeberg then turned to fire his stern tubes, again at *Saganaga*, which produced the hoped for results. When he heard those torpedoes explode, Rüggeberg circled around still submerged, but in manoeuvring around *Lord Strathcona* in only 100 feet of water, he collided with the ship's stern, damaging his conning tower and some equipment there, fortunately not his periscopes. This was the thud that Chief Engineer Henderson and others had heard. Getting this sorted out and his bow tubes re-loaded in about fifteen minutes, he then fired three fish at the somewhat larger *Strathcona*, one of which failed to detonate, but the other two sinking the ship.

Rüggeberg, well satisfied with his results, and having expended his ready-use torpedoes, turned away south and west, circled Bell Island again and departed, still completely unseen. The DEMS gunner crew of *Rose Castle*, who had been ashore, also rushed back aboard and fired a round or two at possible periscope targets up Conception Bay. *Rose Castle* had escaped undamaged, but only for two months.

At this point the Army's 4.7-inch guns mounted for the defence of the Wabana anchorage and piers began firing at what they too imagined, at a half to one mile's distance, to be a briefly glimpsed periscope, or anything that looked like a periscope. They even got off a couple of rounds at an inoffensive pilot boat down the shore. Bofors heavy anti-aircraft machine guns were at once moved to the area and then opened up at any swirl in the Bay that looked likely or suspicious. The *Evelyn B.* (which had just been circling and preparing to anchor to await her turn alongside), observing the havoc in the anchorage, immediately weighed anchor and began a swift retreat to the west of Bell Island, weaving about the anchorage, her DEMS gunner and crew getting off a series of rounds at what they took to be a periscope. At least two of these ships' rounds ended up ashore near houses on the island itself, fortunately failing to explode. The sound and fury of the Battle of the Atlantic had suddenly arrived in Conception Bay.

All this shooting was without effect as *U 513* made her way submerged for the fifteen miles out of the Bay, unseen by the RCAF's aircraft, a Hudson from Torbay and a Digby from Gander that arrived about thirty-five minutes later but were hindered by the 200-foot cloud ceiling that barely cleared the hills of the island. An American Digby bomber even arrived at 1350 with a colonel from their operations staff aboard to see if they could help.

Once clear of Conception Bay, the U-boat surfaced and her crew were able to make some vital repairs to the damage on the conning tower from the collision with *Lord Strathcona*. Fog hampered any further sightings by the U-boat until 19 September when she encountered and damaged but didn't sink the British *Ocean Vagabond* off St. John's. With no further successes Rüggeberg departed the area on 10 October, arriving in Lorient on 22 October. The U-boat made two more patrols, the last under a new CO, and *U 513* was sunk by USN aircraft off Uruguay the next summer. Rüggeberg survived the war as commander of a U-boat flotilla from mid-1943 on.

Those lost: None aboard *Lord Strathcona*

Sources: Tucker, *The Naval Service of Canada, Vol. II*; Hadley, *U-boats Against Canada*; Notarized statements by Captain Stewart and Third Officer M.B. Glasgow, PRO, Kew; Parker, *Running The Gauntlet*; Wynn, *U-Boat Operations*; *Lloyd's Register, 1941-42*; correspondence with Capt. Joe

Prim, St. John's; Neary, *The Enemy On Our Doorstep*; McIsaac Inquiry; USN Survivor Interview transcript; D Hist Form SA; Newfoundland Constabulary Report.

ROSE CASTLE

Ship: 7,803 grt, 455 ft. bulk ore freighter. Built in 1915 by Short Brothers, Sunderland, England. Owners were Rose Castle Steamship Company Ltd. of Sydney, N.S., a subsidiary of Dominion Steel & Coal Company.

FATE: Torpedoed and sunk by *U 518* on 2 November 1942, off Bell Island, Conception Bay, Newfoundland. Up to thirty-five casualties.

This ship's duties and fate are tragically similar to *Lord Strathcona*'s above. She too was an older coal and ore carrier, in the trade between the mines on Bell Island and the steel mills in Sydney. She carried iron ore southbound and when sunk was also at anchor off the island, with another familiar nearby, the French-owned and crewed but, for wartime, British managed and registered *PLM 27*. *Rose Castle* was a near sister to *Lord Strathcona* in size and appearance, and had been in the coal-iron ore trade since her launching. She was not glamorous, but essential.

After *Rose Castle*'s close call in early September, many were reluctant to serve aboard these local ore-carriers, often inadequately escorted, so there was quite a crew turnover. However several of the survivors of *Lord Strathcona* transferred to her, including the First Mate, Walter J. MacDonald of Toronto who became *Rose Castle*'s

Rose Castle, lost at anchor like *Lord Strathcona*, showing her in her early war condition, with an emergency liferaft seen on the rigging of the king posts just before her bridge. (Greg Pritchard)

new Master. As well, with all the changes, there is some variation in records as to numbers of the crew on board and confusion in whether the DEMS gunners were included in figures as well, but it appears there were forty crew on her books plus three DEMS gunners.

In mid-October, on passage in ballast from Sydney back to Newfoundland and Wabana by the east and north-about route, in a storm she became separated from her small convoy, WB-9, and had a torpedo fired at her which evidently hit the but failed to explode. She was the target of KL Ulrich Gräf in *U 69*, who was just departing those Canadian waters after the torpedoing of the Sydney–Port aux Basques ferry *Caribou*, with tragic loss of life. An American destroyer came out from the USN base in Argentia as a result of *Rose Castle's* urgent radio call for help (which the German *B-Dienst* listening service also picked up, telling them where Gräf had got to). The destroyer shepherded her into the south coast port of Argentia until she could be escorted in safety around to Bell Island again. She arrived at the Wabana anchorage on 31 October, and went alongside the loading piers at 0830 on 1 November.

There she loaded 10,200 tons of ore and, like her predecessors, at 5 p.m. local time also moved to the anchorage, about a mile southeast of the loading docks, as before toward Little Bell Island. The anchorage was still almost completely unprotected except for the Army's two guns on the clifftop. *Rose Castle* anchored near *PLM 27*, just as *Strathcona* had done less than two months earlier. Unlike earlier in *Lord Strathcona*, a full watch of firemen and trimmers was in the engine spaces to ensure steam for maneuvering if needed. Also at anchor but further north near the loading piers was the somewhat smaller ore ship *Anna T*. The British freighter *Flyingdale* and another ship, the *Panos*, lay alongside one of the loading piers. The Navy had now begun to furnish at least a nominal standing anti-submarine patrol of 108-foot Fairmile B motor launches to provide some protection for the area at Bell Island, but their elementary 123-type asdic sets were not very effective in detecting U-boats if the latter were careful. There were still no anti-submarine net or underwater electronic loop defences installed, which at least would have given warning of an intruding U-boat.

Naval patrol orders had been issued to provide an escort in and out of Conception Bay by corvettes, Bangors and Fairmiles. And when ships were loading at the pier a corvette and the Fairmiles would patrol offshore for protection. In fact on the night of the next uproar, the corvette *Drumheller* and one of the two Fairmiles, *Q 078*, were patrolling offshore but several miles to the north and east of the island, not really where the loaded ships were anchored. The other ML, *Q 057* was lying at Topsail Head on the mainland, across from the north end of Bell Island on standby. Conditions at the anchorage, between Bell Island and the mainland were not good for asdic sweeps, cluttered with echoes from the previously sunken ships, rocks and other debris. The Governor of Newfoundland, Vice Admiral Sir Humphry Walwyn, RN (Retired), on visiting the Conception Bay area earlier that very day, horrified at seeing laden ore carriers lying once again in the open and unprotected anchorage, had telephoned Captain Roger Bidwell, the naval command's Chief of Staff in St. John's.

At about 0103 a.m. on 2 November, on a pitch black, moonless night, havoc erupted once again off Lance Cove. With no premonition of any problems, let alone the presence of an enemy, suddenly a tremendous flash of an explosion, a huge column of water and debris, destroyed a section of the Scotia loading pier, close to the bows of *Flyingdale*. This broke windows and rattled houses for a mile around, waking the whole neighbourhood.

Before anyone could determine what had happened, *Rose Castle* was hit with two torpedoes, and a minute later *PLM 27* with two more. It was an almost identical attack to that in September on the *Lord Strathcona* and *Saganaga*, but in somewhat closer sequence. *Rose Castle* was hit first, just forward of the bridge, then a few yards further aft in the engine room, where the watch of stokers, firemen and trimmers became trapped. As before, both ships sank within a minute or two, but with no time to launch any lifeboats, although the Captain did manage to fire two "snowflake" illuminating rockets. Some rafts were knocked loose or floated clear when the ships foundered, but most of the survivors of both crews were left swimming in the bitterly cold water, trying to grab onto floating debris. In *Rose Castle* many were trapped below, the ship rolled to port, broke up and sank so quickly. In *PLM 27* only ten or so failed to get away. Of *Rose Castle*'s complement of forty-three, twenty-eight seem to have been lost plus at least two DEMS gunners, either in the explosions or in the water. This included her Master, W.J. McDonald, formerly with *Lord Strathcona*. Fifteen survived. British records indicate only twenty-three and one DEMS gunner were lost, while American records indicate sixteen crew and two DEMS gunners survived. This long after the event, it is almost impossible to verify either record.

PLM 27 had a crew of forty-nine under Captain Jean Batiste Caharel, of whom twelve died and thirty-eight were eventually saved. Perhaps fortunately for him Captain Caharel was ashore for the night, arriving at Lance Cove with dozens of others after his ship had disappeared. All those rescued mention their recollection of the freezing water, their inability to even walk properly, talk, or open their mouths when they reached shore. While most life jackets had small lights on the shoulder to help rescuers locate swimmers, of those who had managed to grab one, many men were too cold or too disoriented to even switch them on.

A raft floated clear from *Rose Castle* and some seamen and Engineers who had jumped clear struggled onto it. A few swimmers from both ships were picked up by the two Fairmiles that appeared on the scene within about half an hour, after an abortive sweep around the anchorage looking for the attacking submarine. They hunted about the area for men in the black water. But many were in the water for several hours, time that seemed in retrospect to have been most of the night. Those that didn't have their life belts or jackets on at the time of the torpedoing rarely survived. Since *PLM 27* had been somewhat closer to Bell Island, some of her crew swam the three-quarters of a mile to the island and crawled onto the shore. The huge explosions had awakened everyone on that side of the island once again, so all inhabitants were awake and soon assisting survivors. Suzie, a black Labrador from *Rose Castle* swam to the shore with a sailor clinging to her, then returned to the area where the ship had gone down and ended up on a raft there with survivors. She lived out her life peacefully afterwards at Lance Cove.

The Fairmile took its rescued crew members in to Lance Cove just at dawn, and the villagers wrapped the shaken personnel in blankets, took them to their homes or to the local outport hospital and warmed them with a drink—in some cases the infamous "Newfy Screech!" It was some days before the survivors were able to travel, and with the imposed secrecy about the attack, families were often left with no news, or only knew *Rose Castle* had been sunk but not whether a relative had survived. The story is told of one man who had been serving aboard *Rose Castle* with his son, but was in hospital in St. John's with pneumonia. A nurse came in with the cheerful news that "You won't have to worry about going back aboard that of yours. It's just been sunk!" It took almost a week for the father to learn his son was one of the few survivors. Of those from the *Rose Castle* who died, five were Newfoundlanders, sixteen were from the Maritimes and Alberta and the rest from England, Estonia, Denmark and India. Most of the twelve lost in *PLM 27* were from France.

A funeral was held for the twelve men whose bodies were recovered by the next day, 3 November. Five were buried in the little Anglican churchyard and six at the Catholic church in Lance Cove. One man's body was returned to St. John's.

Proper defences were then placed at the wharves in December 1942 and in May of 1943 more permanent net defences for ships anchored off were installed. However, there were no more serious attacks on the anchorage.

A Board of Inquiry was ordered by RAdm Leonard Murray, the Flag Officer Newfoundland Force. Sitting in St. John's on 4 November, only two days later, it examined the circumstances of this second series of sinkings in Murray's territory. It was presided over by Cdr G.A.M.V. Harrison, RN, the CO of the base at St. John's, HMCS *Avalon*, with an RN lieutenant commander from a destroyer and Lt Tony Griffin, RCNVR of the corvette *Pictou* as members. There was some fairly strong criticism in their final report of the apparent lack of standing orders to direct *Drumheller* as to procedure during events such as this torpedoing, and of the Fairmiles' decision to rescue survivors floundering in the water when their primary duty should have been hunting the submarine. But neither *Drumheller*, nor the Bangor escort *Chedabucto* which came to assist in a few hours, nor the Fairmiles ever found the slightest sign of the departed *U 518*, which had slipped away west then north out of Conception Bay. For the Fairmiles' young RCNVR skippers, Lieutenants John Finlayson and John Gallagher however, it would have been asking too much for them to ignore the merchant seamen dying in the waters off Lance Cove on the off chance of catching their antagonist.

And at Lance Cove, where many of the survivors from all four ships landed and were tended, and where considerable damage from the torpedo explosions occurred, an anchor resurrected from the bay was mounted in November 1994 to commemorate those days and the lost seamen—an anchor raised from the wreck of the *PLM 27*, *Rose Castle*'s neighbour that night.

The U-boat that caused this second havoc, *U 518* (in some write-ups incorrectly listed as *U 578*) was a large Type IXC boat commanded by OL Friedrich-Wilhelm Wissmann. He was in fact on his way to the Baie des Chaleurs between New Brunswick and Quebec, near New Carlisle, to land a German agent, Werner A. Waldmar von Janowski, supposedly to be a spy in Quebec. In the 1930s Janowski had worked on a farm near London, Ontario. News reports of Quebec's disaffection with the war effort and dissatisfaction with the lack of naval protection in the St. Lawrence had encouraged the German espionage people to plan on landing two agents to stir up trouble.

Wissmann had left Kiel at 0700 on 26 September 1942, stopped off at Stavanger/Kristiansand, Norway to top up with fuel, and left there on the 28th, passing into the Atlantic via the Faeroes-Iceland Passage on 3 October. He entered Newfoundland waters on 18 October in almost continual fog. He looked into the Strait of Belle Isle to the northwest, submerged by day and surfaced at night, but found nothing worth attacking. He then elected to see what could be done in Conception Bay, while awaiting a dark moon period with a rising tide, the necessary conditions for landing his agent in the Gulf of St. Lawrence.

Wissmann was just following the lead of Rüggeberg's *U 513* in September, which BdU had encouraged by suggesting but not ordering two other boats to consider her example. Wissmann entered the bay after dark on 1 November trimmed down on the surface, with misty rain falling. He made his cautious way close around Bell Island's southeast end, just like his predecessor KL Rüggeberg. In fact he was aided by Army searchlights that swept the bay at regular ten minute intervals. These in fact only served to illuminate and then silhouette the ships at anchor, making it easier for Wissmann to identify them and take careful aim. At one point, fearing he had probably been seen, he turned away, but was reassured by no activity and altered back, now seeing all three ships in the increasing moonlight.

Despite this, his first torpedo fired at the *Anna T.* with zero deflection angle missed her, passed close under the bow of *Flyingdale* and hit the loading pier, the first startling explosion, destroying several yards of the massive pier and damaging *Flyingdale*. Still on the surface he adjusted his point of aim and within seconds fired two torpedoes and hit *Rose Castle*, which began sinking quickly. He fired a third at *Rose Castle* which seems unidentified in the confusion but was probably the first that hit *PLM 27*. Wissmann then fired one more at *PLM 27* which also sank within minutes. As Rüggeberg had done, after sinking the two ore carriers Wissmann also departed as he records in his log "at full speed, passing close to the southern corner of the island." The first and ready duty Fairmile did not arrive on the scene until fifteen minutes after *U 513* had left. Although there were some reports of sightings of "something" and periscopes, no one had seen the U-boat sufficiently clearly to direct the aim of the clifftop guns.

The intensive anti-submarine air patrols this second attack triggered in fact located *U 518* a few days later off Cape Race, running on the surface. RCAF Digby X of 10 Squadron just missed her with four aerial depth charges as the U-boat dived. They did only slight and repairable damage. Fog prevented any further attacks, and Wissmann continued into the Gulf.

Wissman landed Janowski as planned on the Quebec shore, and slipped away for home, encountering westbound Convoy ON-145 off Nova Scotia where he sank one ship, later two more. His boat survived a thorough depth charging in mid-Atlantic when caught unawares and arrived safely in Lorient. The agent Janowski was caught within two days by suspicious locals through using out-of-date Canadian money. Wissmann survived the war as a flotilla training officer but his *U 518* did not, being sunk by USN destroyers on 22 March 1945 off the Azores, with no survivors.

As an aside to demonstrate we never seem to learn from history, the author was NCSO St. John's for a NATO Control of Merchant Shipping exercise during the early 1970s and elected to anchor several (mythical) deep draft freighters in Conception Bay off Bell Island, as they could not enter St. John's harbour because of their draft. Knowing the above story, to see what the reaction would be, he reported that one of them appeared to have been (mythically) torpedoed by a "Red Force" attacking submarine. There was no reaction of any kind from the exercise controllers in Halifax. The report was ignored, even mythically.

Those lost: As *Rose Castle* was sunk close to shore, quite a few of her crew who died were given burials ashore, including three Muslims, in the Anglican cemetery. Most of the names below are those seamen who died in the waters of Conception Bay and were not found. However those indicated by * come from a list in D Hist files and do not appear in either the Merchant Navy *Book of Remembrance* (the source of all other names), or with the Commonwealth War Graves Commission. But the total below is still less than the number of fatalities usually mentioned. Certainly there seems to be only one potentially Muslim name below. Between various lists there are some spelling inconsistencies.

Walter J MacDonald, Master

		Said Ali
A. Bagnell*	Reginald Bennett	A. Burke*
Fred Burt	A.A. Driscoll*	William J Dwyer
W. James Fillier	Albert E Gabriel	John R Green

Charles Hardy	C. Hardy* (dupl?)	William Henderson
Henry C King	Angus MacLeod	Robert D MacPherson
Robert A Mann	M. Matheson*	Patrick McMullin
Michael J McPherson	G. Meadows	James Miles
Viggo S L D Pherson	R A Ross	Gerald M. Stromsoe
Jean Suga	Arthur J Vatcher	Leonard B Wasson

Plus at least one DEMS gunner, AB William G. McLennon RN

Sources: Hadley, *U-boats Against Canada*; Parker, *Running The Gauntlet*; D Hist File RCN Monthly Report #11 and Form SA; correspondence with Alf Emmerson; *The Wiarton Echo,* 2 Aug. 1995; *Legion Magazine,* Jan. 1995; *Lloyd's Register, 1941-42*; War Graves Commission Register No. 23; correspondence with Capt. Joe Prim, St. John's; Neary, *The Enemy On Our Doorstep*; USN Survivor Interview transcript; Reid, *The Arming of Canadian Merchant Ships in the Second World War.*

CHAPTER 5

Shinai: A Unique Seizure and Loss

The victims of this unsavory chapter seemed to have been innocent bystanders of low degree who were unfortunate enough to stand within reach.

—Thomas B. Costain, *The Last Plantagenets*

SHINAI

SHIP: 2,410 grt, 251 ft., two-deck freighter. Built in 1920 by Collingwood Shipbuilding Ltd., in their affiliated yard in Kingston, Ontario as *Canadian Beaver*, for the Canadian Government Merchant Marine.

FATE: Captured by Japanese forces near Kuching, Sarawak on 24 December 1941. Later sunk by USAF 17 Sep. 1944. One recorded casualty as a POW.

The *Shinai* when still serving as *Canadian Beaver* at a west coast port sometime just after the First World War.
(Vancouver Maritime Museum)

There is almost nothing inscribed in Canadian records of the loss of this Canadian-built and registered freighter to Japanese forces at Kuching on what was then the western Sarawak coast of the island of Borneo, now a part of Malaysia, 400 miles east of Singapore. Much of the information has been derived from secondary sources, such as newspaper reports.

Shinai had been built for the Canadian Government Merchant Marine as one of the continuing run of ships with "Canadian" as part of their names, started just before the end of the First World War and only stopped in 1921. To further complicate her shadowy past, in the published history of the Collingwood shipyard-built vessels, there is no record of *Canadian Beaver*. This is because she was built 200 miles east at a Kingston shipyard where Collingwood Shipyard's owner, Roy M. Wolven, had a financial interest. The firm also owned yards in Port Arthur and Midland at that time. Her engines, though, were produced in Collingwood and shipped to Kingston for installation. These yards were all acquired in 1945 by Canada Steamship Lines Ltd. from the Wolven estate upon his death.

Her brief history is mentioned in S.C. Heal's book on these Canadian-named ships, together with their First World War counterparts with War names (and the Second World War Fort, Ocean and Park ships.) At least the *Canadian Beaver*, he records, tended to considerable instability when loaded with deck cargo, and a photo of her in the early pre-war days shows the ship burdened high with a deck cargo of lumber and leaning drunkenly against the jetty. Part of this load had to be jettisoned when on a trip south she threatened to capsize in only moderate weather. After the First World War the *Beaver* and her sister *Canadian Farmer* were taken over by the CNR, under D.B. Hanna as President, the arm of government that actually operated ships for the Government Merchant Marine. Hanna set up two companies with share capital, one being Canadian Beaver Limited, to operate in their freighting business.

Canadian Beaver was re-named *Shinai* in 1934 when George Shaw of Foochow, China, bought the two ships, the *Beaver* from CN (which allowed the Beaver and Farmer Companies to lapse), and the *Canadian Farmer* from a Finnish company to which CN had sold her during the Depression. Although *Shinai* was registered in Vancouver to G.L. Shaw, with a Vancouver office address and still flying the Canadian-crested red ensign (and thus included here as a Canadian ship), Shaw's principal business interests in 1941 were in China, as George L. Shaw Ltd. In addition to *Shinai*, by 1941 Shaw owned five other small motor lighters and elderly freighters (one dating from 1894), registered in Hong Kong, Singapore and Shanghai, plus the afore-mentioned *Canadian Farmer*, now named *Shin Kuang*. This latter was sunk by Japanese warships in the Bay of Bengal on 6 April 1942.

After the declaration of war between Britain, the Netherlands and Japan in December 1941, the huge island of Borneo, which included the independent states of Sarawak and Brunei, was a target for Japanese seizure, in part because of its oil refineries. Otherwise its continued occupation by British and Dutch forces would have threatened the Japanese southern and seaward flank in their intended drive into the south Pacific islands after Pearl Harbor.

Borneo and Sarawak had only modest defences, despite the oilfields and refineries in the northeast at Miri and Seria in Brunei. A ship was bombed by Japanese aircraft at 9 a.m. local time on December 8th 161 miles off Kuching, Sarawak, and by that day's end, the oilfields and refineries were being destroyed by their staffs, anticipating a Japanese landing in force.

On 4 December 1941 *Shinai* was on a freighting voyage from Palembang in northeast Sumatra bound for Shanghai, China and Manila with a cargo of 3,300 tons of coal. On that date, with the volatile political situation, she was re-routed to Hong Kong by the Admiralty, sailing again from that port on 7 December. With Japanese forces soon sweeping southwards down the Malay Peninsula, attacking the Philippines and offshore shipping, the ship's Master, Captain George C. Walker, who at first had planned to shelter in Manila, resolved to await events eastward in Miri, Brunei, where *Shinai* arrived on 13 December. There, with the likelihood of a Japanese invasion, she was ordered to help evacuate the civilian population, some Indian Army troops and armed local volunteers, others of whom had hurried inland. She and two other RN requisitioned ships (one formerly the Rajah of Sarawak's yacht), took aboard a large contingent of locals and sailed at 2100 on the evening of 13 December, southwest toward Western Sarawak or even "the fortress" of Singapore. All of the ships were attacked by Japanese twin-engined bombers on the 14th, with some casualties in the small armed escort HMS *Lipis* where five were killed and twenty-nine wounded. *Shinai* was discovered and bombed in two attacking runs, probably by the same aircraft, which then flew past and fired machine guns at the ship, killing a fireman and wounding a policeman and a cabin boy. Although the bombs missed, the engine room crew panicked, shut off the steam and tried to seize a lifeboat. They were driven back to their posts by troops of the Sarawak Volunteers who also fired with Lewis guns and their rifles at the aircraft.

Shinai arrived off Tajung Po, near the mouth of the Sarawak River leading up to the capital of Kuching at 0330 on the 15th, and the next morning picked up a pilot to take her up the tortuous, winding river. She was bombed again during the day, although again the bombs missed their target, and two Dutch fighter aircraft arrived to drive off the attacker. She arrived at Pending, on a wide tributary near Kuching on the 16th. There her crew refused to work her any further, believing a Japanese force was gathering offshore, although the ship was ordered to Shanghai by local naval authorities.

Borneo was invaded by Japanese Southern Army troops, estimated at up to 10,000, carried in Japanese freighters and protected by destroyers of their western naval force. They landed at Miri and Seria in northeastern Sarawak and Brunei, just down the coast a few miles, on 16 December 1941 with only minor opposition. It was however a somewhat hollow victory because the refinery at Lutong and nearby oilfields had been sabotaged by the retreating British. Also, a major storm developed and many of the attackers perished before they were able to get ashore.

Another section of the attacking force landed further southwest on 24 December, on the coast of Sarawak, north of Kuching, ten miles up the Sarawak River. That force, the Kawaguchi Detachment, consisting of the 35th Infantry Brigade plus supporting arms, was fortunate to be able to reach their disembarkation point at the mouth of the Kuching River. All three transports were hit by torpedoes fired by the Netherlands "Kolonies" type submarine *K-XIV*, commanded by LCdr C.A.J. van Well Groeneveld. While the Dutch submarine records two of the three ships sunk (*Katori Maru* and *Hiyoshiri Maru*) and the other, *Hokkai Maru*, damaged, the US/Japanese Monograph says all landed most of their troops, although some had been killed and injured in the attack. By 1640 that day, the 24th, the area ashore was in Japanese hands.

The force then turned west by the 26th on their way to seize the oil ports in western Borneo. The Dutch submarine *K-XIV* survived the war, patrolling and attacking in the same area until April 1942 when, after a refit she returned to the Far East and more successful patrols from March 1944 until the war's end.

Japanese planes were flying over the Kuching area each day from the 13th. A search of records in Japan revealed no details whatsoever of the attack that involved *Shinai*. Nor are there any files in the Public Record Office at Kew or in the Department of History and Heritage in Ottawa. However, Monograph #26, translated from the Japanese and held by the Historical Section of the US Army as background for its own history of battles in the area, gives the details of the Japanese attack. And the ship's fate is described in a February 1957 edition of *The Sarawak Gazette*.

Because of the Japanese landing, *Shinai*, now cut off from access to the sea, was taken down the Sarawak River and into a tributary, the Kuop River, and placed so that when the tide went out she would ground on rocks, and a fire was started in No. 3 hold. The Japanese however soon seized the ship and the fire was extinguished. Subsequently the ship was refloated and *Shinai* was later towed to Singapore for repairs after that city's fall to the Japanese in February 1942, some of her original crew being pressed into serving aboard. Her Master rendered a brief post-war report in February 1946, although it has not been located. All her crew were evidently made prisoners by the Japanese. It is likely her seamen and stokers were mostly Chinese, although a Mate, Lo Chien, was also Chinese and certainly survived.

Shinai was re-named *Shinai Maru* after her repairs and used for freighting, until she was sunk by USAF bombers at Starhang Gulf in the Celebese, just east of Borneo, on 17 September 1944. And no histories of the US 5th, 7th or 13th Air Forces, which by then were operating in the area on their road to attacking the Philippines, record an attack on *Shinai* specifically. One vague report indicates that *Shinai Maru* was sunk by a mine, which in fact could be possible as a result of the extensive aerial mine-laying operations undertaken by the USAF, which effectively choked off almost all Japanese shipping by mid-1945.

There were no deaths during her capture, although the Merchant Navy *Book of Remembrance* shows her Chief Engineer, Robert E. Shaw died on 13 February 1942. This occurred while he was a Prisoner of War "for want of medical attention" for what the Japanese recorded as heart failure. His is the only name recorded. The name of the fireman killed during *Shinai's* flight from Miri to Kuching is nowhere recorded. If some of her Chinese crew died as POWs they are naturally not noted in Canadian crew records.

Those lost: Robert E Shaw

Sources: *Lloyd's Register, 1941-42*; correspondence with Masahiro Kawai of the Japanese National Institute For Defence Studies; Official *British Vessels Lost At Sea 1939-45*; Jablonski, *Airwar, Vol. 2*; Collard, *Passage To The Sea*; translated Japanese Monograph #26, US Army Historical Section (Dr. Robert Wright); Dull, *The Imperial Japanese Navy*; Heal, *Conceived in War, Born in Peace*; Website for "Dutchsubmarines.com"; NAC RG95, Vol.1222; correspondence with Mike Cooper and John Henderson; Vincent Foo, *The Story of the Sarawak Steamship Co.*, and *The Sarawak Gazette*.

CHAPTER 6

Two Ships Lost to Heavy German Warships in the Same Month

If I should meet thee
After long years,
How should I greet thee?
With silence and tears.

—Lord Byron, *When We Two Parted.*

The German U-boats were by far the greatest danger to Allied merchant shipping. Around the United Kingdom and in the Mediterranean enemy aircraft accounted for sinking a great many vessels, some of them Canadian. Also around the UK coasts mines were a hazard, sinking two of the Canadian vessels, the *Robert W. Pomeroy* and *Collingdoc*. But almost eighty percent of the losses in these stories were caused by the U-boats.

However, in the early days of the war Germany put to sea most of its large armoured ships from time to time; battle cruisers and heavy cruisers, hoping to seriously disrupt the North Atlantic convoys as well as the sailings of independents in the southern oceans. Grand Admiral Erich Raeder, the *Kriegsmarine's* Commander-in-Chief, was more attuned to surface gunnery ships than was Dönitz with his U-boats, and prepared to scatter them across the oceans to cause major problems for his enemies. The story of the battle between Commodore Henry Harwood's three cruisers and the armoured *Admiral Graf Spee* off Uruguay in mid-December 1939 is well known. So is the destruction of the British battle cruiser HMS *Hood* and the subsequent search, chase and eventual destruction of the huge German battleship *Bismarck* in May 1941. Both of these German ships were operating strictly as commerce raiders before they were caught and sunk. They were not looking to engage in pitched naval battles but to attack merchant shipping. In fact all of them tried hard to avoid any naval confrontations.

Not counting a couple of elderly armoured coastal defence ships, the *Kriegsmarine* employed seven battleships and battle cruisers and two heavy cruisers which caused much anxiety for the Royal Navy and its Allies until the end of March 1941. In all, six of these ships sank forty-eight British and Commonwealth merchantmen, causing disruptions of convoy sailings and major efforts by the RN to hunt them down. Only the mighty *Bismarck* did not sink any merchantmen. And the huge German battleship *Tirpitz* was of concern until its final destruction in October 1944. The problem was not so much the total number of ships sunk by these warships and the heavily armed merchant raiders, but the need for the Allies to counter the threats from these ships all over the world. They bled away badly needed Allied warships from more vital areas. Admiral Raeder knew this and used his ships to advantage.

In the early days of the eastbound convoys, anti-submarine protection was only provided for a day or so as convoys formed up and left the Canadian ports in case U-boats crossed the Atlantic (which it turned out they did not), and in Britain's Western Approaches where they operated in growing numbers. Most convoys of any size or value were accompanied where possible for their voyage by an elderly, usually First World War vintage RN battleship or battle cruiser such as HMS *Royal Sovereign* and HMS *Renown*. This was good protection against possible attack by German armoured ships, which could not afford to risk even modest damage so far from home or air protection or friendly ports for repairs.

Then by late 1941 the German Navy could no longer face the hazards of the unequal surface numbers. Or rather Adolf Hitler would not permit his Naval Commander-in-Chief to risk their warships' destruction and thus the embarrassment of unfavourable publicity. Their surface fleet then became more of a threat-in-being that could be used, requiring large Allied forces to ensure that these ships would be met with superior force if they did attack. The RAF, the Fleet Air Arm and Allied Air forces lost dozens of aircraft and valuable crews trying to destroy or at least seriously damage this handful of heavy warships in their lairs. The attempt for several years to cripple the massive battleship *Tirpitz* in her northern Norwegian fjord attests to the success of this policy of threat-in-being.

Only two Canadian registered merchantmen fell victim to these warships, half a world apart. One was lost in the Indian Ocean and one in the west-central North Atlantic, but amazingly only one day apart, in February of 1941.

CANADIAN CRUISER

SHIP: 7,178 grt, 430 ft. passenger freighter built by Halifax Shipyards Ltd. in 1921. Owned by Montreal–Australia–New Zealand Lines of Montreal when sunk.

FATE: Sunk by explosive charges placed aboard by the armoured (*panzerschiff*) *Admiral Scheer* on 21 February 1941 in the northern Indian Ocean, 600 miles east of Mombasa, Africa. No casualties.

Owned by the Montreal-based firm MANZ, the *Canadian Cruiser* was one of a large number of Canadian-built ships ordered in early 1918 that continued to come off the ways even after the First World War ended. In fact, the Canadian government did not even start to contract for this series of sixty-eight merchantmen of three

Canadian Cruiser, although built under the same arrangements as *Shinai/Canadian Beaver*, is quite different in bridge, funnel and mast arrangements. Dressed overall for some holiday occasion.
(Murray Manson, Halifax Shipyards)

dimensions until March of 1918. This was one of those destined to replace the losses suffered during the war itself. She was of the largest size, about 8,800 deadweight tons, originally owned by the Canadian Government Merchant Marine, which had been incorporated in December 1918. The later was technically owned by CNSS, Canadian National Steamships, which became an operating subsidiary of the CGMM, to some extent vice versa. While originally fitted to carry both freight and twelve passengers, when requisitioned after the start of the Second World War she was to be employed mainly to carry freight. And some records show she was owned by Canadian Tramp Shipping Company Ltd., but at this late date it is almost impossible to determine who should be shown as "owner" as different from "charter manager" or parent company. The Canadian historian Ken Mackenzie refers to ownership as "a byzantine world of shell companies and various layers of ownership," so it is difficult to be certain. The Montreal, Australia & New Zealand Line (MANZ) was incorporated in 1932 to take over CNSS's money-losing Australian service which they had been operating to make use of these surplus First World War ships. MANZ itself was a new company formed on one-third shares each for Cunard's Port Line, Ellerman & Bucknall, and the New Zealand Shipping Company and *Canadian Cruiser* was one of their few remaining elderly ships by the beginning of the Second World War.

After a relatively normal freighting voyage with army supplies to India, on 13 February 1941 *Canadian Cruiser,* under Captain George R. Nuttall and his crew of thirty-five, left Colachiel on India's southwest coast bound for Durban, South Africa with a cargo of iron ore. Aiming to approach the African coast north of Madagascar and then follow it south, the intercepted a radio distress call "R-R-R" indicating a surface raider was in the vicinity. Despite her Canadian registry, the ship was disguised with American flags painted on either side of the hull amidships, on the bridge and also right aft, and she flew the American flag. This *ruse de guerre* was employed by both protagonists.

At about 1800 local time on 21 February, smoke was seen on the horizon from an unidentified warship. While it is not recorded in the *Canadian Cruiser*'s later reports, a small scouting aircraft, an Arado float plane from a German warship, had detected them and reported back. The warship whose smoke they had noted then rose over the distant horizon, steamed rapidly toward them and flashed *Canadian Cruiser* by signal projector in the gathering dusk, asking for her secret recognition letters, and telling them to "STOP FOR CONFIDENTIAL ORDERS."

The Master at first altered toward the distant ship, almost fifteen miles away, signalling "WHAT SORT OF ORDERS?" The warship signalled "PUT ABOUT TO FACILITATE RECEPTION. I WILL SEND A BOAT."

But then recognizing from her massive upper works that she was a large warship, unlike any British ship he knew and more likely the raider of which they had heard, Captain Nuttall altered directly away again and increased to maximum speed—not more than 10 or 11 knots. When challenged Nuttall had given the coded four-letter secret response of the day. This was shortly identified aboard the raider as a British

The German 16,200-ton armoured *Admiral Scheer, Canadian Cruiser*'s unequal nemesis. (Heinrich Dettmer photo)

coded reply, not American. Several more signals were exchanged, each more suspicious, the unidentified ship still pretending she had orders. But Captain Nuttall was now sure he was dealing with an enemy. He increased speed and had his Canadian Marconi wireless operator, Floyd Domina, send the "R-R-R" raider message and his own identity and location several times. The radio transmissions were promptly answered by shore stations at Mombasa, Aden and Zanzibar—also heard aboard the warship and reported to her Captain.

The ship, for it was the massive 26-knot *Admiral Scheer*, was then close enough to illuminate the merchantman by searchlight in the gathering gloom. They were not taken in for a moment by her American disguise. The warship fired a round or two ahead of the merchantman from her 11-inch guns from a range estimated at ten miles (although it was probably less). Then as the merchantman still sailed on, she opened fire with her 3.7-inch anti-aircraft guns, hitting the bridge and wireless office several times and causing most crew to abandon the midships area for the *Canadian Cruiser's* foc's'le. It was patently impossible to escape, so the ship was stopped and her boats prepared for lowering. The German ship slowed nearby, guns trained on the hapless merchantman, and dropped a large motor cutter which came alongside. Soon its officers, led by the English-speaking navigator, determined the ship was assuredly not American, although none of the *Canadian Cruiser's* officers were forthcoming and Captain Nuttall continued vociferously insisting the ship and its crew were all Americans. A search of his cabin however produced the ship's true papers and crew list, most of them of course British seamen. As the crew prepared to leave, *Scheer's* men brought aboard explosive charges, while the Merchant Navy crew waited until more of the warship's own boats arrived to take the last few of them off. No one had been injured so far, and the whole crew of *Canadian Cruiser* were taken aboard *Admiral Scheer*.

German seamen placed explosive charges in her bottom spaces, and, although the prisoners did not see it happen as they were now locked below, the *Canadian Cruiser* sank three minutes after the explosives detonated. With responses heard to the "R-R-R" signals, *Admiral Scheer* advised Berlin that she had sunk the British *Canadian Cruiser*, disguised as an American. Berlin responded by awarding Captain Theodore Kranke of the *Scheer* the Knight's Cross of the Iron Cross, as well as 10 Iron Cross First Class and 100 Second Class to the crew for the successes of their cruise to date. They were ordered home. The ship had been away from Germany almost exactly four months, roaming the whole Atlantic and Indian Ocean at will.

The *Canadian Cruiser's* crew joined those of two other ships, *British Advocate* which was retained and sent back to France by the Germans as a prize, and the Greek *Georgios II* which they sank after searching her cargo, stated to be Red Cross supplies but which was in fact machine guns, armour plate and aircraft tires. The next day they added to their numbers a mostly Malay Dutch crew from the small refrigerated *Rantau Pantjang*. Most of these captives were later transferred to the German supply ship *Ermland* with other prisoners from ships sunk or seized by other German armed merchant raiders operating in the Indian Ocean and South Atlantic. However Captain Nuttall was sent to Germany with one or two others in the blockade-runner merchantman *Portland* because Captain Kranke of the *Scheer* considered him a potential danger if left with others of his own crew, his stern uncooperativeness indicating a possibility of organized rebellion. In fact while crossing the Bay of Biscay later Nuttall did succeed in starting a smoky fire in an adjacent hold, trying to reveal the home-bound ship to searching aircraft. It didn't work, but Kranke's caution was justified.

Leaving the Indian Ocean for the Atlantic, and steaming along the Brazilian coast, the *Admiral Scheer's* captives eventually reached Bordeaux, France, and from there went into the internment camp for naval and merchant navy prisoners, Marlag und Milag Nord in north Germany. All the crew of *Canadian Cruiser* survived their more than four years in captivity, except for Seaman W.H. McArthur, who contrived to escape, reached Gibraltar via Spain and was able to tell authorities what exactly had happened to *Canadian Cruiser*. The had just been listed as missing until he arrived in Allied hands with the details.

The *Admiral Scheer*, a "pocket battleship" of the Deutschland class was the epitome of the *Kriegsmarine's* plans for armoured, high speed, long range commerce raiders. They were specifically intended to bring Germany political respectability on the world naval stage. The three ships, *Admiral Scheer*, *Deutschland* (soon re-named *Lützow* in case she should be sunk!) and *Admiral Graf Spee* had in fact relatively unspectacular careers, although *Admiral Scheer* and *Admiral Graf Spee* did succeed in causing some short term turmoil along shipping routes, as planned. *Admiral Graf Spee* was, however, sunk off the River Plata in mid-December 1939, and the other two confined to German waters from early on in the war.

From her foray into the Indian Ocean and her destruction of the *Canadian Cruiser*, the *Admiral Scheer* arrived in Bergen on 30 March after five months at sea, and went on to Kiel on 1 April. There, a few days later, she was damaged in an RAF raid. Again, in April 1945, the ship was bombed and sunk alongside her dock. The area was simply filled in, with the battleship's remains left beneath the rubble, where it presumably lies today.

Those lost: None.

Sources: SCS interview, W.M. McArthur; official *British Vessels Lost At Sea*; Lenton, *German Surface Vessels 1*; Schmalenbach, *German Raiders;* Halford, *The Unknown Navy*; Kranke & Brennecke, *Pocket Battleship*; Koop and Schmolke, *Pocket Battleships of the Deutschland Class;* Heal, *Conceived In War, Born In Peace*; discussion with Floyd Domina, January, 2001; website for Commonwealth & Dominion/Port Line history, <www.red-duster.co.uk>.

A.D. HUFF

SHIP: 6,219 grt. 410 ft. two-deck freighter. Built in 1920 by Ames Shipbuilding & Dry Dock, Seattle, Wash. as *West Jester*. When sunk she was owned by Atlantic Transportation Company of Montreal and on charter to Canadian International Pulp and Paper Company, also of Montreal.

FATE: Sunk by gunfire of the battle cruiser *Gneisenau* on 22 February 1941 in mid-Atlantic, 610 miles east of Newfoundland. Two casualties.

This standard freighter had had a somewhat varied career, having carried the names *West Jester*, *Oran* (for the Oriental Navigation Company of New York) and *San Anselmo*, also American, until acquired by Atlantic Transportation Company in 1940 and chartered to the Canadian International Pulp & Paper Company (CIP). As the war's shipping losses led to requisitioning of shipping, *A.D. Huff* was swept up like the others. In her case she had a largely Canadian crew. She made a freighting trip or two in convoy to the UK, and in December 1940 as she was leaving England on the way back to Canada she was hit by two bombs during an air attack, one destroying one wing of her bridge, the other fortunately failing to explode. In this shape she reached Halifax again and went into Halifax Shipyards dock for running repairs, which did not include a full replacement bridge. She had an ancient 4-inch gun installed and one crewman recalls the ammunition casings were green with age. Her Master, Captain Woodward, also left for a larger ship.

When ready to sail she went to Dartmouth, Nova Scotia for a part cargo of iron ore ingots, thence to Dalhousie, New Brunswick for her normal cargo of newsprint for CIP, loaded some pit props for Welsh coal mines on top and steamed back to Halifax to await convoy. She crossed safely, arriving eventually in the Thames to

A not too clear photo of the *A.D. Huff*, loaned by one of her POW survivors. As she only served under that name for a year and a half, other photos are non-existent.
(George Shaker)

discharge. For ballast she took on some stone rubble that originated from the Coventry blitz. Again, leaving in mid-February 1941, she crossed safely about half way. Since the U-boats were not yet operating in the western Atlantic in early 1941, the convoy she was in broke up on the 21st and ships proceeded toward their final destinations on their own, the *A.D. Huff* at a modest 8 knots. Her Master, Captain Hugh McDowall, a newly joined Scot recently promoted from First Officer, planned to arrive in Halifax in a few days' time. She carried a total crew of forty-two and her personnel included one DEMS rating for the single gun located aft on her poop deck.

Although there were radio indications that a raider was in the general area, nothing much could be done about that. In late morning of February 22nd a small biplane flew over the ship and dropped a message. It was the pocket battle cruiser *Gneisenau*'s scouting Arado aircraft, and the message told the ship to stop. Captain McDowall of course ignored this and hastened on his way at his best speed— still only about 8 knots. In fair weather and with no other vessels in sight, at 1244 local time ship's lookouts reported a ship on the horizon astern. Almost at once there was the distant thud of heavy guns and two huge shell splashes landed in the *A.D. Huff*'s wake, close astern. Captain McDowall kept his ship moving away west and weaving at her maximum speed, but within a quarter hour their opponent was seen to be a large battle cruiser-style warship which continued periodic shelling of the merchantman with 11-inch guns. The Master dropped smoke floats which seemed of little use, and ordered his puny 4-inch after gun fired at the oncoming vessel, but the DEMS gunner probably wisely refused. One colourful account even tells of Captain McDowall firing a pistol from the bridge at the gun's crew and calling them "colonial cowards" to encourage their defence of his ship, but this is probably apocryphal.

Then enemy fire began to hit the ship, one directly on the *A.D. Huff*'s large anchor windlass on the forecastle, showering her decks with dangerous chunks of flying steel debris. By now the *Gneisenau* was hitting the merchantman with her secondary 5.9-inch armament, her Captain, KzS Otto Fein considering it was unnecessarily wasteful to use his 11-inch guns at this range. Eventually it would seem that the merchantman was hit some thirty-two times, the most damaging being two hits in her engine room, before the Master stopped the vessel and ordered his crew away in lifeboats. The Radio Officer, George Shaker, in fact an employee of CIP, had tried to transmit the raider warning signal R-R-R, but *Gneisenau*'s operators jammed the signal. As the ship's boats drew clear, *Gneisenau* approached to within 100 yards and hastened the *A.D. Huff*'s demise with further gunfire until she sank. Two men had been killed in the engine room when it was hit, the fourth Engineer and a fireman, and the First Officer was badly burned. One boat got away, and then another of the four ship's boats, carrying in all forty surviving officers and crew. After sinking the ship, *Gneisenau* approached the boats—which had started under the Master's direction to row to Newfoundland, 600 miles west—and took all the crew aboard.

A.D. Huff's adversary, the huge German pocket battle cruiser *Gneisenau*. (Heinrich Dettmer)

Treated reasonably well by their German captors, the crew were housed three decks below the upper deck in large spaces cleared for prisoners. They joined the crew of the freighter *Lustrous*, sunk earlier in the day, and before it was over they were joined by two other crews, some of them quite badly wounded. In one case after sinking a tanker, picking up some seamen from a lifeboat and steaming off, the *Gneisenau's* Captain was told there were other survivors swimming around the sinking ship. Captain Fein turned back and illuminated the area by searchlight to rescue the swimmers. Three days later these prisoners were transferred to the supply and prisoner ship *Ermland*, already with men from the *Canadian Cruiser* on board. After a further sweep southward in this transport for several days, *Ermland* set off for France, which they reached at La Rochelle on 31 March. After ten days in a dreadful ex-Foreign Legion barracks at St. Medard-en-Jalles, where they were fed infested ship's biscuits and many contracted diarrhoea, all these prisoners were moved northeast by train in regular passenger cars, but without seats, for Holland and Germany. *A.D. Huff's* Bosun, Ernie Shackleton, and AB Percy Coe were two of twenty men that were able to jump from this train at a stop in a village near Aachen. Although most were shortly recaptured, these two eventually made their way south via unoccupied Vichy France to Spain and Gibraltar, reaching Greenock, Scotland on 14 August, almost six months after their ship had been sunk. Only then were the Allies able to determine what had actually happened to the *A.D. Huff*. The rest of the captives passed on northwest to Bremerhaven and Wilhelmshaven for interrogation, and then fourteen months in Stalag XB. The Merchant Navy prisoners then were moved to the much more amenable naval and merchant marine camp Marlag und Milag Nord near Bremerhaven for the rest of the war. They even put on concerts, musicals and plays, with printed programs, which survive. They were finally released on 27 April 1945 by the British Second Army's Highlanders.

Gneisenau was a 31,800 ton displacement battle cruiser, 771 ft, with nine 11-inch and twelve 5.9-inch guns, capable of 32 knots, under Captain Fein with a crew of about 1,800. She was a sister ship to *Scharnhorst*, with whom she had sailed from Kiel on 28 December 1940, the two under command of RAdm Günther Lütjens. Due to storm damage, the two turned back and departed again on 23 January via Norway, and aimed to get into the Atlantic through the Iceland-Faeroes passage. But they encountered a patrolling British cruiser squadron at long distance, so the pair doubled back around Iceland and down the Denmark Strait into the Atlantic. The aim of the operation was to disrupt the vital convoys throughout the Atlantic area. The two encountered east-bound convoy HX-106 but found it protected by the formidable, although elderly, 'R' class battleship HMS *Ramillies* with 15-inch guns, so they prudently withdrew. Two weeks later, on 22 February they encountered the dispersed ships of *A.D. Huff*'s convoy and the two pocket battle cruisers sank five ships in all. Realizing that the hunt would now be on in earnest, the two heavy warships went southeast to the African coast with their two supporting supply ships. There they sank other freighters, doubled back to the convoy lanes for more sinkings and eventually arrived in Brest on 22 March after two months at sea.

After a refit at Brest, *Gneisenau* and *Scharnhorst* were being prepared for another raid on the Atlantic convoys, when the RAF managed to score a torpedo hit on *Gneisenau* as she lay at anchor in the outer roads, followed by four bomb hits when she was placed in the local drydock. She was never to contribute to the war at sea again. After escaping up-Channel in February 1942 with *Scharnhorst* and the cruiser *Prinz Eugen* in the daring and, to the British, highly embarrassing and costly "Channel Dash" *Gneisenau* was again hit by a large bomb in a drydock at Kiel and immobilized. As the war ended she was scuttled in the harbour entrance in Gdynia in April 1945.

Those lost: William A. Smith and Roy Tustain

Sources: Hughes & Costello, *The Battle of the Atlantic*; Official *British Vessels Lost At Sea*; *Lloyd's Registers, 1922 & 1938-39*; SCS interview with Bosun Ernest Shackleton; Parker, *Running The Gauntlet*; von der Porten, *Pictorial History of the German Navy in World War II*; Lenton, *German Surface Vessels 1*; Ruge, *Der Seekrieg*; Kemp, *Escape of the Scharnhorst and Gneisenau*; discussion with George Shaker, Nov. 2000; notes in D Hist file.

CHAPTER 7

N.M. Paterson Loses Eleven Ships to War

When sorrows come they come not single spies
But in battalions

—Shakespeare, *Hamlet*

The Paterson fleet of lake ships was one of the most severely savaged during the war, the company sending sixteen off for war service, losing five outright to U-boats, another sunk, salvaged and used as a blockship, one sold to the US and sunk, and four more lost to war-related causes. Only five ships returned to the company after the war.

N.M. Paterson & Company was formed in 1908 to buy grain at the lakehead for shipment to eastern Canada. A first storage elevator was built at Fort William (later Thunder Bay) in 1912. Patersons were eventually to own some 100 elevators throughout the west.

A wooden steamer *D.R. van Allen* was their first ship. Steel ships joined the fleet in 1923, then in 1926 Norman Paterson bought eleven bulk carriers from Interlake Steamship Company and formed Paterson Steamships Ltd. All were then given the names of cities plus the ending of "doc." Mr. Paterson, being a strongly supportive federalist, informed people subsequently that the extension stood for "Dominion of Canada." More ships were then ordered, to be built for the firm in the UK. The fleet carried coal, ore and newsprint as well as grain in a competitive market, surviving the downturns of the Depression.

Early in September 1939, on the announced outbreak of war, Mr. Paterson sent a cable to C.D. Howe, then Minister of Transport: "Will you please accept this offer of my loyal support and my services and those of our staff and ships in whatever capacity the Council may deem appropriate."

The offer was accepted, and the first ships were requisitioned on 31 May 1940. They were all canallers, smaller ships capable of passing through the modest locks of the St. Lawrence River below Kingston. The first three taken up were *Collingdoc*, *Kenordoc* and *Portadoc*. None of them ever returned. Paterson continued running the larger upper lakes freighters in their normal trades.

The requisition telegram stated: "By authority of power delegated to me by Minister of National Defence under Regulation Number 48 Defence of Canada

Regulations your vessels *Collingdoc*, *Kenordoc* and *Portadoc* are hereby requisitioned for hire on a bare boat basis by the Government of Canada for service overseas under direction of Ministry of Shipping of the United Kingdom. STOP. Your vessels above mentioned are to be drydocked as soon as possible for steamship inspection and alterations deemed necessary." This presumably referred to engine room changes to allow for operating in salt water, and strengthening to allow fitting of defensive armament and protection.

Thus the requisitioned ships were still owned by Patersons, but on charter only, and with "interest payable at not over five percent." Some Paterson crews went with their ships, or at least with other Paterson ships, and fifty-eight of them were to lose their lives during the war. Few Canadian Paterson crewmen volunteered to go with the British chartered ships as the wages paid were considerably less than the Canadian rate. In addition to these requisitions, Paterson sold some ships, such as *Soreldoc* to the US Maritime Commission for their Army's use. In part because of this unstinting loyalty, Mr. Paterson himself was nominated to the Senate in May 1940.

Later in 1942 and 1943 a number of canallers from various companies were requisitioned by the American War Shipping Administration through Canadian assistance and placed under time charter to Saguenay Terminals and Alcoa Steamship Company. These included six other Paterson ships. But then in early 1943 four canallers were returned to Paterson for Great Lakes service. Trade in Great Lakes bulk commodities still had to be maintained, war or no war, if at all possible. Several of the requisitioned ships were later sold outright, although Patersons bought back *Ganandoc* in 1953 for $275,000 from her American owners.

KENORDOC

SHIP: 1,780 grt, 261 ft bulk canaller freighter. Built in 1926 by Furness Shipbuilding Company Ltd., Haverton Hill-on-Tees, England as *George R. Donovan* for Interlake Steamships Ltd. Owned in 1940 by Paterson Steamships Company, Fort William, Ontario.

FATE: Shelled and sunk by *U 99* on 15 September 1940, 330 miles west of northern Scotland. Seven casualties.

Kenordoc, acquired in 1939, was a late purchase by Patersons, but was the first of the Paterson ships to go on war service, and the first lost. She was manned entirely by British seamen, or at least men appointed by the Ministry of Shipping, under Captain Charles E. Brown as Master.

On 2 September 1940 the ship left Sydney, Cape Breton around noon, in Convoy SC-3 bound for Bristol on her first overseas delivery voyage, fully loaded with 500 standards of timber. The ship carried no armament, but the wheelhouse had been provided with concrete slabs covering its sides and windows for protection from small arms fire in case of attack by aircraft during her work around the United

With the distinctive Paterson P on her funnel,
Kenordoc in the St. Lawrence River system Galops Canal in 1940.
(Gene Onchulenko)

Kingdom. During the night of 5/6 September, in mid-Atlantic, she had to drop out of her convoy with machinery troubles in the pump room, in part caused by heavy seas which proved too much for the little laker. She lay stopped for thirty-six hours while her engine room staff repaired the problem, before setting off again, still in what seemed to her crew to be very heavy seas, at a strenuous 8 knots.

They sighted the convoy in the distance at 1100 on 12 September, six days after they had left it, but had to reduce speed to 6 knots because of the heavy seas. They trailed along, again dropping out of sight of the convoy which could hardly delay or risk all the other ships for the one little laker struggling along behind. This went on for three additional days, until 0925 on 15 September. Then the bridge watch sighted what they thought was a trawler on the horizon, dropping back from the convoy. When examined through binoculars it was soon obvious that the small object was the conning tower of a U-boat. In fact it was *U 99* that had been following the SC-3 convoy herself after having successfully attacked it the previous night. Earlier records say it was *U 48*, but her position when examined post-war did not accord with *Kenordoc*'s and the assessment has been changed.

The Master altered around and put *Kenordoc*'s stern to the U-boat while it was still four or five miles off and worked up to about 7 knots. But the U-boat's surfaced speed of some 15 knots allowed him to swiftly overhaul the ship, approaching within 200 to 300 yards of her port beam. There her CO commenced shelling the little freighter at point blank range with his deck gun. The U-boat commanders would use gunfire if the risk was minimal rather than their small stock of much more costly and (to the intense annoyance of COs) quite unreliable torpedoes. The Master threw overboard his confidential books and ordered all the engine room crew on deck as the first shell hit the bridge right forward, shattering the concrete shelter and injuring the helmsman. Geoffery T. Barker, the twenty-one-year-old wireless operator from Lancashire, England, had already got away the "S-S-S" submarine attack message and their position, staying at his set until he was sure it had been received. He was killed by another shell fired deliberately at the wireless office to silence him, which demolished the little space. The Master as well was evidently wounded or killed in this exchange.

The U-boat shelled *Kenordoc* for ten minutes, firing about twenty-five rounds, all of which seemed to hit the ship. The port lifeboat had been more or less destroyed when knocked out of its cradle and davits, so with the Master dead, the Chief Officer, Mr. Donald Kerr, ordered the starboard boat away, into which all but the Chief Officer, the Third Engineer and one seaman clambered, pushing off into the heaving seas. Kerr shortly after threw overboard the wooden gangway and tried to push over the seaman clinging in terror to the rail, who refused to jump clear. Another shell's explosion blew Kerr himself over into the ocean, where he swam to the gangway and was soon joined by the Third Engineer. The ship settled by the stern before anything further could be done to help the remaining seaman on board.

With the ship evidently sinking, the U-boat approached the lifeboat and "a young-looking Captain who spoke perfect English" asked the name of the ship and its cargo. Without noticing the two officers clinging onto the grating, the submarine moved away to the westward. It was two and a half hours before Kerr and the Engineer were picked up by the lifeboat which came back for them, despite the heavy seas. It now contained thirteen men, six of them injured by the shell fire or in abandoning the freighter. With a strong wind blowing they were all wet and cold so Kerr had the ablebodied take turns rowing—toward Ireland!—to keep their circulation going.

At about 1630 that day the RN destroyer HMS *Amazon*, no doubt alerted by the S-S-S call, came along and picked them up. Kerr felt most of them would not have lasted the night because of the cold and waves slopping into the boat. Since *Kenordoc*'s bow was still showing, buoyed by her lumber cargo, *Amazon* shelled it until the ship sank. The destroyer's crew treated the distressed seamen most kindly, the wounded being accommodated in the officers' bunks. The survivors were landed at Greenock two days later.

For his efforts in taking charge, saving the crew and getting them away after the Master was killed, Donald Kerr was awarded the OBE and Lloyd's Medal for Bravery, while the young radio operator Barker was awarded a posthumous commendation and also Lloyd's Bravery Medal.

Although *U 48* is taken in most records to be the boat that sank *Kenordoc*, there was some doubt about this. And recently this loss has been attributed to KL Otto Kretschmer's *U 99*. Jürgen Rohwer had earlier credited *U 48*, the war's most successful boat, with fifty-four ships sunk on twelve patrols and another four damaged, forty of the sinkings under her two commanders Rösing and Bleichrodt. However, it seems more likely it was Kretschmer, who had left Lorient on 4 September, tried to attack Convoy SC-2, was driven off, attacked and sank an independent ship, joined *U 48* in tracking SC-3, encountered *Kenordoc* and sank her. This time he returned to Lorient on 25 September, but was himself sunk six months later, just after sinking the Canadian *J.B. White* in March of 1941. He was taken prisoner for the rest of the war.

Those lost: (all from Britain)   Charles E Brown, Master
                     Geoffrey T Barker   John P Barrow   Thomas Dodds
                     Robert Kilgour   James J Moralee   Stanley Scott

Sources: SCS interview with Mr. D. Kerr, PRO; DND D Hist records; Seedie, *Merchant Navy List*; Trembley, *How Great The Harvest Is*; Rohwer, *Axis Submarine Successes*; Wynn, *U-Boat Operations, Vol. 1*; correspondence with Rob Fisher, D Hist.

PORTADOC

SHIP: 1,740 grt bulk canal freighter. Built in 1924 by Cammel Laird & Company Ltd., Birkenhead, England, as *Eugene C. Roberts*. Named *Portadoc* by Patersons after Port Arthur.

FATE: Torpedoed by *U 124* on 7 April 1941, 175 miles off Freetown, Sierra Leone, West Africa. Eventually two casualties, as POWs.

Another little laker requisitioned for overseas service, *Portadoc* had originally been renamed *James B. Foote* in 1925 as soon as she arrived in Canada from her builders. She was rebuilt and modernized somewhat in the 1930s, and bought by Patersons in 1939 as business improved following the Depression. She was typical of her type, with a small high wheelhouse over a cabin right forward with a mast close behind; right aft was another rectangular deckhouse with a tall thin funnel rising from it and another mast. On the funnel even in wartime black could still be seen the shadow of the distinctive large white P, used by the firm until its last ships were disposed of in 2003.

On 14 July 1940 the minutes of the Canadian Shipping Board recorded that the new licences for operation of twenty-one lake vessels requisitioned by the Canadian government were "for and on behalf of the British Ministry of Shipping." On 14 January 1941, an application had been made by Canadian Import Company of Quebec (who were to be *Portadoc*'s temporary managers) for "supply of a ship for a freighting voyage, Sydney, Nova Scotia, Saint John, New Brunswick and to Sierra Leone for and on behalf

Portadoc in the Galops Canal in 1939 or 1940. The plume of smoke from her coal-fired boilers demonstrates the problem these ships had whereby the dark smudge attracted U-boats from beyond the horizon.
(Ron Beaupré/George Deno)

of the British Ministry." Even then all was not smooth sailing, for her first British crew refused to sail the little ship for distant Africa. They were removed and another crew appointed—unfortunately for them to some extent. Thus *Portadoc* went to war. Under her Master, Captain J.E. Jones she carried a Canadian crew, not Paterson men but appointed by the Shipping Authority, men obtained from a merchant seamen pool in Nova Scotia. At least two came from Ontario, from Meaford and Port Colborne.

Portadoc loaded coal in Sydney, topped up with other cargo in Saint John and at the end of March 1941 set off down the US coast and then alone across the Atlantic toward the west African coast and Freetown, Sierra Leone. She was scheduled to be docked in that British colony as a bunker for coal-burning merchantmen, halfway between South Africa and the United Kingdom. Not a glamorous occupation, but a necessary one that would require a minimal merchant naval crew. She was destined never to even arrive in Freetown.

At about 3:30 local time, when quietly plodding along at about 7 knots some 175 miles west of Freetown the deeply laden ship was hit by a torpedo fired by an unseen U-boat. None of the crew were seriously injured, although it was quite apparent that the ship, loaded to her Plimsoll marks with heavy coal, was quickly sinking. About twenty men, most of the crew, hastily abandoned into one lifeboat. A raft was also released, onto which Bosun Fred Jones and Harry Lachapelle scrambled after jumping into the sea. The U-boat then surfaced, motored toward them and called the raft alongside. The Captain in very passable English called down

"Come aboard and we'll check you over." The two men scrambled aboard the wallowing U-boat with some difficulty, had some cuts and bruises treated and were given a glass of brandy. When another of *Portadoc's* empty lifeboats drifted near, two German sailors dove in, swam to it and bailed it out. The U-boat then towed it over to the overcrowded first lifeboat. The Captain gave the survivors extra provisions and told them they were about 176 miles west of Freetown. He added "But there is a 3 knot southerly current along this coast so you had better steer a little north." With a wave from those on the conning tower, the submarine then turned away and shortly after submerged again. *Portadoc* had sunk by this time.

The crew divided themselves between the two boats and set off sailing east. On the second day they noted a periscope again, presumably the same U-boat checking on their progress, which soon disappeared. However their course adjustment had been too great or the current was less, for in six days they landed at Benty in French Guinea, north of Sierra Leone, where they were subsequently very ill-treated by the French and abused by their Singhalese guards.

The local French were loyal to Vichy, and bitterly opposed to anything British, or even to the Free French of the almost unknown General De Gaulle. This animosity was largely due to the highly controversial destruction of French warships at Oran the previous July and an aborted attack on Dakar in October by the Royal Navy to prevent those valuable warships from falling under German control. This sorry attack had killed many French. The *Portadoc's* crew were grilled like enemy captives at Conakry for six days. Then, with survivors from the British ship *Tweed*, they were mustered and seven *Portadoc* and five *Tweed* men, under age eighteen or over forty-eight, were told they were to be released. Returning the thirteen miles to Benty, they were given one of *Portadoc's* lifeboats under command of a *Tweed* officer, some supplies, and told to sail south to Freetown. After some arguments between the British and Canadian crews, and stranding on sandbanks, this little group arrived at Lungi, fourteen miles from Freetown. There native crews succoured them, they were able to reach Freetown and eventually Britain in the *Britannic*.

The other survivors of *Portadoc*, *Tweed* and the Danish *Samsr* were then sent by train to a rough straw hut prison camp inland, seven km west of Kindia. There they suffered from malaria, dysentery and scurvy, receiving a few handfuls of rice per man per day, but no cooking facilities to heat water. In the makeshift hospital there *Portadoc's* Second Engineer, Lewis Elliott died on 25 May, on his fortieth birthday. He was buried in his uniform in a rough Army coffin.

In the same camp were prisoners from another six or more sunken Allied merchantmen, all treated severely by their erstwhile Allied captors. Some of the ex-Vichy French merchantman *Criton's* deck officers, whose ship was seized by the British and then in a mistaken fit of zeal sunk by their own Vichy French sloops, refused to say they had scuttled their ship and were convicted of "piracy" and transported further inland to Timbuctoo.

A very long six months and eighteen days after their capture, on 8 June most of the men were told they were being exchanged for French troops captured in the Allied seizure of Lebanon and Syria. They were taken by truck thirty-five miles south toward the Sierra Leone border and a further eight miles along a dirt path with a French guide, to a simple dirt road crossing in the jungle. There the sorry lot were released with no food or supplies whatsoever, and merely told they were four days' march from Freetown. While struggling along the rough road, another unidentified crew member died and was buried in the jungle. He was evidently not a crewman from *Portadoc*. The survivors reached a river where a passing British boat picked them up and took them down to Freetown. There they were in hospital for six weeks, and these *Portadoc* men repatriated to Canada. One man, Fireman Schou, was too ill to travel and remained behind for some time. Their supposed arch-enemy in the U-boat had been notably kinder to these survivors than those who should reasonably have been at least neutral friends.

Portadoc's attacker had been *U 124*, KL Georg-Wilhelm Schulz, aged thirty-six, who had been in the merchant marine before joining the *Kreigsmarine*. This was probably the reason for his considerate treatment of his victims, which he evidenced in at least one other case a few days later. This was his fourth war patrol, leaving Lorient on 23 February 1941 for patrol in the central Atlantic area, along the routes between South Africa and the United Kingdom. He had sunk four ships, replenished from a German merchant raider near the equator, went north again and sank two more, and then attacked *Portadoc*. Schulz was to continue and sink another four vessels over the next six days, then, all torpedoes expended, he headed back to France, arriving at Lorient on 1 May. Evidently Schulz had picked up one of *Portadoc*'s round life-savers, for it is noted in a German film clip of *U 124* returning to Lorient, hanging with others, from her conning tower.

This U-boat was to make another eight war patrols, sinking twenty-seven more ships under Schulz and another CO. *U 124* was sunk in early April 1943 off the Portuguese coast by RN ships, with no survivors. Schulz had already had a very lucky escape when his previous boat, *U 64* had been sunk by bombs from a Fleet Air Arm Swordfish in Norwegian waters. He and most of the crew escaped using emergency breathing apparatus. He survived the war as commander of a training flotilla.

Those lost: Lewis Elliott

Sources: Trembley, *How Great The Harvest Is*; DND D Hist notes, *Merchant Ships: General A-Z*; Reader's Digest, *The Canadians At War*; Leonard J. McLaughlin, *The Desperation Fleet*; Greenwood, *Namesakes*; Wynn, *U-Boat Operations, Vol.1*; notes from Fr. van der Linden; War Graves Commission website, <www.cwgc.org.uk>; correspondence from Bernard de Neumann; Ken Mackenzie notes from NAC DoT files.

Collingdoc, supposedly on one of her last down-bound trips, with a full cargo of pulpwood, and in the days before air pollution was a major factor!
(Ken Thro/Gene Onchulenko)

COLLINGDOC

SHIP: 1,780 grt, 253 ft. Built in 1925 by Furness Shipbuilding Company Ltd., Haverton Hill-on-Tees, England, as *D.B. Hanna* for Union Transit Company. Owned by Patersons from 1939.

FATE: Mined and sunk on 13 July 1941 off Southend Pier, 200°, 800 yards in River Thames. Salvaged, not repaired, and expended as a blockship in the Orkney Islands. Two casualties.

Collingdoc was another of Patersons' first group of ships taken up by the Canadian government, with *Kenordoc* and *Portadoc*. She was the company's smallest ship lost, the only one under 1,900 grt. She had been acquired in 1939 by Patersons from the Union Transit Company and given the traditional Paterson "doc" name. She had been used by her previous owners in the canal trades hauling grain, coal and pulpwood, which was continued by Patersons.

On being turned over to the Canadian government she was managed briefly for record purposes by the Montreal Shipping Company, who applied for a one trip licence for her and others "to carry timber, etc. to the United Kingdom, thence in trading between UK ports and other locations." She was manned by a British crew who came over to pick her up. *Collingdoc* was used by the British Ministry in the coal trade around the UK, to release larger vessels for ocean trading.

On 13 July 1941, with a British crew under Captain R.T. Robinson, having discharged a coal cargo in London, England, she was outbound down the Thames in ballast for the River Tyne in northern England. Then, just southwest of the long pier at Southend-on-Sea, *Collingdoc* either struck a mine or passed over a bottom-laid magnetic mine dropped by German aircraft. She foundered almost at once. The various records are unclear as to how many casualties there were, but recent research shows there were two killed and one badly injured. Those who died were both British Engineer officers. The Second Engineer, William Edward Stuchbury, had gone on deck for a cigarette and was blown over the side by the explosion. When the ship sank moments later another crewman swam to him, but on finding he was so badly injured he would not survive, left his body in the Thames. Stuchbury's body was never recovered, but the first Engineer's body was found when the ship was raised, and he is buried near his home in the South Shields (Harton) cemetery in Durham. He was fifty-one years old. A donkeyman was badly injured and reportedly never fully recovered. No Canadians lost their lives.

Since she was in relatively shallow water, the ship was salvaged and refloated on 21 July, only eight days after the mining, towed to nearby Gravesend and placed in the King George V Dock for possible repairs. But the cost of salvaging and repairing her did not warrant making her seaworthy as an operational ship again. Thus she was patched, converted to a hulk and towed north up the North Sea coast later that summer, at first to Rosyth on the Firth of Forth. Then *Collingdoc* was towed north again to Scapa Flow and expended as a blockship, her hull used to help block one of the southeastern entries to the huge naval anchorage in Scapa Flow. She was sunk by explosives in Water Sound between the north side of South Ronaldsay and Burray Islands, close to the Ronaldsay shore. She joined several other expendable hulks, the total eventually reaching forty-three such ships.

Two years previously, on the night of 13/14 October 1939 the German submariner KK Günther Prien in *U 47* had crept into the Flow through the inadequately blocked Holm Sound and torpedoed the battleship HMS *Royal Oak*. To prevent this happening again the naval authorities were looking for ships to sink in the several rarely used passages into the Flow to ensure it was completely blocked except for two carefully controlled south and west entrances for its own warships. The channels thus blocked were later made impregnable by "Churchill barriers," a series of concrete causeways just inside the line of sunken ships. *Collingdoc* is now almost completely buried in shifting sands and mostly dry as a result of sand build-up on the seaward side of the barrier. Part of her bridge can still be seen, with its concrete protective bridge panels still visible.

The German mines which sank *Collingdoc* were a plague along all of the British coast throughout the war. German aircraft of *Luftflotte* 3 began mining the Thames almost from the first day of the war, followed shortly by ship, E-boat and even submarine-laid mines at harbour approaches and in channels. It was close to

Southend that the very first magnetic mines were dropped. After several ships were mysteriously mined in October 1939, an unexploded mine was discovered at low tide on sand flats in the area, dismantled at great risk, its secret mechanisms ascertained and counter-measures developed. In July of 1941 when *Collingdoc* was mined eleven other ships were lost or damaged by mines around the British Isles. At least one sank on 3 July, within sight of the location of *Collingdoc*'s demise ten days later. Mines accounted for over eleven percent of all enemy-caused losses in 1941.

Those lost: William Martin Wilson and William Edward Stuchbury

Sources: Trembley, *How Great The Harvest Is*; notes from Fr. van der Linden; Greenwood, *Namesakes*; *British Vessels Lost At Sea*; *Lloyd's Register, 1941-42*; correspondence with Mike Cooper, England, for *Lloyd's War Losses* and Dr. Neil Stuchbury; corresondence with Zoe Cuthbertson of Scapa Flow Diving Charters; Ferguson, *The Wrecks of Scapa Flow*.

SARNIADOC

SHIP: 1,940 grt, 259 ft bulk canaller freighter. Built in 1929 by Barclay, Curle & Company Ltd., Glasgow, Scotland for Patersons.

FATE: Torpedoed and sunk by *U 161* on 14 March 1942 in east central Caribbean, 160 miles west of Dominica. Twenty-one casualties, no survivors.

Sarniadoc. Lost in March 1942 with not a single survivor. (Gene Onchulenko)

This was one of the second group of sixteen Paterson canallers requisitioned by the Canadian government for transfer to British or US control. *Sarniadoc* plus *Hamildoc*, *Farrandoc* and *Coteaudoc* were on time charter to companies requiring bauxite for their aluminum smelters, in this case to Saguenay Terminals Ltd. of Montreal, on behalf of the Aluminum Company of Canada. Their contract was on a daily rate basis for twelve to eighteen months. Later, in July of 1941 *Soreldoc* and *Prescodoc* were added; soon there were eleven more. Some of these were at first involved in moving general cargoes southward along the coast of Canada and the US, and even in bringing cargoes of cryolite, used as a flux in smelting aluminum, from Ivigut, Greenland to mainland ports.

On 14 March 1942, *Sarniadoc* was moving northbound from Trinidad, bound for the original transshipment base at St. Thomas in the American Virgin Islands. A new depot was to be built shortly at Port of Spain, Trinidad but was not yet in operation. She was fully laden to her marks with bauxite, maybe a bit more given the calm seas in the eastern Caribbean. She was commanded by Captain William A. Darling of Collingwood, Ontario, with a crew of twenty. Then at about 2130 local time she was hit by one or more torpedoes fired by *U 161*, commanded by KL Albrecht Achilles. As there were no survivors whatsoever and no other ships in the immediate area, we have only Achilles' reports to go by. He recorded his target as a tanker, the type of he and other U-boat commanders in his group had been told to attack. The error is not too surprising, given *Sarniadoc*'s low mid-ship, uncluttered profile, rather like that of a small tanker.

The crew were largely Canadians, and are all listed on Patersons Seamen's Memorial in Thunder Bay, so the firm had considered, for a change, that they were Patersons seamen. Seven in fact hailed from British Guyana, where coal-burning ships often made up their engine room crews of oilers, firemen and trimmers. Sadly, two of the lost Canadian seamen were brothers, John and Gordon Newton of Bras d'Or, Nova Scotia, both "wheelsmen." As well the Chief Officer, Lewis Dalgety, aged forty-two and himself a qualified Master, was only making the trip in replacement of another officer who was off sick when *Sarniadoc* was due to sail. Even today, Captain Dalgety's daughter recalls an officer coming to their house in Sarnia to talk to her mother after the ship was sunk, but she does not know if he was from Patersons. But she remembers that they received a rather curt and unfeeling letter announcing his death, but giving no details since there were none until the U-boat's reports could be examined post-war.

Achilles, aged twenty-eight at this time, had departed on his and *U 161*'s first patrol on 24 January 1942, bound for the Caribbean as part of the five-boat Neuland Group, tasked to attack the tanker traffic and fuel shipping facilities there. They were in position off the Caribbean by 13 February, each boat then acting independently, with *U 161* initially assigned to Port of Spain, Trinidad. There he boldly entered the shallow harbour at night, torpedoed two tankers and calmly departed, on the surface until he was clear. Because of the shallow water, the two ships were subsequently salvaged. Achilles then torpedoed another tanker on the 21st, was bombed by a naval aircraft without damage and returned to finish off this tanker with another torpedo. He torpedoed a merchant without sinking it (although it later sank when under tow), was bombed again by a US bomber, suffering slight damage this time, and then sank another tanker.

The determined Achilles moved on to Port Castries, St. Lucia where he again entered the harbour at night, this time even showing running lights similar to a small fishing boat. Again, he torpedoed two ships alongside the wharves, the Canadian CNSS *Lady Nelson* and the British *Umtata*, both to be subsequently salvaged. Departing unscathed, even unattacked, he moved into the central Caribbean and on the night of 14/15 March he sank *Sarniadoc*. Continuing to move north, the next day south of Haiti he sank the US naval lighthouse tender USS *Acacia* by gunfire. All torpedoes spent, Achilles returned to Lorient on 2 April.

He made four more patrols to the central and south Atlantic areas, sank sixteen ships in total, and then when his luck ran out, was lost with his entire crew off Bahia on the east coast of Brazil on 27 September 1943. He was attacked on 26 September by a USN Mariner aircraft that damaged his U-boat, and, located by another on the 27th was depth charged and sunk, although his anti-aircraft gunners succeeded in injuring two of the aircraft's crew with return fire. There were no survivors of the U-boat's crew of fifty-two.

Those lost:	William A. Darling, Master		Ephrem Audet
	Alex Belford	Jean R. Breton	Joseph Briand
	Alexandre Corriveau	Lewis Dalgety	Roy Da Silva
	Jerome De Freitas	John De Freitas	J. Fayard
	A. Fernandez	Richard A. Husbands	Cecil Keeping
	Albert Lebrecque	Camile Levesque	Gordon Newton
	John William Newton	Jascintho Phillippe	S. Piatowski
	Edmond Picard		

Sources: DND D Hist notes, R. Fisher and Skip Gillham; Trembley, *How Great The Harvest Is*; correspondence with Gene Onchulenko, Thunder Bay and Alan Mann, Sarnia; Rohwer, *Axis Submarine Successes*; Kurowski, *Knight's Cross Holders*; Wynn, *U-Boat Operations, Vol. 1*.

TORONDOC

SHIP: 1,927 grt, 253 ft., bulk canaller freighter. Built in 1927 by Swan Hunter & Wigham Richardson of Newcastle, England directly for Patersons.

FATE: Torpedoed by *U 69* early on 21 May 1942 100 miles west of Martinique in the Caribbean. Twenty-three casualties, no survivors.

Torondoc, another Paterson ship sunk by a U-boat with no survivors. (Gene Onchulenko)

This is another tale of a torpedoed ship with only a partial story of her loss, since, like *Sarniadoc* sunk a couple of months earlier in the same location, there were no survivors to report what had happened on board, and no other ships nearby.

Torondoc was a Paterson-ordered that was requisitioned in July of 1941 for use in the Caribbean bauxite trade. In her case this was after fourteen years of Great Lakes service hauling bulk cargoes of grain, ore and coal for the company. She was valuable in the bauxite trade like the other little canallers with their modest draft and flat bottoms. They could navigate the offshore shallows and bring the cargo to transshipment points such as St. Thomas. There the ore would be stored and carried north to the smelters in larger, deeper-draft ocean ships.

On 20 May *Torondoc* was northbound from Trinidad to St. Thomas, with François Xavier Daneau as Master and a crew of twenty-two, of which eight were from British Guyana; some were seamen, some engine room staff. *Torondoc* was following a track about 100 miles inside the Leeward Islands, was unarmed, had no direction finding equipment and steered by magnetic compass, unlike the more modern ships which were changing to the more accurate gyro compass. According to the later report of KL Ulrich Gräf, commander of *U 69*, he tracked and attacked her at about 0253 in the early morning of 21 May. Many reports including the

Merchant Navy's *Book of Remembrance* show her sunk on the 20th, but Gräf's records state it was at 0753 Central European Time which the U-boats kept, five or six hours ahead of eastern Caribbean time.

There is no indication that Gräf contacted any of the survivors, or that they had made it into lifeboats. With her load of densely packed bauxite the ship would have gone down swiftly.

Gräf was *U 69'*s last CO, departing St. Nazaire on 12 April 1942 on their first patrol, to operate in the western Atlantic around the Lesser Antilles and eastern Caribbean. On the way, south of Bermuda, *U 69* was topped up with diesel fuel from a supply submarine, and that same day encountered and sank the Canadian trading schooner *James E. Newsom* by gunfire (see Chapter 13). Near the West Indies he engaged a US Coast Guard cutter without damage to either, moved into the Caribbean and sank a tanker off Dutch Curaçao to the south. He then moved 400 miles northeast, encountered and sank *Torondoc* about 100 miles west of Martinique, then left the Caribbean for home. On the way he sank an abandoned tug and arrived at St. Nazaire on 25 June.

Gräf and *U 69* made two more patrols, both in the north Atlantic and in Gulf of St. Lawrence waters. There on his second patrol he sank the Canadian/ Finnish *Carolus* (see Chapter 16) and the Newfoundland ferry *Caribou* (see Chapter 17). On his last patrol he and other boats of his group were unsuccessful in locating the convoys for which they searched, and when he was shadowing Convoy ON-165 he was detected and sunk by HMS *Viscount* on 17 February 1943, with no survivors.

Thus Ulrich Gräf's record of seven ships sunk or at least hit during his career as a CO included five Canadian vessels, for on 20 October 1942 he had hit *Rose Castle* but his torpedo failed to explode.

Those lost:	F Xavier Daneau, Master		Gaetan Besner
	Lawrence Bourne	Alfred C Brett	Joseph Cottreau
	Sydney Crichlow	Antonio De Freitas	F Gardiner
	Lionel Garneau	M Giraud	Reuben Holder
	Augustus Jardine*	Marcel Karnequin	Armand Letourneau
	Joseph Lewis	Marcel Mondou	Frank R Morisutti
	James Paraig	Marcel Poitras	Harry Redmoth
	Joseph V Rodrigues	Michael Sokoluk	Urban D Watts*

* All except these two names, both of men from British Guyana, appear on Patersons memorial cairn in Thunder Bay. Jardine and Watts may have been recruited locally by Captain Daneau on that last voyage.

Sources: Correspondence with Gene Onchulenko and Ken MacAskill, Thunder Bay; notes from Fr. van der Linden; *Lloyd's Register, 1941-42*; Rohwer, *Axis Submarine Successes*; Wynn, *U-boat Operations, Vol.1.*

TROISDOC

SHIP: 1,925 grt, 259 ft. bulk canaller freighter. Built 1928 by Swan Hunter & Wigham Richardson, Wallsend-on-Tyne, England for Patersons.

FATE: Sunk by gunfire of *U 558* on 21 May 1942, in Caribbean forty miles west of Jamaica. No casualties.

Troisdoc was another little Paterson laker in the bauxite trade, taken up and in appearance almost identical with the *Torondoc* sunk earlier the same day under similar circumstances 1,100 miles to the east. She too had been ordered new-built from Swan Hunter, although at a different yard than *Torondoc*. She was named after Trois Rivières, Quebec, from which Paterson ships carried newsprint to customers around the Great Lakes. For her wartime service she was on time charter to ALCOA Steamship Company, the American Aluminum Company's shipping arm.

On 21 May 1942, she was southbound at a modest 6 knots from Mobile, Alabama with a general cargo of 55,700 bags of cement, vegetables, 1,600 cases of beer plus some cartons of cigarettes for American installations in Georgetown, British Guyana, planning to then move inland up the Demerara River to load bauxite. The crew were evidently (at least in part) Canadians, her Master was Roland Gignac, according to the Second Mate, Mr. Gordon Palmer, who was interviewed in Halifax after the sinking. She carried a crew of eighteen in all (one report says) and had no defensive armament nor a radio.

Shortly after 1100 that morning, when *Troisdoc* was about forty miles west of Jamaica the ship was hit by a torpedo that failed to explode—evidently an electric model rather than one driven by air pressure, as it was noiseless and wakeless. The submarine then surfaced about a half mile on *Troisdoc*'s port quarter and, not

Troisdoc in the Welland Canal pre-war. (J.N. Bascom/J. Kidd)

wishing to waste another costly torpedo on such an easy target, opened fire on her at first with a heavy machine gun, scoring what *Troisdoc's* crew estimated as 200 hits. The ship was stopped and *Troisdoc's* crew abandoned her into one of her boats and a liferaft. The U-boat then circled and fired more rounds, including several from her 4-inch deck gun until the vessel was sinking. The crew all got away safely and there is no mention of anyone injured in the shelling.

The submarine, *U 558* commanded by KL Günther Krech (as was discovered much later) approached the boat and questioned the survivors as to their ship and its cargo. Mr. Palmer reported the bearded questioner spoke good English and translated the replies to about ten others on the conning tower beside him. An officer also took photos with a small camera. Palmer was able to describe as well the profile of a man's head painted in white on the front of the conning tower, plus the word "Holzauge," meaning "wooden eye."

The submarine then departed and submerged. The survivors were picked up that evening at about 2100 by the RN Flower class corvette HMS *Clarkia*, on loan to the USN to try to help prevent the slaughter along the coast and in the Caribbean. The survivors were transferred on 24 May to the CNSS passenger ship *Lady Nelson* which took them back to Mobile on the 29th.

U 558 was Krech's only command, and her only CO, for ten patrols. He sank twenty-three ships, including the corvette HMS *Gladiolus*, and the A/S trawler HMS *Bedfordshire* off the North Carolina banks. When he encountered *Troisdoc* his boat was on her seventh patrol, having left her base in Brest on 12 April. After sinking the laker, Krech hit but didn't sink another merchantman in the Caribbean and sank two more ships by gunfire. On the way home, after refuelling south of Bermuda he sank another merchantman and was back in Brest on 21 June.

On his tenth and last patrol, on the way home off Cape Ortegal in northwest Spain he was attacked over a period of two days by aircraft, and on 21 July 1943, the U-boat was sunk by depth charges of a Liberator of the USAF and an RAF Halifax. Only five crew survived, forty-five were lost. Krech and his Engineer were able to climb aboard a liferaft with three crewmen and thus were saved.

Three days later they were sighted by an RAF Liberator and an emergency pack was dropped to them. On the 25th, four days after the sinking, they were plucked from the sea by the Canadian destroyer HMCS *Athabaskan*. She had been on anti-U-boat and anti-destroyer "Musketry" patrols in the Bay of Biscay with two other destroyers and a cruiser, and was on her way back to their base in Plymouth. While the was picking up Krech, they were signalled by a Sunderland that yet another U-boat was sinking nearby, and the ships then went off and rescued another thirty-seven men from *U 459*, also sunk by aircraft, as well as a Wellington Coastal Command bomber's tail gunner whose aircraft had been shot down during the attack on *U 459*. The survivors and the prisoners were taken in to Plymouth. Günther Krech survived the war and died in June 2000.

Those lost: None

Sources: D Hist files, incl. DNI message; Burrow & Beaudoin, *Unlucky Lady*; Greenwood, *Namesakes*; Onchulenko and Gillham, *The Paterson Fleet*; Rohwer, *U-boat Successes*; Wynn, *U-boat Operations, Vol. 2*; notes from Fr. van der Linden; USN Survivor Interview transcript.

PRESCODOC

SHIP: 1,938 grt, 253 ft. Built in 1929 for Patersons at Swan Hunter & Wigham Richardson Ltd. Sunderland, England. Engines from Swan Hunter's Newcastle yard.

FATE: Torpedoed by *U 160* on 29 July 1942, 175 miles north of Georgetown, British Guyana. Sixteen casualties.

Prescodoc was the last Patersons ship lost to the enemy. She was almost identical with the other ships lost in May, on charter at a daily rate to Saguenay Terminals Ltd. for twelve to eighteen months. Like the other Canadian lakers of several firms *Prescodoc* was hauling 2,820 tons of bauxite from the Demerara River in British Guyana to the new transshipment port at Port of Spain, Trinidad. Travelling at a modest 6 knots, she carried a crew of twenty under Captain John C. Prouse, was unarmed, and was not even equipped with a radio.

On 29 July she was not zigzagging, in fairly calm weather in good visibility. Some 100 miles off the coast of British Guyana, just as dawn was showing on the

Prescodoc. (Gene Onchulenko)

eastern horizon, she was torpedoed at about 0440 in the morning with no warning of any kind. No torpedo track was seen, and it hit near the starboard bow, evidently blowing it off, as the ship sank almost immediately by the bow. None of the bridge staff survived. In fact there were only five survivors, who managed to clamber into a lifeboat that had either been blown clear or floated off when the sank.

The U-boat was evidently on the surface when she fired her torpedo at *Prescodoc*, for the survivors saw her almost at once. She approached to identify the just as she sank. In this case the U-boat's CO did not bother to contact, interrogate or help the five men swimming toward the lifeboat. He then altered away and made off to the northward after fifteen minutes.

The five shocked crewmen were discovered in their lifeboat by chance by the small Yugoslav steamer *Predsednik Kopajtic* at about 1200 that same day and taken to the West Indies and safety.

KL Georg Lassen had been a submariner since just before the war broke out and when under training at Danzig survived a serious fire in *U 160* which killed seven of his crew. This patrol was his second of three as CO. Departing his base in Lorient on 20 June, he crossed the Atlantic to the West Indies, sank a tanker on 16 July, then a freighter, another tanker, then moved down to the South American coast. There he sank the small freighter *Telamon* and then *Prescodoc* on the 29th. Patrol records show he evidently tracked *Prescodoc* for over an hour and a half before reaching a position to torpedo her. Lassen then started northward for home, sank yet another freighter and hit a tanker that was shortly after sunk by an Italian submarine. He arrived back in Lorient on 24 August.

Lassen made two more highly successful patrols, was awarded the Knight's Cross with Oak Leaves, and survived the war as a flotilla training officer. *U 160* however did not, being sunk by USN carrier aircraft south of the Azores on 13 July 1943. Because of some operational confusion in BdU as a result of Allied attacks on *milch cow* U-boats, *U 160* had been sent to a rendezvous which no longer existed. There were no survivors of her crew of fifty-four.

Those lost:	John C Prowse, Master	Henry Austin	Joseph Burton
	William Chiasson	Jean-Marie Coté	Roland Desjardins
	Henry Dugas	Lionel Fraser	Raymond Gaudin
	Roger Goulet	Armand Guilbert	Napoleon C Hattote
	Frederick B King	E Raymond Koenig	Noel Olliver
	Edward Wilsterman		

Sources: SCS Interview with un-named crew; Form SA in D Hist; *Lloyd's Register, 1941-42*; Onchulenko & Gillham, *The Paterson Fleet*; notes from Fr. van der Linden; Rohwer, *Axis Submarine Successes*; Wynn, *U-boat Operations, Vol.1*; Busch & Röll, *German U-Boat Commanders*.

The Sailors' Memorial in Thunder Bay, honouring men lost from
Paterson ships during the Second World War.
(Gene Onchulenko)

One of the three plaques
on the Paterson Memorial,
listing those who gave their lives.
(Gene Onchulenko)

CHAPTER 8

Four Imperial Oil Tankers Sunk

Our wasted oil unprofitably burns,
Like hidden lamps in old sepulchral urns.

—William Cowper, *Conversation*

The Imperial Oil Company of Toronto operated a large fleet of tankers before the war, including lakers, coastal and ocean-going vessels. The company itself was founded in 1880, acquiring its first ships in 1899 when Imperial bought three barges and the next year a tug to tow them, to supply crude for their only refinery at Sarnia, Ontario. These purchases were its solution to local transportation problems that had developed.

Until the turn of the century the refinery had depended on railway shipments to bring in crude oil from Canadian and northern US well-heads and then to refined products to their markets. But water transport was proving much more economical in the wider sphere, so Imperial Oil at first contracted for ships to bring oil from US fields to Sarnia and to distribute the products, then began to operate their own small tankers. The first actual self-propelled, self pumping bulk oil tanker was the *Imperial* of 1902. By 1918 the company had established four new refineries, in Halifax, Montreal, Regina and Ioco, British Columbia. As well the company had ordered five tankers built at Collingwood Shipyards, Ontario specifically for Great Lakes service, where Imperial Oil's principal trade was located. These were, for their times, quite large tankers, of over 2,700 dwt.

By 1939 Imperial was not only operating twenty-five tankers in their own name, but had set up and then sold at least two operating companies for tankers between South American fields and their coastal refineries and customers. Of their own ships, four were on the west coast, nine on the Great Lakes, three on the St. Lawrence and east coast. Nine were ocean-going, two steam and seven diesel powered. It was, naturally enough, this latter diesel-powered group of large tankers that were quickly appropriated by the government when war broke out and thus suffered all the company's losses of their truly Canadian ships.

By the end of August 1939 (thanks largely to the preparations in Halifax by Commander R.H. Oland, DSC, in controlling merchant shipping and providing for escorted convoys in the western Atlantic), instructions had been issued to all

Imperial Oil's ships of the action to be taken if war was declared. Their ocean tankers were spread from the coasts of South America to Europe, yet on 3 September, when the message was received that Britain and Canada were at war with Germany, that night they ran for friendly ports without any lights, not even port and starboard navigation lights, to the considerable worry of their Masters and crews who were not used to this utter blackness.

The company was asked to reroute its tankers for overseas service and also, as the only Canadian company operating Canadian-registered tankers, to take over operation of seventeen Panamanian flagged, usually US-owned tankers transferred to Canadian and British administrations. These ships all continued to sail from the supply ports, the crude oil terminals in South America, the US coastal ports, and even from the Iraq pipeline at Haifa, but now under a centralized government control. The crude, and the refined diesel, gasoline, furnace fuel oil and other products were destined for refineries and depots in the UK and, at first, France, one of the larger refining countries. The refined fuels, if not utilized locally, went to storage depots or directly to user pipeline terminals worldwide. At first Imperial's ships travelled almost always in convoy, for not only were they valuable, but they were not particularly fast. These voyages at first had only the minimal escort protection that could be scrabbled together in the earlier days.

Unlike many merchantmen taken over in wartime, the tankers continued under the ownership and the management of Imperial Oil, which largely supplied the crews, certainly the Masters and Chief Engineers. As vacancies occurred these could be made up from manning pools, but just as often from Imperial's own resources and other ships of the fleet. Imperial's ships, although their cargoes were considered dangerous, were popular with the crews, for the company cared for its men, the ships were clean and efficient and the food was good. While refined fuel was a dangerous cargo, heavy diesel was not, under careful controls. But when empty, a very real risk with these tankers was from any remaining fumes in the tanks after they were pumped out, and "purging" of these fumes by air blown through the tanks was vital. But due to the pressures of time and urgency of turn-around, time was not always available to properly purge the huge tanks.

While tramp freighters, usually equipped with simple steam triple expansion engines, could be manned to a large extent by untrained assigned crews, these tankers were much more sophisticated, with diesel engines and complicated pumping arrangements, and required experienced hands. As well, pre-war, they offered full time employment, unusual in the ocean shipping trades. During the war the company allowed leaves of absence for those who had made several ocean trips in the war zones.

As well, when the Canadian shipbuilding industry began turning out new-built wartime tankers, thirteen Park ships, out of a total of seventeen built, were assigned to Imperial Oil to crew and manage, although ownerremained with the Canadian

Government Merchant Marine. Technically the Imperial Oil tankers were "owned" by Imperial Oil Shipping Ltd., a subsidiary company.

The ocean-going ships were all diesel twin-screw, and according to some of their Engineers the continuous steaming with almost no layovers even for repairs meant that one engine was usually broken and being repaired by the crew on board, even making new parts if necessary, while the other drove the ship.

It was a tough war on men and ships. Imperial paid the price with the loss of four: *Calgarolite*, *Canadolite*, *Montrolite*, and *Victolite*, with the loss of seventy-three crew. Another forty-four men were captured and made prisoners of war. Two of the Panamanian-flagged ships were lost as well, the *James McGee* and the *Joseph Seep*, both mined (see Chapter 18). And, typical of all seamen's contracts, when their was sunk their wages ceased. In Imperial's case this applied only to the supplement paid to men serving in tankers. In order to retain skilled seamen familiar with tanker operations, Imperial kept them on the payroll.

CANADOLITE

SHIP: 11,309 grt, 511 ft diesel bulk tanker. Built 1926 by Frederik Krupp A.G., Kiel, Germany for Imperial Oil.

FATE: Captured 25 March 1941 by German armed raider *Kormoran* in mid-Atlantic, just north of Equator. No casualties.

Canadolite was the only Canadian merchant or warship captured and retained by the Germans during the Second World War, although the Japanese forces captured the Canadian registered *Shinai*. Like her compatriots *Canadolite* had been

A builder's photo of *Canadolite* from 1926.
The only Canadian merchantman captured on the high seas.
(Murray Manson)

carrying crude and refined products to the refineries and storage depots in North America and Europe.

Under Captain Thomas V. Ferns, in April-March 1941 she had carried a full cargo of refined naval fuel (usually called FFO, furnace fuel oil) from Aruba, Netherlands Antilles to Freetown, a major refuelling port on the West African coast for escorts and merchantmen. Leaving Freetown on 21 March, she steamed almost straight west in ballast for Aruba again—at a very modest 8 knots hampered by a heavy growth of weed on her hull. Her course was somewhat to the south of the normal traffic route, and despite her slow speed and considerable value she had no escorts or other vessels in sight.

Just before dawn on her third day out, about 5 a.m. on 25 March, her watch sighted a suspicious ship closing her from the west on the opposite course. The ship, which looked like a smallish passenger liner was fully illuminated, which was unusual in wartime, and carried no country's flag. The stranger passed but then circled around astern of the tanker in thirty minutes or so to follow *Canadolite*, and the Master, suspecting trouble, told the wireless operator to transmit "R-R-R", the general warning of an enemy raider. The other was indeed the largest of the German raiders, *Kormoran*, armed with six 6-inch and anti-aircraft guns as well as torpedoes, all hidden behind folding side plates. *Kormoran* pulled level to starboard of *Canadolite*, illuminating the tanker by searchlight, while Captain Ferns continued edging away from this unknown vessel. She then signalled Ferns by light to stop,

The innocent-appearing German raider *Kormoran*,
her guns and torpedo tubes well hidden behind bulwarks.
(Heinrich Dettmer)

which he ignored, turning away and continuing to make off. At this point *Kormoran* unmasked one of her guns and fired a shell across *Canadolite's* bow, which, when Ferns ignored that as well, was followed by several more.

At this Captain Ferns was forced to reconsider. He had only one elderly 4-inch gun aft in the way of armament with which to fight back, his speed was probably less than half that of this opponent, and his was empty but the tanks still contained very volatile fuel oil fumes, as they had not taken time to purge them after leaving Freetown. If a shell hit one of these, it would likely result in a massive explosion that could quite possibly destroy the ship and her crew. Captain Ferns ordered the confidential books thrown overboard, and the DEMS gunner to throw over his weapon's breech block. He himself threw over his navigating instruments and ordered the ship abandoned in her boats. It was not practical, with her large empty tank spaces, nor had it been pre-arranged, for him to sink his ship. The whole crew of forty-four climbed down into two lifeboats alongside and rowed away, expecting the raider to shell and sink *Canadolite*.

But Captain Theodor Detmers of *Kormoran* had other plans for this valuable and undamaged ship. He sent a prize crew aboard the tanker, and a motor lifeboat manned by armed sailors after *Canadolite's* boats, towing them back to their own ship. While taking Captain Ferns, the Chief Engineer, the senior Wireless Officer and the DEMS gunner aboard *Kormoran*, the rest were told to climb back aboard their ship. Then, after a careful examination of the ship, with an armed prize crew of sixteen Germans *Canadolite* was ordered by a round-about route back to France, taking with her several sick crewmen of the raider.

Although now fitted with explosive scuttling charges to prevent her recapture, the tanker made her way undetected back to Bordeaux on the Gironde River in southwest France where she arrived on 13 April, nineteen days after her capture. The Canadian crew went to a desolate prisoner of war camp near Bremen in Germany, Marlag und Milag Nord, where they were reunited with the ship's officers who had been sent back in another support ship. A few seamen and the second Engineer who had become ill while in the camp were repatriated through Lisbon in July 1943. The Red Cross was able to advise the Allies that the crew were prisoners, but could offer no information on what had happened to *Canadolite*, which had just disappeared. Then on 30 May 1941 a Washington intelligence report noted that *Canadolite* had been captured, confirmed in July by the Canadian High Commissioner to Vichy France. The details of her capture were not available until that information arrived with the repatriates. It had naturally been presumed at first that she had been sunk when her crew was captured.

All survived their four years in captivity. They were released by advancing British soldiers in April 1945. One prisoner from that camp, Gordon Olmstead, became a leading voice in efforts to secure better recognition from the Canadian government for these merchant seamen who served in the war at sea every bit as much as the naval seamen. Imperial Oil hosted a dinner at Halifax for their returned seamen, and re-employed any who still wished to work in tankers.

The *Canadolite* was renamed *Sudetenland* and primarily used as a fuel oil storage facility in French ports. She was sunk in an RAF bombing raid on Brest on 14 August 1944 and her hulk broken up after the war.

At the time of *Canadolite's* capture, *Kormoran's* fuel supply was getting very low and Detmers' engines needed repair work so he dared not steam at high speeds for any long period. The raider continued south, sank five freighters and captured one, and was able to refuel and get supplies from a German merchantman, *Rudolf Albrecht*, on 3 April. She went on south to sink another five freighters, and her final victim was the Australian cruiser HMAS *Sydney*. Pre-war *Kormoran* had been the almost new ex-German HAPAG-Lloyd passenger freighter *Steiermark* built in 1938. She was also known in the German Navy as *Schiff 41* and known in British Intelligence as *Raider G*. She could stay at sea for almost a year if need be, and carried a crew of about 400. In addition to her heavy gun armament and torpedoes, she carried two small aircraft for reconnaissance and a motor boat equipped to fire a torpedo, to extend and vary her attacks. Her end was even more dramatic than her capture of *Canadolite*.

On 19 November 1941 the cruiser *Sydney*, commanded by Captain Joseph Burnett, RAN, became suspicious of a freighter she encountered 250 miles west of the coast of Western Australia. When Captain Burnett queried her identity by signal light, KK Detmers in *Kormoran* told his signalman to say he didn't understand, then gave misleading identification and turned away from *Sydney*. *Sydney* herself was armed with eight 6-inch guns and torpedoes and had almost twice the speed of the raider. This cat-and-mouse game continued for several hours, the cruiser keeping up with but distant from the freighter, her guns still well hidden but the turrets trained now on the ship. Without positive identification, Burnett was reluctant to fire at an unidentified and evidently unarmed merchantman, but he hesitated to get too close, just in case she was an armed raider, of which he had been warned in general terms. This continued, with Detmers refusing to stop and pretending to be suspicious of this warship in his turn.

Then *Sydney*, hoping to resolve the impasse, came within range of *Kormoran's* torpedoes. Detmers appreciated it was now or never, dropped the shell plating hiding the tubes and his guns, changed instantly from a neutral flag to the *Kriegsmarine* ensign and opened fire with all his weapons. Although *Sydney* replied almost as quickly, it was too late, for *Kormoran's* well drilled gunners swept her bridge and upper decks and set her well afire. Both ships continued firing, now both alight. *Kormoran* had taken only two serious shell hits, but in the engine room, severing vital connections. These, even if the fires were put out, would prevent her continuing her voyage. With seventy-six dead, Detmers ordered the ship abandoned into her remaining boats and they rowed away from the now blazing ship. The *Kormoran* exploded an hour or so later when the fire reached her ammunition magazines.

The *Sydney* also steamed away over the horizon, also now well on fire. That was the last ever seen of the cruiser or any of her 645 officers and crew. Probably the fire aboard her also reached her magazines and she blew up, destroying every soul on board. Nothing was ever found except for some life belts and an empty Carley float despite a wide search .

After several days 317 survivors of *Kormoran* eventually reached the Australian coast, hungry, thirsty and many wounded, and were made prisoners. Captain Detmers survived the war and died in 1976.

Those lost: None in *Canadolite*.

Sources: Holman, *The King's Cruisers*; Schmalenbach, *German Raiders*; Brown, *WarLosses of World War Two*; Hogan, *Esso Mariners*; Parker, *Running The Gauntlet*; *Imperial Oil Review, Fall 1943, Fall 1944 & Fall 1988*; Readers Digest, *The Canadians At War 1939/45, Vol. 2*. RN memo in D Hist file; Woodward, *The Secret Raiders*.

MONTROLITE

SHIP: 11,309 grt, 511 ft., diesel bulk tanker. Built 1926 by Frederick Krupp A.G., Kiel, Germany for Imperial Oil.

FATE: Torpedoed by *U 109* on 4 February 1942, 260 miles northeast of Bermuda. Twenty-eight lost, twenty survivors.

The *Montrolite* was a sister of *Canadolite*, also carrying light diesel crude from Venezuela, but in her case to her home port refinery in Halifax, under her Scottish-born Master, Captain John White. The Chief Engineer, John Lundy, had been born in Belfast, Northern Ireland.

Montrolite, a clear photo of a typical large Imperial Oil tanker. (Murray Manson)

Montrolite had left Venezuela at the end of January and Captain White, on the instructions of the local NCSO, set his course well out into the Atlantic northbound, keeping clear of the mayhem already occurring along the American coastline in the concentrated German *Operation Paukenschlag* attacks. She was alone, without escort, making about 10 knots, and as one of her watch officers reported, zigzagging, but only about twenty degrees every hour, just enough to bother a following U-boat, but not frequently enough to throw off a determined one. On the night of 3 February it was rather stormy and rough as they passed east of Bermuda, and in view of the weather and poor visibility no trouble was anticipated.

At about 1945, just after dark and with no prior intimation of danger, a torpedo hit *Montrolite* on the starboard side just aft of midships, tearing a huge gash in the ship with a flash of explosive. Fortunately her cargo of diesel fuel did not catch fire, and the three remaining undamaged lifeboats were launched quickly at the Master's orders with some crew in them. Others jumped into the sea and were pulled aboard the boats as the wind and breaking seas from aft pushed the boats forward along the ship's side. The boats pulled clear as the ship slowly settled. Then the U-boat, still unseen by survivors, passed around to the ship's port side and fifteen minutes later put another torpedo into her. This one set the fuel cargo and the ship's fuel afire in a huge blaze, but in about half an hour the tanker sank by the stern and all that was left was some burning fuel on the ocean surface, a pall of black smoke blown away in the wind, and the three lifeboats.

One boat reportedly had only three survivors in it, another was very crowded with twenty-five and a third with twenty. In the dark stormy weather, the first two boats and their twenty-eight souls simply disappeared. In these boats were Captain White, the Chief Engineer, a DEMS gunner and twenty-five of the crew. No trace whatever was found of them or the boats.

The other boat, holding mostly seamen and engine room personnel with the fourth Engineer officer in charge, was driven north in a half gale of wind, rain and sleet for three days. In the weather they didn't try to sail but used the boat's canvas as a sea anchor to keep her head to windward. They were bailing much of the time and rowing to the west when seas and wind moderated or they were not too cold and exhausted from bailing.

Then about noon on the third day an elderly British merchantman that was a straggler from a distant convoy came across them by chance. Fortunately that ship's carpenter happened to see the little lifeboat wallowing in the breaking seas between the and the horizon and informed the bridge watch. The ship, unidentified in reports, turned to the boat, put a scramble net over the side and quickly helped the half-frozen survivors aboard. There they were warmed, fed and clothing shared out. The survivors were taken into Halifax in a few days, landing on 10 February.

The U-boat which attacked them was *U 109* under KL Heinrich Bleichrodt. She had departed her base at Lorient on 27 December 1941, one of the first five boats assigned to *Operation Paukenschlag*. It was her fifth patrol, and Bleichrodt's fourth in command of this boat. So far in the previous patrols, although patrolling in wolf packs along the Atlantic convoy routes, he had had no success in hunting. But on this patrol, on 1 February he sank an American freighter, then short of fuel and on instructions from BdU, refuelled from another boat north of Bermuda and came across *Montrolite* by chance on the 4th. Bleichrodt was evidently a stubborn man, for on the 6th he encountered the modest-sized Panamanian freighter *Halcyon* and decided to sink her by gunfire. To do this he expended 300 rounds of his 4-inch shells! He arrived back in Lorient on 23 February.

Bleichrodt, who had already commanded two earlier U-boats and sunk sixteen ships, took *U 109* on three more patrols, sinking eight ships, one of these with an expenditure of eight torpedoes, some of which failed to run or explode. He was ill when he returned to France in January 1943. He was awarded the Knight's Cross with Oak Leaves, and later commanded 22 U-Flotille, surviving the war. *U 109* was lost with all hands and a new CO in May 1943 in an attack by an RAF Liberator northeast of the Azores.

Those lost:	John White, Master	Albert J Aubie	Frederick W Bowdridge
	Martin B Burke	James B Clannon	Peter M Clannon
	John W Dunne	Peter A Dunseith	Leslie S Flynn
	Roland Frechette	Roy W Gillespie	Norman E Hammond
	Daniel James	Robert S Kinkaid	Gaston J Lachance
	Henry A Liot	James P Lundy	Arthur R Mason
	Alphonse Melanson	Leo A Murphy	Louis A Pierre
	Martin L Sampson	Walter H Smith	Harold W Sponagle
	Alexander W Suttie	James E Thompson	Herbert F Wilson

1 DEMS gunner at least, AB Axel W Hukkanen.

Sources:	Hogan, *Esso Mariners*; Wynn, *U-Boat Operations Of The Second World War*; Parker, *Running The Gauntlet*; DND *Montrolite* file, Form SA.

VICTOLITE

SHIP: 11,410 grt, 510 ft. diesel bulk tanker. Built 1928 by A. Stephen & Son., Glasgow, Scotland for Imperial Oil.

FATE: Torpedoed by *U 564* on 10 February 1942, 240 miles northwest of Bermuda. Forty-eight casualties, no survivors.

Victolite, although built in a different shipyard than the other Imperial Oil tankers above, was also a near sister in power, size and capacity. In her case, the loss is only known in general terms, as there were no witnesses apart from the U-boat's CO and no survivors to record how it happened.

Victolite, just after her completion in 1928. Another ship lost with no survivors, in this case exploding when a torpedo sparked the lingering gas fumes in her hold.
(Murray Manson/W. Ralston, Glasgow)

Victolite had discharged her cargo of diesel crude at the Imperial refinery in Halifax and sailed on 4 February 1942 under Captain Peter M. Smith. She was heading south in ballast for Las Piedras, Uruguay, a few miles inland from Montevideo, to load light diesel oil. Like other tankers at that time she also had been routed well out into the Atlantic, just clear of Bermuda, to keep her away from the U-boats then attacking shipping close along the American coast from Maine to the Carolinas. She had no protective escort, and her routing was not enough to keep her safe. Despite her relative newness and diesel engines, she was not a fast ship, and was slowed somewhat by sea growth on her hull.

Six days out of Halifax, running south at last light, at about 2238 local time on 10 February, the ship was evidently attacked by gunfire by *U 564*, herself southwest bound. The radio operator only had a chance to signal her call letters and "S-S-S" indicating she was being attacked by a submarine. KK Reinhardt "Teddy" Suhren, by this time one of the German U-boat aces, had run out of torpedoes on a couple of previous patrols and as a watch officer in the very successful *U 48*. So if practical and if he was not likely to be attacked by surprise himself he would try to sink his targets by gunfire before using his torpedoes. It is likely this is how he tackled *Victolite*, but shortly decided the was worth a torpedo and fired at least one.

Victolite, in ballast and with empty tanks, had likely not had enough time to fully purge them of the volatile gas fumes left when she was pumped out at Halifax. With the torpedo detonation the ship evidently exploded. Nothing further was heard of or her forty-eight-man crew, and Suhren reported no contact with any boats. There is a mountain in south central British Columbia named Mount Reid after twenty-four-year-old Roy Reid, one of *Victolite*'s junior Engineers. The circumstances of the ship's disappearance were not released to families and the public until after the war, over three years later.

U 564, a Type VIIC boat of 1 U-Flottille had left La Pallice on 18 January 1942 on her fifth patrol, to look initially off Newfoundland for targets. Finding none, Suhren sailed south and west to join the hunting off the southern US, and encountered *Victolite* about 240 miles northwest of Bermuda. Suhren, at the time twenty-five years old, had already accumulated an impressive score of ships sunk and damaged, first as a watch officer in *U 48*, then nine ships as CO in *U 564*. He went on to sink another nine and ended the war as Commander U-boats in Norway and the Arctic. He died in 1984. *U 564* was sunk in the Bay of Biscay on 14 June 1943 by Coastal Command aircraft, but not before shooting down two of her attackers. Her new CO and seventeen men were saved by another U-boat, but twenty-nine of her crew were lost.

Those lost:

Peter M Smith, Master	Antoine J Arsenault	John F Ball
Raymond Bell	Phillippe Bourbonnais	George W Boynton
Thomas J Buckingham	John W Burke	George C Burt
Edwin M Chisholm	Judson J Cross	Wilfred E Dauphinee
Graydon Dempsey	Kenneth Driscoll	Claude W Ettinger
Richard C Geddes	Frederick Getson	Harold F Getson
Jean-Jacques Goulet	David P Harries	Eugene A Hilchey
Fraser H Latimer	James C Lee	Peter MacMillan
Arthur Marchand	Francis Marshall	Gerard R Martell
Albert L Mattatall	Victor McCrea	Neil Munro
Joseph A Ouellet	Roger Pharand	John Polygach
John T Pommerelle	Fred C Raymond	Roy Reid
John T Rowland	Fritgof Soderberg	Thomas J Spofforth
Daniel R Stone	Reginald A Stratton	Frank G Taylor
Samuel Taylor	Charles H Tooker	Owen H Vaughan
Donald A Wright		

2 DEMS gunners, AB William Manzell, RCN and AB John R A Lawson, RN

Note: The Getsons were cousins, both from La Have, Nova Scotia. Two more Getsons from La Have were captured and made PoWs when *Canadolite* was taken by *Kormoran* in 1941. The Taylors were not related.

Sources: Hogan, *Esso Mariners*; Parker, *Running The Gauntlet*; *Imperial Oil Review, Winter 1945*; *Legion Magazine, July/Aug., 1992*; Mann, *Wallaceburg News, Aug. 1996*; Kurowski, *Knight's Cross Holders*; Rohwer, *Axis Submarine Successes*; Wynn, *U-Boat Operations, Vols 1 & 2*; *Lloyd's Register, 1941-42*.

Imperial Oil's *Calgarolite*, showing an unusual amount of smoke for a diesel-engined tanker.
(Murray Manson/USCG)

CALGAROLITE

SHIP: 11,941 grt (16,500 dwt), 542 ft. diesel bulk tanker. Built 1929 by Furness
Shipbuilding Company, Haverton Hill-on-Tees, England for Imperial Oil.
Machinery aft.

FATE: Torpedoed and shelled by *U 125* on 9 May 1942, in northwest Caribbean,
about 120 miles south of Cuba. No casualties.

Calgarolite, a large ocean tanker, had made several convoy passages from North
and South American ports to refineries in the US, England and France. The ship was
slightly damaged in a bombing attack at Le Havre just as France fell to the Germans
in 1940. Then on 30 April 1942, on charter to Standard Oil of New Jersey, she left
New York at 4:00 a.m. southbound for Cartagena, Colombia in water ballast, to load
light crude oil.

Unescorted, she passed down the coast, through the Florida Strait, around the
northwest tip of Cuba and south into the Caribbean, travelling at 12 knots. Her
Master was Captain Thomas J. Mountain. He was forty-three years old, and had been
Master of various Imperial ships for seventeen years. She carried a crew of forty-five,
including ten deck and engine room officers, plus two naval DEMS gunners.

At 0215 on 9 May, blacked out and with the First Officer on the bridge with two
lookouts (who saw nothing), she was hit on the starboard side by two torpedoes in
quick succession. Fortunately *Calgarolite* had purged her tanks of volatile fumes

during her trip south and was in water ballast so that no explosion resulted from the torpedoes' blast. One hit just under her bridge amidships, the other aft in a bunker oil tank.

Flooding quickly through huge breaches in her empty cargo tanks, she began to list to starboard. While the lifeboats on that side had been damaged, two port side lifeboats were lowered efficiently, albeit with difficulty because of the increasing list and damaged plates that had buckled outwards in the torpedo explosion even on that side. At the Master's order, the confidential books and papers were thrown overboard in a perforated and weighted box by the First Officer. *Calgarolite* was abandoned and the boats pulled half a mile clear. Just then the periscope of the submarine was seen approaching and the U-boat surfaced. Circling the slowly sinking tanker, she then fired another torpedo, hitting the ship close to the stern, in the engine room. The U-boat, *U 125*, ignored the lifeboats and shelled the tanker with about thirty rounds from a deck gun to ensure the ship's destruction. *Calgarolite* rolled onto her side and sank, about an hour and thirty minutes after the initial attack. No lives had been lost, since the first hits were in her tank spaces, and fortunately the ship did not catch fire. The U-boat then turned and motored away to the east on the surface without contacting the survivors.

Given the prevailing winds, the boats made sail northward toward the Isle of Pines, Cuba, but became separated at night. The Master's lifeboat with twenty-two crew and one DEMS on board reached the island at 1400 four days later, on 13 May, being towed the last forty miles by a Cuban fishing boat. The other boat, commanded by First Officer J. Gair, with twenty-three crew and another DEMS gunner, sailed considerably farther to the west and landed at Puerto Moreios, Mexico, on the tip of the Yucatan Peninsula on the 12th. Thus all survived. Captain Tom Mountain went on to skipper a series of government-owned Park Steamship tankers, most administered by Imperial Oil.

U 125, commanded by KL Ulrich Folkers, was part of the 2 U-Flotille out of Lorient, having sailed on 4 April 1942 for operations in the Caribbean. This was her third patrol, second under Folkers. His first foray had been as one of the first wave of five boats in the hugely successful *Paukenschlag*, against minimal opposition, almost none of it skilful at that stage.

On this patrol Folkers sank an American freighter south of Bermuda, entered the Caribbean and sank four more ships around the Caymans before her attack on *Calgarolite*. After that she sank three more in the same general area, one of them another tanker, then departed for home, arriving back in Lorient on 13 June. Folkers and *U 125* carried out another two patrols, one in the central Atlantic, another in the Caribbean, sinking a further six ships. Folkers was awarded the Knight's Cross on 27 March 1943. He was twenty-eight years old.

Then on 13 April 1943 *U 125* left for operations in the North Atlantic convoy routes, but on 6 May was discovered on the surface while trying to attack Convoy ONS-5 southeast of Newfoundland and rammed by the RN destroyer HMS *Oribi*.

While she survived this attack and submerged, she was then located and depth charged to the surface by the destroyer *Vidette* and sunk by gunfire. There were no survivors.

Those lost: None

Sources: Hogan, *Esso Mariners*; *Lloyd's Register, 1941-42*; Wynn, *U-Boat Operations, Vol.1*; Parker, *Running The Gauntlet*; SCS interview with Captain Mountain; USN Survivor Interview transcript; *Imperial Oil Review, Fall 1944*.

Calgarolite's crew abandoning after the first torpedo hit. (P. de Villers)

CHAPTER 9

CNSS Loses Two Lady Boats and One Freighter

In war only submarine commanders who possess distinctive tactical knowledge and ability will be successful in the long run.... In addition, complete success as a result of a thorough exploitation of the weapon can only be achieved if all the officers in charge of it are trained to think along the same tactical line.

—*The U-boat Commander's Handbook, 1943*

Since the late nineteenth century Canada has had a strong trading relation with the West Indies, encouraged by the British who hoped this would lessen their own subsidies for those island colonies. In the 1960s there was even a minor movement for some of the West Indies to become an eleventh "province" of Canada, mostly supported with considerable amusement by those who saw the islands as a low cost holiday aspiration. While in the post-First World War period Canada-West Indies trade was stable, it was not always sufficiently profitable for private enterprise, and the Canadian government subsidized it from time to time. Scheduled services were provided, but often somewhat irregularly, between Montreal, Charlottetown, Halifax and Nassau, other islands, Mexico and Cuba. A Nova Scotia company operated on the route for a few years, and many maritime and Newfoundland schooners traded back and forth on their owner's own accounts when the fishing season was over. In 1920 Canada and Jamaica agreed to jointly sponsor a regular freight/passenger service, extended to Bermuda and the British Honduras in 1922. The Canadian Government Merchant Marine (CGMM) acted for Canada, forming the Canadian National (West Indies) Steamships Ltd., providing services using ships constructed during the First World War, the "Canadian"-named ships.

In 1922 the British Royal Mail Steam Packet Company (RMSPC) won a five-year competitive contract to carry mails on this same route, and the Canadian sponsored freight-only services declined. But the ships of both RMSPC and the CGMM were mostly elderly and unreliable, inadequate for the service. Subsidies, particularly the West Indies' proportionate share, were insufficient to cover the losses being suffered, and the RMSPC did not re-bid on the contract on its expiry in 1927.

Few Canadians realize that in 1925 a formal trade agreement was signed between Canada's Liberal government and the loose affiliation of the British West Indies. Under its terms Canada was to provide the ships for a reliable, efficient fortnightly passenger and freight service. Subsidies were assured by Canada and each of the West Indies islands, plus Bermuda, British Honduras and British Guyana (then spelled Guiana). Tenders were called for two services, Eastern to the outer Leeward and Windward Islands and as far south as Georgetown, British Guyana; and Western to the Bahamas, Jamaica and Belize in the Honduras in the Caribbean. The contract was put out to tender.

CN Steamships won the contract and at first provided the service with ex-wartime "Canadian"-named ships. These soon proved inadequate, having no refrigeration and only accommodations for twenty-eight passengers. Then in 1927 an act was passed providing $10 million to order new ships for the two routes and to refurbish the older ones primarily for a continuing freight service.

This allocation funded the building contract with Cammell Laird & Company of Birkenhead in England for the two groups of Lady boats. They were of two sizes; the slightly smaller *Lady Drake*, *Lady Hawkins* and *Lady Nelson* (the latter considered to be the flagship) were 7,831 grt, and served on the eastern, outer islands route. The larger (at 8,184 grt) *Lady Somers* and *Lady Rodney* served the more heavily travelled western route, to Bermuda, Nassau, Jamaica and Belize. All were named after the wives of former British admirals who had been connected with the West Indies in the earlier historical days. The ships' officers were encouraged to join the RCNR, although only *Lady Somers* initially had enough such officers to entitle her to fly the Blue Ensign. Each had 270,000 cu. ft. of cargo space, 13,000 cu. ft. of which was refrigerated, and this was later enlarged with more temperature controls for carrying bananas northbound. At about $1.6 million each, they were expensive ships to build, and not economical to operate without the subsidies. Each carried about 130 first class passengers and 132 second class and deck passengers.

The CNSS also continued to operate several freighters on the same route, some able to accommodate up to twenty passengers. One of these was *Cornwallis*, ex-*Canadian Transporter*, whose story is told below; others were *Chomedy* and *Colborne*, also both ex-*Canadian* post first war ships. They were referred to as "The Vagabond Ships" since their schedules were not absolute and they called in at whatever islands—British, French or American—offered cargoes for inter-island, northeastern US or Canadian ports. In fact, in the twenty-six years between 1929 and 1955 this CN(WI)SS service operated at an accumulated loss to Canada alone of $3.3 million.

In the Lady boats' peacetime roles it took thirteen days to go from Halifax to Bermuda and on to St. Kitts, Antigua, Barbados, Trinidad and Georgetown, eleven stops in all. They returned along the same route on a strictly maintained schedule. And no one now can say why these ships seemed to have always been called "boats" rather than the more traditional "ships" for vessels of this size.

During the war four of the Lady boats at first maintained the Canada-West Indies passenger/freight service, as vital to the general war effort. Because the CNSS could afford to dispense with one in the slow recovery period immediately following the Depression, *Lady Somers* was sold to the Admiralty in 1940 as an armed boarding ship. She was however sunk by the Italian submarine *Morosini* on 15 July 1941. *Lady Nelson* was torpedoed and sunk in the harbour at Castries, St. Lucia but raised, repaired and put to use as a hospital ship for the rest of the war. *Lady Drake*, *Lady Hawkins* and *Cornwallis* were all torpedoed and sunk with considerable loss of life.

LADY HAWKINS

SHIP: 7,831 grt, 438 ft. three-deck passenger/freight liner. Built in 1928 by Cammell Laird & Company, Birkenhead, England. In peacetime could carry 262 passengers.

FATE: Torpedoed by *U 66*, on 19 January 1942, 165 miles east-southeast of Cape Hatteras, North Carolina. Two hundred and forty total casualties; eighty-eight to ninety-two of them crew.

This ship was named after the wife of Admiral Sir John Hawkins who had made a comfortable fortune in the slave trade to the West Indies (to the intense annoyance of the Spaniards, who considered it their prerogative) and is better known for his participation in the defeat of the Spanish Armada in 1588. He died later during a more respectable commercial voyage to the West Indies. *Lady Hawkins* was the first of the Canadian National Steamships sunk and had the greatest loss of lives of merchant seamen in any Canadian-registered ship sunk during the Second World War. She was

Lady Hawkins at anchor in a West Indies bay pre-war, her accommodation ladder down for her passengers.
(CNSS)

one of the first vessels sunk in the German U-boat campaign along the almost undefended US eastern seaboard in *Operation Paukenschlag* which began on 12 January 1942, only a week before *Lady Hawkins'* loss.

Given Britain and Canada's experience in two and a half years of anti-U-boat warfare, it is shocking to realize how few preparations were in place along this coast when America declared war on Germany. With the Atlantic U-boat war now over two years old, preparations in the US were minimal and ineffective: air patrols at dawn and dusk, of which the now-skilled U-boat COs were well aware; cities, lighthouses and other sea marks all still brightly lighted; all ships sailing independently, some even with their steaming lights on. There were very few useful anti-submarine escorts available, even fewer with any current anti-submarine training, except for the odd destroyer that had been involved in escorting American troops to Iceland.

For twenty-eight months of war *Lady Hawkins* had plied her trade much as she and her sister ships had done in peacetime. Painted a medium grey rather than the pristine white of peacetime, she sailed without upper deck or navigation lights of any kind, was armed with only one 4-inch manual breech-loading gun aft and one naval DEMS rating in her crew, the rest of the gun's crew to be made up of men from the ship. At a service speed of 14 to 15 knots, she was not usually provided with an armed escort, as any ship capable of over 13 knots was considered by naval authorities to be safe steaming on its own.

She left Halifax as usual at 1530 on Thursday 15 January for the south, via Boston and then Bermuda, under Captain Huntley O. Giffin who had been her first and only Master. Unlike the other Lady boats, the *Lady Hawkins* flew the Blue Ensign rather than the more customary Red Ensign, since Captain Giffin held a commission in the Royal Naval Reserve. Her Chief Officer Percy A. Kelly had been Master in other CNSS ships, and was assigned to do one trip in *Lady Hawkins* before assuming another command. She reportedly carried a crew of 109 in total including the one DEMS gunner, although she may have had a few more crew. Eventually there were 211 passengers. Many were Americans boarding in Boston, hired to construct their new naval base in Trinidad which had been established under the destroyers-for-bases agreement of two years before. The passengers included a contingent of eighty-three Royal Navy men heading for Trinidad for training, a group of eleven British Army soldiers as well as a hundred and fifteen civilians, including the construction workers; eighty men, twenty-nine women and six children. Leaving Boston at 1530 on 16 January, on a course as far as possible from waters where U-boats might be anticipated, *Lady Hawkins* passed through the Cape Cod Canal, Vineyard Sound and the East River of New York as far as the Ambrose Channel and then out to sea. Escorted for a brief period by a USN destroyer, she travelled south until opposite Cape Hatteras then turned southeast for the 500 mile solo run to Bermuda. By Sunday the 18th her radio operator was picking up distress calls from ships torpedoed or attacked along the American coast. The day was clear and calm, and the ship sighted the occasional US aircraft and naval blimp before dark. In the evening and overnight hours there was a modest wind and slight seas on a dark, moonless but starry night. The ship zigzagged along a base course.

Then at 0135, with no prior sighting, a small searchlight to port illuminated the *Lady Hawkins*, and in its glow could be seen a submarine running parallel to her. It was in fact KK Richard Zapp making sure of his target, sighted strictly by chance against the faint night sky. The light went out and Captain Giffin altered away, but was unsure what to do under the dark conditions. The ship's officers could not see the U-boat which was better able to keep track of the far larger ship. Zapp pulled ahead and fired two torpedoes from his stern tubes, both of which hit *Lady Hawkins* after an eighty-second run within a few seconds of each other, at 0143. One hit forward in No.2 hold, the other just at the critical bulkhead between No.3 hold and the engine room.

To the crash of the explosion was added the chaos as the ship rolled violently to port and then partly upright again, settling at about a ten degree list as she began to flood. Her mast came down with a further thunderclap, and all internal lights went out. Evidently there were many of the passengers and crew on deck and a lot of these were thrown directly into the cold sea by the roll. The ship stayed lurched over to port as spaces flooded, and boats on her high starboard side could not be launched. Only three port side boats evidently got clear before the ship sank, about twenty minutes after she was hit. Many of the passengers, unfamiliar with the ship's layout in the utter blackness below, never found their way onto the upper decks, or were trapped by distorted doors in cabins and mess spaces. Almost all who did reach the open decks had to jump into the sea to escape, and many of these swimmers were never seen by the three boats in the utter blackness of the night. Because all the radio sets had been smashed, no emergency message had been possible.

As so often happened when there was considerable loss of lives, there were in the *Lady Hawkins'* case at least three pairs of merchant seamen brothers serving together in the same ship: the Dixons, the Harfords and the Seales, all from the West Indies. Three other West Indian pairs were also likely related as each pair came from the same village and all were stewards—the Breretons, Nurses and Phillips. No one was spared from death in these circumstances—women such as stewardess Lillian Cook-Gorbell, aged forty-nine, or youngsters aged sixteen and seventeen were among those lost.

The thirty-foot lifeboats were crowded with the few survivors, both crew and passengers. The U-boat lay stopped on the surface about 500 yards off, with a searchlight sweeping over the boats and watching *Lady Hawkins* disappear as she continued to roll to port and then sank swiftly by the bow. Shortly after, the U-boat motored away on the surface without contact with the boats or any swimmers struggling in the cold debris-littered sea. Lit only occasionally by calcium flares that had fallen into the ocean, the lifeboats were within sight of each other for a time. No.2 boat was now commanded by Chief Officer Kelly, who fished half-frozen swimmers out of the sea when they could be found. His boat, certified to carry a maximum of sixty-three persons, eventually carried seventy-six in all: twenty-three *Lady Hawkins* crew members, twenty-four RN seamen and officers, five Army personnel, twelve construction workers and twelve passengers including two-and-a-half year old Janet Johnson of Trinidad with her civil servant father and her mother. The rather large percentage of naval and military personnel reflects perhaps their more disciplined approach to abandoning the ship in an emergency than the completely unprepared civilian survivors. Several were quite badly injured.

Eventually the boat was so jammed they had to pull away from other swimmers to avoid being swamped and capsized. Kelly's boat became separated from the other two in the moderate easterly wind and those boats and whatever shaken survivors they had rescued completely disappeared; neither were ever seen again. Possibly they had been swamped by panicking survivors in the water. The only account of the sinking and of the survivors comes from those in Kelly's boat.

Everyone was wet and cold as a result of having to leap into the ocean and swim to the boat. It was crowded, with only room for some to sit on the thwarts or even in the water over the bottom boards, the last of which could not easily be bailed out. Others were standing huddled together for mutual warmth. Those who had the foresight to wear greatcoats wrapped others in them, including little Janet. The bartender, Steward Bill Hague, had brought off three bottles of rum but lost two before reaching the boat. Otherwise there was a small bottle of brandy, some tins of condensed milk, two water casks and a tin of biscuits. The boat carried a small first aid kit, but no practical spare equipment such as canvas for a shelter from sea, cold or sun. Such unanticipated problems or lack of useful equipment would be later remedied at least in part as a result of future reports from the survivors. This boat already lay to the westward of the other two and the floating wreckage from the *Lady Hawkins*, and although the breeze tended to push them slowly further west, they could hear some shouting from the water, and between the other boats, indicating they too were loaded with survivors. While Kelly was anxious to take advantage of the 6 to 7 knot winds that arose and sail west toward a chance of rescue, in the dark with many of his people completely unfamiliar with boats or even with the sea, and all shocked at their sudden drastic change, he dared not hoist sail and cope with sailing over the swells and seas in the dark.

By dawn, five hours later, the two other boats could not be seen. The Chief Officer took stock of their situation and immediately established a list of his people, organized his group to man the oars, and later had everyone sit as low in the boat as possible. There were seventeen Americans, a couple of civil administrators and some missionaries, at least one of whom was a lady whose husband had not survived to reach her boat; also one ships' wireless operator, plus the twenty-four RN seamen who were under Lt(E) Harry E. Barrett (himself a keen yachtsman and experienced small boat sailor who prepared a fourteen-page detailed report when he landed a month later in Trinidad). Of these seventy-six persons, five died over the next five days at sea: two elderly passengers, one of the construction workers, a black crewman and the ship's bartender, Bill Hague.

After first light, between 6:30 and 7:00, the sails were rigged and crewmen Charlie Bolivar, an experienced Nova Scotia doryman, and Bill Burton took turns steering to the west with an oar, as the rudder had been lost overboard before it could be shipped on its fittings. They were later spelled off by two Royal Navy seamen, ABs Squires and Rice. It was estimated they were up to 150 miles from shore, and if the wind failed or increased too much it might take two weeks to reach it, although it was quite possible they would be sighted by another or searching aircraft. Water slopped into the boat frequently and it was necessary to bail continuously, at which all took turns. Kelly organized his survivors' duties and even their positions, some standing, some seated. Breakfast was half a biscuit and a part dipper of water, lunch a mouthful of condensed milk taken in a flashlight cap, later diluted with some water, especially for Janet, and supper the same as breakfast. Each meal took almost two hours to distribute. Many soon developed colds and fevers, including Janet, as a result of being everlastingly damp and cold. Then the bottle of rum was produced and passed around to all for a sip, about an ounce a person on the honour system, with Kelly getting the last few drops. The sharing included a little, diluted, for Janet, which brought on fits of laughing, to the delight of the other survivors. In a few hours her fever subsided, so the cure worked. She and her mother were sheltered in a tiny three-by-four-foot cuddy right forward used for storing boat's supplies.

Prayers were said each noon before the milk issue. On the second day the wind further increased, and the sail had to be struck for safety, the boat riding reasonably well to just a jib overnight, as a sea anchor the boat carried had been damaged. With dawn and the easing of the winds they sailed on. A steward, Austin Riviera, died the second morning, having fallen into a coma. He was probably injured internally. His useable clothing was removed, and his body slipped sadly over the side with a few prayers. There was rain, thunder and lightning overnight and on Wednesday 21 January two other elderly passengers died and their bodies were committed to the empty sea. The water ration had to be reduced when one of the barricoes was found to be only half full, and another survivor, Bill Hague, whose rum bottle had been a lifesaver, also died, followed by one of the American construction workers, both possibly injured in the evacuation of the *Lady Hawkins*. By dawn on the fourth day the storm had abated and under sail again the boat was making reasonable progress, although many were showing signs of weakness, and sores and boils were developing.

Then late in the evening of their fifth day in the boat, 23 January, the steering oarsman cried out "A ship! A ship!" and all could soon see the dark outline of a ship not far off. Amidst general shouting they lit a flare and waved a flashlight, but to their utter despair the ship altered away from them. Realizing the ship's suspicion that their lights might belong to a U-boat, the survivors shone the light across their sails to show what they were. The ship altered around and approached the crowded boat.

Their rescuer was the 7,000-ton American passenger freighter *Coamo* bound for Puerto Rico, under Captain Nels Helgenson. He had indeed suspected the initial flashing light to be a U-boat ruse, but then saw the sails of the lifeboat. He came as close as possible and opened a lower shell door about ten feet above the water. The lifeboat sailed and rowed up to the opening, where a rope and a rope ladder were lowered to them. In twenty minutes all were on board, climbing on their own or helped by others, some even confused at what was happening. Chief Officer Kelly hurried to the bridge to say they were all aboard and not to remain stopped. As the turned away, Kelly in particular was saddened to see the derelict lifeboat, which had been their saving, wash astern. No one had thought to pull the plug in the bottom to sink it. The survivors were fed, the injured well and professionally treated by the ship's doctor and two physicians among her passengers, and all given beds. Seventy-one had survived from the *Lady Hawkins'* 321 persons. After arriving in San Juan, Puerto Rico on the 21st, two stewards whose feet had been in water for most of the five days had to have them amputated; others required treatment in hospital for salt water boils and aggravated cuts. But survive they did; their nightmare was over. Even little Janet survived and was well. No trace of the other boats was ever found.

On behalf of all the survivors, Lt. Barrett drafted a handsome letter to Chief Officer Kelly, thanking him and crediting him for their survival: "You had terrible decisions to make and you made them calmly and wisely and with such tact that everyone agreed...you saw to it that the humblest got equality of treatment and shared in what little comfort was available....You kept our spirits steadfast....You held us together. As an officer, seaman and Christian gentleman...a man amongst men... We shall never forget you."

Lt. Barrett wrote to CNSS strongly recommending Kelly for a decoration for his leadership, seamanship, strength and courageous actions. Chief Officer Kelly was later awarded an MBE and Lloyd's Bravery Medal, and on Kelly's recommendation Bolivar, Burton and Robert Clayton, the radio operator, received commendations for their valiant work in handling the steering oar and sails of the lifeboat.

KK Richard Zapp and his Type IXC *U 66* of 2 U-Flotille had left Lorient 15 December 1941 on his fourth patrol for the first efforts in *Operation Paukenschlag* on the American coast. Of his first three war patrols, mostly off Freetown and in the central Atlantic, Zapp had sunk four ships, all during the second patrol. This time, just off Cape Hatteras on 18 January he sank an American tanker, *Allan Jackson*, and expecting intensified searching had moved out to sea during the day and early evening, where he encountered *Lady Hawkins* strictly by chance shortly after midnight. After torpedoing her, he returned the next day to search off Hatteras, sinking three more ships, one British and two American in that area on the 22nd and 24th. Never attacked during the patrol, he returned to Lorient on 10 February 1942.

Zapp left *U 66* after one more very successful patrol in the Caribbean where his targets were mostly tankers. He survived the war in command of a Naval Defence Regiment at La Rochelle, France. *U 66*, under another belligerent CO was sunk west of the Cape Verde Islands on 6 May 1944, with thirty-six survivors in a dramatic gunfight, the German submarine even ramming and boarding the USN destroyer escort USS *Buckley*.

Those lost: Typical of several sinkings, the record of those lost does not correspond exactly from one source to another. The ship supposedly sailed with one hundred and nine in her crew plus 1 DEMS, and Kelly's boat rescued twenty-three less the two crew who died, or twenty-one. Thus eighty-eight crew should be on the list; but there are ninety-one names in the Merchant Navy's *Book of Remembrance* and below. Possibly the figure of one hundred and nine was not correct. But these are the Merchant Seamen lost, including West Indian crew serving as stewards and firemen.

Huntley O Giffin, Master		Frank A Archer
James Archibald	Percy Avery	Robert A Bell
Bertrem G Bennett	Donald S Blake	Charles H Blanchard
John N Brereton	Samuel Brereton	James Brown
Henry B Bush	Frank C Butcher	Fitzherbert Cadogan
Byron Calder	Lawrence G Callaghan	Witson B Campbell
Wilfred E Cannell	Henry J Cassidy	Godfrey Cherebin
Lillian C Cook-Gorbell	Carl H Coolen	Thomas P Cubitt
E Danglar	Clifford A Daniels	Joshua A Dewever
Coolridge C Dixon	Daniel Dixon	Henry Dumouchel
James A Dunne	George E Edward	Edmund O Forde
Edward Greenridge	William A Hague	Lloyd K Hall
William T Hamelin	Frederick Harford	Sedley Harford
Donald S Hayman	Harry P Houghton	Howard Ingram
Effrage Jacob	Ernest A James	Obyrne J Jones
Dale S Kent	Rene A Kuhl	Peter Lee
James A Leurs	Evans C Linton	Ivan D MacKinnon
Dudley DeC Mayers	Aubrey F Maynard	Stanley Mayo
Thomas McDonald	Ulric V McRae	Walter W Merriman
Leopold D Moore	Ovila Morin	Lewis N Morrison
Ephraim E Newell	Herman St.C Nurse	John W Nurse
John E Parker	Gordon Paul	George W Phillips
Laurie J Phillips	Armand C Prevost	Renwick Ramdayhan
Austin O Riviera	John Roberts	Donald B Ross

Bruce E Royer	Francois X St.Pierre	Jean Sanfillipo
Donald O Seales	Ralph H Seales	Jacques Shillingford
Edward Silverton	Herbert Singleton	Frederick A Slaven
Albert O Smith	Thomas A Smith	Shamont Sobers
Philip M Stone	Michael Sylvester	John Thompson
Harold E Tyrrell	Lorne Whitby	Hermanus Willemstyn
Oswald E Willoughby	Fred D Younkers	

plus DEMS gunner AB Ralph E Marryatt, RCNVR

Sources: D Hist copy of Lt(E) Barrett's Report; Hannington, *The Lady Boats*; Gannon, *Operation Drumbeat*; Reader's Digest, *Canadians At War, Vol.2*; Rohwer, *Axis Submarine Successes*; Wynn, *U-Boat Operations, Vol.1*; Busch & Röll, *German U-Boat Commanders*; Hickham, *Torpedo Junction*; Paquette & Bainbridge, *Honours & Awards*; Mike Cooper, e-mail re: corrections to *Honours & Awards*. Website, Cabinet Documents, No.58-56 of 6 Mar.1956; unidentified magazine article by Gregory Pritchard.

LADY DRAKE

SHIP: 7,831 grt, 438 ft. passenger freighter. Built in 1928 by Cammell Laird & Company, Birkenhead, England for CNSS.

FATE: Torpedoed and sunk by *U 106* on 4 May 1942, 90 miles northwest of Bermuda. Six Merchant Navy, six passenger casualties.

Lady Drake at the Halifax pier pre-war. In wartime these ships were painted a dark grey overall.
(Murray Manson/CNSS)

Like the *Lady Hawkins*, the *Lady Drake* continued with her role of providing service to and from the West Indies which was even more necessary in wartime. Many troops were stationed there for training and as a safeguard against possible German intrusion. The ships' cargo capacity was essential. Thus they were not requisitioned, although their cargoes and passenger list were assigned by the authorities. They were only supplied with additional seamen and engine room personnel from manning pools if there was a shortage.

The only concessions to the war raging throughout the Atlantic was their grey paint, a requirement to operate at night with no lights, and a routing established by the NCSO to keep clear of the US coast where U-boats prowled.

In April 1942 the *Lady Drake*, under Captain Percy Kelly (formerly the First Officer in *Lady Hawkins*) proceeded south via Boston and Bermuda to the West Indies, to Trinidad and Georgetown. She had no escorts, being considered fast enough on her own, and the USN assured the Captain they were watched by aircraft, although none were ever actually seen.

Northbound again in the last days of April *Lady Drake* took aboard a contingent of British Fleet Air Arm naval ratings bound eventually for the United Kingdom, and fifty-one Barbadian technicians. At St. Lucia the crew were sobered by the sight of *Lady Nelson* sitting half submerged on the bottom of Castries harbour, victim on 10 March of a U-boat torpedo even within that supposedly safe shelter. The *Lady Drake* even picked up some of the *Lady Nelson*'s crew, as well as ten "distressed seamen" from other lost ships for return to Canada. From there they had a corvette escort for a day and a half because of the numerous U-boat sinkings around the islands, and went in to St. Kitts for additional cargo. Then they headed straight north, without an escort, to Bermuda which they reached in safety. More passengers and cargo were picked up for Halifax and a fortunate few persons dropped off.

Captain Kelly asked for escort protection for the next leg, en route for Saint John, New Brunswick, knowing there were U-boats frequently passing through the area between Bermuda, Boston and Nova Scotia. But none was available, and the NCSO assured him the danger of encountering a U-boat was not great. Kelly intended to sail in the early evening out of Bermuda on 3 May, to be well clear of that way-point, maybe 125 miles, by dawn the next day. However the ship was delayed in cargo loading, in fact only by about twenty minutes, and when he sailed Kelly could no longer see the essential buoys marking the tortuous channel through Bermuda's northeastern reefs, so had to anchor for the night in the outer harbour. By this time *Lady Drake* had aboard 151 passengers and 121 crew.

The next day, 4 May, was clear, sunny and calm, with only a modest swell. They were escorted by occasional aircraft until about 10 a.m. From then on they were on their own. The fuel they had picked up in Trinidad was of poor quality, and at any speeds of over 12 knots they trailed a notable pall of smoke astern. The Radio Officer reported two German signals close by, and the ship zigzagged along a base course for

New York, passing in the afternoon some wreckage of a previous sinking. After dark Kelly altered directly for Boston at a maximum speed of about 14 knots. Although by dark they had managed 186 miles of steaming because of zigzagging, they were only about 100 miles northwest of Bermuda.

Then at 9:00 p.m. local time a torpedo track was seen by after lookouts to pass astern of the ship by a scant fifty feet. Before the bridge could be warned a second torpedo hit the *Lady Drake*'s No.3 hold next to the engine room, both of which flooded through the ruptured bulkheads, cutting off all power when the engines were stopped. All was in complete blackness, although the ship only rolled slightly to the injured side.

Order was maintained because the crew had expected trouble, and boats were turned out ready for launching. At first it was hoped the ship might be saved, but when she began settling quite quickly, Kelly gave the order to abandon ship. The boats were lowered, and while one had been smashed, five others got away within ten minutes, carrying the 260 survivors, including one woman, evenly divided between them, an average of fifty-five people crowded into each, almost their full capacity. Twelve persons had been lost, six in the engine room with the torpedo explosion, the other six evidently passengers, although how they were lost is not known. Possibly they were trapped in the utter blackness below decks, as happened in *Lady Hawkins*. The ship dropped by the bow and sank within twenty minutes of the torpedo hit.

Captain Kelly maintained a firm control of his situation, haunted by the *Lady Hawkin*'s terrible experience of missing lifeboats only three and a half months before. He insisted the boats be kept close to each other and remain in the area throughout the dark hours, a ship's senior deck officer in charge of each boat. With dawn the boats searched the area for any other survivors, but there were none, so the boats all hoisted sail and set off southeast in company for Bermuda. Fortunately it remained relatively peaceful, with enough wind to fill the sails but not endanger the boats. There was enough food and water in each boat to sustain them for at least some days.

At dawn on the second day there was much excitement when a very large ship appeared over the horizon, travelling toward them and weaving at high speed. She was soon recognized as Cunard's great liner *Queen Mary* on her way to New York. At almost 30 knots, she passed quickly not far off, not daring to stop, as the *Lady Drake*'s officers explained to their terribly disappointed mariners, because of the U-boat danger to such an inviting target. But from her lofty bridge flashed an Aldis light "I WILL REPORT... I WILL REPORT." This was some comfort to the survivors, who continued on their way toward Bermuda under sail.

A message was received by the British Routing Office in New York the next day, 7 May from the local NCSO officer: "The R.M.S. *Queen Mary* arrived New York at 0830 today and Captain Bissett immediately sent a message ashore to me that at

10:00 a.m. on the 6th of May he had sighted in position 35° 27′N 64° 22′W five boats loaded with survivors under sail, and had further passed an overturned lifeboat in the same vicinity. The boats when last seen were steering to the southward."

For those in the boats there was considerable anxiety as to what would happen and when help might arrive, if indeed it were sent. And they were only safe as long as the weather held and food and water supplies lasted—not many more days. Even at night the boats kept close, those that had, like Percy Kelly, survived previous sinkings boosting the morale of all.

At 0600 on the 7th an aircraft flew over the boats, the survivors waving and shouting to attract attention. The American plane turned, passed low over them, dipped its wings in acknowledgement and flew on, searching for U-boats, but radioing to its base the location of the lifeboats. Three hours later the elderly little American Lapwing class minesweeper USS *Owl* (1918) arrived from Bermuda, where she had just arrived a few days earlier for towing and general duties. Guided by the plane's signal, she picked up all 260 of *Lady Drake*'s people from their boats, crowded into her length of only 188 feet. All were taken aboard and the set off for Bermuda.

On arrival four of the injured were hustled to hospital, and the others were accommodated by Bermudians until arrangements were made for their onward transportation to Canada or elsewhere. The *Lady Rodney* was in Bermuda by this time, awaiting orders, the authorities now reluctant to sail her without escort protection, given the *Lady Drake*'s fate. A corvette was sent south from Halifax as escort. The thirty-one West Indian members of the *Drake*'s crew were sent back home in the Alcoa Company's *City of Birmingham*, and in an unusual gesture for the day, given two months' wages by CN(WI)SS, despite the established routine that all wages stopped when a ship was lost. CNSS even gave their Canadian crew members a month's paid leave. In addition to the loss of a good ship, the CN's annual report noted a direct cost of $36,009 attributed to the sinking—all in fact paid for by the Britannia Steamship Insurance Association Ltd.

For his successful rescue of all these survivors, as well as his exploits in saving at least the one boat load from the *Lady Hawkins*, Captain Percy Kelly was made an MBE in January 1943, as well as being awarded the Lloyd's Bravery Medal. And the little USS *Owl* also survived the war.

Given that by now CNSS had lost four of their *Lady* boats, although *Lady Nelson* was salvageable, one can sympathize with the plaintive tone of a letter from R.C. Vaughn, CNR's President, to P.J.A. Cardin, the Canadian Minister of Transport: "All our vessels, as you know, have been sailing under the direction of the Navy. Our Captains, of course, would like to have had convoys or escorts, but that appears to be impossible. Perhaps you may wish to take this matter up with the Navy with a view to seeing if some arrangements could not be made to protect the *Lady Rodney* and the freight vessels."

Their attacker had been *U 106*, KL Herman Rasch who completed six patrols in this boat, of which this was the third. He had departed Lorient on 15 April planning to go to the Gulf of Mexico. He was detected and attacked by the destroyer USS *Broome* on the way without being damaged, then encountered *Lady Drake* by chance as he continued westward toward the US coast. After this success he passed through the Florida Straits, sank two tankers and a minesweeper in the Gulf of Mexico near New Orleans, then two more and left for home. Rasch refuelled on the way east-northeast of the Azores, rescued a single lonely merchant ship survivor and arrived back in Lorient on 29 June.

In a later patrol his U-boat was attacked by a Czech Wellington aircraft, during which one officer was killed and Rasch wounded. He returned to his base and left the boat. Rasch survived the war in command of a flotilla of the *Kleinkampfverbände* small two-man submarines. *U 106* was lost on her 10th patrol to two RAF Sunderlands north of Spain which sank her with depth charges on 2 August 1943. Twenty-five men were lost and thirty-five picked up by German torpedo boats that had been sent out to escort her in.

Those lost:	While records indicate twelve lives were lost, only six names, Canadians and West Indians, are listed in the Merchant Navy *Book of Remembrance* and on the Seamen's Memorial at Halifax. The other six were passengers.

Graham Carter	Emanuel Crozier *	Harold Stanley
Hewley E White *	David Wilbourne *	Anthony Yearwood

Passengers lost:	A. Bradsmace	O. Greenridge	M. Hambline
	L. Mercier	O. Reid,	plus one unidentified

* West Indians

Sources:	Hamilton, *The Lady Boats*; Reader's Digest, *Canadians At War, Vol.2*; Paquette & Bainbridge, *Honours & Awards*; MacKay, *The People's Railway*; Tucker, *Naval Service of Canada, Vol.2*; Rohwer, *Axis Submarine Successes*; Wynn, *U-Boat Operations, Vol. 2*; Kurowski, *Knight's Cross Holders*; Hazegray website, <www.hazegray.com>; USN Survivor Interview transcript.

CORNWALLIS

SHIP:	5,458 grt, 400 ft. two-deck freighter, 20 passengers. Built in 1921 as *Canadian Transporter* for CGMM by J. Coughlan & Sons Ltd., Vancouver; engines by J.G. Kinkaid, Greenock, Scotland.
FATE:	Torpedoed by *U 1230* on 3 December 1944 in the Gulf of Maine, 10 miles south of Mount Desert Island. About forty-two casualties, including DEMS; five survivors.

The CGMM freighter *Canadian Transporter* in 1926. She became CNSS's *Cornwallis*.
(Murray Manson)

The good sized freighter *Cornwallis* was one of the Canadian government-ordered ships of 1918 that continued to roll off the ways even after the First World War was over. The Vancouver firm of Coughlans that built her burned on 30 August 1924. Canada and the rest of the Allies had lost a vast number of merchantmen during the period of unrestricted U-boat warfare in 1916 to early 1918, before convoy was accepted as the only way to protect trans-Atlantic shipping.

For ten years, as *Canadian Transporter* she was managed by CGMM, then transferred to the CN operations and renamed *Cornwallis* for employment in their West Indies freighter trade, as were five other ex-Canadian-named ships, to supplement the Lady boats. At 8,390 dwt she was capable of carrying twenty passengers on the Vagabond Cruises and operated out of Montreal from spring to fall via Halifax. Once the demands of war arose *Cornwallis* was used on more extensive freighter voyages as well, one being to India.

Her first U-boat encounter came as a tremendous shock not only to the ship's crew but to the authorities. On 11 September 1942 she was lying at anchor off the jetty in the sheltered harbour at Bridgetown, Barbados, awaiting escort south to Trinidad, with anti-torpedo nets out along her sides. At about 5:30 p.m. local time KL Hans-Jürgen Auffermann gently brought his *U 514* into the Barbados roads on the surface, hidden in the late afternoon sun's path. He calmly slowed, to let his gunners open fire on the merchant ship's net supporting rigging until it collapsed. Auffermann then torpedoed the ship in No.2 hold. Although he claimed another hit, there is no record of this and his other torpedo probably exploded against the shore. Auffermann then calmly reversed course and left, without even being fired on.

Although *Cornwallis* was provided with an elderly 4-inch gun, her gunners were not prepared and in the sun's brilliance did not see the attacker anyway. The CNSS's *Lady Nelson* had suffered the same fate five months before, when torpedoed in the harbour of Port Castries at St. Lucia.

As *Cornwallis* began to settle, fortunately with some steam up, her Master, Captain Duncan MacLeod was able to move her into relatively shallow water where she came to rest on the bottom. Because of the actions of several of her ship's company the vessel was saved from major flooding damage. She was then patched and towed to Mobile, Alabama for repairs. Two months later she was again put into service for CNSS. Six members of her ship's company who had remained aboard and helped save the received medals for their efforts: Captain MacLeod (MBE), Chief Engineer H.H. Jenkins (OBE), additional Chief Engineer E.G. Griffith (OBE—he had also helped previously to save the CNSS *Colborne* when she was heavily bombed in England), AB Claude Freeman, Carpenter J.J. Murray and Bosun Harold Gates (all BEMs).

Cornwallis returned primarily to her West Indies trade, now provided with considerably more armament: a 4-inch gun on her stern, a 3-inch forward on the fo'c'sle, Oerlikon heavy machine guns and some anti-aircraft rocket launchers. They were to prove of little value however in her next encounter with the enemy U-boats.

By the beginning of December 1944 Operational Intelligence in NSHQ in Ottawa had developed a fairly clear picture of recent U-boat operations along the Nova Scotia and northern US coasts. These location identifications were based on ULTRA, D/F bearings, sightings by ships and aircraft and even a few attacks. A report noted that "there was an increase in enemy submarine activity in the Canadian coastal zone" and the Intelligence group correctly located *U 1228* in the Cabot Straits, *U 1231* off Gaspé, *U 1230* in the Gulf of Maine, south of the Bay of Fundy, and *U 806* at the eastern limit of the area. (Interestingly, *U 1231* in the Gulf of St. Lawrence had attacked several ships but had had repeated torpedo failures, as well as icing of her schnorkle and thus had sunk no ships.)

Despite this potential threat, *Cornwallis*, northbound under a new Master, Captain Emerson H. Robinson (formerly *Lady Rodney*'s Chief Officer), left Barbados on 20 November 1944, carrying a cargo of bagged West Indian sugar and barrels of molasses. She left her convoy off New York and moved up the coast toward Saint John, New Brunswick to offload. Just before dawn about 0600 local time, in chilly 44°F weather, about ten miles south of Mount Desert Island off the Maine coast she was hit with no prior warning by probably two torpedoes from *U 1230*, commanded by KL Hans Hilbig. Her boats had been swung out as a precaution, but she rolled onto her side and sank so quickly, in less than five minutes, that no boats could be launched in those brief terrible moments. Her Bosun, AB John Buffett, had been concerned at just this possibility, commenting to one of his mates that "if torpedoed, to hell with the boats", and as planned he knocked the securing pin off a liferaft, let it fall into the sea and jumped in after it. The gallant radio operator only had time to send a brief partial signal, "S-S-S OFF DESERT..." before the power failed.

In the flat calm but frigid December sea, few survived. The bosun climbed onto his raft and paddling about awkwardly was able to pull only five others up with him: another Danish seaman, Soin Christensen; a fireman, Elmer Crossman; two West Indian deck boys; and a cook, Ormond Rocque. Even with the radio signal warning that a ship was likely sunk, the only clue to narrow the search area, the word "Desert," could refer to several places along the coast.

A fishing vessel and one of the search aircraft sent out in response to the distress signal found debris at 1134 the same morning but no survivors; two USN destroyers and a Coast Guard cutter sent shortly after also found nothing. It was not until almost 1330, seven and a half hours after the sinking, that the New England fishing vessel *Notre Dame* came across the raft and plucked the five survivors from the sea. Rocque, the cook, had died on the raft from exposure or injuries, and his body was not recovered. The survivors were taken into Rockland, Maine for treatment at a USCG hospital. Forty-two lost their lives, including DEMS ratings and possibly a few passengers. Four bodies were recovered and also landed at Rockland. The crew hailed from all across Canada, from England, Scotland, Wales, Northern Ireland, and from New York City. And notably a significant number were French Canadians, as were many on the lists of merchant seamen lost from other ships.

It was a tragedy not far short of the CNSS's *Lady Hawkins'* loss three years before. Sadly, similar to the *Lady Hawkins*, two brothers were lost in the sinking, Fifth Engineer Wayne Jessop, aged nineteen and his brother Donkeyman George B. Jessop, aged eighteen from Chatham, Ontario. The Battle of the Atlantic continued to exact a sorry toll even in its last year.

KL Hans Hilbig's Type IXC *U 1230* only made one war patrol, and only sank one ship, *Cornwallis*. This was also Hilbig's first and only appointment as a U-boat CO. Leaving his base at Horten, Norway on 8 October 1944. he crossed to the Nova Scotia coast, ran south as far as Cape Cod, then returned to Mount Desert Island, Maine, where Bar Harbour is located. He cautiously approached the shore at periscope depth on the north side at Frenchman's Bay, for he had on board two agents to be landed as spies, a German and an American. They were put ashore by small rubber boat on the night of 29 November, but were detected by Coast Guard patrols, followed to their contacts in New York, arrested and executed in short order.

Meanwhile Hilbig slipped out, and by the night of 2 December had encountered *Cornwallis* heading north offshore. He torpedoed the ship, identified her, but did not contact the survivors. He likely didn't even see them. Being on the surface that close to the US shore in daylight by this time in the war would have been suicidal. He remained in the area for a few more days, then left for mid-North Atlantic, where he had weather reporting responsibilities until mid-January in connection with the German plans and execution of the "Battle of the Bulge" in southeast Belgium at

Bastogne. He arrived back in Kristiansand on 13 February 1945 and he and *U 1230* did not go on operations again, being surrendered in May 1945. The boat was sunk by naval gunfire in Operation Deadlight west-northwest of Ireland on 17 December 1945.

Those lost: The total number lost again varies slightly with different reports. Thirty-six are listed in the Merchant Navy *Book of Remembrance*, and there are references to seven DEMS gunners lost, forty-three in all. Forty are listed on the Seamen's Memorial at Halifax, including six DEMS, leaving thirty-four merchant seamen. Even so there would seem to be thus two unlisted names in each source. The list below is a combination of the two, giving thirty-seven merchant seamen lost, plus the six DEMS gunners.

Emerson H Robinson, Master		James W Barry
Alden R Brewer *	Lawrence D Cleveland **	J Gerald Comeau
Roy L Couves	Thomas S Cyr *	P Harry Dine
Stephen Fowler **	William Gaythwaite	Oswald Hamilton
Herbert Harding	Jacob G Hodder	Kenneth V. Hopfe ***
George B Jessop	Wayne Jessop	Patrick J Kearney
Norman H Kenny	Eric J C LaCouvée	Leandre LeBlanc
Francis E T Lyons *	James B E MacDougall	Roy MacDougall
Wendell G MacLellan	Edward J Maughan *	Harold B D May
James McLaughlin	John J Murray **	George F Olsen
Andrew P Pantoff	Marcel Perron **	Chesley Perry
James G G Peterkin *	William J Quilty †	Ormond Rocque
James A Roy	Herbert E Scott	Roger G Smith
David H Stewart	Nick Szuszwal *	John W Wallace
John J Walsh	George Whalen †	Joseph L Williams

Note: DEMS gunners (* above). Five bodies were recovered (** above). Quilty and Whalen (†) were serving under the names of Dunn and Keif in *Cornwallis*, as they had been members of the Naval RCNR and deserted in May 1944 to join the Merchant Navy—an unfortunate decision.

Sources: Hannington, *The Lady Boats*; *Lloyd's Register, 1941-'42*; DND files, *Merchant Ships A-Z*; Hadley, *U-Boats Against Canada*; David Syrett, *The Battle of the Atlantic and Signals Intelligence*; Parker, *Running The Gauntlet*; Paquette & Bainbridge, *Honours & Awards*; Mike Cooper, e-mail re *Honours & Awards* corrections; Wynn, *U-Boat Operations, Vol.2*; Rohwer, *Axis Submarine Successes*; Gannon, *Operation Drumbeat*; Gentile, *Track of the Grey Wolf*; McLean & Preston, *Warship, 1997-1998*; Busch & Röll, *German U-Boat Commanders*; USN Survivor Interview transcripts; copies of message traffic concerning *Cornwallis* in D Hist files.

CHAPTER 10

Canadian Pacific: Two Losses, Few Casualties

You are going through a great trial, but I know you
are doing everything you can and are resolved to
continue to do so.

—Lord Mayne, Secretary of State for the Colonies,
in the *Singapore Sunday Times,* 15 Feb., 1942

The Canadian Pacific Railway Company (CP Rail) since its incorporation in February 1881 had developed into a full service company. That is, in addition to building rail lines to the west coast the directors had extended its interests into shipping in order to make use of and encourage rail traffic. Its first ships on the Great Lakes in 1884, with the traditional CP names of Empress, Princess and Beaver, were to assist with the construction of the railway itself. Then, even before rail lines had actually reached the British Columbia coast CP appointed agents in Japan and China to encourage traffic from the Orient. They would bring cargoes and passengers to Canada, transship them by rail across Canada to its eastern cities and the US, then onward to Europe. It was "The All Red Route," referring to the red colour of the British Empire on most maps. By 1886 sailing vessels were arriving at Port Moody near Vancouver, the CP's western terminus. The large, opulent and fast Empress liners acquired early on received a substantial Royal Mail subsidy, and with CP's negotiations, connected through the Orient with the Trans-Siberian Railway.

From this enthusiastic beginning the company expanded so that by the outbreak of the Second World War it had not only a large fleet of many types of ocean-going ships on the Atlantic and Pacific, but also had ships on lakes and rivers, particularly in British Columbia and the Great Lakes. CP had also acquired several other shipping companies, built hotels, lodges and other properties to be served by and encourage use of their rail network. Unlike its chief rival, the government-owned Canadian National Railway, it operated largely without direct subsidies and was a profitable business operation. As its pre-First World War President Shaughnessy said, "The railway was to be clear of any political entanglements." CP stock on the market was considered a bellwether of the Canadian financial climate. Much of its financing was arranged in England, and thus most of its larger ships were registered and crewed there rather than in Canada.

CP could abandon services that did not prove financially supportive. CN often could not, or face a politically unacceptable storm. In the First World War CP had provided some forty-eight liners and cargo ships for war service, thirty-seven of them under Admiralty direction, with some on contract or sold outright to the Admiralty and other interests. Fifteen were lost to enemy action, mines or marine war hazards.

By the start of the Second World War, not counting inland lake steamers, tugs, service barges and small ferries for use between the B.C. Gulf islands, Canadian Pacific Steamships (CPSS) was operating about thirty-five ocean ships: the six large Empresses, four Duchesses, eight merchant ships or combination merchant and passenger vessels, and fifteen Princess ships on the west coast. However most of these, all but the *Empress of Asia* and *Empress of Russia* and the Princess ships, were British registered in London, and flew the unadorned British red ensign. While ten of these British ships were lost to enemy action or wartime marine accident—such as the *Empress of Britain* and *Empress of Canada*, two Duchess ships, and the freighters *Montrose* and *Beaverburn*—their stories do not concern us as they were not Canadian registered ships. Their losses are covered briefly however in Chapter 18.

In total it has been estimated that CP's ocean ships during the war carried 977,133 tons of cargo and almost 1,010,000 passengers, steaming over 3,615,000 miles. (George Musk, *Canadian Pacific Afloat, 1883-1968*.) The two Canadian registered ships CP lost were sunk under somewhat unusual circumstances.

EMPRESS OF ASIA

SHIP: 16,909 grt, 590 ft.(overall), passenger liner. Built in 1913 by Fairfield Shipbuilding & Engineering Company Ltd., Glasgow, Scotland; four coal-fired steam turbines and quadruple screws, for 20 knots. Accommodation for 384 first and second class and 808 "Asiatic" steerage passengers and 476 crew.

FATE: Bombed and set afire by Japanese aircraft 5 February 1942 when in Convoy BM-12. Anchored and sank just off Singapore, Malaya. One of the crew identified as having died.

Almost as soon as the *Empress of Asia* was launched and completed her trials in 1913 she left for Hong Kong via Cape Town on her maiden voyage. She had cost, like her sister the *Empress of India*, $5 million to build. At Hong Kong she was requisitioned by the British government immediately on the outbreak of the First World War and provided with guns as an armed merchant cruiser (AMC). She was to patrol Chinese and Indian Ocean areas, then was sent as part of the blockade of Manila Bay in the Philippines where fourteen German supply ships were hoping to join von Spee's squadron in the Pacific. She was fortunate to survive and be operating in those eastern oceans, as seventeen other similar AMC ex-liners were sunk during

Empress of Asia in CP colours, leaving Vancouver in peacetime.
(Vancouver Maritime Museum)

that war. As the German ships loose in the Pacific were rounded up, these AMCs became unnecessary there, so they were moved to the Atlantic. The *Empress of Asia* was returned to company service in March of 1916, but was used by CP as an Atlantic troopship until the war's end. Her last trooping voyage was to Vancouver via the Panama Canal with 1100 returning Canadian troops. She was returned to CP's use in February 1919.

During the inter-war years she was employed continuously on trans-Pacific liner service, by January 1941 completing her 307th and last scheduled crossing at the remarkable age of twenty-seven. She could carry 1180 paying passengers, taking eight days, fifteen hours from Japan to Vancouver. With the outbreak of the Second World War, on government contract she at first carried troops and passengers to Hong Kong. On 14 September 1940 while in the Gulf of Tokyo she had been bombed by a Japanese aircraft, and several Chinese crew in the galley were wounded. "An accident, to be accepted" the Japanese said, although their consul in Vancouver paid damages to CP.

On return to Vancouver the *Empress of Asia* was requisitioned in February 1941 by the British Ministry of Shipping for service once again as a troopship. Having landed those of her crew who were Chinese and with a hundred or more Canadians as volunteers (thirty from the Owen Sound and Collingwood areas of Ontario in response to an ad), she left that month via the Panama Canal for the UK. At Liverpool where she had been built the ship was again taken in hand for conversion and arming. In her role as a troopship she was eventually to carry 7923 troops and 3495 tons of cargo in total. She was armed with one 6-inch gun, one 3-inch anti-aircraft gun, six Oerlikons, eight Hotchkiss .303 machine guns, four PAC rockets and depth charges. By this time the ship was elderly, still coal-fired, and in her urgent trooping role tended to become shoddy and infested with the usual cockroaches and rats. Before she even left Liverpool seven of the new stokers, now tough Liverpudlians, had deserted.

Under Captain J. Bisset Smith, the ship sailed from Liverpool on 12 November 1941 (the Ontario volunteers returned home, replaced by British sailors, although other mostly west coast Canadians remained), making one trip to New York and Halifax, then back to Liverpool and on to the Far East, taking troops via Freetown and Durban to Bombay. Already another seven of her crew had deserted or been arrested, attesting to difficult conditions in her stokeholds and boiler rooms. At Bombay she embarked 2235 troops of the British 18th Division for Singapore for the defence of that fortress garrison. These consisted of the 125th Anti-tank Regiment, a medical unit and infantry, plus a cargo of military supplies. She departed Bombay in convoy on 23 January. Thus, despite the Japanese attacks of a month and a half before, she was involved in the last attempts to add military firepower and troops to bolster Singapore's defence. Even with the Japanese already sweeping down the Malay Peninsula and its army's skill of movement seriously underestimated, it was yet hoped that Singapore could be successfully held. Or at least, to save face with the oriental Allies, it could be valiantly defended to show Britain's commitment. Before the fortress fell there had been seven escorted convoys sent in, totalling forty-four ships, carrying 45,000 fighting men of all services. Several of these previous convoys had included CP's other British ships, *Empress of Australia*, *Empress of Japan* and *Duchess of Bedford*.

The *Empress of Asia*'s circumstances were not helped much by the questionable abilities of some of her engine room personnel. One report notes that with the Chinese stokers she could maintain a steady 18 knots; with the inexperienced Canadian replacements only about 16 knots, but with their tough but mostly inexperienced and recalcitrant Liverpool replacements the best that the boilers could produce was steam for 10 knots. There were even reports after her loss that this was in part because the unruly stokehold crew was not able to maintain enough steam for the speed needed to keep up with her convoy BM-12, and was only in part the fault of poor steaming coal.

That convoy consisted of an ex-French liner, the Bibby-managed *Félix Roussel*; a Dutch 6000 ton passenger the *Plancius*; the large Bibby liner *Devonshire* and the *Empress of Asia*. They were joined by another group of eight ships going to Batavia in Dutch Java which broke away a couple of days later, although one of that group, the 8300-ton *City of Canterbury* continued on to Singapore with them.

On 4 February the *Empress of Asia* was the last in her convoy of five, steaming in a single line at 12 knots. Her Master was still Captain Smith, with a crew of 416, including eighteen Navy and seven Army DEMS gunners. Their escorts were two RN cruisers, HMS *Exeter* astern of the merchant ships and the older HMS *Danae*, two destroyers, and two sloops, HMAS *Yarra* and HMIS *Sutlej* off the convoy's bow. At 1100 local time that day the convoy was passing through Banka Strait between eastern Sumatra and Bank Island, 350 miles southeast of Singapore, in clear weather with a few high thin clouds. They were sighted by a V formation of about eighteen Japanese aircraft and bombed from about 5000 feet. There were no direct hits, although there were ten near misses on either side. There was little damage aboard the *Empress of Asia* except to some of the lifeboats pierced by splinters and some broken saloon windows. All the bombs dropped in clusters near the *Empress of Asia* except for a couple which fell out toward *Yarra*. All ships opened fire, escorts and merchantmen, but without any observed results.

At this time many of the stokers downed shovels and refused to remain in the stokehold, crowding in a noisy group on an after deck. Colonel Dean from the army was able to temporarily recruit some ex-Welsh miners as stokers until the recalcitrant group were driven back to their jobs at pistol point. It was not a good omen for the morrow.

That afternoon of the 4th, the Dutch *Plancius* and the *Devonshire* pressed on ahead, aiming to arrive in Singapore by first thing in the morning of the 5th. By this time *Empress of Asia* had dropped astern of the remainder, unable to maintain convoy speed.

The next day, again in good visibility and calm seas, the three remaining liners were steaming east at a reduced speed of 5 or 6 knots, waiting for the *Empress of Asia* to catch up and planning to pick up a pilot about fifteen miles out of Singapore. They were now protected only by *Danae* and the two sloops. At almost the same time as the day before a larger force of twenty-four Japanese planes passed high overhead and into some clouds, dropping no bombs. But at about 1100 the planes returned, singly and in pairs attacking all three ships in the convoy from all directions. Captain Smith felt that because his was the largest ship, and with its distinctive three funnels was well known to the Japanese from its pre-war voyages to Japan "they bore the brunt of the attacks." Some of the troops attributed this to their position, still astern of the others. The French *Felix Roussel* was hit with one bomb which did not succeed in stopping her.

The aircraft dove from about 15,000 feet, at an angle of not more than forty-five degrees, down to about 3000 feet, dropping large bombs which could be easily followed until they hit the water or a ship. The Master noted that it was difficult to differentiate between near misses and hits when standing on the bridge as each shook the vessel severely. By 1105 there was a thick volume of black smoke issuing from the vicinity of the forward funnel, evidence of a hit. At once the first officer and fire parties closed on the area to see if anything could be done.

The first stick of bombs had hit, one going through the ornate dome over the main lounge and into the B deck dining room; another destroyed her radio equipment, others damaged the engine room. The attack lasted for about an hour and the *Empress of Asia* suffered at least three major hits, causing serious fires that covered the boat deck in dense smoke and steam. All her guns, and those of the other liners and escorts, were firing at the attackers, but no aircraft were noted as being shot down. The dense clouds of escaping steam and smoke drifting along the ship's side made it almost impossible for the gunners to aim at anything except the noise of diving aircraft.

By 1125 the First Officer reported to Captain Smith that the fires were uncontrollable. There was no water available through the ship's fire hydrants as the water mains had been shattered by the bombs. While pumps were operating at full pressure and there were some fire extinguishers, this was entirely inadequate to control the fires now burning throughout the midships accommodation and spreading easily via the old varnished woodwork. By 1130 the Chief Engineer advised that the engine room was filling with smoke and his crew could no longer remain below. He was thus advised to evacuate the engine room, leaving the engines still turning, but slowly.

Captain Smith advised the officer commanding the troops to muster them right forward and right aft on A deck. To prevent too great loss of life, the Master resolved to anchor just outside the channel, near a lighthouse on Sultan Shoal, south of the swept channel through the British minefields which protected the entrance to Singapore itself. The *Empress of Asia* was still moving slowly through the water as he conned her around toward the shoal. By this time also the lower bridge and officers' accommodation was afire and the bridge watch had to abandon it because of smoke and heat. They could no longer use the bridge ladders leading aft so had to slide down a rope onto the foredeck. Captain Smith threw overboard a weighted box containing all his confidential signal books, secret charts and codes and then slid down the rope as well. The engines were stopped and the ship slowed.

By 12:15, an hour after the start of the attack, the ship was anchored just off the shoal in shallow water but not quite aground, eleven miles from Singapore. The whole midships section was now afire and covered in smoke, including some of the lifeboats, so Captain Smith decided it was too impractical to order abandoning by lifeboat. The two ends of the ship, largely undamaged, were packed with soldiers and crew, quite a few of them wounded. While all the armed ships and Dutch aircraft fired continuously at the Japanese aircraft, again no hits were noted.

While a few of the Japanese aircraft were still about, within minutes they flew off, chased by Hurricane fighters which arrived overhead. No British aircraft had appeared during the actual attack mainly because there was simultaneously a Japanese air attack on the Singapore airport and the British had a shortage of fighter aircraft.

Shortly a host of small craft came out from Singapore and sent boats over to the liner. These took off loads of survivors, taking them over to the Sultan Shoal, returning for further boat loads. Other ships in the convoy, carrying on into the city, also dropped their lifeboats. The small Australian sloop HMAS *Yarra* in a neat feat of seamanship came right alongside aft and took off about 1500 troops and crew including most of the injured.

Captain Smith, despite burns to his hands, superintended the abandonment of his ship and was the last to leave her at about 1300, by motor launch to HMS *Danae* which was also standing by. He transferred to HMIS *Sutlej* and made a sweep around the *Empress of Asia* just to ensure no one had been overlooked in the rescue. They then went on into Kepple Harbour, Singapore, by about 1420, no other ships being damaged in the attack. Those survivors who had been landed on Sultan Shoal were also transported into Singapore by the day's end.

Two days later on 7 February two officers, including the captain, came out again and boarded the burning and now foundering ship to assess if it was possible for the invading Japanese to salve her. He deemed this unlikely as the fires by then had extended into the ship's coal bunkers. Exploding ammunition drove them off the ship once again. The *Empress of Asia* eventually rolled onto her side and settled in shallow water.

Only one Caucasian crewman had been seriously injured in the bombing, a pantryman named Douglas Elworthy, who shortly after died in hospital and is buried in Singapore. Fifteen soldiers were later unaccounted for in the confusion of abandoning ship and transporting men from to shoal to Singapore, although the Master and Colonel Dean thought that some would probably turn up. Some were certainly badly injured and a few killed. Many of the crew were cared for by the Salvation Army, which provided food, blankets and a place to sleep. After, in rain and cold, they were moved to army camps. There were also sporadic air raids, as by this time the advancing Japanese were shelling installations on the island from the mainland. On 6 February the port shipping Master arranged for 127 of the rebellious firemen and one steward to depart that day on the French *Félix Roussel*, which got away safely.

The Japanese landed on the island of Singapore on 8 February. On the 10th the director of medical services appealed to the *Empress of Asia*'s catering department to help tend the hundreds of injured in the local hospitals. The ship's doctor and all of her 147 catering staff volunteered at once to help and all were taken prisoner when the city fell four days later. It has not been possible to identify how many of these valiant volunteers subsequently died at the hands of the Japanese. In fact 153 were later reported as POWs. One name has been added recently to the *Empress of Asia*'s casualties: galley boy H. Smallwood is recorded as dying on 29 March 1944 in a POW camp.

On the afternoon of the 10th a port naval officer arranged with Captain Smith for all the other surviving deck crew to take over three small coastal steamers of 100 tons each that had been abandoned by their Chinese crews. They were brought

The only name appearing on the Thames Embankment Merchant Navy Memorial for the
Empress of Asia, but not lost during her sinking. Douglas Elworthy is not listed
because he is buried in a known grave in Singapore.
(F. Redfern)

alongside to take on stores although because of the air raids they could not obtain
any more fuel. On the 11th these vessels left for Batavia (now Djakarta) in Java, 550
miles to the southeast. Two of them reached that port on the 15th. The third one,
the Straits Steamship Company's *Ampang*, was navigated by *Empress of Asia*'s First
Officer and navigator, Len Johnston, who running short of fuel put in to Palembang
on Sumatra's north coast. But because of the arrival of Japanese paratroops in the
area, they could not get the fuel to continue. The *Empress of Asia*'s crew got away
again, this time by bus and then train overland through the mountains to the south
coast and eventually also to Batavia, just ahead of the invading Japanese. From there
they and the earlier arrivals took the little freighter *Whangpoo* to Freemantle,
Australia. The Canadians arrived back in Vancouver via New York four months later.
On 15 February Singapore, "Fortress of the East," surrendered to the Japanese infantry
after five days of confused and hopeless fighting.

The other three merchant ships of the last convoy into Singapore survived the
war. In fact of all the ships in the seven convoys sent in to Singapore, the *Empress of
Asia* was the only one sunk. As well the RN destroyer *Jupiter* sank one Japanese
submarine at the time, although she herself was sunk shortly after in a minefield on
27 February 1942. The insurance underwriter's rights to the wreck of the *Empress of
Asia* were sold to the International Salvage Association Ltd. in October 1951. They
removed the wreckage for its scrap value over the next year.

Captain J.B. Smith was awarded an OBE for his services, as the citation reads,
because "Later he was successful in navigating a small coastal steamer from Singapore

to Batavia under exceptional conditions." The *Empress of Asia*'s Chief Engineer, Donald Smith was also awarded an OBE, and the first officer an MBE. Donald Smith's and First Officer Leonard Johnston's citations are similar, in that in addition to assisting with the defence of the *Empress of Asia* and supervising her largely successful abandonment, Donald Smith commanded and Johnston helped navigate "a small coastal steamer carrying some of the vessel's crew (*Empress of Asia*'s) in an endeavour to reach safety. This small vessel was under constant air attack and both food and water were exhausted. They had to abandon this when attacked by enemy naval units and parachute troops. [They] successfully led the party of 41 overland to safety."

Those lost: (Merchant Navy) Douglas Elworthy, buried at Singapore
                H. Smallwood (as a POW)

Sources: Roskill, *The War At Sea, Vol. II*; Musk, *Canadian Pacific Afloat* and *Canadian Pacific, The Story*; Paquette & Bainbridge, *Honours & Awards*; Lamb, *Empress to the Orient*; PRO SCS interview with Captain J.B. Smith; McKee & Darlington, *The Canadian Naval Chronicle*; Newbolt, *A Naval History of the War*; notes from AB Geoff Tozer; Attiwill, *The Singapore Story*; Veterans Affairs Canada website <veteransaffairs.gc.ca>.

PRINCESS MARGUERITE

SHIP: 5875 grt, 350 ft., coastal fast passenger ferry. Built in 1924 by John Brown & Company Ltd., Clydebank, Scotland for CP. Capable of 21 knots.

FATE: Torpedoed, set afire and sunk by *U 83* on 17 August 1942 in the Mediterranean north of Port Said, on the way to Cyprus. No crew lost.

A CP postcard of the *Princess Marguerite*. (Author's collection)

Named after The Hon. Marguerite Kathleen Shaughnessy, daughter of former president of the CPR Baron Thomas Shaughnessy, the new *Princess Marguerite* cost the CP just over $570,000, as did her sister *Princess Kathleen*. It was the first time the CP's Princesses had not been named after Royal Princesses, and they are probably unique in both being named after the same person. The Hon. Marguerite Shaughnessy herself was the sponsor at *Princess Marguerite*'s launching, her mother sponsoring the sister ship.

In 1925 *Princess Marguerite* reached the west coast after an 8826 mile trip in twenty-six days, arriving on 20 April. With her sister they were specifically planned as replacements for the aging *Princess Victoria* and *Princess Charlotte*, built in 1902 and 1909 respectively. In May the new ships began the CP's well known "Triangle Run"—Victoria, Vancouver and Seattle—and remained on this duty for sixteen years, until requisitioned for war service in the fall of 1941. The reliability and intense use of these two is demonstrated by *Princess Marguerite*'s service for the year from May 1938 to April 1939, when she maintained a continuous day and night twice daily service, except for three days in drydock on one occasion. The longest period in port each day was two and a half hours. In the eleven months she sailed a total of 81,144 miles. The *Princess Kathleen* sailed in the opposite direction on a similar schedule. This operation was

An unusual wartime photo of *Princess Marguerite* burning, August 1942.
Evidently taken from HMS *Hero*, one of her rescuers.
(Author's collection/CPR)

continued from 1909 until 1949 with various ships. In the spring of 1939 the *Princess Marguerite* carried HM King George VI and Queen Elizabeth from Vancouver to Victoria during their triumphant Royal Tour.

The Princess ships were quite luxurious for those days, and were promoted as the ship-of-choice for those travelling on the triangle run, with a dining saloon that would seat over 170 persons, a library on the boat deck and an observation room with a repeater gyro compass for the interest of the passengers. They had staterooms for 1947 first class passengers and provision for another 325 seated on benches. They could carry 30 cars as well. During the mid-Depression years the two ships were sometimes laid up during the winter months and smaller CP ships employed on the run.

Because of the necessity to maintain the ferry services the Princesses and other CP ships provided on the west coast, only *Princess Marguerite* and *Princess Kathleen* were requisitioned of those ships. The large ocean liners and the Beaver and "Mont"-named ships were nearly all put to war services. The *Princess Kathleen* served as a troopship in the Mediterranean until the war's end and survived. The *Princess Marguerite* was spectacularly lost on 17 August 1942.

With a speed of over 21 knots with her geared turbines and passenger capacity of 347, the *Princess Marguerite* was a natural for trooping services. On 7 September 1941 the two Princesses were requisitioned at the end of their normal summer schedule. Refitted at Esquimalt for war service and a long ocean passage, the two left in November for the Mediterranean, initially via Hawaii, intending to go westward-about through the Indian Ocean. However the worsening Japanese situation in late October caused them to be re-routed eastward via the Panama to Europe and the Mediterranean.

In that theatre they made many trooping trips, until mid-1942. On 17 August *Princess Marguerite* left Port Said at about noon with soldiers of the 8th Army bound for Famagusta, Cyprus. She had a total complement of 1124 on board, of which some 400 were crew, commanded by Captain Richard A. Leicester of Vancouver.

At 3:00 p.m., despite screening by an armed merchant cruiser, HMS *Antwerp* and three destroyers, she was hit in an oil fuel tank by a torpedo fired by *U 83*, which the escorts had not detected. The explosion set the ship afire at once, the engine room soon filled with smoke and steam. All interior lights went out as the ship continued to forge ahead. Two of her British Engineer Officers, E.E. Stewart and W.B. Harris were able to grope their way to the throttles and stop the engines. The fire spread rapidly and the ship was soon a blazing inferno from midships to her stern. This soon reached the ammunition stowage which began to explode, adding to the hazards. However it was still possible to lower many of the ship's boats and get all the crew and most of the troops away.

The destroyer HMS *Hero* picked up a large number of the survivors, and despite the number of troops on board who were unfamiliar with routines for abandoning ship there was a remarkably low loss of life, fifty-five being unaccounted for, of which perhaps forty-nine were British soldiers. There appear to have been no Canadian merchant seamen lost. There is one reference to her sister *Princess Kathleen* also rescuing some survivors; quite possible, as they were on the same general trooping duties in the same area, although this is not confirmed.

The ship floated ablaze for forty minutes and then sank just as the last of the survivors were being rescued. The ship's loss was not announced officially until 22 January 1945, although the award of an OBE to Captain Leicester was announced in November 1943 for his leadership that day in getting so many off the ship with so few casualties. MBEs went to Engineer Officers Stewart and Harris, announced in March 1944, again with no mention of the name of the ship at the time.

U 83 was a Type VIIB U-boat operating out of the Italian port of La Spezia on the northwest coast of Italy, commanded by KL Hans-Werner Kraus of 29 U-Flottille. She was not a particularly successful U-boat, damaging two ships that were salvaged and sinking three sailing craft and a small patrol vessel. Kraus was her first CO, taking the U-boat on two Atlantic war patrols where he sank a Portuguese ship, and then on seven patrols in the Mediterranean, sinking the sailing vessels. *Princess Marguerite* was the only large ship he actually sank. Kraus had thought the ship was an armed merchant cruiser. On 4 March 1943 this boat, under a new CO, was attacked and sunk by depth charges off Algeria in the western Mediterranean by a Hudson aircraft of 500 Squadron of the RAF. There were no survivors of her crew of fifty. Kraus survived the war, but as a POW when his next U-boat, the new Type IXD *U 199*, was sunk off Brazil by USN and Brazilian aircraft with only twelve survivors.

Those lost: No Canadians. No record was seen of British Army troops lost.

Sources: Musk, *Canadian Pacific Afloat*; Hacking & Lamb, *The Princess Story*; *Vancouver Province*, 22 Jan. 1945; Wynn, *U-Boat Operations, Vol.1*; Halford, *The Unknown Navy*; correspondence with Mike Cooper; Busch & Röll, *German U-Boat Commanders*.

CHAPTER 11

Upper Lakes and St Lawrence Transport Loses Six Little Lakers

Here am I laid, my life of misery done.
Ask not my name, I curse you every one.

—Plutarch, *Lives of the Noble Romans*

The origins of the Upper Lakes and St. Lawrence Transportation Company can be traced back to 1840, when Captain James Norris formed a partnership with Sylvester Neelon and bought their first ship, in order to ship grain from mills in southern Ontario. This led eventually to acquisitions of the mills themselves (later to become Maple Leaf Mills Ltd.) and to the formation in 1932 of Upper Lakes & St. Lawrence Transportation, the present Upper Lakes Shipping. Under the name ULS Group of Toronto, employing some of the largest self-unloaders worldwide, it now has shipping interests both on the Great Lakes and the world oceans.

In 1928, with the opening of the larger Welland Canal, elevators were established at Toronto by Toronto Elevators Ltd., and in November the first laker arrived directly from the west. Gordon Leitch, now managing the grain business, appreciated that its transportation was a vital component of the company's profitability. To ensure reliable supply he arranged to buy his first vessel and formed the Northland Steamship Company and by 1932 this was the Upper Lakes and St. Lawrence Transportation Company. In partnership with American interests ships began to be acquired, slowly and carefully, usually from other companies having financial problems as a result of the Depression, such as the Eastern Steamship Company. Upper Lakes tended to retain the purchased vessels' original names, considering as some seamen do that changing names might bring bad luck. Most of the earlier ships were named after men who had a financial involvement with either the Eastern Steamship Company or ULS.

With the outbreak of the Second World War ships of many companies such as Upper Lakes Shipping were requisitioned by the Canadian government on behalf of the British. The ULS firm owned and operated 28 lakers, many quite old. Of these 17, or over 60% of Upper Lakes' fleet, were to see war service: seven just in coastal trade in the lower St. Lawrence and over to Newfoundland; two went on charter to the US Wartime Shipping Administration for east coast employment; and eight were sent overseas, some to the United Kingdom, mostly for coastal UK coal shipping to relieve larger vessels. Others, as with the CSL lakers, were pressed into the bauxite trade between northeast South America and the Caribbean.

Their ships were "bare bones" chartered, that is without crews, between the company and the Director of Marine Services for Canada "for the account of the Ministry of Shipping of the United Kingdom for the duration of the war and three months after." The Ministry was to pay the owners the charter fee directly, with interest at five percent on any unpaid balances. If the ships were lost, this interest charge continued until the insurance on them was paid. The first ships, *Albert C. Field*, *Edwin T. Douglass* and *William H. Daniels* were requisitioned for charter on 9 July 1940 and *Robert W. Pomeroy* and *Watkins F. Nisbet* on 27 July, at a rate of $125 per day (plus a one-time payment for the value of any coal and stores still on board), on ships valued at $250,000 for insurance purposes—somewhat surprising, given their original costs of $45,000 to $60,000. If necessary each was to be delivered to a suitable drydock (in this case Montreal Dry Dock) for repairing to normal Canadian steamship standards at the owners' expense, and then fitted out for Atlantic crossing and war service at the Ministry's expense. The Ministry also assumed insurance costs, in the *Robert W. Pomeroy*'s case from 27 July.

Marconi Radio fitted *Robert W. Pomeroy* with $1,380 worth of new radio receivers and transmitters, plus a cost of $150 for its installation. This was equipment not considered necessary when she was simply running on the Great Lakes and along the upper St. Lawrence. Liferafts, to a value of $250 per were provided, and this ship's refit cost almost $29,900 (after an initial estimate of about $20,000) for docking, repairs and new fittings, such as fitting ten watertight doors. All these details are included in the voluminous file on this one in the National Archives' papers. She left Montreal Dry Dock at 10 p.m. on 20 August for Carleton, New Brunswick in the Baie de Chaleur to load a cargo of timber for England.

Of the eight small ULS lakers that were to be employed in Atlantic waters in1940, all of about 1750 tons and some 260 feet in length, only two ever returned. They were the *William H. Daniels* which had been largely employed in the coastal coal trade around the UK, although she was also taken up for carrying supplies for the Normandy invasion beaches; and the *Edwin T. Douglass*, which was employed as a stationary coal depot at the Scottish naval base at Scapa Flow in the Orkneys. The *William H. Daniels* was not returned until 1950.

One ship, the *Watkins F. Nisbet*, acquired by ULS in 1936, was lost shortly after her arrival in England, after she was damaged in a convoy and was deliberately run aground near Llanddyn Island, South Wales in the Bristol Channel on 6 December 1940. There were apparently no casualties. She could not be fully salvaged, but the stern was cut off and eventually towed to Birkenhead where her engine machinery was removed for installation in another vessel. Whether she should be classed as "sunk by war causes" is certainly a debatable point.

The other five little lakers, designed only for work in the Great Lakes and adjoining canals, have sadder histories. After the war ULS was paid $1.5 million from the insurance plan for their six lost ships, over half a million more than the 20 canallers had cost Leitch in 1936. But then ULS had to replace the losses with post-war construction.

GEORGE L. TORIAN

SHIP: 1754 grt, 261 ft. bulk carrier. Built 1926 by Earle's Shipbuilding
& Engineering of Hull, England.

FATE: Torpedoed by *U 129* on 22 February 1942, off the Venezuelan coast
southeast of Trinidad. Four survivors; thirteen Canadian seamen lost, and
probably two others.

The *George L. Torian* was built for the Buffalo-based Eastern Steamship Company for use in the canal trades. Eastern fell on hard times during the Depression, and when its president died in early 1936 its twenty ships were put up for sale. Ten in the first lot were bought by ULS for $60,000 each. *George L. Torian* was in the grain trade for ULS until requisitioned in 1941 by the Federal Minister of Munition and Supply, C.D. Howe, for employment in the bauxite trade in the West Indies–northeast South America area.

On 22 February 1942 the *George L. Torian* was northbound from Paramaribo, Dutch Surinam with a full load of bauxite. At about 1720 the ship was torpedoed with evidently no warning by *U 129* (KL Nicolai Clausen), and sank almost at once. The violent explosion blew one crewman on watch, James Stillwell, into the sea, where he was able to grab onto a wooden hatch cover, also blown off. Three others also escaped in some fashion and joined Stillwell on his precarious perch. The vessel

George L. Torian in Upper Lakes ownership. (J.N. Bascom/J.M. Kidd)

disappeared beneath the sea in minutes, and the U-boat turned and left without seeing the survivors. They clung to the makeshift raft for twenty-four hours before they were saved. One source says they were picked up by a passing American ship, but in a later interview by USN authorities it appears a US Navy aircraft, reportedly a PBS-1 Sikorsky (a large experimental flying boat) sighted these men and landed in rough seas, took them aboard and flew them to Trinidad and safety. Two were eventually returned to New York, including Stillwell, one stayed in Trinidad and the fourth went to Brazil.

KL Asmus Nicolai (Nick) Clausen had first served in minesweepers, then transferred to the U-boat arm. He was thirty when he was on his fourth war patrol in the early stages of the *Paukenschlag* operation, sank seven ships in the area in a period of two weeks including the *George L. Torian* and the CSL laker *Lennox*, and eventually became one of the most successful U-boat commanders, with a total of twenty-two ships of some 67,500 tons to his credit. He did not survive the war, however, being lost on 16 May 1943 while commanding *U 182* in a convoy attack off Madeira, sunk by depth charges from the American destroyer USS *Mackenzie*. *U 129* however survived the war under two other COs, lying battle-scarred in Lorient after July 1944 and captured there.

Those lost: Seventeen total crew seems an unusually low number when the total was usually twenty-one or twenty-two, so there may have been four or five more West Indian or Guyanese crew as well, who are not listed in this ship's record, although they often are found for other ships.

Captain John Allen, Master		Hugh Allan
Edward Bond	Andrew Ellis	Walter Harrison
Gordon P Hilliard	Jaaks Julkenen	Leo Lefebvre
Eileen Pomeroy	Frederick N Pomeroy	Robert Stevens
James W Weeks	Eldred Whitely	

Note: the Pomeroys were second cook and chief cook in the ship, but records do not indicate if they were related. The Allans came from the same area near St. Catharines, Ontario and Hugh Allan was Chief Engineer.

Sources: Wilcox & Gillham, *Ships of Upper Lakes Shipping*; Rohwer, *Axis Submarine Successes*; notes from Fr van der Linden; DND *Torian* file; Kurowski, *Knight's Cross Holders*; Wynn, *U-boat Operations, Vol.1*; USN Survivor Interview transcript.

ROBERT W. POMEROY

SHIP: 1724 grt, 261 ft. bulk carrier. Built in 1923 by Earle's Shipbuilding, Hull, England for Eastern Steamship Company.

FATE: Mined on 1 April 1942 in the North Sea off Norfolk. 1 DEMS gunner killed.

The *Robert W. Pomeroy* was originally acquired in April 1936 by Upper Lakes Shipping under the same terms as the *George L. Torian* from Eastern Steamship Company. In this case, the ship was named for a prominent Buffalo lawyer who had been instrumental in setting up the Eastern Steamship Company. She was requisitioned for war service in 1940 for use in the coastal coal trade around the British Isles.

On 31 March 1942, having delivered a load of Welsh coal for London's supplies, the ship left Southend on the Thames at 0845, and proceeded north in Convoy FN-70, heading for Blyth on the Yorkshire coast, then Tyneside. The convoy was in two columns, with *Robert W. Pomeroy* the third in the starboard column. She was armed with an Oerlikon 20mm machine gun plus another three .303 machine guns, a Holman Projector and four PAC rockets and towed a barrage balloon on a wire from her stern, all for protection against potential German air attacks.

At 0230 on 1 April the convoy was just south of The Wash off Norfolk, with a slight sea, Force 3 winds and good visibility in clear moonlight. In the supposedly swept channel and in station in 11 fathoms (66 feet) of water, with Captain J.M Fryett on the bridge, there was suddenly a strong but muffled thud of an explosion in the

Robert W. Pomeroy in Buffalo in August, 1937, after purchase by Upper Lakes. (GLHS)

bunkers amidships on the port side. The Master reported that although there wasn't much water thrown up by the explosion, it blew off the hatch covers and the port side of the vessel was opened outward in a gaping twelve to fourteen foot hole. The ship's engines stopped and she slowed, just drifting while Fryett considered what should be done as the ship so far did not seem to be actually sinking. Four minutes later there was another terrific explosion that seemed to be about thirty feet off the port quarter, this time throwing up a huge column of water with a brilliant flash and causing further machinery damage. The Master realized that mines must be responsible, not torpedoes, which would have had to hit the ship. He also seemed to recall afterwards yet another minor thump of an explosion just before the second one which seemed to do no damage by itself.

After the first explosion some of the crew, fearing they would be sucked down with a sinking ship, promptly jumped overboard. One of the convoy escorts, the little armed trawler HMS *Basset*, altered to pick them up. However the second explosion drenched her in the cascade of water and its concussion damaged her steering, for the moment preventing her from reaching the floundering men. This second explosion also apparently killed one DEMS gunner. In spite of all this commotion the swimmers by this time had reached one of the ship's boats which had also been blown clear and clambered into it. With the second explosion this boat was capsized, throwing its crew into the sea again. They struggled back to the overturned boat and were clinging to it when they were shortly rescued by the *Basset*, mobile once more.

All the other boats and rafts were, as Captain Fryett says, "blown away by the first explosion" and those crew who were forward were unable to get aft across the torn up deck. The *Robert W. Pomeroy* was by now obviously sinking, as she was almost broken in two. Then the little 1260 ton Danish SS *Marx*, their next astern in the convoy, valiantly closed the stricken ship despite the threat of mines, lowered a boat and took off Captain Fryett and nine other survivors.

HMS *Basset* took her group in to Hull just to the north, but the *Marx* carried on with the convoy and arrived next day in Blyth at 0200 with her survivors. Two of the seamen who had jumped overboard were injured, one by the second explosion and one who had become entangled in wires beneath the surface. Apart from them, the missing DEMS gunner was the only casualty of the twenty-three on board.

Captain Fryett noted especially the brave actions of Royal Naval DEMS gunner John Butler, who had rescued one of the firemen knocked unconscious by the explosions in the ship's boiler room. Butler re-entered the ship, despite its now obviously sinking condition and pulled the fireman to safety, into the water and to a boat. He was awarded the BEM, gazetted in the 30 July 1942 honours list, and the Lloyd's Bravery Medal as well for his rescue efforts that day.

There has been no record found of who laid the mines, U-boats or E Boats. The channels were swept regularly, but the Germans knew this and were often prepared to re-lay mines after the sweepers had passed.

ULS records suggest that the *Robert W. Pomeroy* was severely damaged in heavy weather on this same date, incapacitated and safely abandoned, the ship then sunk by an attending destroyer to prevent her drifting east and into enemy hands. However this must be a confusion with some other casualty, as the story above is confirmed by Captain Fryett's interview with the Shipping Casualty Section within days of the sinking, and in British records.

Those lost:　1 DEMS naval gunner, unnamed.

Sources:　　PRO SCS interview with Captain J.M. Fryett; Wilcox & Gillham, *Ships of Upper Lakes Shipping: Seedie's Merchant Navy List*; National Archives *Pomeroy* file; *Weekly Intelligence Report (WIRs) 10 Apr.1942.*

FRANK B. BAIRD

SHIP:　　1748 grt, 261 ft. bulk carrier. Built in 1923 by Napier & Miller, Old Kirkpatrick, Scotland for Eastern Steamship Company.

FATE:　　Sunk by gunfire of *U 158* on 22 May 1942, southeast of Bermuda. No seamen lost.

Frank B. Baird. This laker was sunk by U-boat gunfire with no crew casualties.
(Ron Beaupré/Alf King)

This was another laker obtained for $60,000 from Eastern Steamship Company and put to grain carrying in the lakes. She too was requisitioned in 1940 for service in the Caribbean bauxite trade, under Captain C.S. Tate.

In May of 1942, while in the south, she had suffered some damage in a storm that required major repairs. So, loaded with 2457 tons of bauxite, instead of going to Trinidad where the cargo would normally be transshipped, she was routed from St. Lucia on 16 May home to Sydney, Nova Scotia for repairs after delivering her cargo at an American seaport. She travelled at a very modest 5 knots for that 1800 mile voyage, which would have taken her over two weeks. She had no armament.

At 2300 on 21 May her steering rods, connecting the wheelhouse to the steering gear aft, were damaged in stormy weather. To repair them the ship lay stopped some 450 miles southeast of Bermuda, on a route that was hoped would keep her clear of the U-boats scouring the American coastline. Captain Tate waited for daylight to allow the repairs to be made.

But at 0815 a large U-boat surfaced about 200 feet to starboard and almost immediately opened fire on the freighter with her deck gun. It was the Type IXC *U 158*, KL Erwin Rostin, and it was only by chance that he had encountered *Frank B. Baird* on his way to his assigned patrol area in the Caribbean. Already on the 20th he had had a confrontation with the British motor tanker *Darina* 200 miles east and sunk her. Aboard the *Frank B.Baird*, one shot cut the whistle lanyard which flailed about and brought down all the radio aerials before the radio operator, who was aft in his cabin, could even reach the set. Port and starboard lifeboats were lowered aft and all the crew except the Master abandoned ship, somewhat precipitately.

The Master, in the little wheelhouse right forward meanwhile, conscientiously threw overboard the ship's confidential signal books in a weighted bag (which he noted floated at first, although he assured worried naval authorities it sank later and was not seen by the submarine.) He put some brandy, cigarettes and ship's papers in a small wooden liferaft, released it and jumped over the bow when the U-boat continued shelling the freighter aft to open up the hull. He made for the floating raft, but it was damaged and sank, and he was left swimming about in the warm ocean for an hour. The ship now obviously sinking in one of the deepest parts of the open Atlantic, *U 158* eased toward Captain Tate and threw him a line, hauling him aboard. Tate commented later that the crew he saw looked smart, clean-shaven and in uniform but that the CO did not, with an unkempt beard, wearing an old coat and no hat. An English-speaking officer asked what they were doing so far from home and in such a little ship. He added "I am sorry we cannot take you along with me." Tate replied that he did not in the least want to go. The officer continued "We are sorry we have to sink your ship, but it is war."

He then wished Captain Tate good luck and good weather, the crew gave him some black German bread, sausage, a packet of German cigarettes and French matches. They then put him in *Baird's* port lifeboat, turned away and promptly submerged. Tate noted that the submarine looked in good condition and was painted a light grey, with a shield badge painted on the conning tower, as well as an animal's head with its tongue sticking out—all grist for the intelligence mill.

The elderly Chief Engineer was in the starboard boat with the native West Indian crew, and it rapidly pulled away from the U-boat and the Master's port lifeboat. This Engineer's boat was discovered later in the day by the Norwegian freighter *Talisman*, bound from New York for the Belgian Congo. When the survivors were picked up the Engineer Officer was so out of breath and disturbed that he had trouble convincing the *Talisman*'s Master that there was another lifeboat. And when the Master heard that the *Frank B. Baird* had only recently been sunk by a U-boat in the area, he was reluctant to hang about and search for it. But after some persuasion he turned back and was able to locate the port lifeboat and they too were rescued. Captain Tate tried to have the Master of the *Talisman* drop off the native crew members in Barbados, but the ship's Master firmly refused to turn aside from his course when another "S-S-S" warning radio signal was picked up. He set off southeast for Africa at his maximum 18 knots on a zigzag course. After arriving at Point Noire in French Equatorial Africa, there was considerable travelling about on the West African coast for the crew survivors, but all twenty-three of the *Frank B. Baird's* men eventually arrived back safely, the West Indians to their homes in the Caribbean, the rest to England.

KL Rostin and *U 158* had a successful time in the Caribbean and Gulf of Mexico on this patrol, sinking eleven vessels (bringing his total to sixteen, totalling 91,700 tons in two patrols). On the way home to France, southwest of Bermuda he encountered the Latvian freighter *Everalda* and sank her by boarding and opening her sea cocks, but not before the freighter was able to send off a submarine alarm with her position. This was evidently unheard by the U-boat's radioman, and an American USN Mariner aircraft of VP-74 located the still-surfaced U-boat—with crew casually sunbathing on deck—and depth charged her. One of these charges lodged in the conning tower and when the boat submerged it exploded, sending her to the bottom. There were no survivors.

Those lost: None from *Frank B. Baird*.

Sources: Wilcox & Gillham, *The Ships of Upper Lakes Shipping*; Wynn, *U-Boat Operations of the Second World War*; McKee & Darlington, *The Canadian Naval Chronicle*; Rohwer, *Axis Submarine Successes*; PRO SCS interview with Captain Tate.

JOHN A. HOLLOWAY

SHIP: 1745 grt, 261 ft. bulk carrier. Built 1925 by Earle's Shipbuilding & Engineering of Hull, England.

FATE: Torpedoed by *U 164* on 6 September 1942, in the central Caribbean north of Dutch Aruba. One crew member lost.

The *John A. Holloway* also came to Upper Lakes Shipping from the Eastern Steamship Company. Eastern had put their second and final lot of ten lakers up for sale in December 1936 and Gordon Leitch and his partner of ULS, having found their earlier acquisitions to be good carriers, bought the second lot as well, including the *John A. Holloway*, for a modest $45,000 apiece. In 1940 she too was requisitioned, and sent to the Caribbean for the bauxite trade, although when sunk she was being employed as a general transport. She was technically on time charter to the US War Shipping Administration and re-chartered to Alcoa Company, the huge American aluminum manufacturer, although she still flew the Canadian merchant marine red ensign. Unlike some of her consorts, she was armed with a 3-inch gun aft and two 30 calibre machine guns, but was not fitted with any wireless apparatus.

Her early wartime Master, Captain J.V. Norris had commented on an earlier occasion that apart from the U-boat danger, he didn't think his little canaller should be out in the open Atlantic at all: "The seas were mountainous high, our charts floated in a foot of water, we weren't able to get fresh water and had to drink fruit juice and beer."

The *John A. Holloway* when serving under Eastern Steamship colours before 1936,
in the Welland Canal, Bridge 5.
(Jay Bascom/J.M.Kiddd)

On 3 September 1942 the ship left Guantanamo, Cuba for Trinidad, having loaded in early August in Mobile, Alabama. She was carrying around 2200 tons of general cargo, mostly construction materials for US bases in Trinidad. Now under a new Master, Captain James L. Holmes, she had a crew of twenty-three plus one USN convoy signalman. While she had departed in a small convoy, she was unable to keep up with its speed of 8 knots, and those in charge were not prepared to slow to 5 to 6 knots for her, and by the next morning the convoy was out of sight ahead.

With no advance warning, at 1645 local time she was hit by a torpedo port side amidships that opened her up and blew up the decks. The *John A. Holloway* was soon sinking, so the Master threw overboard his bag of weighted confidential books (later the first question officials always asked was if this had been done, before considering the crew's fate!), and her two boats were promptly launched, although many of the crew just jumped overboard. The little freighter sank stern first in six to eight minutes. It was found that one man was missing, Fireman William Davis from Trinidad, presumably blown overboard or killed when the torpedo hit. One boat capsized but was righted, and the twenty-three survivors scrambled into the two of them.

The U-boat, *U 164*, KL Otto Fechner, then surfaced about a mile off and approached the ship's boats, as by this time the *John A. Holloway* had sunk. The crew were politely asked by several of the U-boat's personnel who spoke good English the name of their ship, its nationality, tonnage and nature of its cargo. The submarine then turned away and made off at about 1700. The Master in later questioning was able to give a good description of this Type IXC boat, although he thought her smaller than that class. She appeared in good condition, the crew fit.

Several small rafts had floated free as well when the *John A. Holloway* sank, so these were rounded up and their supplies divided between the two lifeboats. They then set sail south for Colombia. They became separated as the crews alternately rowed and sailed as the winds allowed. The Master's boat approached Santa Marta, Colombia at 1930 on 12 September, six days after the sinking, where a Colombian fishing vessel picked up the weary survivors and brought them in. The second boat was also found offshore at midnight on the 13th by the Port Captain's launch on the information given by the Master. While all the crew were suffering to some extent from exposure, there were no serious cases, and all eventually reached their homes.

U 164 was one of the less successful *Kreigsmarine* boats. Under only the one CO, Fechner, she sank three ships in one and a half patrols out of Kiel. Already she had been attacked and slightly damaged by an American Hudson bomber, and when she left the Caribbean she was damaged enough by depth charges from another bomber to force her home on 13 September. On her next patrol off Brazil, during which she sank a small freighter, on 6 January 1943 she was depth charged by a USN Mariner and broke in half. Only two men were saved, who became POWs, while fifty-four perished.

Those lost: William Davis, fireman

Sources: Wilcox & Gillham, *Ships of Upper Lakes Shipping*; Report of British vice
consul, Santa Marta, Colombia; McKee & Darlington, *The Canadian
Naval Chronicle*; Wynn, *U-Boat Operations of the Second World War*;
Rohwer, *Axis Submarine Successes*; Macht, *The First 50 Years*.; USN
Survivor Interview transcript.

ALBERT C. FIELD

SHIP: 1764 grt, 261 ft. bulk carrier. Built in 1923 by Furness Shipbuilding Company,
Middlesbrough, England.

FATE: Sunk by aircraft torpedo on 18 June 1944 in the English Channel off
St. Catherine's Point, Isle of Wight. Four men lost.

The *Albert C. Field* was yet another of the first batch of Eastern Steamship
Company's ships bought by ULS for $60,000 each in 1936 and employed in shipping
their grain. She too was requisitioned in 1940, in her case to the UK for coastal work
in the coal cargo trade.

Albert C. Field after purchase by Upper Lakes & St. Lawrence Shipping,
although still showing as registered in St. Catharines rather than Toronto.
(Ron Beaupré)

She had an adventuresome career around the British Isles, for she went aground off Flamborough Head in northeast England in February 1941 but was refloated. Then on 29 March 1941, heading for Hartlepool, she had engine trouble, was making only 2 knots when discovered and bombed by a German JU 88, which missed her by only ten yards. However the *Albert C. Field* survived until June 1944, just after the D-Day invasion of Normandy.

On 16 June the ship left Penarth in south Wales at 1600 under Captain John R. Bramley. She joined Convoy EBC-14 in Barry Roads that night at 2300, scheduled to go to the Normandy invasion beaches. There were twelve ships initially but more joined as they progressed down the Bristol Channel and around Land's End until there were about twenty, although some then departed until the remainder, about twelve again, pressed on across to Normandy. The *Albert C. Field* had a cargo of 2500 tons of ammunition for the troops ashore, and also 1300 bags of US mail for their men. The crew consisted of sixteen British seamen, seven Arabs (presumably engine room Lascar stokers), five Army Marine Regiment RA and five Naval DEMS gunners, thirty-three in all. She was equipped with five Oerlikon 20mm machine guns and four PAC rocket projectors.

At about 2340 (British double summer time) on the 18th the *Albert C. Field* was travelling east as third ship in the starboard of two columns, shepherded by several small escorts, when aircraft engines could be heard. Shortly after, in the deep grey dusk, a plane was sighted, at least by the Chief Officer, Mr. C.W. Robson, who later rendered a report. It was flying at 200 feet about a quarter of a mile out on their starboard beam, parallel to the ship's course. The first presumption was that this was an Allied aircraft hunting for submarines and it didn't seem to be attacking the convoy, so no ships of the escort or convoy opened fire. This despite an air raid warning an hour before and guns' crews on the alert.

The escort trawler HMS *Herschell* was between the *Albert C. Field* and the aircraft when it evidently dropped a torpedo, without even turning toward the ships, and made off over the horizon. On later consideration Mr. Robson decided the aircraft was probably a JU 88. After entering the water the torpedo altered course toward the ships and at 2340 hit the *Albert C. Field* on the starboard side amidships, right between two of her large holds. No one had seen the track and no action was taken even in the reasonable visibility and calm sea. While a large hole had been opened, there was little water thrown up and no flash of an explosion. "It was rather like a very heavy depth charge (detonation)," recalled Robson. The bags of mail in No. 2 hold caught fire, and the two lifeboats on the poop deck were blown over the side and were seen floating upside down.

Half the crew jumped overboard at once, expecting the ship might explode at any minute if the fire reached its ammunition cargo. The seamen forward could not get aft because of the fire, so jettisoned two rafts from their stowage on the forward rigging, although a third jammed in its distorted launching guides. Within three minutes the ship hogged at the point of the explosion, broke in two and sank. Two explosions of ammunition, or possibly her boilers, did take place just as she broke and went down.

Mr. Robson could not swim so stayed with the ship until forced into the sea, where he struggled toward a raft and climbed onto it. Other seamen were clinging to floating scorched mail bags and other debris. Robson tried to manoeuvre his unwieldy contraption, rescuing the Third Engineer, although because of the clutter of floating debris he could not reach the steward who was shouting for help. Shortly he came upon the other raft holding Able Seaman Nevin and they lashed the two together.

The *Herschell* approached and lowered her boats, picking up survivors floundering in the water. The *Herschell's* CO commented that the little red battery-powered lights on the shoulders of the life jackets and the whistles with which they were equipped greatly expedited the rescue. Forty minutes after taking to the sea, the men on the rafts were picked up as well. The Master of the sunken ship was missing, as were three members of the crew, two able seamen and an Arab fireman. Three of the survivors were picked up by another naval vessel. The Master evidently was trapped when the ship sank as he was last seen struggling to release the third raft when the ship broke up and slid beneath the surface.

Some reports, including one company history, record *Albert C Field* as sunk by a mine in the channel, raised and used as a sunken breakwater for the Mulberry Harbours at Normandy. But this must have been some other ship. There is no official record of the *Albert C. Field* being raised. Divers who have been down to the wreck in recent times say the sea bed is strewn with a carpet of flattened shell cases, now green with age.

HMS *Herschell* took her survivors into Portsmouth where they arrived at 1000 the next morning. In total there were thirteen British crew rescued, the five Army and five Naval gunners, and six of the seven Arab firemen, a total of twenty-nine. Four men were lost.

Those lost: John R. Bramley, Master; two British able seamen and an "Arab" fireman, unnamed, listed as such on Thames Merchant Navy monument.

Sources: Wilcox and Gillham, *Ships of Upper Lakes Shipping*; PRO SCS interview with Mr. C.W. Robson; correspondence with diver Bill Butland; USN survivor interview transcripts.

CHAPTER 12

Two Ships of Markland Shipping Lost

About four U-boats are now operating in the
Caribbean and there are indications that two
more are on passage to that area. Three or
four ships have been attacked. On 19 April
Curaçao was shelled.

—U-boat Situation Report of 20 April 1942

The Markland Shipping Company of Liverpool, Nova Scotia was a subsidiary of the Mersey Paper Company, a paper-maker of long standing in Nova Scotia. Post-war the firm was bought by the Bowaters Paper Mills Ltd. of England in 1956. The company still operating the large paper mill in Liverpool is now Bowater Mersey Paper Company Ltd.

Between the two wars, Mersey Paper Company's paper-making operation on the river at Liverpool was dependant on shipping for both its incoming pulpwood and coal supplies, and its shipment of final paper products. These ships were at first mostly occasional local freighters, even schooners and brigantines bringing in loads of pulpwood, and chartered freighters carrying rolls of newsprint to their customers on the open newsprint market. In 1929 Mersey Paper bought the freighter *Markland*, and formed the Markland Steamship Company to operate her and successor ships acquired during the Depression.

Cargoes of newsprint went twice a month to New York for their primary customer, the *New York Herald-Tribune*. Later in 1933 when that paper did not require the full mill output, the *Liverpool Rover* was bought to carry newsprint rolls to New Zealand.

When the war started demand for newsprint increased, and yet at the same time the non-company ships Mersey Paper had been chartering were no longer available on the market, requisitioned by the British government for war purposes. So in March 1940 the company's President and Marine Superintendent, Captain Charles Copelin went to Hog Island, New Jersey where several vessels of First World War vintage were still laid up as a result of the Depression, but were in good shape. There the company arranged to buy the American freighter *Sapperino*, but they had to assure the authorities she would only be used for neutral trading, as American neutrality regulations were very strict, with severe penalties for selling ships to belligerent countries for war purposes. So through the Panamanian consul in Halifax they arranged to register their new purchase at first as Panamanian, with the very non-Canadian company title of Cia. Scotia de Vapores S.A. She was renamed *Vineland*, and arrived in Liverpool with the words *Vineland–Panama* boldly painted on her side together with two Panamanian flags, hopefully to deter searching U-boats as well.

Similarly, Markland Shipping bought the Montreal registered freighter *Sonia* in the early summer of 1941. She too had been US-owned recently so was then registered in Panama, sailed to Liverpool, Nova Scotia, but promptly re-registered in Canada as the *Liverpool Packet*. By mid-1941 the USA was softening its neutral stance and was not quite as meticulous about the activities of Canadian ships or owners.

At this time Mersey Paper also bought another ship from this source, renaming her *Liverpool Loyalist*. The company had other ships as well, which survived the Second World War. But two were to be torpedoed and lost. After the war, as replacement for their lost ships, Mersey Paper acquired two of the Park ships, *Argyle Park* and *Champlain Park*.

VINELAND

SHIP: 5587 grt, 250 ft., geared steam turbine freighter. Built 1919 by American International Shipbuilding, Hog Island, NJ.

FATE: Torpedoed by *U 154* on 20 April 1942 northeast of the Windward Passage between Cuba and Haiti. One man killed.

Although in 1942 the Mersey Paper Company still relied on freighters to bring in pulpwood and coal supplies, and for shipping their newsprint, early in 1942 their available ships including *Vineland* were requisitioned for what were considered vital war purposes. Only the bare minimum of ships were left under the parent company's control.

On take-over by CGMM *Vineland* was registered as Canadian and the Panamanian names and flags removed. The government presumably had some problems with pretending the ship was Panamanian when she was registered in Montreal. She was to be managed by the large British firm of Furness Withy & Company and put into the bauxite trade, bringing cargoes from the transshipment point at St. Thomas in the US Virgin Islands mostly to Portland, Maine.

Her first trip was from St. Thomas to Portland, which passed without incident. On her second trip she went to St. Thomas again, loaded bauxite and headed north out into the Atlantic via the Windward Passage between Cuba and Haiti. Her Master was Captain Ralph A. Williams of Halifax, with thirty-three crew, mostly from Nova Scotia. Williams was a sea captain of considerable experience, and his brother

Vineland alongside Mersey Paper's wharf at Liverpool, Nova Scotia, and still in their hands, disguised as a Panamanian "neutral" with flags boldly painted.
(C.W. Copelin/Mersey Paper Co.)

Charlie commanded another of Markland Shipping's ships. As well the *Vineland* carried three RCNVR DEMS gunners for her armament.

On 20 April, just after 2:10 p.m., in the open Atlantic in a modest sea swell and fine weather, with no sighting of a submarine at all, *U 154* hit *Vineland* with a single torpedo in No.4 hold, between the mid-ships engine room and the poop deck aft. Although she was fitted with a defensive 4-inch gun, there was no target to fire at, no time to even man the gun. The explosion also wrecked the ship's wireless so that no "S-S-S" alarm or even an "S-O-S" was sent out.

A second torpedo missed astern, by which time the crew were already launching two remaining lifeboats. When the crew were in the water a third torpedo hit amidships and the ship was doomed. Only one seaman was killed, Oiler Lawrence Hanson, possibly from debris thrown up by the second explosion. His body was pulled from the sea into a lifeboat and brought back to Nova Scotia for burial.

Once the crew were in the boats, many of them covered in oil that had been stored on deck for the galley stove, they rowed clear of the slowly sinking *Vineland*. The submarine surfaced, then fired about a dozen rounds from her 4-inch gun into the ship's bow to ensure her sinking, which took about twelve minutes. The U-boat then approached the lifeboats. Captain Williams threw his braided cap away, fearing that if he was recognised as the Master the U-boat might take him prisoner. The Germans appreciated that experienced senior officers were an asset to be removed from Allied control if practical. The U-boat commander, now known to have been KK Walther Kölle, asked for the ship's identity, cargo and where bound. The U-boat crew took pictures of the survivors, asked if they needed any first aid, threw down some cigarettes, and then motored off to the east on the surface.

Vineland's boats set off south, rowing and sailing as winds allowed, aiming for the Turks and Caicos Islands ninety miles away. After five days the two boats, which had managed to keep close to each other, were discovered by local fishermen who towed them in to the beach on the Turks Islands. Although sunburned and dehydrated, the survivors were in reasonable shape. The authorities there advised the NOIC in Trinidad that *Vineland* had been sunk. The survivors were taken to Grand Turk Island where they awaited a Dutch inter-island steamer for thirteen days, then were taken into Willemstad on Curaçao where they were provided with clothing and even some funds. After three more days they were able to take another Dutch steamer which eventually returned them to Nova Scotia by early June. Most of them at once sailed off in other Mersey Paper ships, or in some cases joined the Navy so they could fight back for a change.

U 154, a larger Type IXC boat commissioned in August 1941, was on her second patrol out of Lorient, as part of 2 U-Flotille. She had departed on 11 March for Caribbean operations where Kölle sank two tankers off Puerto Rico in early April and two more ships in the eastern Caribbean on the 12th and 13th. The sinking of the *Vineland* was her last success on this patrol and she returned to Lorient by 9 May. Most of the crew of *U 154* transferred to *U 105* after their boat's next patrol and were lost in that boat in June of 1943. KK Kölle was not among them and was eventually on staff with the *Wehrmacht* at the war's end. The *U 154* did not survive, being sunk on 3 July 1944 by USN escort forces near Madeira, with no survivors.

Those lost: J Lawrence Hanson

Sources: Raddall, *The Mersey Story*; correspondence from Cdr C.W. Copelin, Nov. 1998–Aug. 1999; article by Capt Charles Copelin in *Mersey Quarterly*, Winter 1983; Parker, *Running The Gauntlet*; Wynn, *U-Boat Operations, Vol.1*; Rohwer, *Axis Submarine Successes;* NAC crew list.

LIVERPOOL PACKET

SHIP: 1188 grt, 248 ft. coastal freighter. Built in 1926 by Swan Hunter & Wigham Richardson Ltd., Newcastle-upon-Tyne, England.

FATE: Torpedoed by *U 432* on 30 May 1942, twelve miles south of Seal Island at southeast tip of Nova Scotia. Two men lost.

Liverpool Packet in February, 1942, just three months before she was sunk. With her startlingly tall funnel she is evidently flying her convoy position flags, the "Blue Peter" and a pilot flag just before sailing.

(Murray Manson/USCG)

This ship, named after a famous War of 1812 Nova Scotia privateer, had been bought by Markland Shipping Company/Mersey Paper in the summer of 1941 from Frank K. Warren of Halifax. She had changed hands several times, being at one time the Swedish-owned ex-*Nidarnes*, then *Delson*, then Warren's *Sonia*. She was one of the smallest ships involved in ocean trading that was lost, and although still manned largely by a Markland Company crew of twenty-one and commanded by their Captain Norman E. "Dynamite" Smith, she was on charter to the Canadian government and, like *Vineland*, managed by Furness Withy & Company for use as a stores and supplies carrier, taking stores from northeastern US ports to Newfoundland. She was unarmed.

On her final voyage the *Liverpool Packet* had left New York City on 27 May 1942 with a 1945-ton general cargo of US government supplies destined for their air bases in Newfoundland, via Halifax, her course assigned by the Naval Control of Shipping Officer (NCSO) in New York. Despite her modest speed of 7 knots, there were too few escorts available and none was provided. On 30 May she was just off the southeastern tip of Nova Scotia staying close to the coast. She was travelling alone, not zigzagging, in moderate seas with two-mile visibility and light northeast winds.

At about 8:30 p.m. local time, with the Third Officer on watch and the others having a tea break, the ship was hit in the starboard side of the engine room by a torpedo from *U 432*, without the U-boat being sighted, even though there were three lookouts on the bridge. The explosion destroyed the ship's wireless so no emergency signal could be sent. The ship began to break in two and sink rapidly. Her one remaining lifeboat was promptly launched, the crew scrambled into it and began to pull the other survivors from the water. There was not even time for the Master to collect and dispose of his secret papers and route charts. But he was later able to assure the worried naval officers interviewing him that they had certainly gone down with the ship, which had sunk in about five minutes. Two men in the engine room had been killed in the attack and two other seamen injured.

The submarine now surfaced and approached the crowded lifeboat to determine the identity of their victim. A German officer called down to the Master's boat:

"What are you?"

"*Liverpool Packet.*"

"What cargo?"

"General."

"Where were you bound?"

"I don't know!"

At this, with machine guns trained on the boat from the submarine's conning tower, the crew remonstrated with their captain who then replied "Halifax." Then Captain Smith asked "Are you German?"

"Yes." The German officer pointed out the direction to row toward shore, and the submarine, after a slow circuit around the floating debris, turned away. The crew, thus encouraged, broke into a boisterous version of "There'll always be an England." But when the U-boat seemed to turn back toward them again they thought better of it and desisted. By 9:30 the U-boat had disappeared over the horizon on the surface.

The crew then started to row toward Seal Island, about twelve miles away, just on the horizon. There was considerable difficulty using the long and awkward oars because of the crowding in the boats. After half an hour one of the hands heard a shout and the boat turned back to come across the First Mate clinging to a large wooden potato storage box from *Liverpool Packet*'s upper deck. He was pulled aboard as well and they set off for shore again. They drifted and rowed all night and off and on all the next day, the morning's damp fog leaving them cold and many of them wet.

About 4:00 p.m. the castaways were sighted by four men in a lobster boat setting traps off Seal Island. They towed the boat into the small harbour where the tired and cramped survivors were helped ashore, fed and given dry clothes. On 1 June they were taken to the mainland to a hotel at Barrington Passage, and over the next days all made their way home.

U 432 was a Type VIIC boat, commanded at this time by KL Heinz-Otto Schultze, part of 3 U-Flottille out of La Pallice, France. This was the boat's seventh patrol, and already Schultze had sunk fifteen ships, two of them neutral Brazilians. After finishing off the *Liverpool Packet* on this patrol he sank two fishing trawlers by gunfire and damaged another freighter before returning to La Pallice. In two more patrols Schultze sank another two ships. He was awarded the Knight's Cross in July

1942, having had other successes in *U141*, but lost his life in his third command, *U 849*, when she was sunk by a USN Liberator southeast of Ascension Island on her way to the Indian Ocean. There were no survivors found. *U 432* also did not survive the war, being sunk by the Free French corvette *Aconit* just after the U-boat had sunk HMS *Harvester* during a North Atlantic convoy attack. Twenty-six of her crew were lost, twenty made prisoner.

Those lost: Norman B Atwood and Burns Williams

Sources: NCSO Halifax report; Form SA; Raddall, *The Mersey Story*; correspondence from Cdr C.W. Copelin, Hunt's Point, Nov. 1998–July 1999; Richardson, *B. Was For Butter*; Wynn, *U-Boat Operations, Vol.1*; notes from Fr van der Linden.

CHAPTER 13

The Bullying U-boats Sink Seven Fishing Vessels

The Ship That Never Returned

A ship set sail with a cargo heading
for a port beyond the seas...
There were fond farewells,
there were sweet loving signals
while her form was still discerned;
For they knew it not at the solemn parting
of the ship that never returned.
It was a dream of hope in a maze of danger
while her heart for her youngest yearned.
Yet she sent him off with a smile and a blessing
on the ship that never returned.

—Old Newfoundland folk song

The sinking of smaller fishing vessels, schooners and one barquentine by the marauding U-boats always seems a case of bullying the defenceless. But they were considered legitimate targets when encountered by chance and larger merchantmen were not accessible. Allied submarines and surface ships sank enemy fishing trawlers in the same way. There were several cases of neutral Spanish fishing vessels being sunk, even by RCN warships, merely on the suspicion they were secretly providing the German U-boats with information on passing Allied shipping or with food supplies. Official complaints were lodged in these cases with no result.

The Canadian and Newfoundland fishing and freighting schooners in this chapter were sunk by U-boat gunfire, offering too small a target for an expensive torpedo. Thus the crews were usually allowed to escape into dories or dinghies before firing began, although not in all cases. It depended on the mood and personality of the U-boat's commander and the urgency of disposing of the target. Many of the crews' deaths occurred not from the German enemy directly, but their old adversary "the cruel sea" when storms were subsequently encountered while in small lifeboats.

And because their ships were not "merchantmen" in the accepted sense, nor did they sail in organized convoys, their stories tend to be only available from secondary sources such as published survivor memories rather than formal naval interviews or post-convoy or Shipping Casualty Section survivor interview reports. In some cases there is almost no account of the loss, only the briefest of records. Photos of a few of these ships have proved impossible to find; many were difficult to trace. It is sad to note that in fact there is usually much more information available from German U-boat logs and BdU records than Allied reports.

As well, many fishing and trading schooners were owned on "shares," always sixty-four shares in such cases, of which the Master or his family and friends at home often owned several, with members of the crew also sometimes owning a few. Thus company reports were not required, and when a vessel was lost, the survivors simply reported this to the other shareholders and the case was closed. Even insurance was often a local arrangement. Several Newfoundland schooners were insured by a local firm set up on the Burin Peninsula, the Western Marine Insurance Company.

In addition to the seven recorded here, there may in fact have been other enemy-caused losses of fishing vessels. Such ships were always faced with the hazard of North Atlantic weather, and a simply listed as "Missing, presumed lost due to stress of weather" may have been sunk by a U-boat with any survivors unable to reach land to report. And if the U-boat was then sunk before reaching home port, there would have been no reports on either side. As far as it has been possible to trace, however, there are no other unidentified U-boat caused losses.

ROBERT MAX

SHIP: 172 grt 127 ft. wooden two-masted, auxiliary engined Grand Banks schooner. Built in 1920 by McKay Shipbuilding Company Ltd. of Shelburne, N.S. Owned by Grand Bank Fisheries Ltd. of St. John's, registered in St. John's.

FATE: Sunk by gunfire from *U 126* on 4 August 1941, 250 miles southeast of the Azores, opposite Gibraltar. None lost.

In some records, including Lloyd's Register, this banks schooner is shown as *Robertmax* but evidence from Newfoundland sources indicates that her name was actually *Robert Max* of Grand Bank, Burin Peninsula, Newfoundland. She had previously been the *Clara B. Creaser* of La Have, near Lunenburg, named for her then-owner's sister, and had been employed fishing on the Grand Banks. Then in 1929 the schooner was bought on shares by a well known Newfoundland fishing skipper, Captain John Thornhill, who named her *Robert Max* after two sons who had died earlier of diphtheria. She has the unhappy distinction of being the first Newfoundland or Canadian fishing schooner sunk by the *Kriegsmarine* in the Second World War.

The Newfoundland Grand Banks fishing and trading schooner
Robert Max leaving Grand Bank, Newfoundland for fishing on the Banks before the war.
(Robert Parsons/Robert Stoodly)

Put to trading with cargoes for Britain when the war broke out, *Robert Max* was to make five trips across the Atlantic from Newfoundland before her loss. On this, the fifth voyage, under Captain Harry A. Thomasen, a Danish-born forty-three-year-old skipper who had lived in Grand Bank, Newfoundland since he was a teenager, she set off with a crew of five from Bay Bulls in late July 1941 with another schooner, *Helen Forsey*. Their cargo was dry salt cod, destined for Portugal. But being different sailers the ships had become separated on the way.

Aboard the *Robert Max* on 4 August about 400 miles off the southern Portuguese coast and 300 miles from the Azores, Thomasen was taking a sun sight about five p.m. In moderate rolling seas a U-boat surfaced a mile from the *Robert Max*'s port bow and fired two warning shots from her 88-mm deck gun. Captain Thomasen calmly finished his sun sight and calculated his longitude on a piece of paper which he put in his pocket, suspecting he would need that figure later in his lifeboat. He ordered the vessel rounded up into the wind where she lay gently rolling in the swells, her sails flapping lightly in moderate winds. The U-boat approached closer and the schooner's skipper was called on board by loudspeaker. He put some confidential charts in a weighted box and told his cook to throw them overboard if he gave a secret arm signal from the U-boat. Thomasen was then rowed over by two of his crew in the ship's dory, which then stood off, waiting to see what would happen.

Thomasen gave the CO, KL Ernst Bauer of *U 126*, details of his ship's cargo and destination. But Bauer told him that he must sink the ship as it was providing food for the Allies, despite Thomasen's remonstrance that Portugal was neutral, not an ally. The German crew exchanged a few friendly words with the Newfoundlanders, gave them some tins of Turkish cigarettes, and allowed them five minutes back aboard *Robert Max* to collect supplies and belongings. The cook having jettisoned the box on the side away from the U-boat, stores were put in the dory and the six crew abandoned the vessel. With a couple of dozen rounds that set fire to the ship's bow and then smashed open her stern near the engine the schooner was sent to the bottom in a welter of woodwork and canvas. Bauer offered to tow the dory for a bit toward land, which Thomasen independently refused, figuring that if the U-boat was discovered and attacked, his dory would suffer as well. Bauer called down "Give my respects to Winnie Churchill" and Thomasen replied "There'll always be an England!" With a wave of his arm, Bauer turned the U-boat away and then dove out of sight.

Reasonably well provided, the experienced small boat crew set off for the Azores, about 297 miles to the southeast, with favourable winds and currents helping them along. The crew were organized into three two-man shifts for rowing and watchkeeping, with a small improvised sail to help when practical. Hard bread, corned beef, and carefully allocated amounts of water from five ten-gallon barricoes at regular intervals allowed them to survive for the three days it took them to reach the islands, although all were sore and stiff by the end of their exertions.

On 6 August about 1:30 in the afternoon land was sighted, albeit it took them another twelve hours to get close enough to identify Sao Miguel Island, near Ponto Delgado. On a lee shore in the dark, with high cliffs and a heavy ocean swell breaking in huge waves, they did not dare try for a landing until daylight. They anchored offshore in deep water for the night, lying most uncomfortably on the boat's bottom boards. For fear of again being accosted by a German U-boat, Captain Thomasen had not allowed his crew to light matches, so they could not smoke at night during their trip. And the crew had been worried that the German's cigarettes might somehow be deliberately drugged or poisoned, designed to make them ill. Now they took a chance and luxuriated in a night's smoke—a relief for normally hard-smoking Newfoundland fishermen.

When dawn broke, they rowed in closer to the beach where fishermen could be seen netting sardines. A small boat came out, followed by a somewhat larger one which took the survivors in through the surf, even rescuing their dory and landing them on the open beach beyond the surf. Somewhat reluctant to abandon the dory that had saved their lives, the crew were taken to a town seventy kilometres away and cared for at a local hotel. In a week they left by freighter for Lisbon, where three of them, including Captain Thomasen, sailed for Newfoundland and home in the schooner *James Stanley*, another Grand Bank vessel. Those three were followed a week later by the three remaining crew who returned in the *Helen Forsey*, herself to be lost to a U-boat's gunfire thirteen months later.

U 126, a type IX boat, had only commissioned in March 1941 under "Dwarf" Bauer, so named to distinguish him from two other Bauers in U-boats. On this his first patrol, he left Kiel on 5 July, operated without success against a convoy sighted by Kondor aircraft, then sank two ships from Gibraltar-bound convoy OG-69 on 27-28 July off the Spanish coast. Moving away to avoid countermeasures, he encountered *Robert Max*, sank her, attacked a home-bound convoy but was driven off, then sank an independent freighter and returned to Lorient on 24 August. Bauer made four more patrols, sank twenty-six ships in all, was awarded the Knight's Cross in 1942 and ended the war commanding training flotillas at Pillau on the Baltic. Held in a military hospital at Mürwic after the war, he was released in December 1945. *U 126* however was sunk two years later by an RAF Leigh-light Wellington aircraft's depth charges northwest of Spain on 3 July 1943. There were no survivors.

Those lost: Nil

Sources: Parsons, *Toll of the Sea*; *Lloyd's Register, 1941-42*; Rohwer, *Axis Submarine Successes*; Wynn, *U-Boat Operations, Vol.1*; Busch & Röll, *German U-Boat Commanders*; Kurowski, *Knight's Cross Holders;* correspondence with Captain Joe Prim.

JAMES E. NEWSOM

SHIP: 671 grt, 178 ft. four-masted trading schooner; no motor. Built in 1919 by East Coast Company, Boothbay Harbour, Maine, for American owners Crowell & Thurlow. When sunk owned on shares by Lunenburg citizens, including the Master.

FATE: Sunk by gunfire from *U 69* on 1 May 1942 in the North Atlantic about 250 miles northeast of Bermuda. No casualties.

The trading schooner *James E. Newsom* was part owned by her skipper, Captain Dawson Geldert and part by Zwicker & Company, both of Lunenburg who had bought her from American interests in October 1928 and registered her in Canada. In some reports she is shown as *Newsome* with the "e" but her name as above is correct. She had retained her American name throughout her career, *J.E. Newsom* being a Boston fruit and produce merchant. Also, technically by the time she was sunk she was Barbados registered, not Canadian. But she had made the trip south as a Canadian vessel, was still partly owned in Canada, and thus is included in this record.

On one pre-war trip in 1937 the *James E. Newsom* carried lumber to Preston in England and returned with Welsh hard coal, a return trip that took forty-six days to reach Charlottetown in a series of tremendous gales. She could carry 1100 tons of coal or 750,000 board feet of lumber in her 14-foot, 10-inch-high holds, and sailed

The Lunenburg trading schooner *James E. Newsom*.
(McBride/Shipsearch)

well "light" as well as laden so required no ballasting when empty. Her sailing crew consisted of the Master, two mates, a cook and four able seamen.

In war as in peace she continued in her trade of carrying cargoes southward as far as the West Indies and back, as she had done for years. These could be lumber, hay or other Nova Scotia products in exchange for sugar or molasses. On at least one occasion she brought a load of coal from New York to Halifax.

In the middle of January 1942 Captain Geldert and a crew of eight took her south empty to collect a cargo of molasses. On arrival in Barbados they discovered the molasses shipment was not ready, so the crew worked intermittently on keeping the ship up and spent much time on the Barbados beaches.

Then Captain Geldert, hearing of the U-boats now operating along the American and Canadian shores and attacking even the oil port of Aruba, decided his investment in the *James E. Newsom* was not worth the risk and sold his share to a local Barbados company, H.O. Emptage & Company, and flew home. The senior mate knew of a schooner skipper back in La Have, Nova Scotia who was between jobs, and John R. Wilkie was flown south to take command, with his son Eugene also coming along as one of the crew. The molasses at last arrived and the full cargo of puncheons, barrels and "tierces" was taken aboard, destined for St. John's, Newfoundland. *James E. Newsom* sailed on Sunday 12 April 1942 directly north for Halifax, bypassing Bermuda to the east. For nineteen days the voyage was uneventful.

Then just after 11:30 a.m. local time on Friday 1 May, the ship gliding along in light winds in good visibility, the man at the wheel shouted out "Captain, there's a submarine coming up astern!" No one had noticed it before so the submarine must have just surfaced. At first the crew ignored it, thinking it might be American, until the submarine fired at them, a shell pitching into the water just ahead. Then the schooner was allowed to round up into the wind while the U-boat fired at them a couple of more times to make her point. The sailors then threw gear and food into their lifeboat slung across the ship's stern and it was lowered into the long oily swell. The nine crew clambered down into the boat, the falls were released and they dropped astern of their ship, leaving all her sails set but flapping in the light airs.

The U-boat, trimmed down so her decks were just awash, altered toward them at first, which caused some crewmen to prepare to jump out of the boat into the ocean if need be. But she then swung toward the *James E. Newsom* and continued firing, cutting halyards and bringing down the sails then firing at the hull. After what was estimated as about thirty rounds, the schooner rolled on her side and sank by the bow, leaving a welter of floating wooden debris. The U-boat then coasted nearer to the lifeboat, again scaring the crew, but someone called out to ask if they had any food. When the Captain replied "Some," a German seaman secured to a lifeline climbed down onto the casing and threw them some cans of bread. These were found later to be mouldy. No questions were asked about cargo or destination and soon the U-boat simply turned away and disappeared over the horizon.

Their lifeboat, about twenty-six feet long had a sail, motor and oars. When mounted on the stern the motor would not start because its battery was long dead, so to save weight they threw it overboard along with a tank of gasoline they had plucked from the debris. They hoisted sail and set off southwest for Bermuda. Captain Wilkie had taken his sextant and was a skilled navigator, and figured they had about 250 miles to go, about six days' sail, allowing for the north-setting Gulf Stream. Apart from the German bread they had some fresh bread the cook had just baked, together with some tins of sardines and other supplies, plus one keg of very old water. They alternated sailing and rowing for three days. On the fourth a ship was seen on the horizon that evidently did not see them and passed on.

Then on the sixth day, 7 May, first one then a second aircraft flew over, which they tried to signal with the flashing lid of a sardine can. A float plane turned to pass close over the little boat and then landed nearby on the smooth sea. The pilot told them he could not take them aboard, but gave the boat what supplies he had, and said he'd signal for the shore authorities to send a boat for them. He was asked by Captain Wilkie "Where is Bermuda in relation to us?" "About 20 miles to the sea buoy, right ahead of you." Remarkable navigation after a week at sea with only a sextant for longitude, from a small boat.

Soon a USCG 90-foot cutter arrived and picked them up. "We were pretty stiff after six days in the boat," commented Eugene Wilkie. They were given some soup and cautioned not to drink too much water—futile, given their long spell with very little. Landed in Hamilton, Bermuda that same afternoon, the crew were housed in the British Sailors' Home, the captain in a hotel, and each given £5.00 from a Distressed Seamen's Fund to buy additional clothing. They waited for six or seven days and then were split up for onward travel to Halifax in the slow and elderly little tanker *Cities Service Fuel* and the much newer and faster Norwegian *Britain Sea*, with an elderly four-stacker ex-American destroyer for escort.

Both ships arrived safely, the Master of the *Britain Sea* becoming fed up with their plodding progress and when fog was encountered hastening on ahead, followed into port half a day later by the tanker. The crew were annoyed at officialdom for delaying their departure for their homes because they had no identification or passports, but as soon as they reached home, most were off to sea again within days.

The U-boat had been the Type VIIC *U 69* under KL Ulrich Gräf on his first patrol out of St. Nazaire, who took over the boat from two previous successful COs who had completed eight patrols in her. Gräf's first target on the way to the American coast was the little *James E. Newsom*. He went on to be attacked without damage by a USCG cutter, sank two ships by torpedo and gunfire, then the Canadian laker *Torondoc* on 21 May in the Caribbean, then an abandoned tug, and returned to base on 25 June.

Gräf and *U 69* seem now to have been a particular nemesis for Canada, for in addition to *James E. Newsom* and *Torondoc*, in two more patrols he sank two more ships, both more-or-less Canadian, the ex-Finnish *Carolus* and the Newfoundland ferry *Caribou*. In addition the Canadian *Rose Castle* was lucky when she too was fired at by Gräf but the torpedo failed to explode. But then the U-boat's luck ran out on 17 February 1943. *U 69* was sunk east of Newfoundland by HMS *Viscount*, with no survivors, including Gräf.

Those lost: None

Sources: Parker, *Running The Gauntlet*; D Hist, R. Fisher notes; *Lloyd's Register, 1941-42*; Wynn, *U-Boat Operations, Vol.1*; Rohwer, *Axis Submarine Successes*; files from the Fisheries Museum of the Atlantic, Lunenburg.

MILDRED PAULINE

SHIP: 245 grt, 132 ft wooden 3-masted fishing schooner. Built in 1919 by Placentia Shipbuilding Company Ltd., Placentia, Nfld. Owned by A.G. Thornhill (R.T. Sainthill & Sons, managers) of Sydney, Cape Breton.

FATE: Sunk by gunfire from *U 136* on 7 May 1942, about 600 miles southeast of Nova Scotia. Seven lost, no survivors.

In this sinking at least seven seamen lost their lives, including the Skipper, Abraham Thornhill of Newfoundland. There are no records of any survivors being seen and of course no newspaper reports of interviews with anyone reaching shore. The War Graves Commission notes that the twenty-one-year-old Second Engineer,

Mildred Pauline, owned in Newfoundland but registered in Sydney, Cape Breton, seen at Trois Rivières, Que. in September, 1939. (Richard Breeze)

George Thornhill, was the son of the Master, both lost from one family. The members of the crew were all from Nova Scotia or Newfoundland. *Mildred Pauline* was at first just reported missing on a fishing voyage after 1 May. Then, judging from post-war U-boat records, *U 136* was in the area, and was the only boat that recorded sinking a fishing vessel about that time. After her sinking stories circulated at home that the crew were killed by U-boat small arms fire, but since there were no survivors or bodies located, this would appear to have been understandable resentment at the loss by family and neighbours.

In fact in a bizarre turn of events, an American transcript of a German radio broadcast provided the only detail, and confirmation, on the loss of the *Mildred Pauline*. On 12 June,1942, just over a month after her actual destruction, Berlin Radio broadcast a positive propaganda interview with a U-boat commander, KL Heinrich Zimmermann. He told how, on his way back from a patrol on the American coast he had encountered a schooner just south of Nova Scotia. While regretting, as a sailor, he had to sink a lovely schooner, he commented "But when the enemy has to resort to such means to carry their freight, there is nothing left for me to do." It was quite dark, and the crew seemed to have been sleeping, so didn't see the U-boat until it opened fire. There is no evidence in his interview whether or not Zimmermann gave the crew time to abandon their ship, but in the absence of any reference to such a humane gesture, one might presume he did not, and many could have been killed by his gunfire. The schooner sank in half an hour.

The transcript of the broadcast was obtained by R.T. Sainthill, who identified their ship although it was not named, and passed the information on to Angus L. MacDonald, the Minister for Naval Affairs in a furious letter. It was the first the Department had heard of the broadcast or the details of the schooner's loss. Mr. Sainthill referred to "the cowardly and callous destruction of the ship and crew... by such cowardly commanders or murderers as they would best be known or should be," even suggesting the story would make good propaganda "to stiffen up the spines of some jelly fish that still remain in the doldrums in Canada."

While the U-boat's reports do not indicate she was responsible for the death of the crew, it is also possible some of them took to their boats and were lost in stormy weather trying to reach Nova Scotia or New England, about 500 miles away—at least ten days' sailing, more if they were rowing.

The Type VIIC *U 136*, KL Heinrich Zimmermann, left the base at St. Nazaire for its second war patrol on 24 March 1942 for operations in the western Atlantic. On his first patrol in February Zimmermann (who had previous service in German minesweepers) had already sunk two naval corvettes, HMS *Arbutus* and the Canadian HMCS *Spikenard*, as well as one freighter in attacks on four

Aboard the *Mildred Pauline* at Trois Rivières, l. to r., Skipper Abe Thornhill (who with the rest of his crew did not survive her loss), a river pilot and photographer Richard Breeze. (Richard Breeze)

convoys. This time out he sank two freighters close in to the American coast and damaged a third, then was attacked unsuccessfully by a USCG cutter and USN aircraft. It was on the move north before returning to St. Nazaire that he evidently sank the *Mildred Pauline*, although the log only refers to "a fishing vessel" sunk off southeast Nova Scotia. There is no reference to any survivors in Zimmermann's report. His estimate of his position is about 600 miles or more southeast of Nova Scotia.

On *U 136's* next patrol, while setting up to attack Convoy OS-33 with other U-boats off Madeira, this U-boat was located and sunk on 11 July 1942 by two RN ships and a Free French destroyer, with no survivors, including Zimmermann.

Those Lost: Abraham G. Thornhill, Master

J.E. Landry	Norman E. Landry	MacGregor MacKinley
Samuel Pierce	James B. Purves	George G. Thornhill

Sources: D Hist notes from R. Fisher, including transcript of German broadcast; *Lloyd's Register, 1941-42*; McKee & Darlington, *The Canadian Naval Chronicle*; correspondence with Richard Breeze, Greg Pritchard.

MONA MARIE

SHIP: 126 grt, 127 ft wooden fishing schooner. Built in 1920 by J. McGill Shipbuilding & Transportation Company, Shelburne, N.S. Although registered in Shelburne, she was owned in the Barbados when sunk.

FATE: Sunk by gunfire from *U 126* on 28 June 1942 just east of Grenada in the Caribbean Windward Islands. None lost.

This schooner was the only vessel shown in Lloyd's Register in 1941–42 as still owned by Mr. Ritcey of La Have, just outside Lunenburg. She was a "knockabout schooner," that is, not fitted with a bowsprit. *Mona Marie* had been built by Lemuel Ritcey of Riverport, N.S. with ownership by fifty-three shareholders until 1933. On completion she was put to fishing, and in that same year of 1920 was considered to be fast enough to be one of the five official Canadian contestants in the first of the Halifax-sponsored International Fishermen's Trophy Races, later made famous by the successes of the *Bluenose*. She did not win and in fact that first race was won by an American schooner, the *Esperanto*. By 1933 *Mona Marie* had been sold to Newfoundlanders. After a steering problem, she was resold to Barbados interests that year. But since she was still Shelburne registered and flying the Canadian Red Ensign (when she flew a flag at all!), her story is included here. The change in her registry to Barbados never reached Lloyd's however.

When she was sunk her Skipper was Captain Laurie Hassell of Barbados. The schooner was involved mostly in local coasting trips around the Caribbean, whatever trade could be picked up. Cargoes northbound back to Canada and Newfoundland

Survivors such as these, about to be rescued from their rafts, were the lucky ones.

(Author's Collection)

were usually sugar or molasses when in season. When lost she had departed Barbados on Sunday 28 June southbound with a cargo of empty oil drums destined for a refinery in Trinidad. Apart from Captain Hassell there was a crew of six and one passenger, Stanley Henricks along for the short trip.

About sixty miles southwest of Barbados, as Captain Hassell was chatting to Henricks on the after deck on the first evening out, he noticed his vessel was being overtaken by a surface-running submarine. As the crew watched to see what would happen, the approaching U-boat fired both her deck gun and Oerlikons at the schooner, wounding a couple of the crew with flying splinters, although the Master stopped the ship as soon as the firing began. One larger eighteen-foot lifeboat, although damaged by gunfire, was dropped over and the crew and their passenger abandoned into it, with the wounded crew's injuries bound with ripped-up shirts. The schooner was soon floating with her deck almost awash. The lifeboat, also now filling with water through several splinter holes, was rowed over to the submarine, *U 126*, and the survivors were told by a *Kriegsmarine* officer in excellent English to climb onto the U-boat's fore-casing, which they did.

Captain Hassell was asked the schooner's name and registry, and then whether they, the *Mona Marie*, could spare his naval crew any coffee or flour. Hassell explained there had been very little on board as they were just coasting from island to island, although this was not exactly the case—he was simply determined to be unhelpful. He then asked to go back aboard his foundering craft and release the smaller but undamaged lifeboat. This the U-boat's captain, KL Ernst Bauer, allowed, motoring over to run his bow alongside the stern of the schooner and allowing the sailors to jump back on board, warning them they had only five minutes before he opened fire again, and to cut down the flapping sails. The sailors dropped the sails, released the other boat, and in a scramble they soon piled into the fifteen-foot Moses lifeboat, after tossing in some stores. The U-boat then fired several dozen rounds into the schooner which broke up and sank, leaving a litter of shattered wood on the surface. As some of the U-boat's crew watched from her conning tower, Bauer turned away and disappeared over the horizon.

Since they were not far from the Windward Islands, and the light wind and current carried them along to the island of Mustique in the Grenadines, all of *Mona Marie*'s crew survived, landing two days later, on Tuesday the 30th. They returned via St. Vincent to Barbados. Captain Hassell had another brush with a U-boat later in the war, in September 1942, when KL Hans Auffermann in *U 514* put a torpedo into the CNSS freighter *Cornwallis* in a harbour in Barbados. Hassell helped man a small patrol craft that went after the departing U-boat but without success, since the submarine was faster. The *Cornwallis* survived this attack, but was sunk as related in Chapter 9.

Ernst Bauer, known as "Zwarg" or "Dwarf" Bauer to distinguish him from other Bauer U-boat COs (he was the only one to survive the war), was on his fourth war patrol when he encountered *Mona Marie*. In three previous patrols he had already sunk fifteen merchantmen and one fishing vessel (the *Robert Max* above), and damaged two more. In October of 1941 Bauer succeeded in saving 308 German seamen when the raider *Atlantis* was sunk by HMS *Devonshire*. *U 126* had been refuelling from her and when *Devonshire* appeared, the 1st WO dove the U-boat and remained nearby, as Bauer himself was aboard the raider having breakfast. Rescued from a lifeboat, Bauer took 107 men aboard the U-boat and towed another 201 in lifeboats until met by the raider *Python* which took on the survivors.

On this patrol, Bauer had already sunk two large tankers, two other merchantmen and a British fishing vessel before encountering *Mona Marie*. He went on to sink another and damage one more before returning to Lorient on 25 July. He made another patrol later in the year, adding another three ships to his total, before being transferred to command a training flotilla. *U 126*, under a new CO, was sunk by depth charges of a Leigh-light Wellington of 172 Squadron while returning from a patrol on the night of 3/4 July 1943. There were no survivors of the crew of fifty-five. Interestingly, Captain Hassell got in touch with Frau Thea Bauer just after Ernst Bauer died in 1989 and kept up correspondence with her.

Those lost: None

Sources: *Lloyd's Register, 1941-42*; *Trident* monthly newspaper, MARCOM; Rohwer, *Axis Submarine Successes*; Wynn, *U-Boat Operations, Vol.1*; Kurowski, *Knight's Cross Holders*; D Hist notes, Merchant ships: General, A-Z; Busch & Röll, *German U-Boat Commanders*; files of Atlantic Fisheries Museum, Lunenburg; correspondence and discussion with Captains Earle Wagner and Cecil Ritcey; *Barbados Advocate*, Oct. 28, 1991; *The Lunenburg Times, Vol.3 No.2*.

LUCILLE M.

SHIP: 54 grt, 75 ft. swordfishing trawler schooner with auxiliary power. Built in 1918 at Meteghan, N.S., owned by Fred Sutherland of Lockport, N.S. and registered in Yarmouth.

FATE: Sunk by gunfire from *U 89* on 25 July 1942, 110 miles southeast of Cape Sable Island, N.S. None lost.

Only brief mention is usually made of the loss of this little trawler when working at the northern edge of George's Bank, southeast of the southern tip of Nova Scotia, under Captain Percy Richardson of Shelburne, N.S., although the schooner worked out of Lockeport. And in DoT registers her name is sometimes spelled Lucile M. with one "l", but this is incorrect. Earlier in February of 1942 the vessel had come across a half submerged lifeboat with six survivors and a dead body of one crew member from the torpedoed British freighter *Silverray* and brought them in. Several schooners out of Nova Scotia had encountered U-boats, one Lunenburg schooner's crew even talking to the U-boat's crew before it motored off leaving them unmolested.

But by July 1942 the Americans had learned a sorry lesson and there now were far fewer valuable merchantmen sailing singly and unescorted. The U-boats sent to the American coast were at last being attacked more frequently from the sea and the air. To find targets they now had to attack escorted convoys, or move closer inshore. The easy pickings of *Operation Paukenschlag* were over, and the fishing vessels at least provided occasional targets of opportunity.

The sombre crew of the sunken schooner *Lucille M.* after their rescue, from a photo in *The Canadian Fisherman* for August, 1942.

(Maritime Museum of the Atlantic)

The eye-witness accounts of the loss of *Lucille M.* come from a newspaper article in the *Canadian Fisherman* of August 1942, published surprisingly soon after the event. It includes a photo of seven of the surviving crew members, all looking rather dour! There are also official reports, the DND Form SA ("Particulars of Attacks On Merchant Vessels By Enemy Submarines") and the USN's Survivor Interview report.

At about 3:00 a.m. on Saturday 25 July 1942, as the schooner lay stopped and most of the crew were asleep, some heard the deep throbbing of heavy diesel motors in the distance in quite a thick haze. They presumed it was some patrol vessel. But just after dawn at about 5:00 a.m. a submarine appeared, later established as *U 89* and commanded by KK Dietrich Lohmann. It was this boat recharging her batteries they had heard during the night. She stopped about 100 yards off the resting schooner and opened fire at once on the ship, hitting her first in the fore-rigging, then in the stern. Only a watchkeeper, Hughey Locke of Jordan Bay, N.S. was on deck at first, the rest of the crew still in their bunks below. As the U-boat continued shelling the ship, the crew of eleven under Captain Richardson hastily abandoned into two dories, but not before four crew members were injured by flying shrapnel or wood splinters. They pulled clear, and lay close to the U-boat, which ignored them. Captain Richardson could hear clearly the clang of the gun's breech working, the clatter of ejected shells onto the deck and an occasional splash as one fell into the sea. He even heard one crewman say in English "The damned thing won't sink." Then for almost forty-five minutes the submarine shelled *Lucille M.* until she did in fact sink, taking two tons of swordfish to the bottom with her, as the news accounts record with considerable annoyance.

After firing what Captain Richardson estimated were about 200 rounds at the ship, the submarine came within hailing distance. In good English someone on her conning tower (later found to be Lohmann) told the crew he regretted having to shell their ship, but he was under orders and had to obey. Someone fired a machine gun near the dories which injured some seamen, and then the U-boat sailed off. This much is quoted in newspaper accounts.

In a phlegmatic display of endurance, first aid was rendered to the injured and the crew then set off to row almost 100 miles to the Nova Scotia coast, although hampered by currents and tides the distance was considerably more. They reached the Cape Sable lighthouse in safety the next day and rowed on in to Clarke's Harbour at the southeastern tip of the province. The injured were treated and one man, Everett Scott, removed to hospital at Bridgewater, while the rest were taken to Halifax. All of the crew had survived.

And on 3 June 1943, ten months later, Captain Richardson was awarded an MBE for his "courage and leadership" in succouring the injured and getting his crew to safety.

These attacks on Canadian and American fishing vessels could not be kept secret for long as survivors reached shore, and there was some publicity in newspapers such as the *Halifax Herald* and Montreal's *Le Soleil* asking what the Navy was going to do about them. But there was little the Navy could do about single, independent, small fishing vessels that were now also being attacked.

This was the third U-boat Dietrich Lohmann had commanded although the first two were training boats. *U 89*, a Type VIIC boat was his first and only operational command. This was her first war patrol, and *Lucille M.* his only victim, after a futile attempt to attack a convoy near Gibraltar. After sinking the trawler he searched along the American coast south of New York and back to Canadian waters with no success, returning to Brest on 21 August 1942 after a seventy-seven-day patrol that had netted very little. Admiral Dönitz was reportedly disgusted with this performance by KK Lohmann and considered appointing him elsewhere. But Lohmann and *U 89* made three more patrols in which he sank three more vessels and again had problems attacking well-defended convoys, in which his boat was damaged on two occasions. On his fifth patrol while attacking Convoy HX-237 on 11 May 1943, *U 89* was discovered on the surface and attacked by Swordfish aircraft from an escort carrier. Lohmann dove his boat and was then depth charged by the destroyer *Broadway* and the frigate *Lagan*. The U-boat did not survive these attacks, and Lohmann and forty-seven men perished. In the same series of attacks another two U-boats were also sunk, with a cost of three ships from the convoy. The tide was turning against the U-boat arm.

Those lost: None.

Sources: Hadley, *U-Boats Against Canada*; *Canadian Fisherman*, Aug. 1942; Paquette & Bainbridge, *Honours & Awards*; *Trident* monthly newspaper, MARCOM; Halford, *The Unknown Navy*; Rohwer, *Axis Submarine Successes*; Busch & Röll, *German U-Boat Commanders*; Dunmore, *In Great Waters*; USN Survivor Report transcript; Gentile, *Track of the Gray Wolf*.

HELEN FORSEY

SHIP: 167 grt 123 ft., wooden two-masted Grand Banks fishing schooner with a gasoline engine, although in trade when sunk. Built by Smith & Rhuland of Lunenburg, N.S. in1929. Owned by William Forsey of Grand Bank, registered in St. John's.

FATE: Sunk by gunfire from *U 514* on 6 September 1942 in the open Atlantic southeast of Bermuda. Two killed.

The *Helen Forsey*, named after the owner's daughter, in peacetime was a "banker", fishing with dorymen on the Grand Banks northeast of Nova Scotia, and referred to as "a 100-tonner" because her net tonnage was ninety-eight. In the winter and in wartime she was in trade to the West Indies to make up for the ships withdrawn from that business or sunk in maintaining it. In April of 1942 *Helen Forsey*

The launching of the *Helen Forsey* at Lunenburg in 1929.
(Memorial Univ. of Nfld. photo)

under Captain John Ralph had rescued forty-four sailors of a crew of forty-seven from the British freighter *Loch Don*. That freighter had been sunk by *U 202* on April 1st when some 400 miles northeast of Bermuda while the schooner was on the way back to Nova Scotia from Barbados.

On her last voyage, still under Skipper John Ralph with a crew of five, she had carried a cargo south to Barbados, and took on a shipment of molasses for St. John's, Newfoundland, setting off sailing straight north up the open Atlantic, planning to pass east of Bermuda. On Sunday 6 September at about 6 a.m. just before dawn, when about halfway to Bermuda, she was sighted by the large Type IXC *U 514*, KL Hans-Jürgen Auffermann, on its way to the hunting ground off the American coast. Surfacing and intending to rapidly dispose of this target of opportunity, the U-boat opened fire at the schooner at once, hitting the foremast. A crewman on watch, Leslie Rogers ran forward to grab some personal belongings from the crew's mess under the fo'c'sle, as it was obvious they were not to survive this attack. Another shell struck the forward companionway, killing Rogers; Arthur Bond, also from Newfoundland, was killed in the shelling which injured Captain Ralph as well. The remaining three men launched their small lifeboat and pulled clear, only to see

Captain Ralph, whom they had left for dead, waving and shouting from the wallowing schooner's deck. They pulled back and rescued him, then stood off while the U-boat put half a dozen more shells into the hull. The *Helen Forsey* sank by the stern under the weight of the molasses and her engine.

The U-boat pulled close to the little lifeboat, and someone called down to speak to *Helen Forsey*'s Captain. Crewman Bill Keating, afraid the Germans might want to kill him, called out that their Captain had been killed in the shelling. Someone fired a burst of machine gun fire around their boat, presumably just to frighten them, then the submarine turned away without further questioning and submerged.

The little boat had providentially been supplied with emergency food and water as Captain Ralph knew there could be danger along their course, so they set off north northwest for Bermuda. Water was their chief concern, although they caught enough in their oilskins in occasional rain squalls to allow the little group of four to survive thirteen days, rowing and sailing, until they were picked up by a just off Bermuda. There Captain Ralph was treated to remove several pieces of shrapnel and splinters, and eventually the survivors reached home in Newfoundland.

Skipper Ralph and two of the other survivors were eventually to lose their lives as well in other fishing vessels lost to the ever present dangers of the seas in 1949 and 1955.

Auffermann had earlier been acting commander of *U 69* when his CO became ill, but *U 514* was his—and the boat's—only command. He made four war patrols, and on this, his first, had departed Kristiansand, Norway, on 15 August 1942 for western Atlantic operations. He encountered the *Helen Forsey* by chance, sank her, and continued on, to also come across CNSS's freighter *Cornwallis* in harbour at Bridgetown, Barbados, damaging her as well, although she was raised and repaired. He sank another freighter, was in turn attacked by USN aircraft and a destroyer with slight damage, and continued patrolling further south in the area off the Amazon River where he sank another three ships. *U 514* was again detected by USAF aircraft, but escaped to return to Lorient on 9 November, a patrol of almost three months.

Auffermann made four more patrols, but on his fourth, when just off Cape Ortegal in northwest Spain he was surprised on the surface by an RAF Liberator of Coastal Command, forced to dive by rocket fire and then sunk by depth charges and one of the air-dropped new homing torpedoes. There were no survivors of the U-boat's crew of fifty-four.

Those lost: Arthur Bond and Leslie Rogers.

Sources: Parsons, *Lost At Sea, Vol.2*; *Lloyd's Register, 1941-'42*; Rohwer, *Axis Submarine Successes*; Wynn, *U-Boat Operations, Vol.2*; notes from Capt. Joe Prim; discussion with Jack Keeping, Grand Bank, and Captain John Smith of Ottawa.

ANGELUS

SHIP: 338 grt., 126 ft. three-masted barquentine originally French owned by Felix Chevalier, Cancale, France. Built in 1921 by Tranchmere at La Richardais. When lost, managed by a Sydney, Cape Breton firm and technically owned by Montreal Shipping Company on behalf of the CGMM.

FATE: Sunk by gunfire from *U 161* on 19 May 1943 in North Atlantic, 375 miles south of Nova Scotia, opposite New York. Eight men lost.

This French-owned barquentine was employed even after the war started in the fishing and shipping trade, still being operated by her owners in western France. After the fall of France in June 1940 and the subsequent British attack on the French naval base at Dakar in September (to ensure the substantial French fleet did not also fall into German hands), there was understandably the greatest hostility between the French and the English-speaking Allies. While nearly all French citizens were strongly anti-German, many supported the Vichy régime that had made peace with the German conquering armies in the northern half of the country. They did not necessarily embrace the newly forming "Free French" operations of the aloof and then-unknown General Charles De Gaulle. Thus the French ships at sea, from an Allied viewpoint, were suspect. At least one newspaper article suggested that the barquentine *Angelus* "had been used by the Nazis as a supply for their submarines." Although highly improbable, this was the prevailing "spies and fifth

The ex-French barquentine *Angelus*, although abandoned without casualties when sunk by *U 161*, lost all but two crew from her boat in subsequent storms. (A poor reproduction of a newspaper photo from the Lunenburg Fisheries Museum)

column everywhere" attitude of the day. In fact, *Angelus* was on a normal fishing voyage out of St. Malo to the Grand Banks for her French owners and intending to return there when she was seized by the Canadian Navy. Her previous trip's cargo of salt fish had been seized by the German occupiers when she arrived back in France.

On 31 August 1941, *Angelus* was encountered in the centre of the Grand Banks by the new Canadian corvette HMCS *Prescott*, Lt H.A. Russell, RCNR. He ordered the vessel stopped, put a prize crew aboard and had her taken in to Sydney by 4 September. There her French crew were released, some returning to then-neutral Vichy France, others joining Free French forces in London, a few remaining temporarily with the ship. In October, after an Admiralty court decision awarded the to Canada, the departing French crew were replaced by Canadians familiar with sail, from Newfoundland, Nova Scotia and New Brunswick. *Angelus* lay in Sydney harbour for a considerable period, undergoing repairs and having her sails mended. She then went into the Nova Scotia to West Indies trade, carrying products of those countries back and forth at her leisurely sail pace. All shipping by late 1941 was vital, even a sailing vessel. In actual fact paperwork involving her seizure, completed in July 1942, had taken almost a year to process. Her first charter voyage was made from Sydney on 15 December 1942 on time charter at $300 per month.

In early 1943, commanded by Captain Edward P. Jensen, a Danish-born resident of Lunenburg, *Angelus* was lying in Louisburg, Cape Breton, at the town dock awaiting a load of barrel staves or "shooks" for West Indies molasses barrels. Her crew were instrumental in saving lives when an American naval patrol boat, *SC 709* drove onto an offshore reef in an icy gale. They rowed out to the wreck in two-man dories, rescuing several seamen. Then in April, with a minimal crew of only nine men and the Master, *Angelus* was towed out of harbour through ice patches for four or five miles then set off under sail for Barbados with lumber piled high even on deck. The ship was old and leaky, so the men on both watches had to man the pumps much of the way. They did this on a diet of potatoes and salt fish because, with no machinery or electricity, there was no refrigeration. It was a scene from the last century; all that was missing was impressment and scurvy. She had no radio or armament.

Captain Jensen arrived safely and delivered his cargo, then loaded molasses in wood puncheons for a Halifax company and sailed from Bridgetown at 3:10 p.m. on 28 April, straight north for Nova Scotia.

Early on the morning of 19 May, twenty-one days out on an empty ocean somewhere opposite New York, Sandy Holmans, son of the ship's Mate Arthur J. Holmans of Newfoundland, was at the wheel. He called out he could see something on the horizon ahead, about four miles off. This turned out to be a German U-boat, the Type IXC *U 161*, that approached them on a converging course and was soon turning parallel to *Angelus*. A shot was fired from the U-boat's deck gun just ahead of the ship, now lying stopped, sails flapping. *Angelus* put out her one small lifeboat and on shouted orders from the submarine, the ten crew abandoned the ship, including the captain's dog. The boat was told to come alongside the submarine, with gunners covering them with machine guns from the conning tower.

Captain Jensen boarded the U-boat and responded to the usual queries as to the ship's name, cargo and destination. He was told his crew could have exactly twenty minutes to return to *Angelus* to collect provisions and navigation equipment. Some reports say Jensen declined, telling the U-boat's CO they had already put those items in their boat. The sailing ship's crew were asked by U-boat men if they had any fruit they could spare, but said no, they had none. Jensen returned to his lifeboat and his crew rowed toward the idling *Angelus*, but soon realized they could not get back off her in the allotted twenty minutes, so they just lay off and watched. Right on time the gunners of *U 161* fired about twenty rounds of their 88mm deck gun into the barquentine in a leisurely manner, in Mate Holmans description, "as though they were engaging in target practice." Eventually the ship rolled onto her side and sank by the bow in a confused mass of masts, wood and sails at about 6:10 a.m. Then the U-boat departed with no further contact with the men in the boat.

In the lifeboat, although it was not fitted for sailing, a make-shift sail lashed to oars was hoisted and a course set for the American coast some 700 miles away to the west. It was impossible to row that far, so the castaways relied on being seen by a passing ship. For three days they made modest progress, cold at night and baked by sun during the day, sometimes in heavy swells, which were not a problem for these experienced small boat seamen. This went on until a heavy storm blew up on the night of 22 May, their fourth day in the boat. At first, for two hours, they were able to keep head to wind and sea in the dark, but eventually a massive wave overturned the boat. The crew were able to right it, although it happened three more times during the night before midnight, with men struggling, weaker and weaker, back into the flooded lifeboat. After the second capsize, the Master, Captain Jensen was missing and never seen afterwards. Nearly all their stores were lost, as they were only able to rescue a small case of corned beef and some condensed milk.

By dawn the survivors began to succumb to exhaustion, cold and hypothermia. First a Newfoundlander died, then six more men, including Mate Holmans' son Sandy, aged twenty, whom the mate held in his arms in tears for a day. They were committed to the surging ocean, as was another who died during the day of the 23rd until only three were left, Arthur Holmans, AB Walter G. Boudreau of Moncton, N.B. and the ship's cook, Harry Boyd. He too eventually went mad, throwing overboard some of their tinned food and then jumping into the ocean himself and disappearing. One of the lost crew's name was not even known to the crew, as he was simply "Frenchy" from Montreal (no doubt J.-P. Brunelle).

The storm abated with daylight, and the two survivors pressed on for four more days, rigging a sail from an oilskin slicker and a pair of pants, which enabled them to keep moving westward, steering by the North Star at night. Now weaker from lack of food and water, the two were occasionally bailing with a bailer fashioned from a piece of canvas. After eight days at sea the two in the boat were sighted by a patrolling US aircraft on 24 May, and picked up by the USN destroyer USS *Turner* later that day. They were taken to Portland, Maine by the 26th. The two crewmen arrived back in Halifax on 30 May. This was Arthur Holmans' third encounter with U-boats, having been shelled twice and torpedoed once before. Yet as soon as he returned to his Newfoundland home he volunteered and was off to sea again: "I can't give up. We've got to finish the job." He had already paid a dreadful price.

U 161 was commanded by KL Albrecht Achilles, a very successful U-boat CO who had joined the *Kriegsmarine* in 1934. He had served in the battleship *Gneisenau* until late in 1940. On his first three war patrols in *U 161* he had sunk fourteen merchant vessels and two schooners and damaged the RN cruiser HMS *Phoebe*. He had torpedoed and damaged another five ships, four of them vessels alongside in supposedly safe harbours, including the Canadian *Lady Nelson* at Port Castries in the West Indies.

On this his fourth patrol, at age twenty-nine, he had sailed from Lorient on 13 March 1943, met the Germany-bound Japanese submarine *I 8* to give her two German officers and radar equipment that would be required to cross the Bay of Biscay inbound. He moved to the Canadian and then the US coast where he was attacked several times and had no success against Allied shipping. Moving toward home he encountered *Angelus* and took out his frustrations on her, arriving back in Lorient on 7 June.

On his next and last patrol to the South Atlantic, after sinking three ships, *U 161* was herself sighted by patrolling USN Mariner aircraft and on 27 September 1943 depth charged and sunk off Bahia, Brazil. There were no survivors of the crew of fifty-two, including Achilles.

Those lost:	Edward P. Jensen, Master	James Boyd	Jean-Paul Brunelle
	Cecil Hardiman	John Hillier	Alexander Holmans
	Clarence Mullins	Francis J. Walsh	

Sources: *Lloyd's Register, 1939-40*; Unnamed newspaper article dated 26 May 1943; DND D Hist files, Merchant Ships, General, Vol 1; USN Survivor Interview transcript; Borrett, *Down To The Sea Again*; Parsons, *Wake of the Schooners*; *Halifax Herald*, 1 June 1943; Rohwer, *Axis Submarine Successes*; Wynn, *U-Boat Operations, Vol.1*; Busch & Röll, *German U-Boat Commanders*; Garfield Fizzard, *Unto The Sea*; Caplan, *Cape Breton Shipwreck Stories*.

CHAPTER 14

The Park Steamship Company Loses Four and A Half Ships

When stately ships are twirled and spun
Like whipping tops and help there's none
And mighty ships ten thousand ton
Go down like lumps of lead.

—Ralph Hodgson, *The Song of Honour*

Shortly after the start of the Second World War those responsible for shipping in the United Kingdom, and soon in Canada as well, presumed that unrestricted U-boat attacks on shipping was to be Germany's method of warfare at sea. A reasonable assumption, brought about when the Donaldson passenger liner *Athenia* was sunk without warning by KL Kemp's *U 30* on the day war was declared, 3 September 1939. In fact this had been against Hitler's and Dônitz's orders. The U-boat commanders were, in the beginning at least, to follow the general "Rules of war" which required that unarmed merchantmen were to be warned before they were sunk.

With forty-six merchant ships sunk by U-boats in the month of September alone, another three seized as prizes and three more damaged, it was soon obvious that many more merchant ships would be required under Allied control. Not only to replace anticipated losses but to carry the vast increase of vital goods and troops needed during wartime. There was also the withdrawal of a significant number of German controlled ships from the available pool, such as the ships of their Hapag-Lloyd Line, a major world shipping company.

While Britain built many replacement merchant ships, her established larger dockyards shortly became fully involved with major warship construction programs and all too soon with repairs to damaged ships. The British Ministry of Transport soon was forced to look elsewhere for merchant ship construction facilities. With the loss of 252 ships to the U-boats between October 1939 and February 1940, plus a mounting toll from mines and aircraft attack, the problem became urgent.

Four main classes of new-built ships can be identified in the inventory of the British Allies:

1. British built, bought or seized shipping with Empire names. This was a large but highly varied group of ships, some aged, some brand new. There were as well the ships still being built for the private shipping companies, usually overlooked in tables of wartime construction.

2. Sixty purchased American-built ships, to a British North Sands design from J.L. Thompson & Sons of Sunderland, named "North Sands" after the area where the first of them was built. They were built in only two American yards, one on the east coast, one on the west coast, on a strictly cash basis of about $1.6 million per ship. In a novel American development the ships were largely welded rather than riveted, and in part pre-fabricated. The first was laid down on 14 April 1941; all were given Ocean names, such as *Ocean Vanguard*. Similar American ships for their own Maritime Commission, the famous Liberty ships, were given people's names. After the US entered the war in December 1941, Lend-Lease arrangements came into play. While manning varied somewhat, the Ocean ships were all British owned and manned, although individuals came from various countries, some manned by Belgians, Norwegians and Danes. A later group of US built Liberty-type ships were turned over to Britain under Lend-Lease; these were American owned but largely British manned, and given names beginning with "Sam," such as *Sampep*.

3. Canada became the source for two very large groups of ships, in a staggering increase in shipbuilding capacity. The first group, built in Canadian yards to British order, and again essentially of the North Sands design but mostly rivetted, were 9300 dwt vessels, although they were referred to as 10,000-tonners, since wartime regulations allowed deeper loading. Each cost about $1.85 million. In total 196 were built, the first contracted in January 1941. Under the Hyde Park Agreement of 20 April, 1941, eighty-seven of these were paid for by the US then transferred to Britain on a "bare boat" charter, the survivors being returned to the US at the war's end. Two were purchased outright from Canada, *Fort St. James* and *Fort Ville Marie*. All were given Fort names, such as *Fort Qu'Appelle*. They were all manned out of British resources, as was the Ocean class. They flew the British Red Ensign although they were still technically Canadian owned ships, but on British registry, control and management. Thus they do not come under this book's coverage (however, see Chapter 18 for brief records of their losses).

4. The second Canadian-built group were to Canada's own account, the Park ships. There were several sizes and types; some were launched as Park ships but turned over to Britain and renamed as Forts in 1944 and 1945. Late in the war some, although technically still owned by Park Steamships of Montreal, were manned and managed in Britain. All were named after federal, provincial or municipal parks in Canada.

The whole matter was a shifting, continuously changing arrangement of outright sales, charters, lend-lease, variations in management, registration and crews, and included changes of names and even changes back to original names. And, as always, there was the odd exception. Almost every list, of ships provided and those lost, vary by a few numbers from other lists.

THE PARK SHIPS

In order to manage these ships rapidly rolling out of a half dozen shipyards across the country for our own ownership and use, the Canadian government formed the Park Steamship Company in April 1942 as a Crown corporation. At its peak it controlled some 183 Park ships. The company was based initially on the resources of Canadian National Steamships (CNSS), although it soon developed into its own corporate entity and had the ships managed on contract by various firms, Canadian and British. After the war, all the surviving Park ships were sold and the company operations wound down or rolled into the Canadian Maritime Commission by 1948.

The Canadian Park ships themselves fell into four main groups and ten types:

1. 121 dry cargo 10,000 dwt, centre island freighters (that is, the bridge in the centre of the ship, with holds fore and aft). These were Victory, Canadian and North Sands types (two of these were lost to U-boats).
2. 42 smaller 4700 dwt, 328 ft. dry cargo freighters; all with coal-fired triple expansion engines (again, two were lost).
3. 19 tankers, of four types, 13 North Sands and Victory types and 6 small laker tankers.
4. One re-built ship, a very elderly tanker that had been a Public Works dredger and was converted in 1943 to a small tanker because of a shortage of such vessels. This was the Polson Iron Works 1905 of 2000 dwt, *Riding Mountain Park*, often omitted or confused in tables.

As an idea of the horrendous losses suffered during the war by the British Merchant Navy alone, it may be noted that 175 Empire ships were sunk, 17 Oceans, and 31 of the Forts, 223 ships in just these three specialist categories. And there were another 61 of these ships damaged and out of service for sometimes a very long period.

In the fall of 1940 the British Merchant Shipbuilding Mission ordered ten ships from Canadian yards, shortly increased to twenty-six. The Canadian order came under the War Supply Board, later to be C.D. Howe's Department of Munitions and Supply. Eventually the yards, many of them new-built or enlarged, turned out 410 merchantmen in total, plus another 300 warships. It was all coordinated by the Canadian government firm, Wartime Merchant Shipping Ltd. Building times improved from an average of 307 days to as little as 112 days by July 1942, and the peak of personnel engaged in shipbuilding reached 57,000 by mid-1943, a five-fold increase at a time when the Armed Services had drawn off another half million men and women. A staggering increase indeed.

These are the stories of the four Canadian-built, registered and flagged Park ships that were lost to enemy action during the war

JASPER PARK

SHIP: 7130 grt, 441 ft North Sands type dry cargo freighter. Built and turned over 24 September 1942 at Davie Shipbuilding & Repair Ltd., Lauzon, Quebec.

FATE: Torpedoed by *U 177* on 6 July 1943, in the Indian Ocean 425 miles southeast of Durban, South Africa. Four lost.

Jasper Park was the first of the Park Steamships to be sunk, only ten months after she went into service. She made an initial convoy voyage to Britain and back with war supplies, then loaded similar supplies in New York for the British Army in India. These she discharged in Calcutta.

Captain M. Buchanan, a Master in his sixties, with a First Officer already seventy, had a crew of forty-five Canadian and British seamen, plus four Maltese. There were also six Canadian RCNVR DEMS gunners embarked for her considerable armament of 3-inch and Oerlikon 20mm guns, for a total of fifty-five persons. She was loaded with a cargo of tea and jute at two ports in western India. On 22 June she cleared Cochin on the southwest coast of India to sail directly across the Indian Ocean to Durban, South Africa. She was travelling alone, not zigzagging, in good

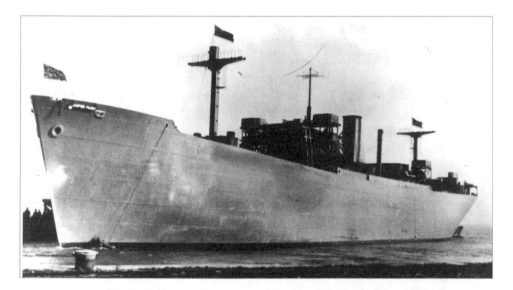

Because the Park ships that were sunk disappeared so soon after their building, good photos of them are scarce. This is *Jasper Park* just after she was launched and while fitting out at Davie Shipbuilding, Quebec.
(Murray Manson)

weather at 11 knots, with no other ships in sight. Being a coal-burner, she left a notable trail of smoke at times. During the afternoon watch from 12 to 4 p.m., a crowsnest lookout, AB Jack Sharkey, had noted an occasional puff of smoke or exhaust on the horizon off the port bow. This he reported, but no action seemed appropriate or necessary (possibly because the lookout had a notation about unreliability in his Navy record). Although the ship was fitted with anti-torpedo nets, they were not down as the gear was being overhauled, and they were unpopular anyway, as there was a rumour that if a ship was sunk these nets would trap seamen trying to abandon her amidships.

At 10:25 a.m. local time on 6 July she was struck by two torpedoes fired by *U 177*, KK Robert Gysae, with no warning whatsoever. There had been a scare the night before when what was thought to be a possible torpedo track was seen crossing ahead. Captain Buchanan altered course ninety degrees for an hour, then resumed course for Durban again. Indeed it had been Gysae's U-boat exhaust smoke that had been seen the day before, and the track of his torpedo, for he had been tracking *Jasper Park* for almost a day when he was finally able to get ahead enough to attack her successfully.

The first torpedo hit her in No. 2 hold just forward of the bridge, the second amidships in the starboard side of the engine room stokehold. The explosions stopped the engines, but the Wireless Officer was able to get off the submarine alarm message, S-S-S, and give their position using an emergency set. Although the ship was armed, no counter-measures were possible because most of the guns were damaged by the explosions, and the U-boat did not even surface until the ship was abandoned. While the starboard side lifeboats had been demolished by splinters, the crew were able to launch the port side boats, and abandoned safely. The Master threw overboard his confidential papers and books in weighted bags, made sure all the survivors were clear after the Chief Engineer told him the watch in the engine room could not possibly have survived, and also went into a boat. Four members of the crew, two British and two from Toronto including the Fourth Engineer had been killed in the engine room spaces by the explosion, but the others left the ship in good order.

While the *Jasper Park* was slowly rolling on her side and sinking by the bow in about forty minutes, Gysae fired another torpedo as a *coup de grâce* to ensure her destruction, and only then surfaced and approached the boats. Coasting to a stop among them and a mass of floating tea chests, he asked questions about the ship's identity, tonnage, last port of call, destination and cargo. In fact the ship's twenty-year-old Second Mate, Canadian Jim Butterfield, jumped onto the U-boat's forward casing with his boat's bow line to ensure his lifeboat was not damaged alongside. In the later report on 13 July to USN Naval Shipping Control Officers, the Master reported that "evasive and contradictory replies were given." They noted that the U-boat, a large one, was very rusty, but the crew looked well, and Gysae spoke halting but adequate English. In conversation, Gysae commented he was surprised that the ship was not protected by her anti-torpedo nets, which were in the raised position, as he had fired at her shortly before midnight but missed.

After this exchange the U-boat crew rescued several of the chests of tea floating about, then motored off to the south on the surface. In the boats, all supplies were gathered from some liferafts that had also broken loose, sail was hoisted and they set off west for South Africa. But as a result of the "S-S-S" signal, the boats were located and all the survivors rescued the next afternoon, after twenty-seven hours, by the destroyers HMS *Quiberon* and *Quickmatch*, sent out specifically to look for them or their attacker. The crew eventually reached England, and the Canadians returned to Canada in mid-September. In fact some of them travelled in the ill fated Convoy ONS-18 when the U-boats initiated attacks on the escorts with acoustic torpedoes, sinking HMCS *St. Croix* and HMS *Polyanthus* and *Itchen* as well as sinking six merchantmen. The survivors of *Jasper Park* were lucky to get home at all.

U 177 was part of 12 U-Flotille out of Bordeaux and was a larger Type IX D-2 class, commissioned a year and a quarter before. She had left on her second patrol on 1 April 1943, after a most successful first patrol under Gysae in the South Atlantic and Indian Ocean, where he had sunk eight ships. On this patrol he was in the same area, sank two freighters and then, giving an idea of the worldwide extent of the sea battle, refuelled south of Madagascar, not far from where he later encountered the *Jasper Park*, from the large tanker supply *Charlotte Schliemann*. That had come around from Japan and a meeting was arranged by BdU's radio net. The *Charlotte Schliemann* was scuttled when caught by warships the following February. After refuelling, *U 177*'s next victim was the *Jasper Park*. He followed this sinking with two more, returning safely to Bordeaux on 1 October.

Robert Gysae was awarded the Knight's Cross and Oak Leaves, left *U 177* on her return, and went on to serve as commander of the 25th U-Flotille until the war's end. In the final days he commanded the 1st Anti-Tank Regiment. *U 177* did not survive the war, being sunk under command of another CO on 6 February 1944 in the South Atlantic by depth charges dropped by an American Naval Liberator aircraft operating out of Ascension Island. Ten of the crew were saved, fifty lost.

Those lost: Richard Carrick, A.J. Nicholson, James D. Walkinshaw and William J. Wood

Sources: Correspondence from LCdr J. Butterfield, Cmdre J.J. Drent & R. Fisher, D Hist; Rohwer, *Axis Submarine Successes*; Kurowski, *Knight's Cross Holders*; Wynn, *U-Boat Operations*; USN Survivor Interview and NCSO Durban transcripts; S.C. Heal, *A Great Fleet of Ships* and *Conceived in War, Born in Peace*.

A 10,000-tonner, the North Sands type *Point Pleasant Park*. (Murray Manson/USCG)

POINT PLEASANT PARK

SHIP: 7130 grt, 441 ft. dry cargo North Sands type freighter. Built Davie Shipbuilding & Repair, Lauzon, Que., delivered to Park Steamship Company 8 November 1943. Chartered to and managed by Elder Dempster Lines, Ltd., Liverpool.

FATE: Torpedoed by *U 510* on 23 February 1945, in the Atlantic 430 miles northwest of Cape Town, South Africa. Nine lost.

Named after Point Pleasant Park in Halifax where the Naval and Merchant Navy memorial now stands, *Point Pleasant Park* had made her first wartime voyage in December 1943 under charter. Through all of 1944 she travelled with no problems, to Trinidad, Capetown, India and back to Montreal. The shortage of qualified officers, partly caused by their loss in the tremendous destructions of 1942 and 1943, is illustrated by the progress of her Third Officer, Paul Tooke of Owen Sound, Ontario. He joined the as an able seaman, was promoted to ship's Bosun in Cape Town and to Third Officer, without a ticket, on return to Montreal.

This time the ship had loaded in part in Montreal. Under Captain Owen Owens, a Welshman and new to the ship, a crew of fifty-one in total plus seven RCNVR DEMS ratings for her single 4-inch gun and four Oerlikons, *Point Pleasant Park* sailed to Saint John, New Brunswick to complete loading and left for African ports on 8 January 1945. Off Nova Scotia she joined a southbound convoy for protection. The ship went in to Trinidad for instructions and on 11 February, as directed by NCSO Trinidad, she set off alone southeast across the Atlantic for Cape Town 3400 miles away. At 10 knots, the voyage would take almost fifteen days. So far south, and so late in the war, the danger of U-boats was considered minimal.

But at 1355 local time on 23 February, in moderate seas and fine visibility, with no implication of peril, she was hit by a torpedo on the starboard side at the after break of the well deck, between the bridge and the stern, wrecking the whole area and flooding No. 5 hold. This broke the ship's propeller shaft so that the engine raced and was promptly shut down as the engine room flooded. The blast also collapsed the after deckhouse with the 4-inch gun on its roof, brought down her wireless aerials and killed eight men in the crew's quarters aft. The S-S-S signal was transmitted but just then the dynamo failed anyway, and the emergency transmitter would not work. Although the ship was fitted with anti-torpedo nets that could be lowered with the cargo booms, they were not streamed. The NCSO Trinidad did not suggest they should be and they were frequently unpopular with the ship's personnel as they slowed her speed by a knot or more and had the reputation for entangling anyone who jumped overboard.

With the ship obviously a loss and a U-boat presumably still nearby, at 1520 the Master ordered the ship abandoned, which was done in an orderly manner, as he threw overboard his confidential books in weighted bags. Men took clothing, officers took sextants and binoculars, the Third Officer even rescuing his greatcoat, uniform jacket and cigarettes. Two crew members brought along cameras, practically unheard of in a wartime abandoning ship.

They were 500 miles northwest of Cape Town and were well outside the normal traffic lane. It had been pure chance that allowed *U 510* under KL Alfred Eick to stumble across *Point Pleasant Park*. In a larger Type IXC U-boat, he was bringing a cargo of valuable tungsten to Germany from Japan via Batavia, himself keeping well away from any anti-submarine patrols along the South African coast and not necessarily hunting for targets.

The three ship's boats with all the survivors on board pulled around to the port side as the ship slowly filled and settled by the stern. It was only then, about 1530, that the U-boat surfaced. She fired a dozen rounds from a 40 mm gun at *Point Pleasant Park*'s bow to hasten her sinking, circled around watching, fired a few more rounds at the ship, and without communicating with the men in the boats, set off to the northwest. The ship sank at about 1615 local time.

The three boats took stock of their position. There were seventeen men in one, ten in another and twenty-two in the third. One boat was fitted with a motor, and all rigged their sails and set off for the African coast 350 or 400 miles to the east. One, the faster sailer, was commanded by Second Officer Ralph Taylor, one by the Captain and one by Third Officer Paul Tooke. This was not Tooke's first time torpedoed, for he had been a seaman two and a half years earlier when CSL's *Donald Stewart* was sunk in the St. Lawrence River. While the boats had emergency hand-cranked radio transmitters which operators tried to use, they could not tell if their messages were received. In fact the signals do not seem to have been picked up by anyone. The sets were not designed for such long distance transmissions.

It took one boat eight days, the other two ten days to reach safety, sailing about thirty-six miles a day. At first they tried tying the boats together, but this proved impractical, the rope becoming entangled in the motor boat's propellor, and No. 2 boat proving a much slower sailer. At night they tried keeping in touch with flashlights, but even before a storm on the eighth day they had become separated, mostly due to different handling qualities of the boats and skills of the crew. One man who had been badly injured in the torpedoing, probably with a broken back, died after a couple of days and was buried at sea from his lifeboat, although his death is recorded as being on the 23rd, the same as his unfortunate compatriots aboard the ship. He was the ninth and last fatality. One of them, a coal trimmer named Joe Bayliss from B.C., was but 18 years of age. Of those who died, all were Canadians except one Scot from Aberdeen. Others were also injured, but survived. On the 26th, three days into their ordeal, the men were more equitably divided between the boats and they sailed on.

The Second Officer's boat was discovered by a fishing vessel, *Boy Russell*, on 3 March off Mercury Island, just north of Luderitz in Southwest Africa. She accompanied it into a bay. The sixteen men in it and the lifeboat were taken into Luderitz, the loss of the reported by telephone to the small naval base at Walvis Bay

Two of the most unusual photos of *Point Pleasant Park* during the war.

Left, Lifeboats of *Point Pleasant Park* setting off for the African coast after their ship was sunk. The boat in the foreground is 3rd Officer Paul Tooke's boat. Right, the survivors aboard their rescuer, the SAN *Africana*, with the *Park*'s Master, Captain Owens at the right.
(Paul Tooke/Murray Manson)

far to the north, and a sea and air search instigated on the 4th for the Master's and Third Officer's boats. The next day, 5 March, those two were found only four miles apart by the South African naval minesweeping trawler *Africana*, Sub Lieutenant S. Thwaits, who took the thirty-three men aboard, gave them bread and jam, and towed the boats into Walvis Bay 225 miles to the north. Aircraft had also been dispatched to search up the coast. All *Point Pleasant Park*'s surviving crew were suffering to some extent from exposure, but all survived from the three boats. They had four days of recuperation, then were transported to Cape Town.

The Canadian members of the crew were returned to Canada, seven not arriving until 6 June in Philadelphia aboard another Park ship, with problems because they had no identity cards. Similarly, another seven arrived in San Pedro, California as "distressed seamen" aboard *Dorval Park*, and after considerable correspondence and long personal descriptions to establish their identities and determine who was to pay the fare, were sent across the continent to Montreal by train. And unusually for the Merchant Navy, five awards were made to crew members: an MBE to Fourth Engineer Frank Rosendaal of Transcona, Manitoba, and BEMs to ABs Edgar Proctor and John Slade, all for entering a flooded compartment in *Point Pleasant Park* just before she sank and rescuing two badly injured seamen; and BEMs to AB Laurent Girard of Pointe au Pic, Quebec and Robert Korogye of Toronto, both badly injured in the torpedoing and who "suffered with unusual patience and courage through wet and cold weather in an open boat for nine days." Sadly, these awards were not recommended until a meeting with the Director of Merchant Seamen on 26 October 1945, eight months after the event. One gets the impression that those making the awards this late in the war were attempting to rectify a past miserliness in awards to the merchant seamen. They were well deserved, but so would have been hundreds more earlier on.

At first records seemed to indicate that the U-boat that had sunk *Point Pleasant Park* had been *U 532*, which had been operating in the same general area, but further out toward Ascension Island. It was not until investigators questioned her CO, FK Ottoheinrich Junker in the mid-1960s that he advised them it had not been his boat that was responsible. It was then traced to Eick's *U 510*.

This U-boat had been on operations since July 1942, now part of 33 U-Flotille operating out of Flensburg on the north tip of Germany. On her previous four patrols in the western Atlantic and Caribbean under two COs, nine ships had been sunk. On this final voyage of the war, Eick left Germany on 3 November 1943 and was sent into the Indian Ocean. There he sank five ships, and then went on to the port of Penang, arriving in April 1944. That summer he moved from Penang to Singapore to Kobe in Japan, then to Batavia (now Jakarta) in what was then Java with engine problems. These took some months to repair, with spares sent out from Germany. It was not until 11 January 1945 that *U 510* set off again, now with a valuable cargo of tungsten ore, to cross the Indian Ocean and pass up the Atlantic for home.

In fact on encountering *Point Pleasant Park* Eick fired two torpedoes, missing with one astern but finishing her off with the other. Eick arrived in St. Nazaire, short of fuel, on 23 April 1945. There *U 510* was seized by French forces on 8 May, and the crew taken prisoner. *U 510* was taken into the French Navy as FN *Bouan* and was not scrapped until 1960. Alfred Eick had been awarded the Knight's Cross in March 1941, and was twenty-eight when he attacked *Point Pleasant Park*.

Those lost: Joseph S Bayliss   Frederick W Breen   George Edwards
             Patrick Guthrie   Ronald Hallahan   Godfrey A M Malmberg
             Robert Munro   Leslie Toth   Louis Wilkinson

Sources: Mitchell & Sawyer, *The Oceans, The Forts and The Parks*; SCS Interview (Second Officer), PRO; D Hist file; Halford, *The Unknown Navy*; Reader's Digest, *The Canadians At War, Vol. 2*; Wynn, *U-Boat Operations, Vol.2*; Kurowski, *Knight's Cross Holders*; Paquette & Bainbridge, *Honours & Awards*; Veterans Affairs websites <www.vac-acc.gc.ca/general> and <www.vac-acc.gc.ca/remembers/sub.cfm>; Bennett, *Survivors*; USN Survivor Interview transcript.

TABER PARK

SHIP: 2895 grt, 328 ft. Scandinavian type North Sands dry cargo freighter. Built by Foundation Maritime Ltd., Pictou, N.S., turned over to CGMM 28 August 1944. Managed by a British shipping firm.

FATE: Torpedoed by a midget submarine on 13 March 1945, about off the Norfolk-Suffolk border in the North Sea. Twenty-eight men lost including four DEMS gunners.

A *Seehund* Type XXVII two-man submarine of the Klienkampfverbande that sank *Taber Park*. No photo of the merchantman has been located. (Mike Maloney/NJ Naval Museum)

It is significant to note that for *Taber Park*, lost less than two months before the end of the war, there is almost no record in the official files or other histories of the circumstances of her loss. Her crew of twenty-eight was almost entirely British under Captain J.J. Parsons and four DEMS gunners were lost as well, but the details of their fate are not available. There is no record at the PRO of a Ships' Casualty Section interview by the Trade Division, no USN transcript. Earlier on, such interviews had provided valuable information about U-boat tactics, crews, defensive measures required and possible counter-measures. But by now, with the U-boats obviously beaten and the war all but over, there was no point in delaying the survivors with extensive interviews. There was nothing more to learn. And the story of the ship's loss has only recently been included in the extensive German U-boat records because her attacker was not, in those authors' initial opinion, really a U-boat. In the Merchant Navy's *Book of Remembrance* the names of the twenty-four merchant seamen lost only appear on Addendum pages—names added late in its preparation.

Taber Park was one of the group of smaller Thompson-designed Park ships, 4000 gross tons, and only 2875 net. Although technically still Canadian, she was in fact on loan and British charter, largely manned by the British Ministry of War Shipping's Trade Division. Sailing from Methil on the Firth of Forth for the Thames with a cargo of coal, on the occasion of her loss she was passing south down the English coastline in Convoy FS-1753. When first hit at almost 0300 local time, it was presumed she had been mined, a not uncommon occurrence in these waters throughout the war. Of her total crew of thirty-six including six DEMS gunners, only four merchant seamen were able to escape, including the Master. This indicates she sank very quickly because of her full load of coal. Since the Chief Officer is also not listed among the casualties it would seem only the bridge watch escaped.

Her attacker was a two-man miniature submarine, a *Seehund* or Seal of the large group classed as Type XXVII B5 of the *Kriegsmarine's Kleinkampfverbände* or "Small Battle Units." These *Seehunds*, unlike their manned torpedoes and other small craft, were true midget submarines, modeled after the British X-craft. Two of those small British submarines, *X-6* and *X-7*, had been engaged in the 1944 raids on the battleship *Tirpitz* in the Norwegian Kaafjord. These two were scuttled there during the raid, raised by the German forces, carefully examined and to some extent copied for their own planned *Kleinkampfverbände* force. The final lot of German *Seehunds* were equipped with a 60 hp diesel Bussing truck engine and a battery-driven 25 hp electric motor, originally designed to be used as a bilge pump motor in full-sized U-boats. As the aerial battering of Germany increased in 1944, and while 1000 *Seehunds* were planned, only 285 units were actually built before the country's collapse. Training on these boats began in September 1944 and the first went on operations in the North Sea and Channel in January 1945. In fact their first success was off Great Yarmouth in February. Between January and when all operations ceased in April, they made seventy sorties, at first in groups of up to ten. But communications and control proved impractical with such small units. Soon they were each operating on their own. In all it is estimated they sank about fifteen ships, including the Free French destroyer *La Combattante*.

Taber Park's attacker was from the *Seehund's* 5th K Division based at Ijmuiden in Holland. They sailed in lots of five to ten on the 6th, 9th and 11th of March. This *Seehund, KU 5*, was manned by LzS Max Huber and LzS(Eng.) Siegfried Eckoff on their first sortie. They were able to put their two G7e electric-driven torpedoes into the ship.

Their small size and very silent running made them almost impossible asdic targets for surface warships. However their sorties were no more successful than regular U-boat patrols by this stage of the war. In March there were twenty-nine *Seehund* sorties, from which nine boats failed to return. They sank three ships— *Taber Park*, another small freighter on the 26th and the little 833 grt coaster *Jim* on the 30th. That month RN MTBs sank two of the *Seehunds*, a frigate sank another and the trawler HMS *Puffin* a fourth, although she was so damaged herself as to be a constructive total loss. Aircraft claimed three more, and two just disappeared, a not uncommon outcome at the time for these small craft.

The names of the British seamen lost aboard *Taber Park*, inscribed on the Merchant Navy Memorial, Tower Hill, on the Thames, London, England. Not included are the Naval & Army DEMS gunners. (Frank Redfern)

Those lost: Twenty-four of these names appear on the Thames Memorial, with residences noted as throughout the British Isles. Only one Canadian has been identified, D.J. Audfroid, from New Brunswick, although there might be one or two others. As happens all too often, there is some confusion as to names. Those marked * appear only on one file list and not on memorials.

Charles Ashton	Douglas J Audfroid	Walter D Begg
J W Chaper*	John R Clegg	H Clifton*
John F Cox	Walter J Crammon	Ian C Dennis
Sidney Dixon	John W Freeman	Fraser Grant
Cyril Harrison	Sidney H Irving	Douglas K Jolly
Richard Kane	Ralph Kilstin*	Thomas McDonald
Joseph Philpot	Joseph Piesse	Leslie M Ranee
John Reck	Fred E Rutherford	William Rutter
George R Soutar	William M Thompson	James Thomson*

Plus C Whetton, an RA gunner, and three other DEMS gunners, not identified but presumably three of the * above.

Sources: Mitchell & Sawyer, *The Oceans, The Forts and The Parks*; Whitley, *German Coastal Forces*; Becker, *K-Men*; D Hist file; correspondence with Michael Cooper, England; Merchant Navy *Book of Remembrance*, Addendum pages; Kemp, *Underwater Warriors*; Rohwer, *Axis Submarine Successes (2nd ed.)*; correspondence with S.C. Heal and Bill Butland.

AVONDALE PARK

SHIP: 2878 grt, 328 ft. North Sands Original type dry cargo freighter. Built by Foundation Maritime Ltd., Pictou, N.S. Turned over to CGMM 13 May 1944. Managed by Witherington & Everett, Newcastle-upon-Tyne.

FATE: Torpedoed by *U 2336* on 7 May 1945 two miles southeast of May Island, Firth of Forth. Two men lost.

The loss of *Avondale Park* is both unique in the war and provides a final tragic note. She was, as it turned out, the last British merchant sunk in the Second World War of a total of over 4285 ships (if one omits those lost to floating mines after the war). The two crewmen killed, the Chief Engineer and a donkeyman, were the Merchant Navy's final casualties, out of a total of almost 40,000 Allied Merchant Navy lives lost. If they had survived one more day they would have been "home free."

A Norwegian-owned ship, the *Sneland 1* was hit and sunk from the same convoy, only moments after *Avondale Park*. And 400 miles to the south the little Norwegian naval minesweeper *NYMS 382* had been sunk earlier that same day. The war had ended as it began with the sinking of the Donaldson liner *Athenia*: ships and lives

A not too clear photo of *Avondale Park*, alongside a dockyard with a barge alongside. (Murray Manson/Admiralty)

lost to the U-boats of the *Kriegsmarine*. The two in the north were lost to Germany's final and most dangerous U-boat design, a Type XXIII; *NYMS 382* fell victim to an essentially pre-war design Type VII U-boat.

On 7 May a small convoy of five ships, EN-91, was assembled in the Firth of Forth in southeastern Scotland for a final passage north around through the Pentland Firth, with *Avondale Park* destined for Belfast. Everyone knew the war was all but over, and in fact the ships were allowed to sail with some lights on, signals were exchanged by light from ships to escorts, unheard of in the previous five and a half years. At 8:30 local time the group moved down the Firth and past May Island at a modest 7 knots in clear calm weather, forming into two columns, with *Avondale Park* leading the starboard column and acting as Vice-Commodore. The Master was Captain J.W.M. Cushnie, with a crew of thirty-four, with four naval DEMS seamen and three Maritime Regiment Royal Artillery gunners. All were British.

Ominously, May Island was the site of the infamous "Battle of May Island" on 31 January 1918, when in a confusion of multiple collisions, fog, darkness, ineptitude and poor use of submarines, two very large Royal Navy 'K' class submarines were rammed and sunk, two more and a light cruiser badly damaged in the space of half an hour, all from the same Navy.

This time the ships just cleared the entrance to the Firth, sixteen miles from the anchorage, when at 2240 local time *Avondale Park* was hit by two torpedoes on her starboard side near the midships engine room. There was no time to get boats away—and anyway at least two had been damaged or were missing entirely because of the blasts—as the ship slowly rolled to starboard and settled by the stern. With the vessel obviously sinking, the Master shouted the order to abandon ship, and the liferafts were released into the water. The surviving crew and gunners jumped into the sea and scrambled onto rafts or grasped floating debris. In under ten minutes the ship was gone.

As she sank, another explosion was heard as torpedoes from the same submarine hit the *Sneland 1* which also sank within minutes. In neither case were tracks of torpedoes seen, let alone a submarine. Two engine room men in *Avondale Park* were lost including her Chief Engineer, and nine from *Sneland 1*. Another of her men was to die from his injuries later the next day. In all, fifty-four survivors were quickly rescued by escorts and landed at Methil on the Firth. Despite a search by escorts the submarine was not detected and presumably made off submerged after her attack.

The U-boat was a new Type XXIII, *U 2336*, one of thirty-nine or forty so-called "electro-boats" which were completed and put into operation in the last months of 1944. Of these boats only six were able to make eight operational patrols between them, sinking three Allied merchantmen and damaging one other, in April and May 1945. Given their small size at 107 ft (with crews of only two officers and twelve men) and nimble underwater handling abilities, they would have been a substantial pest in the waters of the North Sea and Channel if they had arrived on the scene earlier. They are sometimes confused with the full-sized, high performance Type XXI U-boats that had much higher surface and underwater speeds than the previous wartime boats.

U 2336 was with 4 U-Flotille based on Stettin in what is now northwest Poland, although she operated on her one war patrol out of Larvic, just south of Oslo, Norway. She was commanded by KL Emil Klusmeier, who had until recently been a BdU staff officer, developing the attack tactics for these small U-boats. She had sailed on 1 May to operate off the Firth of Forth, sank the two ships and was back in Kiel as ordered by 14 May with no other attacks or sinkings. With the wide ranging air sweeps by Beaufighters and Mosquitoes specifically looking for surfaced U-boats, she remained submerged almost the whole time and Klusmeier did not receive Grand Admiral Dönitz's order to cease offensive operations and return to harbour, sent out late on 4 May. But then it was perhaps subject to interpretation— "A continuation of the fight from the remaining bases is no longer possible... Undefeated and spotless you lay down your arms."—and not absolutely a "cease fire" order. In any case, the Allies' terms for Unconditional Surrender did not come into effect until midnight 8 May, mostly because General Eisenhower would not agree, as the German High Command wished, to allow their armies to continue the fight against the Russians. Klusmeier was within his rights. Even Adelbert Snee, one of the Aces in a new Type XXI boat carried out a trial attack entirely successfully against a convoy—but did not fire.

After the surrender *U 2336* was ordered to Lisahally in Northern Ireland from Wilhelmshaven, and was sunk in Operation Deadlight in the open Atlantic on 2 January 1946.

The threat from U-boats continued right to the very end. As of 4 May, there were still 126 operational U-boats, with an average number of forty-four at sea and on operations in the Atlantic and home waters.

Those Lost: G. Anderson and W. Harvey.

Sources: NCSO Tyne interview and DEMS interviews, PRO; Van der Vat, *The Atlantic Campaign*; Hay, *War Under The Red Ensign*; Rohwer, *Axis Submarine Successes*; Wynn, *U-Boat Operations, Vol.2*; Gröner, *German Warships, 1815-1945, Vol. 2*; Kaplan and Currie, *Convoy*; Tarrant, *The Last Year of the Kriegsmarine*.

While these four are the only Park ships completely lost to enemy action, there was one that was not a total loss. While it should probably be included in Chapter 18 under "Not Lost", her story is somewhat unique and is added here.

NIPIWAN PARK

SHIP: 2400 grt tanker, 251 ft. Built by Collingwood Shipbuilding & Engineering, Collingwood, Ont. in 1943. Assigned to Imperial Oil Ltd. as managers.

FATE: Torpedoed by *U 1232* on 4 January 1945, thirty miles southwest of Halifax, off Egg Island, N.S. Two lost.

A ship only lost in part: the damaged small tanker *Nipiwan Park*, which lost her bow section to *U 1232* off Halifax. (Murray Manson/DND photo)

This small coastal tanker was operated by Imperial Oil Company as managers on behalf of Park Steamships. She was utilized on both the Great Lakes and on ocean voyages along the Canadian and American coasts. Her name has been spelled in various ways in records, although the above is as she was registered. However, the park she was named after, in northern Saskatchewan, is actually spelled Nipawin.

On 4 January 1945, with the war almost over, under Captain M.J. Stafford and a crew of thirty, she was in the Sydney to Halifax local Convoy SH-194 of three ships, two freighters and herself, steaming in line abreast with the more valuable tanker in the middle with the convoy's Commodore on board. Their lone escort, the Bangor escort HMCS *Kentville* was sweeping across the front of the convoy. *Nipiwan Park* was carrying about 2000 barrels of diesel oil for delivery at Halifax. With no anticipation of a problem the ship was suddenly torpedoed at a couple of minutes before 5:00 p.m. with a massive explosion right before her bridge. Fortunately for the tanker she did not catch fire, and the crew, expecting the ship now to sink, were ordered to abandon her in the two boats not damaged in the explosion. Shortly after this her destroyed bow section broke away from the rest of the at No. 2 tank hold just before the bridge, which was also largely wrecked, rolled on its side and sank. However the remaining half of the ship stayed afloat, although down by the "bow."

Her attacker was the Type IXC *U 1232*, KsZ Kurt Dobratz. He avoided *Kentville* without being detected, and neither did a patrolling aircraft covering the little group sight the stalking U-boat. Two men were killed in the explosion, the Chief Officer, John T. Carroll and an AB, H.U. Bazinet. Three others were injured and required hospital treatment, the Master seriously enough to remain in hospital for several days. The convoy hustled on into Halifax, leaving the after half of the ship rocking sluggishly on the ocean waves. Later that same day the tug *Security* was sent out from Halifax, connected to the still floating stern and towed it into Halifax, arriving about 1:00 a.m. on the 6th. Subsequently this section was towed several hundred miles around to Pictou, N.S. where *Nipiwan Park* was rebuilt with a new bow section and sold, more or less surviving the war. She was eventually re-engined and named *Irvinglake* for the New Brunswick Irving Oil Company's Kent Line Shipping.

U 1232 had actually fired at another ship in the little convoy, the elderly Yugoslav freighter *Perast*, missed her and hit *Nipiwan Park*. Dobratz then also torpedoed and sank the small Norwegian steamer *Polarland* from the same convoy, which sank in minutes. The little *Perast* undertook violent evasive steering and escaped, and *Kentville* searched vainly about the area, towing her CAT anti-acoustic torpedo gear (although Dobratz had used contact-fired torpedoes known for their reliability). Dobratz slid quietly away, following the coastline north in water quite shallow for submarines, never detected by the frantic searching above him. In addition there was a serious collision between the Bangor *Burlington* and the ML *Q 116* which had come out to join in the hunt, damaging both. With two ships damaged or sunk out of

All that was left of *Nipiwan Park*'s bridge.
(Manson/DND)

three and, eventually, three escorts damaged, it must be classed as one of the least successful convoy actions of the war.

U 1232 remained in the general Nova Scotia area, sank two ships from another convoy, and damaged a third. Her presence was detected and the submarine actively pursued for almost a day by two Canadian and two USN escort groups, then was rammed by the Canadian frigate HMCS *Ettrick* which only damaged the U-boat and herself. The boat even ran aground off Norway on her way back to base on 14 February 1945. She too survived the war. Dobratz had served with the *Luftwaffe* until 1943 although he was a naval officer, and then commanded only *U 1232*. He later served in the post-war *Bundesmarine*, becoming Commanding Admiral U-boats.

Those Lost: Hercule U Bazinet and John T Carroll

Sources: Hogan, *Esso Mariners*; D Hist files; Blair, *Hitler's U-boat Wars*; Hadley, *U-Boats Against Canada*; Rohwer, *Axis Submarine Successes*; Busch & Röll, *German U-Boat Commanders*; USN Survivor Interview transcript.

CHAPTER 15

Two Captured Ships, Both Sunk

Let me at least not die without a struggle, inglorious,
But having done some big thing first,
For men to come to know of.

—Homer, *Iliad*

The Canadian Navy managed to capture two large merchant ships early in the war and turn them over to the Canadian government for war service, under the Canadian Government Merchant Marine Ltd. (CGMM). They were administered by Canadian National Steamships, although the government dictated the cargoes and the Navies their sailings.

While both captured ships were useful additions to the wartime trans-Atlantic shipping trade, the first captured vessel lasted for some two years; the second less than one. Both vessels had been owned by large shipping firms in their home countries before falling into Canadian hands. And tragically, from both ships when they were later sunk by U-boats there were no survivors.

BIC ISLAND (EX CAPO NOLI)

SHIP: 4000 grt, 370 ft., two-deck freighter. Built 1917 by Workman Clark & Company, Belfast. Steam triple expansion engines by builder.

FATE: Torpedoed and sunk in mid-Atlantic on 28 October 1942 by *U 224*. No survivors, thirty-six crew lost.

While the loss of this elderly freighter and her whole crew was assuredly a tragedy, her "capture" (in some texts shown thus, in quotations) was more in the realm of Italian *opera bouffe*. She had been built in Belfast for British owners initially, and was twenty-three years old when captured, twenty-five when she was sunk. Named *Murdan* until 1937, she then became part of the large fleet of the Genoa firm of Compagnia Genovese di Navigazione a Vapore Soc. Anon., who had twelve or more rather elderly freighters, all with "Capo" in their names. By 1940 she had been renamed *Capo Noli* and with a sister she was freighting for her owners to the St. Lawrence ports in Canada.

When it appeared likely in late May and early June 1940 that the belligerent Italian dictator Benito Mussolini was about to join Germany and declare war on

The Italian freighter *Capo Noli*, before she became *Bic Island*.
(Italian AIDMEN)

Britain and her Allies, including Canada, Italian ships were secretly advised to leave any "enemy" ports as soon as practical and head for home. *Capo Noli* and *Capo Lena* were at Quebec City, and the *Capo Lena* promptly sailed, heading down the St. Lawrence for the Gulf and the open ocean. The *Capo Noli* was not yet ready for sea. However these departures of potential "enemy" ships in various ports had been anticipated by Canadian authorities to some extent. Flight Lieutenant Leonard J. Birchall, RCAF and his Short Stranraer No. 914 flying boat was moved from her station at Dartmouth on 30 May to Gaspé to be available for Gulf searches and await orders. The Stranraer looks to us today like something out of First World War flying, rather similar to the 1916 Felixtowe series flying boats, with its broad 82-foot wing span and many struts and cables. However it had two Bristol Pegasus X engines between the wings that could push it to 165 mph and a long endurance in the air. In fact its entry into RAF/RCAF service dated only from 1936 and it was the last in a long line of reconnaissance flying boats. Despite its appearance this aircraft was designed by R.J. Mitchell who also designed the renowned Spitfire. The aircraft was armed with three .303 Lewis guns and could carry 1000 lbs of bombs.

On 1 June Birchall was ordered up river to search for and shadow *Capo Lena*, which he did for four and a half hours as she made for the Gulf. Birchall did the same the next day, in two flights of almost ten hours, following the ship until it was clear into the Atlantic beyond Cape Breton. Italy was not yet at war, so nothing could be done. Birchall returned to his base in Dartmouth on 3 June, awaiting further instructions.

These came on the 10th, when he went back to Gaspé to refuel and then, with Italy now officially at war with the Allies, Birchall was again ordered to search for the *Capo Noli*, also now hastening seaward. In the afternoon he came across her, 235 miles out on his search up the St. Lawrence, near Ile du Bic, about twelve miles further upriver from Rimouski. Without the aircraft actually attacking the freighter, for Lt Birchall hesitated to bomb the ship without provocation, her Master evidently decided he might as well give up. He ran the *Capo Noli*'s bow ashore on Bic Island and set her afire. Then the crew abandoned the ship in her lifeboats. There is an account by the brother of the ship's Canadian river pilot that he had been unofficially advised not to let the *Capo Noli* escape if he could do something about it, and that it was he who changed the ship's course to run her aground. However it happened, she was firmly aground.

The little RCN auxiliary minesweeper HMCS *Bras d'Or* (Lt C.A. Hornsby, RCNR) had been stationed at Rimouski for shallow water minesweeping. Until the war's start when *Bras d'Or* was transferred to the Navy, she had been a Department of Marine and Fisheries lightship. This day she had also been hurrying upriver toward the fleeing merchantman but had not yet found the ship when Birchall radioed the freighter's position to the Navy. Shortly the *Bras d'Or* arrived on the scene, while Birchall in his Stranraer circled threateningly overhead. *Bras d'Or* gathered up the Italians in their boats and returned them to the freighter, saying in effect, "If you don't put out the fires you started, it will go hard with you!" Hornsby's men ordered *Capo Noli*'s crew back aboard where between them they soon put out the fires. As Joe Schull's official naval history notes, this "served to lighten the general monotony of naval life."

Leonard Birchall was later to gain much fame and honours as "the Saviour of Ceylon" when he flew patrols out of that Indian Ocean island, reported an advancing Japanese task force and, although he was shot down in his Canso and made a Japanese prisoner, allowed preparations to be made that thwarted the Japanese foray. He retired as an Air Commodore, OBE, DFC, CD.

The two ships did not have such a successful ending. The little auxiliary minesweeper *Bras d'Or* was lost with all hands when she foundered that same fall in heavy weather on 19 October 1940 while again shadowing a freighter in the Gulf of St. Lawrence. All thirty of her seamen lost their lives, including Lieutenant Hornsby. A similar fate was to befall the *Capo Noli*.

Returned to a shipyard on the St. Lawrence for refitting, the ship was renamed, appropriately, *Bic Island* and, operated directly by the CGMM, was put to the Atlantic trade carrying goods to the United Kingdom. On her last trip the *Bic Island* loaded up with 3500 tons of what are listed as "liquid explosives" and ammunition at the

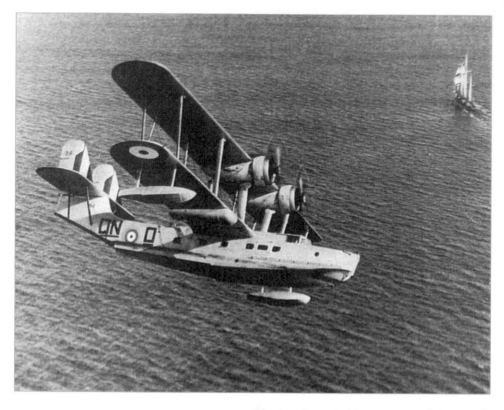

The two improbable capturers of *Capo Noli:*
Left, a Stranraer similar to F/Lt. Birchall's.

HMCS *Bras d'Or.*
(DND)

Dartmouth magazine in Bedford Basin, Halifax, and sailed with Convoy HX-212. She was now under command of Captain James Brown of Vancouver, aged forty-five, and bound for Liverpool. It is likely there were some passengers aboard as well, given her accommodation, and as many as eight or ten DEMS gunners, not identified.

In the last week of October 1942 there were seventeen convoys at sea in the Atlantic: three off Nova Scotia, seven in the central area moving both east and west, two south and west of Ireland and five going to or from Gibraltar and the African coast. At the same time, the Allies had lost their ability to read the German U-boat Triton radio code. This ability had been of great help in determining where the U-boat Wolf Packs were located and their relative strengths. From these advance warnings, many convoys had been re-routed around the worst of the dangers, or extra defence escorts assigned to help protect them. Convoy HX-212 out of Halifax and bound for the UK was to pay a penalty for this lack of foreknowledge. The convoy started out with forty-five ships on 18 October 1942. Although the Allies suspected there was a concentration of U-boats at sea, their whereabouts, plans and actual locations could only be guessed at.

Early in October U-boat group Puma of some eleven to thirteen boats (the number varied depending on fuel and mechanical problems) had been directed to attack outbound (from the UK) Convoy ON-138, located by the German *B-Dienst* code-breakers. Driven off by the aggressive defence of Escort Group B2 (controlled by the later famous Captain Donald Macintyre, RN), the German submariners did not press their attacks as they had now encountered the next following convoy not far behind, ON-139. But only the shadowing and reporting U-boat, *U 443*, was able to attack, sinking two British freighters on 22 October before the convoy was redirected out of harm's way. The U-boat Group then swept westward, and on 26 October the centre of the line of submarines stumbled onto Convoy HX-212 moving directly toward them. The convoy was protected by an American-led Group A3. The elderly *Bic Island* was fourth in the second column as the heavily laden ships slowly ploughed along at less than 10 knots in fairly heavy weather.

Both the weather, which tended to make it very difficult to see or even detect the U-boats, and the relative inexperience of the American Escort Group worked in favour of the attackers. A3 was led by Captain T. Lewis, USCG in the cutter USCG *Campbell* and had under orders the destroyer USS *Badger* and a mixed group of six corvettes, one RN and five Canadian. Of the RCN corvettes three were only attached for passage to the UK for upcoming North African landings. This meant the ships' COs had not worked for long, three not at all, with their Senior Officer or even each other. So despite a close screen of the six corvettes around the merchantmen and the two faster ships sent out scouting ahead, at 1910 local time on the 27th the attacks began, with three ships torpedoed in rapid succession, although only one, the large British whaler *Sourabaya* was sunk. One of those hit, the freighter *Frontenac*, in fact made port safely under her own steam. There were no deterring attacks carried out on the U-boats by the escorts, who could not locate the attackers. Two of the escorting corvettes rescued eighty-two crew and passengers of *Sourabaya*, and *Bic Island* evidently dropped back and picked up some of her survivors as well, but no record of the number now exists. The other ship hit, the American freighter *Gurney E. Newlin* was stopped, but not sunk at that stage.

That same night, at 0145 on the 28th, another attack by *U 606* hit the Norwegian *Kosmos II*, which dropped astern of the convoy, slowly sinking. The British freighter *Barrwhin* bravely also dropped back to rescue the *Kosmos* survivors, when *Kosmos* was finally sunk in a *coup de grâce*. Sadly, two days later *Barrwhin* was also sunk while trying to catch up to the convoy again. There were fortunately some survivors of both.

Lying stopped, now well astern of the convoy at 0602 local time, the *Gurney E. Newlin* was sunk, also by *U 606*. *Bic Island* and the corvettes rescued some of her survivors as well and then set off and tried to catch up to the convoy, still visible ahead. During the day of the 28th there was air cover for some hours by Liberators of RAF's 120 Squadron which helped drive away five U-boats caught on the surface. But at nightfall, still in heavy weather and with the radarless aircraft now departed, Group Puma again attacked. Some German records (Wynn) report *Bic Island* as a straggler, which in a way she was although not by accident. In any case she paid the price of being beyond the convoy's questionable protection. *Bic Island* was still somewhat astern of her column, trying to catch up, but in this next attack two merchantmen were torpedoed, *Bic Island* by *U 224* (KL Hans-Carl Kosbat) at about 1815 local time, and the American tanker *Pan-New York* by *U 624* (KL Graf Ulrich von Soden-Fraunhofen). A seaman in another ship ahead reported that *Bic Island* simply exploded with a tremendous crash and a cloud of smoke blown across the sky. Kosbat had fired a salvo of two torpedoes at *Bic Island* from 900 meters and missed. He then fired a third which hit and destroyed the merchantman, evidently in one thunderous blast.

They were the last ships lost from HX-212 apart from the *Barrwhin*'s loss the following day, for by dawn there was more continuous and effective air cover. Captain Lewis complained later that he was supposed to have had an escort aircraft carrier for the convoy's protection but that these had all been diverted for the North African landings and none was available for convoy protection. Since the attack that sank *Bic Island* occurred well after dark and in those days aircraft from those small carriers could not operate at night, it probably would not have prevented her demise in any case.

Of the thirty-six crew, her DEMS gunners, plus those rescued from the two other ships and any passengers of *Bic Island* there were no survivors. If they did reach lifeboats or rafts even in the weather and cold of late October, no-one ever encountered them. The ship's last moments and those of any of her crew remain unknown, a too-typical loss in that unrelenting year. Eighty-nine Allied merchant ships were lost in the month of October 1942 alone.

This was *U 224*'s first patrol, having left Kiel where she was built, a Type VIIC, on 17 October. After the battle around HX-212 those boats with enough fuel were ordered toward Gibraltar to attack the North African Torch landings. But *U 224* was already low, so remained west of the Irish coast, where on 12 November she sank the Panamanian *Buchanan*. Unlike in *Bic Island*'s sinking, the crew were able to report that seventy-three of them took to four lifeboats, and they were rescued after an epic twelve-day sea and air search.

U 224 returned to Kiel, left again on 3 January 1943 and passed through into the Mediterranean. There on a bright sunny day off the Algerian coast she was detected, depth charged to the surface in a single "by eye" quick attack and then rammed by the Canadian corvette HMCS *Ville de Quebec* (LCdr A.R.E. Coleman, RCNR). The U-boat was sunk in only eight minutes, with one survivor from her conning tower, First Watch Officer W.D. Danckworth. Forty-eight others perished.

Those Lost: The only source for numbers of crew lost is in the Merchant Navy's *Book of Remembrance* in Ottawa, which lists these thirty-six names:

James Brown, Master	William Anthony	Robert Black
Stewart W. Buchanan	Clarence A. Campbell	George E. Cannon
Basil P. Chapman	David Crombie	William Davidson
Edward J. Gilder	Charles Goodspeed	Fred Habib
John M. Hanna	James A. Hannah	Russel J. Kean
Jean Lamontagne	Lawrence D. Long	Lawrence Maloney
Vincent C. McGowan	George McGuffog	James M. McIntosh
George Miller	Reginald C. Naugler	Arthur Pain
Francis H. Pitman	Leslie R. Robbins	Thomas Runciman
Harry J. Secretan	Alex Sinclair	Thomas C. Smith
Knud C. Thers Nielsen	Jack H. Thomson	Henry A.J. Tibbo
Robert Williams	John Wilson	Leslie J. Winn

Sources: Correspondence with L.J. Birchall 28 Oct.1996; *Lloyd's Register of Merchant Shipping, 1941-42*; Tucker, *The Naval Service of Canada, Vol. II*; Milner, *The North Atlantic Run*; Wynn, *U-Boat Operations of the Second World War*; Boutillier, *The RCN In Retrospect*; Parker, *Running the Gauntlet*; Convoy web site <www.uboat.net>; Edwards, *Dönitz and the Wolf Packs*; correspondence with Dr. Achille Rastelli, AIDMEN, Milan; Joubert, *The Third Service*; BdU War Diary, via Rob Fisher.

VANCOUVER ISLAND (EX-WESER)

SHIP: 9472 grt., 487 ft. refrigerated diesel-engine freighter with passenger provision. Built 1929 by Deutsche Werke, Kiel, Germany.

FATE: Torpedoed by *U 558* in mid-Atlantic, 15 October 1941. No survivors of 102 or 103 on board. (Note: One researcher feels this is not what may have happened.)

The capture and later loss of the passenger freighter *Vancouver Island* constitutes one of the more remarkable stories of both the early wartime Canadian Navy and the Canadian lost merchantmen. In some circles her loss is described as obscured by mystery and unanswered questions, with some rather startling theories still being investigated. As far as is recorded in official and generally accepted texts and records, the following tells the story of this ship as it presently is recorded.

She like her sister ship, later the *Elbe*, was built with two small funnels, at Deutsche Werke, Kiel in 1929, as the *Sud Americano* for Norwegian owners. But the ship was returned to the builders after trials as unsatisfactory for failing to reach the contracted speed. Both ships were then chartered for a while to the Blue Star Line, the *Sud Americano* as the *Yakima Star*. After a few years they were laid up at Kiel again as a result of the world-wide Depression, then re-engined to give them a more acceptable speed of almost 20 knots, and funnels were reduced to one large one. They were both bought about 1934 by the large Bremen firm of Norddeutscher Lloyd, and renamed *Weser* and *Elbe*.

Vancouver Island fitting out in Vancouver in November, 1940
(Murray Manson/DND)

In the late summer of 1939 *Weser* departed with general cargo for the west coast of Canada, but by the time she had passed through the Panama Canal in early September war had been declared. So fearing interception by British warships on the Pacific coast, she put in to Puntarenas, Costa Rica to await developments. After about six months she moved up the coast to the more favourable political climate of Manzanillo, Mexico. In these ports she had discharged part of her cargo and taken on 18,000 barrels of oil, coke and peat moss. She was now at the disposal of the *Kriegsmarine*, and was earmarked as a support supply ship for up to six of their merchant raiders in the Pacific. With her speed, refrigeration capacity of over 129,500 cu.ft. and passenger accommodation for thirty to forty passengers (for crew exchanges or captured prisoners), it was a natural role, if she could escape.

While her hull became weed-covered and the refrigeration brine piping deteriorated, by the summer of 1940 opportunities appeared more favourable for a break-out. The British had only one or two ships along that coast to keep watch on half a dozen German merchant ships waiting to slip out of neutral harbours.

In Canada, with the British government's encouragement, the government had requisitioned three west coast liners from the Canadian National Railways' subsidiary CNSS for arming as armed merchant cruisers, *Prince David*, *Prince Henry* and *Prince Robert*, on the understanding that the Admiralty would provide the appropriate guns to arm them. Such ships were a natural, although often not very effective response to the German extensive use of armed raiders ranged on the world's oceans shortly after the war's outbreak. Few of these AMCs could stand up to the larger and much better armed German naval cruisers, their auxiliary cruisers, and certainly not the renowned pocket battleships (although the AMC *Jervis Bay* in fact did so.)

But their presence with a convoy or patrolling along a coastline deterred approach by the enemy raiders, which were vulnerable to battle damage. Their targets were the unarmed merchantmen. While *Prince David* and *Prince Henry* were being given major structural refits and arming on the east coast in Halifax and Montreal, and would not be ready for service until December 1940, the Admiralty was pressing for the completion of *Prince Robert* at Burrard's Shipyard in Vancouver. Two upper boat decks were stripped off, her three funnels reduced to two and a cruiser bridge fitted. For armament she was provided with four ancient 6-inch guns, originating about 1895 in the King Edward class battleships predating the First World War, and also had two 4-inch guns from cruisers of that war, all stored at Esquimalt by the Admiralty in the early 1930s against just such a need for arming AMCs. Although elderly and with no vestige of modern fire control, this armament made these ships the RCN's most powerful warships until much later in the war.

On 31 July 1940 HMCS *Prince Robert* commissioned into naval service, under Cdr Charles T. Beard, RCN with a crew of 241. With some difficulty they began learning the idiosyncrasies of their new ship. But the Navy, pressed by the Admiralty, was becoming more concerned with the number of German ships in Mexican and other Central and South American ports, some obviously preparing for sea. The Allies had only one older RN light cruiser and a few destroyers to patrol and blockade the thousands of miles of coastline, so it was agreed that HMCS *Prince Robert* would reinforce the blockade. On 11 September she went to sea for her first gunnery practice and sailed for the south on the 12th, "in a very unready state!" her CO noted.

She arrived off Manzanillo, Mexico on 18 September. *Weser* had not yet sailed, but had steam up, the British consul reported. So assuming the ship would only attempt to escape by dark and to entice her to do so, during the day the *Prince Robert* lay out of sight to sea or down the coast, and closed the port each evening after nightfall. In those pre-radar days darkness provided an adequate shield for both sides.

On the evening of 25 September when *Prince Robert* closed Manzanillo, lookouts reported the silhouette of a large coming out, just clear of the breakwater. Commander Beard took his ship to the south, close against the land where her own silhouette would be hidden, her crew at action stations. *Weser*, for it was she, continued out, heading for the open sea and as he later recalled, her Captain Beet (his name is not certain) thought the ship he eventually saw close to the land was probably a Mexican gunboat. *Prince Robert* cut in behind the *Weser*, using only her wake as an indication, until they were both well beyond Mexico's three mile limit. Then with no warning, she ran up toward *Weser*'s quarter, fired one rather anaemic starshell from her 4-inch gun, then a 6-inch shell into the water just ahead of *Weser*, and illuminated her by searchlight. A small boarding party of six men, led by LCdr A.M. "Gaffer" Hope, dropped into *Prince Robert's* cutter which had been turned out in preparation, and rowed quickly to the now stopped German ship.

They were concerned about how they were going to clamber up *Weser*'s high sides, but were much relieved to discover that due to her hasty departure, with no sign to be given to watchers in the harbour in the afternoon daylight, the ship's accommodation ladder was still rigged over her side. So their boat was swiftly brought alongside its lower platform and the boarding party of armed men ran up the steps and were aboard in moments. Although *Weser* was fitted with scuttling charges, there had been no time to arm and fire them, and she was seized without further struggle. When challenged by Sub Lieutenant Robert Dundas, the Captain replied in perfect English that "There will be no trouble." Although one of the ship's officers challenged this decision, the Captain's orders not to scuttle the ship prevailed.

With an armed guard aboard and many of the crew removed to *Prince Robert*, the two ships headed north and entered Esquimalt a few days later, the naval white ensign flying triumphantly and very traditionally above the Nazi swastika. A valuable prize had been added to the Allied cause.

Prince Robert continued patrolling the west and east coast for almost three years, without any more significant achievements, except that in the fall of 1941 she escorted the taking the Canadian troops to Hong Kong where, two months later, they were to be captured by the invading Japanese. She was then converted to a well-armed anti-aircraft cruiser, participated in late war convoy battles between Gibraltar and England, returned to the west coast and went out to Hong Kong again to rescue the Canadians still there at the war's end.

The *Weser* required an extensive refit after her year of idleness in a semi-tropical port. The cost of some $206,000 even caused local newspaper comment, but she was a rare, valuable and fast refrigerated cargo passenger ship. The authorities felt it worth the time and effort. Now renamed the MS *Vancouver Island*, she was armed with a 4-inch gun, two Hotchkiss machine guns on the bridge, manned by two DEMS gunners, and later with a 40mm Bofors for her forecastle, manned by four Maritime Regiment Royal Artillery. Now managed by the CGMM, really an arm of the CNR/CNSS, she passed around to Halifax and was sent to the UK with valuable cargoes. Because of her speed, she never sailed in convoy, crossing as an independent, with a zigzag course and speed to protect her from enemy U-boats.

In May 1941 one of her DEMS gunners reports she had a running but inconclusive gun battle with a surfaced U-boat for several hours. Strangely, no reports of such an exchange appear in official records, in Canada or Germany, but it would certainly be possible. The U-boat would be most reluctant to risk any damage by this belligerent, weaving, relatively fast merchantman, and the ship would not be prepared to directly pursue the submarine. She arrived safely that time in the UK on May 16th. In all she made three trips safely.

On 24 September *Vancouver Island* sailed from Montreal, under command of Captain Eric L. Roper. Roper had been born in Liverpool, and since 1925 had been with Canadian National Steamships, latterly in their Lady boats to the West Indies. When the *Lady Somers* was taken over early in the war by the Admiralty to be an armed boarding steamer, Roper and a good part of his crew transferred to *Vancouver Island*. While the cargo is reported in some publications as steel, copper and other metal, this was not entirely so. Her large refrigeration space was taken up with foodstuff, and she had a deck and upper hold cargo of trucks, ambulances, aircraft and spares and other miscellaneous supplies. She also took aboard about thirty-two passengers, many of them US citizens going to Britain to join the RAF.

Coming down the St. Lawrence River the ship accidentally grounded at Grondines above Quebec City. She was at Quebec for a few days for inspection, then on the afternoon of 9 October carried on to Halifax. Leaving that port in the second week of October, she set off across the Atlantic alone.

Several days later, on the 15th according to Canadian, British and German reports, she was by chance encountered by *U 558* (KL Günther Krech) almost exactly half way across, alone and in heavy weather which would make even a surfaced U-boat hard to see at any distance. Krech torpedoed her. A slow convoy, SC-48 was seventy-five miles behind and northwest of the ship. The escort group with that convoy picked up a signal from *Vancouver Island*, saying she was disabled and drifting, but not specifically "sinking." The RCN corvette *Pictou* and HMS

Veronica were sent out to the area the freighter had given as her position and found nothing at all. But then the Canadian corvettes of those days had very poor Canadian-built radar, and even their radio equipment was often less than satisfactory. (One of the group's escorts, HMCS *Shediac*, missed a signal for a convoy alteration of course at nightfall and wandered away for five days, her radio also not picking up calls to her.) Two weeks later HMCS *Agassiz* reported encountering a lifeboat with two dead *Vancouver Island* officers, almost forty miles northeast of the reported sinking position by German records, a not unreasonable drift distance given Atlantic and Gulf Stream currents. None of the crew of sixty-four or five, nor the thirty-two passengers nor the DEMS and Marine Regiment RA men seem to have survived. It is quite possible that the U-boat put a second torpedo into the after she had sent the message, finishing her off too abruptly to transmit a further signal.

Those querying this official record claim that it is possible the ship was captured by prior arrangement by the "attacking" U-boat or another one, and taken into Vigo Spain as a supply depot for U-boats. While some aspects of the last voyage, including the highly unusual lack of any records of that patrol by *U 558* and the exchange of gunfire in May are open to continuing question, for the time being the *Vancouver Island*'s loss is a typical tale, like many others. Among those lost are sadly twin brothers, stewards Jacques and Jean Smets, a doubly terrible blow to their family.

KL Krech was *U 558*'s only CO. He had departed his base at Brest on 11 October 1941 for operations in the Atlantic on his fourth war patrol, having sunk but one ship to date, on his third patrol. His first success this time was the unfortunate *Vancouver Island*. He continued into the Atlantic and sank four more merchantmen before returning on the 25th. In a further six patrols, Krech sank sixteen more ships, but was himself sunk by an RAF Halifax bomber and a USAF Liberator off Portugal on 20 July 1943 and forty-five of the crew perished. Only Krech, his Engineer officer and three ratings survived in a small dinghy, to be picked up by the RCN's HMCS *Athabaskan* four days later. They were made PoWs. Most records say only four survived, but a photo in Burrow and Beaudoin's book on *Athabaskan*, *Unlucky Lady* shows five submariners in their small boat, all wearing the typical U-boat life vests.

Those lost:	Eric L. Roper, Master	George W. Alcock	Charles R. Baguley
	Francis G. Bald	Ross Banning	Carol Alex Bower
	Alfred J. Briggs	Henry O. Brown	Norman H. Budd
	Gordon G. Bunt	Frank Caine	Alfred Callow
	William C. Casstles	Donald J. Cornett	Ernest F. Crete
	Donald Crouse	Joseph Desroches	Harry M. Forbes
	Percy Forbes	Oliver Garand	John Gill
	Victor Gorisky	Roger Gosselin	James V. Graham
	Ralph Green	Gordon Hanna	Howard M. Hutchison
	Ernest Jackson	J.I. Laganiere	Foster A. Lancaster

Douglas J. Lane	Michael Lazor	Lawrence Legacy
Raymond H. Legare	Blowers Loder	Arthur E. Lowson
John MacMillan	Harris MacPhail	Roy McCartney
William McManus	Thomas G. McMullen	Georges H. Michaud
Basil Moraes	Horace Mousset	Michael Myers
Einar L. Nielsen	Frank Pankratz	George Pouliot
William Richter	William Riley	H.B. Rogers
Guy Emil Roy	Thomas A. Shaw	Jacques Smet
Jean Smet	George L.V. Smith	William Sutherland
Herny Thorn	Fred Turner	Bervel B. Vye
Arthur G. Wakefield	Roy G. Williams	Robert Wilson
William E. Wooton	John Young.	

Also lost were two DEMS gunners: John C. Ardaugh, RCNVR, Burris G. McLeod, RCN, and at least four gunners, 7/4 Maritime Regiment, RA: William H. Hopkins, John Roberts, Robert Magill and James Watt.

Sources: Schull, *Far Distant Ships*; McKee, article in *Warship International:* "Princes Three"; Wynn, *U-Boat Operations of the Second World War*; Rohwer, *Axis Submarine Successes*; correspondence with Doug Adams 8 Jul.1999; *Lloyd's Register of Merchant Shipping, 1941-42*; correspondence with Robert Dundas 6 Aug. 1999; Burrow & Beaudoin, *Unlucky Lady*; Reid, *The Arming of Canadian Merchant Ships in the Second World War*.

CHAPTER 16

Five Foreign Ships Borrowed and Lost

Take this my spirit, and loose me from these woes.
My life is lived; the course by fortune given
I have fulfilled, and now the shade of me
Passes majestic to the world below.

—Virgil, *The Aeneid*, "The death of Dido"

In most listings of Canadian ships lost, several names appear of ships that were not Canadian when the Second World War began. As countries of Europe and Scandinavia were overrun by the Russians, Germans, and later the Italians, ships of Finland, Norway, France, Belgium and Greece that were not seized by the Central Powers fled to the relative safety of Allied ports to continue the struggle for their occupied homelands. Some, naturally, went to neutral countries such as the USA, or Mexico or to South America.

As to how the ships were to be managed, the approach of each nation, in fact of each ship, varied. The Norwegian government-in-exile directed all their ships to Allied ports. Then the Norwegians established their own shipping operation for their ships, which continued to fly the Norwegian flag, and they remained Norwegian ships. In fact they were a primary source of revenue for that government-in-exile throughout the war. The Greeks had a similar arrangement. The Danish minister in Ottawa asked that any of their ships that turned up by chance in Canadian ports be taken over under Canadian authority, stiffened, armed and provided with DEMS gunners. But since Denmark was by then in German hands and thus an "enemy," any ships in Allied ports, or even ships encountered on the high seas were to be, at least theoretically, "seized"—such as *Europa*, *Chr. J. Kampmann* and *Erik Boye* which feature in this chapter because they were later sunk, and *Asbjorn*, *Erria*, *Rana* and others which were not sunk. Similarly, two Danish tankers were "captured" by prior arrangement off the Venezuelan coast by the Canadian armed yachts *Husky* and *Vison* because they were destined for occupied Holland. In a bizarre contretemps those two were then re-seized by the Dutch gunnery sloop *Van Kinsbergen*. While some of these foreign crews were nervous about possibly being interned, discussions between the Canadian Navy, the Danish minister and the Department of Justice soon had their ships under Allied control and largely with their own crews as volunteers. One Danish report mentions that "there was a very positive attitude among Danish sailors" to these seizures and that they were happier under Canadian administration than British because of the better pay and food.

French ships were a particularly thorny problem. Vichy France was in theory still "unoccupied," their ships "neutral," and they could thus not normally be seized unless heading for occupied France and German hands. Also, after British naval attacks on the large French fleet at Oran, Dakar and Alexandria to ensure these warships did not fall into German hands, there was strong antipathy among French crews toward the English-speaking alliance. To the surviving French, the British were almost as much "enemy" as were the distant Germans in continental France.

It has not proved possible to determine how many of these ships in total came under direct Canadian control. Thirty-six European vessels were in similar circumstances in then-neutral US ports, under even more confusing situations. Those assigned by the Allies to Canadian management and subsequently lost to enemy action are recorded here just as completely as their truly "Canadian" sisters, their fates described as fully as is known. Some of them were managed by the Canadian National Steamship Company. Others were managed by other steam operating companies, both Canadian and British.

In almost all cases, the ships so transferred kept their own crews, or those that had escaped with the and wished to remain free and not return home, which was most of them. A few, especially French seamen, elected to return to France, even if under the Vichy regime, or join General De Gaulle's Free French. As the war ground on, however, additions and replacements for these crews came out of the various Seamen Manning Pools on an impartial basis.

ERIK BOYE

SHIP: Ex-Danish. 2010 grt, 305 ft. freighter. Built 1924 by A/S Naksov Skibs. for Vendila of Copenhagen.

FATE: Torpedoed by *U 38* on 15 June 1940, west of Land's End, Cornwall. None lost.

This loaned-in Danish freighter has the unfortunate distinction of being the first Canadian-registered ship sunk in the Second World War. She had been owned by D/S Vendila Dampskibsselskabet and managed by Svendsen & Christensen of Copenhagen. But with the fall of Denmark to invading German forces in April 1940, her management and registration was taken over by Canadian National Steamships of Montreal. Evidently the *Erik Boye*'s crew were still mostly Danish, under Captain O. Aggerholm. Unlike the Norwegians who still flew the Norwegian red, white and blue crossed flag, the Danish ships were officially seized and flew the Canadian red ensign, although most Masters and crews supported joining the Allied cause.

On her very first trans-Atlantic trip under Canadian colours, *Erik Boye* was in Convoy HX-47, and carrying 3568 tons of grain bound for Falmouth. She sailed from

The ex-Danish freighter *Erik Boye* at Boston in April, 1939
(W.A. Schell)

Halifax at 0900 2 June 1941. They had been scheduled to sail on the 1st but naval intelligence of a possible U-boat concentration offshore delayed the sailing for a day. Several publications record she was lost from HX-48, but latest research by Arnold Hague, confirmed by convoy file folders in the Canadian Directorate of History, indicates she and two others were lost from HX-47 as it approached the United Kingdom. There were fifty-eight ships on sailing although one returned after colliding early on with another in the convoy. They travelled at a modest 8 knots. For this part of the voyage their only naval escort was the eighteen-year-old ex-Shaw Saville & Albion liner, now armed merchant cruiser HMS *Esperance Bay* armed with seven 6-inch guns. U-boats had not tried to cross the Atlantic as yet in mid-1940 so were not a threat on the North American side. The AMC was sent along to hopefully discourage attacks by any German surface raiders and steamed in the lane between Columns 4 and 5. On 7 June they were joined by a further group of ships coming up from Bermuda and then continued toward St. George's Channel and Land's End.

When about sixty miles west of Land's End Convoy HX-47 had already been attacked by several U-boats. The later famous KL Gunter Prien had sunk the British straggler *Balmoralwood* at dusk on the 14th and KL Heinrich Lieb sank the independently sailing Greek freighter *Mount Myrto* by gunfire and torpedo. Then a couple of minutes after midnight on Saturday 15 June 1940, Lieb in *U 38* fired a torpedo salvo into the convoy, hitting first the Norwegian tanker *Italia* which caught fire, and immediately after the *Erik Boye*. Hit on the starboard side at

No.3 hatch, the ship started to settle at once and the captain judged her doomed, ordered the crew to launch the port side lifeboat and all abandoned ship quickly in an orderly fashion.

Both ships sank shortly after as the following ships swerved around them and continued on. There were no casualties from the *Erik Boye*, although many of her crew were only scantily clad. They were picked up quite quickly by a rear merchantman designated as a rescue ship, reaching safety in England. The *Erik Boye's* history notes that $1,160,000 was paid in insurance! The other ships in the convoy could be considered fortunate, as the U-boat group attacking them included not only Prien and Lieb but the later aces Endrass and Rösing as well.

U 38 was a pre-war Type IXA boat, commissioned in October 1938, and KL Lieb was her first CO. Based with the 2 U-Flottille in Wilhelmshaven, this was their fifth wartime patrol. Lieb had already claimed thirteen victims before his attack on *Erik Boye*, and sank three more on this patrol before returning to Wilhelmshaven. He was eventually credited with sinking thirty-two ships of some 168,500 grt and was awarded the Knight's Cross with Oak Leaves. Promoted to KK, he joined the staff at BdU and unlike hundreds of his compatriots survived the war. So did *U 38*, being relegated to training and experimental roles early in the war.

Those lost: none.

Sources: *Lloyd's Register 1938-39*; Wynn, *U-Boat Operations, Vol.1*; Rohwer, *Axis Submarine Successes*; Kurowski, *Knight's Cross Holders of the U-Boat Service*; Halford, *The Unknown Navy*; D Hist Convoy folder for HX-47; D Hist Merchant Ships: General files; Hague, *The Allied Convoy System*; correspondence with Danish Maritime Museum, Helsingor.

ST. MALO

SHIP: Ex-French, 5779 grt, 385 ft. freighter. Built in 1917 by Kawasaki Dockyard, Japan as *War Wolf*.

FATE: Torpedoed by *U 101* on 12 October 1940 in the North Atlantic northeast of Ireland, off Rockall. Twenty-nine men lost.

This two-deck freighter had been owned by the French company Cie. France-Navigation S.A. and based in Dunkirk, having passed through several owners before that. She was named *Commandant Mages* until 1938. In some registers she has appeared as being initially named *War Elf*, but this appears to be a temporary error corrected in later issues of Lloyd's Register.

After being assigned to CNSS on the fall of France, on 30 September 1940 she departed Halifax at 1400 local time with convoy HX-77. While many of her crew were still technically French nationals, her Master was Captain Charles Finlay of Thedford, Ontario, and he had a crew of forty-three under his command. In this

The ex-French freighter *St Malo*
(Gene Onchulenko)

convoy there were fourteen ships from Halifax plus twelve more coming out from Sydney which joined at noon on 2 October (although three of these had to return because of engine problems and an inability to keep up with convoy speed). Fourteen more joined on 3 October, coming up from Bermuda. The Sydney portion had been accompanied by the RCN armed yachts HMCS *Husky* and *Reindeer*, and the Bermuda BHX convoy by the AMC HMS *Laconia* (a later made famous by her own loss to a U-boat and the subsequent attempts by U-boats to save those aboard—"The Laconia Incident"). But all these defensive escorts returned and the convoy went on eastward with no ocean escort at all until it neared Britain's Western Approaches. *St. Malo* led the third column, and was loaded with general cargo, steel and grain, bound for the Clyde and Glasgow.

The weather turned ugly, typical North Atlantic weather in October, with western gales and heavy seas. Even by the time they were supposed to have met the RN escort the ships were twenty-three hours behind schedule. And the twenty-three-year-old *St. Malo* had already dropped astern, unable to maintain speed with the convoy, which gradually passed her and drew ahead. She thus became a straggler, and paid the price for that. Stragglers, usually unprotected by the scarce escorts, were favourite targets for U-boats as they circled the convoys.

On 9 October FK Victor Schütze in *U 103* had sunk three ships in slow eastbound Convoy SC-6 just north of the rocky sea mount Rockall, 200 miles northwest of Ireland. This was a notoriously dangerous location; the war's first casualty, the liner *Athenia* had been sunk nearby on the first day of the war; most convoys bound for either the docks at Liverpool on the Mersey or Glasgow on the Clyde passed nearby, and the German *Kriegsmarine* knew this. But given the ships' intended ports, it was not practical to avoid the area.

Convoy HX-77, still without any escort protection, was overhauling the slower SC-6 convoy some sixty miles to the south. In that area and directed to operate together, although not yet organised into formal Wolf Packs, were six U-boats. During the evening of Friday 11 October KL Fritz Frauenheim in *U 101* sank three ships in two brisk attacks on HX-77, one the British 8000 grt motor *Port Gisborne* and two Norwegians. During daylight on the 12th he was joined by KL Joachim Matz in *U 59* who sank another British freighter from the same HX-77. Then at about 2125 local time Frauenheim, scouting to the northwest of the convoy, came across, attacked and torpedoed *St. Malo*. She sank quickly, for twenty-eight seamen were lost, including her Master, when boats overturned on launching or men jumping into the bitter Atlantic were unable to reach them. Sixteen survivors escaped in one lifeboat, thirteen Canadians and three Free French. That one surviving boat was under the control of Chief Officer G. Fiddler, with the Third Mate, three seamen and eleven engine room and steward personnel. However in getting clear, that boat as well was partly swamped so they had no oars, sails, compass or any significant amount of food or even drinkable water. They drifted southeastward with the wind and seas, only able to bail out their lifeboat and forlornly hope for an unlikely deliverance. Then occurred one of the most amazing and heartening sea rescue stories of the war.

When the Port line's *Port Gisborne* was sunk on the 11th, three boats had been launched, but her No.3 lifeboat, commanded by her Chief Engineer, capsized and twenty-seven crew were lost. The other two soon became separated in the heavy seas. No.2 boat with the Master, Captain T. Kippins and the First Officer aboard, was eventually encountered by another merchantman on 24 October, twelve days after the sinking, and those survivors rescued.

No. 4 boat was under the charge of a mere crewman, AB Sydney Herbert Light, who not only took efficient charge of the boat but had a good working knowledge of navigation and sailing. With him were nine men, including the ship's Chief Electrician, the Chief Refrigeration Engineer, several engine room hands and stewards—not necessarily experienced seamen. The night of 11 October he had the boat lie to a sea anchor, the survivors bailing out sea water. At dawn, as Light's later report describes it, "they squared away the boat" and set sail to the east in heavy seas. At 1800 on the Saturday again they lay to a sea anchor, as with only Light able to steer with competence in the huge swells and breaking seas, they dared not sail in the pitch black of night. It was that same Saturday evening at 2125 local time that *St. Malo* was sunk, northeast of Light's position. On Sunday, *St. Malo*'s lifeboat simply drifted eastward, the survivors hoping some rescuer might appear. There was not even enough tackle left in the boat to rig a potential small sail. It was a dismal prospect that did not bode well for their survival. *Port Gisborne*'s boat meanwhile sailed briskly northeast, aiming for Ireland.

Then at about 1700 on Monday Light and his *Port Gisborne* boat's crew came across the hapless survivors of *St. Malo* in their drifting refuge and sailed over to them. With evening dusk setting in, the two skippers agreed to simply lie to sea anchors overnight, tied to each other, and see what could be done on Tuesday in daylight. The next day Light again sailed east, but this time towing *St. Malo's* boat at what Light estimated was a very slow 2 knots. Again, at 1800 they lowered sails and lay to overnight. Light, in his seamanlike manner, reported that "At 6:30 on the Wednesday I called the hands" and they shared a very modest breakfast. As the gale had now blown itself out and there was paradoxically now no wind, they set off rowing east, no longer tied together, Light having passed four oars from his supply to Fiddler's boat. It would seem that Mr. Fiddler was quite content to let the capable Light organize their journey. They rowed until 1500, when Light agreed with Fiddler it was too fatiguing and they should quit for the day, to lie to a sea anchor again for the night. On Thursday the 17th there was a light breeze, so they sailed all day and all night, still towing the *St. Malo* boat, although her Third Mate joined Light in his boat to take turns handling the boat in the night watches. This continued through Friday, although the breeze died away and they took to rowing again. Light went into Fiddler's boat to treat some cases of injury and of "trench foot" with brisk massage, which seemed to help. Again they sailed, very slowly, all night.

On Saturday the two skippers agreed that *St. Malo's* boat, because of the previous damage, was becoming unusable and their progress unacceptably slow. They had better join forces. But as the seas were again increasing, it was deemed too dangerous, with cramped, injured and debilitated men, to move from one tossing boat to the other until the weather eased. So again they lay to their sea anchors overnight. At 8:00 a.m. on Sunday the 20th, the remaining fifteen *St. Malo* men transferred to *Port Gisborne's* boat. The boat was now crowded, but the twenty-six crew were efficiently divided into three watches and they set off far more briskly under sail to the east. Light again dealt with cases of trench foot and evidently navigated by stars, as they sailed all night again. Monday they had only begun to sail on when they sighted the British tug *Salvonia*, towing a damaged freighter. This was the Scottish *Blairspey*, loaded with lumber, from Convoy SC-7 which had been astern of HX-77. She had been torpedoed on the 18th, three days earlier, once by *U 101*, KL Frauenheim and then twice by KL Schepke's *U 100*, but she did not sink because of her cargo. *Salvonia* had been sent out from Campbelltown, Scotland, assigned in a normal business deal to try to get her in—even damaged ships were valuable.

Light fired a flare to attract the tug on the horizon, which wasn't seen. Then they dropped their sails and rowed over to intercept the slow progress of *Salvonia* and her unwieldy tow. Already this tug had on board survivors from Convoy SC-7's *Sedgepool* and *Clintonia*, both sunk by U-boats. In a nasty and choppy sea the lifeboat came alongside the tug and the crew were taken aboard by Cdr L.W. Stowager, RNR, the tug's skipper. The seamen were rescued at last after nine and ten days in their boats. *Salvonia*, her tow and the mob of survivors all safely reached the Clyde on 25 October. It was a close to miraculous rescue of those few surviving crewmen from *St. Malo*.

After recommendations by Mr. Fiddler of the *St. Malo*, AB Light was given £10:00 (plus a letter from the Minister of Transport) by the Canadian High Commissioner, Vincent Massey, "As a reward for his courage and resourcefulness in bringing to safety the survivors of the S.S. *St. Malo*." As well, AB Light was awarded the prestigious George Medal in February 1941, equivalent in some respects to the Victoria Cross, except it is awarded for valour not in the face of the immediate enemy. He also received Lloyd's Medal for Bravery in July 1941.

Their attacker, KL Frauenheim and *U 101* were part of 7 U-Flottille out of Lorient, which he had left on 5 October on his fourth patrol. He had already sunk ten ships by this time and went on to sink two more and damage *Blairspey* in Convoy SC-7, coming up the same route a day behind *St. Malo*'s HX-77. The series of attacks on that slow convoy was to result in one of the worst battles of the war in terms of ships sunk per attacking U-boat. This was not too surprising when the group included aces such as Kretschmer, Endrass and Schepke. Frauenheim returned to his base on 24 October. He sank eighteen ships in all and was awarded the Knight's Cross. He transferred to the BdU staff, then was attached to the *Kleinkampfverbände*, the small battle unit miniature submarines, and survived the war. *U 101* was decommissioned as worn out in October 1943.

Those lost:

Charles E. Finlay, Master		Georges Andrieux
Emile Breuil	Louis Carroll	Philip Carroll
Aaron Cleveland	Roland Cousins	William H Davie
John Dickson	Ludger Dufour	Carrol R Gates
Frederick J Hansen	Arthur Knight	Joseph LaCroix
Guillaume LeCornec	Jean F LeSqueren	Frederick McCart
Donald J McDonald	Francis A H McDonald	Fred A E Nixon
Jean Peres	Eugene Phillippe	Henry J Rees
Carmen Richards	Henry A Rose	Medard Surellie
George E Tiller	Donald S Winchester	

The Carrolls were brothers. Also, Lewis McDonald is shown in some lists as lost from *St. Malo*, but not until June 1942. While he was indeed hospitalized for injuries suffered during the ship's evacuation, he was released, but then readmitted with cancer, and died in June. He is buried in Scotland.

Sources: NAC records, RG24, Vol.2529 for AB Light's report; *Lloyd's Register, 1938-39*; Wynn, *U-Boat Operations of the Second World War*; Rohwer, *Axis Submarine Successes*; Kurowski, *Knight's Cross Holders of the U-Boat Service*; Lund and Ludlam, *Night of the U-Boats*; D HIST Convoy folder for HX-77; Hague, *The Allied Convoy System*; correspondence with Rob Fisher.

EUROPA

SHIP: 10,224 grt ex-Danish passenger liner and freighter. Built 1931 by Akt. Burmeister Wain, Copenhagen.

FATE: Bomb damaged alongside in Liverpool in air raids 20/21 December 1940. Gutted by fire and abandoned in air raid 3/4 May 1941 while in drydock.

The Ex-Danish liner *Europa* is by far the largest "Canadian" ship lost of this group, and one with a modest pre-war connection with Canada. She and her three sisters of the East Asiatic Company had plied between Copenhagen and the west coast of North America before the war, with calls at Vancouver on occasion. That company had taken up considerable ownership in commodity production along the coast, thus assuring cargoes for its ships. Also, fortunately, there were no lives lost in her destruction, and her demise is well described in a book on the Liverpool air raids of 1940-1941.

Owned by the large Danish firm Det Östasiatiske Kompagni Aktieselskabet, she was taken over by the Canadian government and assigned to management by CNSS when Denmark was overrun by German forces in 1940. Technically these ships were seized by the Allies, as Denmark was not able to set up an operating company in exile for them as the Norwegians did.

Europa was a handsome medium-sized passenger freighter and a valuable ship for wartime service, with a speed of 17 knots, large holds for cargoes and, in peacetime, accommodation for sixty-four passengers. She was easily identified with her two distinctive squat funnels well aft of her midships bridge. Her Master, the Danish Captain V.L.O. Dahl remained with the ship. She became one of about forty victims of

Europa pre-war visiting Canada's west coast.
(B.C. Maritime Museum)

the massive May 1941 German air raids on the city of Liverpool, an early target with its substantial shipping capabilities, one of the most vital supply ports in the UK.

The first German raids of any consequence in the Liverpool area were in July and early August of 1940 on the suburbs of Merseyside and Wallasea, and then on 18 August on Liverpool itself. Not a lot of damage was done, mostly thanks to inaccuracies in German air navigation at that date and poor bomb-aiming. Raids which caused more damage, particularly fires in the city and in miles of huge dockside warehouses, occurred sporadically in late September and into December.

Then on the night of 20 December 1940 the first of several major raids occurred, by some 205 aircraft, directed specifically at the docks. *Europa* had arrived a week before, and was lying inside Huskisson No.2 Branch dock. She had just completed loading general cargo and aircraft, destined for British forces in the Middle East, and was to sail on the next morning's tide. There was an awkward arrangement required in many Liverpool docks, which were closed in by lock gates to allow the ships to be worked on without coping with the large rise and fall of the tides. A sand barge, *Overdale*, was lying alongside her in the dock, supplying sand for additional ballast. At 2200 a large bomb landed between the two vessels, blowing an eighty by thirty foot hole in No.1 and 2 holds in *Europa* and sinking the barge. *Europa*'s bow settled onto the bottom in relatively shallow water. While most of her cargo was recoverable, her repairs would take some time. The warehouse on the dock, containing mostly sugar, was completely gutted by fire. Also damaged alongside on that same night were the large Cunarders *Britannic* and *Samaria* (in which as a troopship the author's father had crossed in December 1939!). Much of the city and its dock area was set afire, and casualties in the civil population were horrendous. It was the most seriously damaging raid so far, but more was to come, after a mid-winter respite of sorts.

On the night of 12 March another raid of 316 aircraft again created massive damage throughout Liverpool with 303 tons of high explosive and 64,150 incendiaries dropped. A large mine was dropped in the open area just beyond *Europa*, still sitting with her bow on the bottom of Huskisson Dock facing outward. During the morning of the 13th the mine exploded, further damaging her. But she was very much repairable and a valuable asset. A couple of days later the ship was patched sufficiently to raise her and she was shortly towed into the Brocklebank Graving Dock a few hundred yards north of Huskisson's for more permanent repairs. There she settled on the blocks, the dock was drained and work began on her restoration. This was progressing slowly as a consequence of the immense destruction all around in continuing air raids. These not only set fire to vulnerable dockside buildings and offices, but knocked out rail lines, electricity, water and fire services and killed hundreds of skilled workers, not to mention the valiant Liverpudlians.

Then between 1 and 8 May the German forces concentrated on bombing Liverpool into ineffectiveness, with hundreds of aircraft each night flying over the city and across the Mersey to the huge Birkenhead shipbuilding yards. Between the night of 3 May and 7 May 1941, 127 ships, barges, cranes, tugs and other vessels were destroyed or badly damaged in the port area. *Europa* was one. The losses in buildings, ships and lives was appalling, in line with Coventry's destruction in the southeast. When the author visited the city of Liverpool in 1993, over fifty years later, there was still notable evidence of the destruction—large gaps in building areas, others still shored up with immense steel beams, churches with nothing but outer walls reaching skyward and no roofs.

By 3 May, repairs to the ship were now being hastened. The damaged bow plating from the mine explosion had been cut away, leaving a large hole. Sunset was at 2044, and the first air raid siren alert sounded at 2230. It was to be "the worst night of the war for towns on the east bank of the Mersey" says Hughes in his *Port In A Storm*. Some 298 aircraft attacked, dropping 363 tons of high explosive bombs, mines of up to 1000 kg. and tens of thousands of incendiaries. The results were devastating in Liverpool, along the docks, and to the ships still docked there.

At Brocklebanks incendiaries started fires in sheds all around *Europa*, and she was then hit directly by a bomb at 2330. Between 0030 and 0130 she was hit by two more, and a fire started on board. Aircraft were reported as flying low and machine gunning the area. While there were some officers and crew on board, there was naturally no ship's power or water pressure. They only had access to one fire hose leading from shore, and it had been split by bomb damage. With the Fire Service already fully occupied with unprecedented fires raging in the city and elsewhere and hoses too often destroyed by bomb splinters and fallen debris, there was little other practical help.

In addition to the modest efforts of her own crew, men from the CAM *Maplin* and the large minelayer HMS *Adventure*, lying just outside the graving dock, arrived to try and help aboard the now blazing ship. While their ships were also damaged, it was not as serious as *Europa*'s fires, as they had the extra manpower. Often their help consisted of trying to beat out small fires around the outer limits with pieces of wet canvas. While members of the fire brigade turned up about 0600 it was too late. In the terms of Lloyd's Weekly Casualty Report "It was impossible to save the ship." One report records that she burned for three days, even turning papers in the ship's safe to ashes. While initially the dock was dry, it later flooded, either from damage to the gates or it was deliberately flooded in an effort to quell the fires aboard *Europa*. The damage was multiplied when a nearby merchantman, *Malakand*, loaded with explosives, blew up with a huge explosion of devastating effect a day later. At any rate, the shores under *Europa* collapsed and she settled on the bottom leaning against the north dockside.

Even after the "All Clear" sounded the next morning, delayed action bombs exploded periodically throughout the area in addition to *Malakand*'s contribution to the turmoil. The raids continued for several days, and there were others over the next year, but the night *Europa* was lost was the worst. Yet Liverpool continued throughout the war to be a major shipping port. In that May of 1941 alone sixteen convoys of

123 ships arrived and fifteen convoys of 139 ships left, unloaded and loaded again, in the Mersey.

Somewhat later in June, to make the graving dock available, the hulk of the ship was patched enough to be towed to New Ferry Beach further out the Mersey and broken up. Of the company's three sister ships, all were lost during the war: *Canada* to a mine off England in November 1939, and *Amerika* to *U 306* in April 1942.

Those lost: none.

Sources: Hughes, *Port In A Storm*; *Lloyd's Register, 1938-39*; correspondence with Merseyside Museum, 1999, and with Ole Kolborg of Copenhagen; Heal, *Conceived in War, Born in Peace*.

CAROLUS

SHIP: 2245 grt, 296 ft. ex-Finnish registered freighter. Built 1919 by Osbourne Graham & Company, Sunderland, Scotland.

FATE: Torpedoed by *U 69* on 9 October 1942, Gulf of St. Lawrence near Métis Beach. Eleven lost.

This small ship was completed for the Ohlson Steamship Company (Sir Erik Ohlson) of Hull, England, and sold in 1933 to the subsidiary A/B Ohlson Steamship Company, with A/B Nielsen & Thordén O/Y, a Swedish firm as managers, but registered in Helsingfors (Helsinki), Finland before the war. She had been largely employed between Petsamo, Finland and British and European ports. *Carolus* was "seized" by the Canadian government on 31 July 1941, when Finland became a technical, although somewhat reluctant, ally of Germany upon the latter's attack on Finland's bitter enemy, Russia, which had been fighting Finland for two years. The ship was a very minor pawn in the complicated political game.

Her history is also complicated by the fact that her requisitioning in Montreal at the direction of a prize court was not completed until 23 March 1942, when she was assigned to the control of the CNSS on behalf of the Canadian government, as happened with other European ships. She was initially on their books for service in the West Indies trade, but by 1942 was hauling freight back and forth to Newfoundland and Labrador. She retained many of her original crew, judging by the names of those killed in her sinking. She was commanded by Captain V.E.H. Broman, her original Master, with a total crew of twenty-nine, including DEMS. By this time in the war, crew shortages due to promotions, illness or even desertions would have been filled from the general manning pools in Halifax, Sydney, Saint John or other ports, and there were six Canadians on her total muster role of thirty.

On 8 October 1942 she was upbound from the Gulf of St. Lawrence, on passage from Goose Bay, Labrador to Montreal with a cargo of empty oil barrels, in the seven-Convoy NL-9. These convoys were vital to supply the Canadian, British and

American bases established there, in particular the ever expanding Coastal Command aerodromes that provided the minimal but critical air cover for the hard-pressed North Atlantic convoys.

Carolus's convoy consisted of four merchant ships escorted by the three RCN corvettes *Arrowhead*, *Shawinigan* and *Trail* and was travelling at a modest 7 knots, following the south shoreline upriver. At 2138 on Wednesday 8 October, after dark, the convoy was about eight and a half miles northeast of Point Métis, between Matane and Rimouski where the Gulf of St. Lawrence narrows into the St. Lawrence River. KL Ulrich Gräf in *U 69*, moving in from mid-river with his deck awash, encountered first the escorts then ships of Convoy NL-9. He commenced carefully plotting his attack, despite periodic radar contact by the escorts, keeping to the river side of his targets. Eastern Air Command had intelligence information that a U-boat was in the river, and guessed it was probably trying to contact downbound Quebec to Sydney Convoy QS-39, which the U-boat in fact did not locate. The Hudsons of the RCAF's 113 Squadron could not cover the convoys effectively at night, although one flew in the area from midnight on, seeing nothing.

At just before 1 a.m. on 9 October, at a range of just over a mile Gräf saw the ships clearly enough and fired two torpedoes at *Carolus* which was slightly ahead of the other merchantmen in her convoy. One torpedo evidently missed, although it is reported to have passed close astern of *Arrowhead*, which turned up its track dropping depth charges and firing starshell to illuminate the area. The second torpedo hit *Carolus*'s starboard side just aft of No.2 hold, forward of midships. She soon flooded, her engine room also breached, rolled onto her side, broke in two, and sank within two minutes. There had been no time to launch any of her lifeboats. There were eleven casualties, who died either in the initial explosions or from exposure in the cold dark water. The remaining nineteen, clinging to empty gas drums or liferafts and bits of wreckage, were picked up about three-quarters of an hour later by *Arrowhead* and the corvette *Hepatica*. The casualties included at least one naval DEMS gunner, and a sixteen-year-old galley boy from Verdun, Quebec, John Milmine, making his first trip in his first ship.

The portly and cheerful Master of *Carolus* was among those rescued, with his money-belt safe, full of funds gained selling liquor to the construction crews at the outpost at Goose Bay, Labrador. Those rescued were taken on to Quebec City, but told to say nothing of their experience. Authorities were concerned that after similar attacks in September the local populace would raise a political clamour, demanding additional naval protection in the river, which could not be provided because of the shortage of escort forces in the more vital Battle of the Atlantic. However, since residents along the St. Lawrence had already heard the explosions, seen the flames and had in some cases given succour to the merchant ship survivors coming ashore during that summer and fall, newspapers locally, in Quebec, and in Ottawa gave a reasonably accurate description of the loss of *Carolus* within a few days.

Gräf sank no more ships in the river thanks to intensive air patrols and numerous escorts hunting him, although none obtained any contact with his U-boat. However, retreating through the Cabot Strait between Cape Breton and Newfoundland he encountered the Newfoundland-Cape Breton ferry *Caribou* and sank her with heavy loss of life. The escort HMCS *Grandmère* depth charged *U 69* but without inflicting damage.(See Chapter 17.)

This had been Graf's Type VIIC U-boat's tenth patrol, although he had only commanded her since March, operating out of St. Nazaire in France with the 7th U-Flottille. This time he had departed his base on 15 August to lay mines off Chesapeake Bay and patrol off Cape Hatteras. Finding no targets, and having a free rein as to his area of operations, Gräf had elected to enter the St. Lawrence, where he knew compatriots had had some success earlier in the summer and fall. Already he had sunk five ships in the south, including the Canadian fishing vessel *James E. Newsom* and the laker *Torondoc*. *Caribou* was his final victim, although he was robbed of another success when he hit the Canadian freighter *Rose Castle* but his torpedo failed to explode. On his eleventh patrol, while shadowing Convoy ON-165 east of Newfoundland he was detected and sunk by the RN destroyer HMS *Viscount*. There were no survivors of the U-boat's crew of forty-six.

Those Lost:	Verner Andersen	Kurt Andersson	Pablo Cubbillas
	Onni Heino	Nillo Helenius	Runar Karlsson
	Eryitt Kukkonen	John J MacDougall	R F McGaw
	John Milmine	Sulo A Seppala	

Sources: Essex, *Victory in the St. Lawrence*; Hadley, *U-Boats Against Canada*; Lamb, *On The Triangle Run*; Wynn, *U-Boat Operations, Vol.1*; Rohwer, *Axis Submarine Successes*; *Lloyd's Register, 1941-42*. VAC web site <www.vac-acc.gc.ca>; Blair, *Hitler's U-Boat War, Vol.1*; USN Survivor Interview transcript.

CHR. J. KAMPMANN

SHIP: 2281 grt, 306 ft. ex-Danish freighter. Built 1924 by Kjöbenhavens Flydk & Skbs., Copenhagen for the Vendila Company.

FATE: Torpedoed by *U 160*, 3 November 1942 in the eastern Caribbean about 100 miles north of the Venezuelan coast. Eighteen lost, eight of them Danes.

This Danish freighter had been owned and managed by the same firms that owned the *Erik Boye*, D/S Vendila and Svendsen & Christensen, before being seized by agreement when Denmark fell to German forces, passing to the operational control of the CNSS. She had been assigned to the West Indies service that CN(WI)SS had run pre-war. Her full name was *Christian J. Kampmann*, but in records and even when it was painted on her sides before the war it was shortened for convenience.

The *Chr.J. Kampmann*, a sister of the *Erik Boye* and originally owned by the same Danish firm.
(W.A. Schell)

On her fateful last voyage *Kampmann* was in a mixed convoy of merchantmen and tankers, Convoy TAG-18, Trinidad to Guantanamo Bay, Cuba some of which were bound onward for Europe via New York where they would join HX convoys. *Chr. J. Kampmann* was loaded with 3440 tons of sugar and rum, and carried a crew of twenty-seven under Captain Martin Jensen. Several of these valuable tanker convoys, although not this one, had been protected by RCN corvettes and Bangors loaned to the USN's Eastern Sea Frontier until they could gather their own escort forces in sufficient numbers and learn the British and Canadians' hard-earned anti-submarine skills. The Admiralty estimated at the time with quite remarkable accuracy that there were ten U-boats operating in and around the Caribbean and Gulf of Mexico on 2 November when this story unfolds. The U-boats operated individually although sometimes in radio contact with each other.

Convoy TAG-18 consisted initially of twenty-two merchantmen, tankers and freighters, protected only by five small USN escorts: the ex-yacht USS *Siren*, 720 grt and somewhat smaller than a corvette, with LCdr H.G. White USNR as Senior Officer, and four smaller PCs (Patrol Craft) of what the USN themselves derisively called their "Donald Duck" fleet. All had asdic and depth charges, but none had radar. The convoy was in eight columns of two or three ships each.

The *Chr. J. Kampmann* was en route from Georgetown, British Guyana to New York, and had stopped off on the way at Trinidad. The ships had assembled off Trinidad on 2 November, proceeding north toward Guantanamo inside the line of the Windward Islands at 8 knots on a tranquil evening. The sea was smooth with a slight swell, excellent visibility and a light easterly breeze. *Chr. J. Kampmann* was at least a mile astern of the other ships in her assigned column, since the first ships of the convoy had started off relatively briskly at 8 knots as soon as they had cleared the harbour and before the *Chr. J. Kampmann* had a chance to settle into her proper position in the convoy. The 8 knots was about the maximum her elderly coal-fired boilers could manage, so she was not really able to catch up. The ships were not zigzagging. All of this showed some lack of anti-U-boat and convoy experience. *Chr. J. Kampmann* had two lookouts on duty, the bridge watch also keeping a careful watch over the area around and the ships ahead.

The first indication of any enemy presence was the torpedoing of the *Chr. J. Kampmann* at 1515 local time on 2 November. She was hit by two torpedoes, one at No.4 hold, near the stern, and almost at once the other struck just aft of the midships engine room. This broke the ship in half and she sank quickly, with seventeen men killed, either in the explosions or when the ship foundered, including the First Officer and Chief Engineer. There was no time to launch any boats, and the survivors were only able to leap into the sea and scramble onto wooden liferafts that were released or broke free. There is no record of the names of the eight crew who survived, although it is known that the Master did. They were evidently not Canadians. They were picked up by USS *Lea*, a 1918-built flush-deck (Wickes class) destroyer, called out to help the inadequate escort force. She arrived the evening of the 3rd, assumed command of the battle and transferred her survivors to the patrol craft *PC 495* which returned them to Curaçao.

The Master of the tanker *Esso Caracas* in the same convoy reported sighting a periscope within the convoy lanes somewhat later, and told an escort which dropped about five depth charges. While the Master felt that the U-boat was probably destroyed, it was in fact not even damaged.

The attack on the *Chr. J. Kampmann* had been carried out by KL Georg Lassen who was the first CO of the Type IXC *U 160*, operating out of Lorient. Lassen alone did all the initial destruction on 2/3 November. After attacking *Chr. J. Kampmann* he drew off slightly although still undetected by the escorts, then attacked the convoy again at 0130 on the 3rd from within its lanes, sinking the 11,015-ton Norwegian tanker *Thorshavet*, and at 0137 two more ships, the freighter *Gypsum Empress* and the Panamanian tanker *Leda*. Then KK Hans Witt in *U 129* joined, continued the attack on the same convoy on 5 November, having picked up Lassen's reports of success.

In this his fourth war patrol Lassen had already sunk two ships off Tobago before his attack on TAG-18, which he first encountered late on 1 November. After these successes, he withdrew beyond the islands and sank three more ships off Tobago between the 6th and 21st of November. He returned to Lorient safely on 9 December. He completed another successful patrol, sinking twenty-five ships in all for which he was awarded the Knight's Cross with Oak Leaves. He was aged twenty-seven during this patrol, and joined the U-boat training staff after a successful foray into the Indian Ocean in mid-1943. He survived the war as a tactics instructor and naval infantry commander. *U 160* did not, being sunk 14 July 1943 in mid-Atlantic by aircraft of Squadron VC-29 from the escort carrier USS *Santee*, using acoustic torpedoes. There were no survivors of her crew of fifty-seven.

The US Naval staff were justly critical of the defence of this convoy, noting that their escort forces, even in late 1942, had yet much to learn about the subject. No contact whatsoever had been made with any U-boat by asdic (which the USN already called sonar) or radar. Despite the first attack the convoy's course was not changed, nor was it zigzagging. There was no plan in hand to counter any attacks, no illuminating rockets were fired, and escorts only searched their assigned areas. After the first of Witt's attacks two days later, the convoy course was altered for only half an hour then resumed, which would, the Staff noted, have only displaced the ships by about a mile and a half, well within a U-boat's range of visibility.

Those lost:	Reinhold Arndt	William J Bearnes	Justin Bishop
	Muir W Blackmoor	August Christensen	Kristian R Clausen
	John W Coombs	William F Dymott	Christen Mortensen
	Guy F Murphy	Henning P K Olsen	Arthur G. Pope
	Kauko K Rakkolainen	Karl E Soderman	Olaf F Sorensen
	George R Sweeney	Gustav V Wivagg	

Plus at least one DEMS gunnner, AB Josiah Woodward, RN.

Sources: Roscoe, *US Destroyer Operations*; Roskill, *The War At Sea, Vol.II*; *Lloyd's Register, 1941-42*; Rohwer, *Axis Submarine Successes*; Wynn, *U-Boat Operations of the Second World War*; Lenton, *American Gunboats and Minesweepers*; USN Survivor Interview with an unidentified *Chr. J. Kampmann* survivor and the (unidentified) Master of the convoy tanker *Esso Caracas*; correspondence with the Danish Maritime Museum, Helsingor.

CHAPTER 17

Seven Newfoundland Losses

With bowed head and heart abased, strive hard
To grasp the future gain in this sore loss.

—John Oxenham, *Newfoundland Memorial*

Although Newfoundland was not a direct part of Canada until 1949, its maritime affairs during the Second World War were closely tied to Canadian naval operations. Newfoundland seamen tended to join the RN's ranks and the RN had supported and encouraged Naval Reserve training in Newfoundland since about 1903, long before there was a hint of the Canadian Naval Reserves. Merchant ships registered in St. John's were technically British, flew the British un-crested red ensign, but were largely crewed by native Newfoundlanders. Those men and women flowed naturally into many a Canadian also.

The Merchant Navy and the Canadian naval Books of Remembrance show all too many Newfoundlanders' names again and again in British ships—from HMS *Forfar*, an AMC which had been CPR's *Montrose*, sunk on 2 December 1940 to the little A/S trawler HMS *Bedfordshire* sunk off North Carolina on 11 May 1942 while on loan to the USN. And in almost every British or Canadian merchant ship sunk there were Newfoundlanders, ships such as the Nassau-registered SS *Western Head* and a hundred others.

Even though it was not part of Canada, the Canadian Navy established a huge base at St. John's. The administration base was HMCS *Avalon*, with outlying subsidiaries, dockyards, fuel depots and repair slips. Commodore (later Rear Admiral) Leonard Murray operated as the Flag Officer Newfoundland Forces (FONF) from there, administering mid-ocean escort groups for the convoys to and from the UK. Newfoundland may have been a colony, operating under a Commission of Government appointed by the British Parliament, but its ties were very close with Canada. Canadians felt that Newfoundland was a natural extension of their country, taking this affiliation for granted. The Newfoundlanders were a little more distant, suspicious of potential but peaceable Canadian occupation. A local song of the day includes the lines:

Your face turn to England, your back to the Gulf;
Come near at your peril, Canadian wolf!

But it was merely cautionary, not threatening. So it is understandable why their lost ships should be included herein.

Of the eight Newfoundland merchant ships lost during the war, the large ferry SS *Caribou* was owned by the Railways department of the Newfoundland government; four were owned by Bowaters Newfoundland Pulp and Paper Mills Ltd., and three by Anglo-Newfoundland Steamship Company, also a subsidiary of a pulp and paper company. All these ships were registered in St. John's. Of the eight ships, fortunately only four suffered more than one casualty—*Caribou*, *Kitty's Brook*, *Rothermere* and *Livingston*. But the Newfoundland owners lost seven of the eight ships they owned or operated at the war's outbreak in 1939.

HUMBER ARM

SHIP: 5758 grt, 425 ft. two-deck freighter, "strengthened for moving in ice." Built in 1925 by Armstrong Whitworth & Company Ltd., Newcastle, England. Owners were Bowaters Newfoundland Pulp & Paper Mills Ltd. (Variously spelled Bowater's, Bowater)

FATE: Torpedoed by *U 99* when in Convoy HX-53 on 8 July 1940 at southern end of St. George's Channel, northwest of Land's End, England. No casualties.

Humber Arm
(McBride/Shipsearch)

Humber Arm was employed pre-war in carrying pulpwood to Bowaters pulp and paper mills in Corner Brook, Newfoundland and transporting the huge rolls of newsprint to its customers worldwide, as were three other Bowaters ships. In fact much of its product went to the major papers in the United Kingdom, and the ships of Bowaters were specifically built to carry their newsprint paper. In wartime the cargoes were more varied as shipping space demands rose.

On the occasion of her loss the ship, under her Master Captain Jack R. Morbey, had a 7201-long-tons cargo of steel, newsprint, lumber and pulp, bound for Liverpool. The ship was armed with a single 4-inch gun aft, and she had a crew of forty-two plus one passenger. The *Humber Arm* left Halifax on 25 June 1940 in the forty-four-Convoy HX-53 and crossed the Atlantic at a modest 8 knots, albeit this was in theory a "fast" convoy. There were no particular noted problems as the ships crossed the open Atlantic, no serious U-boat attacks developing and no convoy losses. The U-boats had yet to start operating in mid-Atlantic. *Humber Arm* was leading the second column of five ships (two convoy ships had turned back with defects). As they entered the Western Approaches, the group was joined for protection by a British close escort group of four destroyers and two sloops.

She was almost safe home, in good weather although with a heavy rolling sea, when encountered by KL Kretschmer in *U 99*. Kretschmer later became one of the *Kriegsmarine's* most notable aces. On this patrol he had attacked and sunk a couple of stragglers (including the Canadian laker *Magog*) and one out of the preceding convoy HX-52. Continuing scouting southwest of England, he encountered HX-53 just after dawn on 8 July. The only indication in *Humber Arm* that there might be a problem was the order for the convoy to start zigzagging and a destroyer hoisting a large black flag, indicating she was in contact with a submarine. This destroyer then passed aft down between the port outside column and *Humber Arm's* second column. But at 06:53 local time a single torpedo hit *Humber Arm*, when the destroyer was only about 400 yards astern. The devastating torpedo hit the merchantman amidships on the port side, in holds containing newsprint. Captain Morbey could see a large hole in the ship's side just below the surface, with a widening crack extending up to the deck level. The ship's rails there had been blown away, and some of the deck cargo of lumber was blown overboard.

With her heavy cargo of steel and newsprint rolls, this was enough to cause the ship to begin to sink at once, listing about twenty degrees to port, although she then slowly rolled upright again. Her four lifeboats were lowered successfully and without undue panic, the Master waiting until he was certain the ship was indeed sinking, which she did by the stern, about fifty-five minutes after being torpedoed as the last boat pulled clear. She slowly settled aft until almost vertical and then, with the boats well clear and as the crew watched, slipped quietly below the surface. They had seen nothing of the attacking U-boat.

However the explosion had attracted the convoy escorts, which at once turned and located *U 99* by asdic as she passed down the side of the convoy, and over the next nineteen hours dropped some 127 depth charges on Kretschmer's boat. It says much for the builders, Germania Werft in Kiel, that although forced down to the almost unheard of depth for those days of 350 feet (113 m), the boat and her crew survived the pummelling.

The *Humber Arm* survivors were about two hours in their boats, now well astern of the convoy while, as policy required, the escorts hunted around for the attacker, dropping depth charges. Then a destroyer arrived and picked them all up, landing them at Milford Haven in south Wales at 1500 the next day, Tuesday 9 July.

U 99 had departed Wilhelmshaven on 27 June on this second war patrol, after an abortive patrol earlier that month when she had been attacked in error by a German Arado aircraft from the battle cruiser *Scharnhorst*. Kretschmer had sunk *Magog* plugging along astern of her convoy, plus two other independents in the lucrative hunting area just southwest of Ireland. He encountered Convoy HX-53 by chance in the dark of early morning, dove *U 99* until the escorts and the leading ships passed over him as he watched carefully by periscope. He ran on a reverse course to the convoy, firing his torpedoes with 90° angle setting at ships left and right. But lack of experience caused incorrect settings and all forward torpedoes missed. He then fired a stern shot from his single tube, having appreciated and then solved the problem, missed the ship he aimed at but hit *Humber Arm* beyond her.

After surviving his long depth charge attack he was even able to sink another merchantman. He was not known as "Silent Otto" for nothing. He then contrived to capture the 2136-ton Estonian freighter *SS Merisaar*, telling her captain he was going to follow below the surface and if he failed to heed his instructions to head for occupied France he would be sunk instantly without warning. The ship obediently set off as directed, but even this enterprising effort failed when the ship was then bombed and sunk by the German Luftwaffe in an excess of zeal. Sinking one more merchantman on this cruise, *U 99* returned to her new base in Lorient on 21 July 1940.

Kretschmer and *U 99* were eventually sunk by LCdr Douglas Macintyre in *Walker* with HMS *Vanoc*'s help on 17 March 1941. Kretschmer spent the remainder of the war in Canadian and British POW camps. Post-war he rejoined the *Bundesmarine* and rose to command the fleet as a Rear Admiral. He returned to Canada on one occasion as a very popular speaker at a naval dinner.

Those lost: None.

Sources: SCS Master's interview; Robertson, *The Golden Horseshoe*; *Lloyd's Register, 1939-1940*; Rohwer, *Axis Submarine Successes*; Wynn, *U-Boat Operations, Vol.1*; Winton, *Convoy*; Hague, *The Allied Convoy System*.

GERALDINE MARY

SHIP: 7244 grt 438 ft. oil-fuelled freighter. Built in 1924 by Vickers Ltd., Barrow. Owned by Anglo-Newfoundland Steamship Company, with Donaldson Bros. & Black of Glasgow and Liverpool as managers. Registered in St. John's.

FATE: Torpedoed by *U 52* on 4 Aug. 1940 just southwest of Rockall, west of Scotland when in Convoy HX-60. Two crew lost.

The original Anglo-Newfoundland Development Company was formed in 1905 by the Harmsworth brothers of England (later Lords Northcliffe and Rothermere) to ensure a direct control of the supply of newsprint for their thriving newspaper businesses—London's *Daily Mail*, the *Daily Mirror*, and others. The company established mills, and even built up a shipping port at Botwood, twenty-three miles from Grand Falls in western Newfoundland. Anglo-Newfoundland Shipping was a subsidiary company established to operate the purpose-designed ships transporting newsprint to their facilities in England. The AND Company is still in existence, although with no ships of its own, now as Price Newfoundland Ltd., having amalgamated with Quebec City's Price Bros. Ltd.

Their *Geraldine Mary* was named after Mrs. Harmsworth, the mother of Northcliffe and Rothermere. The ship was designed for the trade, with holds dimensioned to handle the huge rolls of newsprint, and bows strengthened for navigation in ice so she could continue most of the winter entering Botwood. In addition to crew space she had accommodation for twelve passengers in six staterooms.

The *Geraldine Mary* at St. John's in very light condition.
(Memorial University)

An unusual photo of a sinking ship.
An RAF photo of the *Geraldine Mary* breaking up just before she sank.
(Botwood Heritage Society Archives)

The *Geraldine Mary* was continuing in her normal peacetime role of delivering pulpwood to the Botwood mills, bringing 6112 long tons of newsprint to her English facilities when sunk, on her 147th voyage. She was armed with a 4.7-inch and a 3-inch gun in part manned by a DEMS rating. Under Captain G.M. Sime she had a crew of forty-six and there were six passengers as well, five Newfoundlanders, including three women. Of these fifty-two people, two crewmen and one passenger were killed, and one crewman injured. The three AND Company ships that were sunk were all being managed by the Donaldson Line, an Anchor Donaldson and Cunard lines subsidiary. At the war's outbreak Donaldson operated twenty-one ships, and were to lose thirteen of that fleet alone.

The ship left Botwood on 19 July 1940, came around south of Newfoundland, joined up with the British freighter *King Alfred* out of St. John's and in a couple of days joined Convoy HX-60 which had sailed from Halifax on 23 July. Despite being a fast convoy, the ships were travelling at 8 knots, crossing the North Atlantic without problems for nine more days, in fine weather, with good visibility.

With U-boats suspected in the Western Approaches area as they neared the United Kingdom, at 0140 on the night of 2 August an "S" message, indicating the presence of submarines, was passed to all the ships. The ships were then ordered to start zigzagging as they entered the Western Approaches. While *Geraldine Mary* started in position 72 (second in the seventh column) she had been moved to 81 on the first day out then back to 71 on 2 August, thus leading her column. Captain Sime then ordered his crew to action stations, and told the passengers to remain in their cabins, fully dressed. Shortly after this *King Alfred* was hit by a torpedo and sank quickly, although only five of her crew were lost. Almost at once a second ship was sunk, victim of the same *U 52*, KL Otto Salman. Then quiet reigned for another five hours, the ships ploughing onward, crews apprehensive. At 0330 the crew of *Geraldine Mary* relaxed a bit, with some crew sent below, but a couple remaining at each gun mounting. First light was about 0400, and gradually the ship's officers relaxed, the Captain finally going to his cabin to lie down.

Then, at 0720 GMT, with quite a rough sea running and while on a leg of the convoy's zigzag, aboard *Geraldine Mary* there was a loud thud and an explosion (although the Master was surprised that there was not more noise). The ship quickly heeled over fifteen to twenty degrees, and on gaining the deck Captain Sime noted that the No.1 starboard lifeboat had been demolished in a torpedo hit just aft of the bridge. He then checked with the wireless officer but was told the set had been completely wrecked. So had the ventilators and samson posts on the starboard side. They were just south of Rockall, some 250 miles from Northern Ireland.

The Master then went down to look at the huge hole created by the torpedo, extending sixteen feet from below the waterline almost to deck level just aft of the ship's funnel. The torpedo had hit in No.3 hold where its bulkhead joined the engine room, the blast passing right through the rolls of paper and blowing a similar hole in the ship's port side, also extending up twelve feet above the waterline. Despite all this damage, the ship's Chief Officer in his cabin on the starboard side of the bridge structure, only about twenty-five feet from the hole, slept through the whole thing, while a passenger just forward of there had been thrown from his bunk!

With the ship now stopped, the Master ordered three surviving boats lowered to water level and all liferafts released but tied by lines to the ship while he considered

The names of the two seamen lost when *Geraldine Mary* was sunk, recorded on the Merchant Navy Memorial on the Thames in London.
(F.Redfern)

whether the ship would survive. He looked into the engine room and even within minutes of the torpedo explosion it was filling with oily water, and the Chief Engineer reported that an Engineer on watch and a fireman had apparently been killed, either with the explosion or flooding. A port side boat was almost sucked into the gaping hole in the surging sea running. All but eight of the crew were sent away in the boats which were ordered to stand clear, while Sime signalled by light from the bridge to the Convoy Commodore in Column 6 "NO WIRELESS." He then went down and checked again on the damage. He found the room one elderly passenger had been occupying right over the explosion was utterly wrecked, with no sign of the man. By now the creaking and groaning of steel plates below in the ship sounded as if she was about to break up so Sime and the Third Officer gave up trying to get forward, four men jumped over and were pulled into lifeboats and the four remaining crew including Captain Sime jumped over from the poop and swam to a liferaft. As they watched, the *Geraldine Mary* tended to right herself, but then broke in two "as she doubled up with her two masts almost touching, turned again onto her side, buckled up again" and eventually sank about two hours after being hit.

One of the escort sloops, HMS *Sandwich*, circled around dropping depth charges, and then picked up the four from the raft about 1130. Captain Sime advised the escort's CO that there were in total three boats with survivors, one of which the sloop found under the Chief Officer with twenty-four men, while another destroyer found a second boat containing four men. The third boat had become separated in the early morning gloom and rough seas and could not be found even after half an hour or more of searching. The escort ships could not risk being away longer from their remaining charges, so had to abandon the search.

After the survivors were landed four days later at Methil on 8 August about 1500, Captain Sime learned that the third boat, under the ship's Bosun, had set sail to the east with sixteen survivors and safely reached the Scottish island of Lewis. Under the circumstances it was a most competent rescue. In all therefore there were only three casualties from *Geraldine Mary* in the sinking, two of the dead from the Merchant Navy.

Salman's *U 52* was on her fifth war patrol under her pre-war submariner captain, when he encountered Convoy HX-60 around midnight on 3 August. He attacked and sank two British ships just after 0230, moved clear in case of counter attack which did not happen, then approached the convoy again and torpedoed *Geraldine Mary* at 0822 local time. These were Salman's only successes on this patrol, although KL Heinrich Schonder in *U 58* sank the Greek steamer *Pindos* from the same convoy 100 miles further northeast at 2020 that evening. Salman returned to Kiel on 13 August. He left U-boats in mid-1941 for BdU administration for the balance of the war, being eventually the Senior A.d.C and Special Advisor to the C-in-C *Kriegsmarine* at the time of Germany's capitulation. Under other COs *U 52* became a training flotilla boat and survived the war.

Those lost: Robert H Barbour, William N Stewart and a passenger, H.C. Thomson

Sources: SCS Master's Interview; Fisher notes, DND; *Lloyd's Register, 1939-1940*; Rohwer, *Axis Submarine Successes*; Busch & Röll, *German U-Boat Commanders*; Wynn, *U-Boat Operations, Vol.1*; correspondence with Capt. Joe Prim, St. John's.

ESMOND

SHIP: 4975 grt, 421 ft. freighter. Built in 1930 by C. Connell & Company Ltd., Glasgow. *Traprain Law* until 1933. Owned by Anglo-Newfoundland Steamship Company Ltd., with Donaldson Bros. & Black (Donaldson Line) of Glasgow and Liverpool as managers.

FATE: Torpedoed by *U 110* on 9 May 1941 when in convoy OB-318 in mid-North Atlantic, 250 miles east of Cape Farewell, Greenland. None lost.

Esmond was the second of Anglo-Newfoundland's ships to be sunk. After delivering a cargo from Canada, she departed Loch Ewe in western Scotland on 4 May in ballast, bound for Sydney, Cape Breton. She was, for 1941, well armed, with a 4-inch and a 3-inch gun, five machine guns of elderly Hotchkiss and Lewis design, two PAC rockets and a kite device. To aid in manning these she carried two DEMS naval gunners and two from the Maritime Regiment, RA. In total, including Captain J.B. McCafferty as Master, there were forty-nine men aboard. All were to survive her sinking.

Seventeen ships had departed Liverpool on 2 May 1941 in Convoy OB-318. They were joined by four more from Milford Haven in South Wales that had come up the Irish Sea, five from the Clyde, and twelve more from Loch Ewe that had already been convoyed around the north of Scotland from east coast ports, including *Esmond*. By 6 May this group set off across the Atlantic steering a northwesterly course, thirty-eight ships in nine columns. The ships were of six nationalities, under Convoy Commodore Mackenzie in *SS Colonial* leading the fourth column. *Esmond* led the starboard column.

Their escort as they crossed Britain's Western Approaches was a strong one, particularly for those days. It came from the 7th (British) Escort Group, B7, comprising three destroyers, a sloop, five corvettes and an A/S trawler, with Cdr I.H. Bockett-Pugh in the somewhat elderly W class destroyer HMS *Westcott* as Senior Officer of the escort. After they had passed well south of the Faeroes and approached 15° West three of the merchant ships broke off from the convoy to head for Iceland.

About this time KL Gerd Schreiber in *U 95* reported an east-bound convoy, SC-29, further to the west. But the Admiralty's Tracking Room, when the U-boat's signal was intercepted, although it could not be instantly broken, thought it might be *Esmond's* OB-318 that Schreiber was reporting. The Admiralty thus ordered a sharp alteration of course to starboard, up to 62° North. However this led it into the view of another searching U-boat, *U 94*, KL Herbert Kuppisch who picked up the ships in the early evening of 7 May. The same afternoon the relief mid-ocean escort group joined—EG-3 under CDR A.J.(Joe) Baker-Cresswell in HMS *Bulldog*, with two more destroyers, three corvettes and two A/S trawlers. This new group included the large ex-liner, the AMC *Ranpurna* in case they were intercepted by a German surface raider. That group brought four more merchantmen out from Iceland to join the convoy and all were efficiently integrated by 10 p.m. on the evening of the 7th, heading west.

The destroyers of the original B7 then left, being short of fuel, a chronic problem of early destroyers. But the sloop *Rochester* and the five corvettes, having refuelled from a ship in the convoy, continued with the new escort group. They were to stay for twenty-four hours then join eastbound convoy HX-123 and return to the United Kingdom. Even with this strong , experienced escort force around the merchantmen of OB-318, in fine weather and ten miles' visibility, *U 94* managed to slip between the two leading destroyers and at 0910 Kuppisch torpedoed two ships, the Holt line's 10,000-ton liner *Ixion* and a Norwegian freighter, *Eastern Star*, loaded with whisky which, sadly, exploded and burned, although the crew were rescued. Kuppisch's boat was detected and attacked astern of the convoy over the next ten hours. Although his boat was damaged, Kuppisch managed eventually to escape by 9:30 on the 8th and pull clear to make repairs and reload his torpedo tubes. Even then he was able to sight another eastbound convoy, HX-126, and report it to BdU and join in its attack, sinking three ships of the nine sunk from that hard-hit convoy. One lost from that group was another Newfoundland freighter, *Rothermere*.

Baker-Cresswell, giving up on his U-boat hunt for the elusive Kuppisch, rejoined the southwest-bound Convoy OB-318 by 4 p.m. local time on the 8th, and released the B7 Group corvettes to go off and help with the HX convoy as planned. For the night he stationed the corvette *Aubrietia* on the starboard wing, the Town class destroyer *Broadway*, the corvette *Nigella*, his own *Bulldog*, another corvette *Hollyhock* and the destroyer *Amazon* across the three mile front of the convoy which was plodding along at its best speed of 8 knots, and the two A/S trawlers, *Daneman* and *St. Apollo* to port and astern of the ships. It seemed a quite adequate defence.

At 8:30 on the morning of the 9th KL Fritz-Julius Lemp in *U 110* and KK Adalbert Schnee in *U 201* had arrived in the area as a result of the sightings and successes reported by Kuppisch. They were now in the convoy's path. As there was no air threat in those early days this far out in the Atlantic, they held a conference on the surface as their two boats rocked close beside each other in the modest ocean swells. Shouting across the space between their boats they agreed that Lemp would attack first and Schnee would follow half an hour later in the confusion of his presumed successes. About 1100 ship's local time, in a short rough sea and moderate visibility, Lemp while submerged closed the convoy from the starboard side. He fired three torpedoes, hitting *Esmond* and the British *Bengore Head* leading the 7th column, 400 yards beyond. Both ships soon settled and were sinking, although with enough time to launch boats and get survivors away.

Esmond had been hit on the starboard side almost immediately in front of the bridge, followed within seconds by a second torpedo just aft. These blew up the hatches from No. 2 and 3 holds, partially wrecked the chartroom and wheelhouse and blew overboard No.1 starboard lifeboat. The force of the explosions passed right through the ship and even punched holes above the waterline on the port side opposite, as had occurred with the *Geraldine Mary*. As the ship began to settle immediately by the bow, the Master gave orders to abandon her in the three remaining boats, although one boat's painter was accidentally released and it drifted away. All the crew got away safely in the other two boats without further trouble. The ship sank about ten minutes after being hit. No.2 starboard boat was shortly picked up by the convoy rescue ship, the Norwegian freighter *Borgfred* which then rejoined the convoy. The men in the Master's boat were rescued by the corvette *Aubrietia* that had circled around in her hunt for the U-boat, and were landed eight days later at Reykjavik, Iceland, from where they eventually reached Canada.

Aubrietia had heard the torpedoes running on her asdics, turned hard a'starboard and at 12:03 gained a contact at once, putting in a ten depth charge pattern attack on Lemp's submerged *U 110* strictly by eye, as there had not been time enough to set up a carefully controlled attack. Although these explosions put his asdic out of commission, the CO cleared the convoy, turned and made another attack at 12:23 on his estimate of where the U-boat would likely be hiding, this time set for depths of 150 to 385 feet. With no asdic, and presuming she had at least driven off the attacking U-boat, *Aubrietia* returned and picked up *Esmond's* survivors from the one lifeboat.

Bulldog and *Broadway* had now swept aft to join in the search and soon got good asdic contacts on the persistent Lemp who had not been able to get away as planned, as his *U 110* had been badly damaged by *Aubrietia's* skilful attacks. The destroyers were setting up an attack when a huge bubble of air and debris arose and Lemp's U-boat surfaced in the middle of it, with men at once leaping down from the conning tower onto her casing. Both destroyers opened fire at once with all weapons, and *Broadway* turned toward the wallowing submarine to ram it. However, Joe Baker-Cresswell appreciated that men were jumping into the sea and the boat was evidently not fighting back but just rolling in the swells. So he called off *Broadway's* plans for ramming by bridge-to-bridge radio. That destroyer sheared aside at the last moment, but not quite soon enough, the U-boat's fore planes slashing into the thin hull plates of *Broadway's* bow and, as she slid down the wallowing submarine's side, also knocking off her port propellor.

All warship commanding officers had been encouraged, if at all possible, to try and board any defeated German U-boat (or surface vessel for that matter) and seize anything such as cypher codes, the Enigma cyphering machine, secret charts or any other equipment and paper of value in the intelligence war. Baker-Cresswell realized that the submarine was being abandoned and although low by the stern did not seem to be sinking. Once again the little *Aubrietia* was assigned to pick up all the swimming U-boat crew, hustling them below while many of *Esmond's* survivors watched with considerable satisfaction. *Bulldog's* whaler was promptly dropped and under S/Lt D.E. Balme and with six sailors, a stoker and a telegraphist, they scrambled aboard *U 110*. Over the course of an hour they removed an absolutely priceless haul of documents, equipment and secret material. The Enigma machine still had the current day's settings on it, subsequently allowing the British at Bletchley Park to break into the German U-boat reporting cypher system. In retrospect it is significant that Captain McCafferty of *Esmond*, who must have watched the whole operation, doesn't mention a word about the subsequent boarding of the U-boat in his Survivor Interview. That secret was perfectly kept until well after the war, in fact for over twenty years. It was vital that the Germans not know anyone had captured or even seen their cyphering tables or equipment, and even more, that the machine codes could be duplicated, which the *Wehrmacht* had assured the Navy would never be possible.

KL Lemp, when he realized the scuttling charges had not detonated and his boat was not about to founder, evidently tried to swim back to it but did not survive. He was the only casualty. And of all those Allies who saw *Bulldog's* boat reach *U 110*, after a serious caution, not a single man mentioned a word of it, and the *Kriegsmarine* never knew that the submarine had been boarded.

Lemp had already caused propaganda problems for the Reich when he sank the Anchor Donaldson liner *Athenia* on the first day of the war, 3 September 1939 with some American passengers aboard. On this last patrol he had left Lorient on 15 April 1941 to operate west of Ireland, sinking one ship, then moved on toward Iceland and encountered Convoy OB-318 on the 8th from Kuppisch's signal, tracking it during the night with Schnee's *U 201*.

Bulldog tried to tow *U 110* for twenty-four hours, but in worsening weather and with the boat leaking from depth charge damages, she foundered during the morning of the next day, 10 May.

With the sinking of two ships just after noon on the 9th, the convoy made two forty-degree turns to port, now steering southeast rather than its planned course of southwest. As arranged, Schnee attacked the convoy, sank one ship and damaged another which nevertheless reached port. Although he heard the distant thud of depth charges, he was unaware of Lemp's disaster and sailed off to continue his patrol. The convoy was attacked again on 10 May just after midnight by *U 556*, KL Herbert Wohlfarth, who torpedoed yet one more which also survived. But he persistently hung onto the convoy and was able to sink two more ships when the convoy, considering it was beyond the operating area of U-boats, was dispersed at first light that morning. Two more of the convoy's ships were sunk by other wide ranging U-boats operating unusually far west on the 24th and 26th of May. Although the hugely valuable cache of secret material had been seized and one U-boat sunk, the convoy had eventually lost eight ships sunk and two more seriously damaged, not counting *Broadway*'s damages.

Those lost: None.

Sources: Captain McCafferty's SCS Survivor Interview; Winton, *Convoy*; *Lloyd's Register, 1939-1940*; Wynn, *U-Boat Operations, Vols. 1 & 2*; Rohwer, *Axis Submarine Successes*; Edwards, *Dönitz And The Wolf Packs*; Roskill, *The Secret Capture*.

ROTHERMERE

SHIP: 5356 grt, 434 ft. freighter, quadruple expansion steam engines. Built in 1938 by C. Connell Company Ltd., Glasgow. Owned by Anglo-Newfoundland Steamship Company Ltd., with Donaldson Bros. & Black of Glasgow and Liverpool as managers.

FATE: Torpedoed by *U 98* on 20 May 1941 when Convoy HX-126 was scattered, 225 miles south of Cape Farewell, Greenland. Nineteen crew lost, plus two DEMS and a passenger.

This almost-new ship was the Anglo-Newfoundland Company's third and final loss of the war, only eleven days after their *Esmond*'s loss, and 370 miles southwest—no great distance in the broad reaches of the Atlantic. She sank so quickly that twenty-two lives were lost. Most of the men came from the United Kingdom.

Like the other ships of Anglo-Newfoundland, *Rothermere* was continuing in her peacetime trade of carrying newsprint to her UK owners, supplemented with a cargo of steel. Bound from Botwood for London she carried 7095 tons of newsprint in

Names of men lost when the Newfoundland freighter *Rothermere* was sunk. No photo of the ship has been located.

(F. Redfern)

rolls, and steel bars. She was armed identically to *Esmond* with 4-inch and 3-inch guns, five machine guns, a PAC rocket launcher and a kite device, again manned by two DEMS and two Maritime Regiment RA gunners. Her Master for this voyage was Captain G.M. Sime who had already survived the sinking of the company's first loss, the *Geraldine Mary* nine and a half months earlier. *Rothermere* carried one passenger and a crew of fifty and sailed 10 May 1941 from Halifax in the twenty-nine-ship Convoy HX-126. All went peacefully until 19 May.

About midnight on the 19th two British ships were torpedoed and an emergency turn was ordered for the convoy, which avoided further attacks that night. However, in overcast but clear weather and in a slight sea, at just after noon on the 20th the freighter *Darlington Court* was hit and sank in about two minutes, followed by the 8500-ton tanker *British Security* which went up in flames, although she did not actually sink for two days. With no U-boats sighted, the Convoy Commodore gave the order to scatter, each ship to make its best speed on diverging courses. From the convoy speed of 9 knots, *Rothermere* soon worked up to almost twelve knots, steering north but weaving as she went. These diversions were not enough to spare the ship and at 1530 she was hit amidships on the port side. A lookout had sighted an approaching torpedo track and had shouted a warning, but too late.

Several hatch covers were blown off, a port lifeboat's whole bottom was blown in and some of the accommodation spaces wrecked. The ship listed to port but then righted herself. The Chief Officer's boat also on the port side had been lifted out of her cradle at right angles and was impossible to launch. Many of these merchant lifeboats weighed a ton or more, with their supplies. The other two boats had problems with launching as, in the confusion and haste, one boat's fore and aft falls were not released at the same moment, pitching some men into the sea when their boat upended. The Captain then ordered the rafts that were secured to the standing rigging released, and most of the crew were able to scramble onto them after jumping into the ocean. The boat that had been swamped when lowered was secured and two or three crew started to bail it out, and others dashed off to get replacement supplies.

Then, about ten minutes after the first, the U-boat put another torpedo into *Rothermere*'s starboard side almost amidships. This explosion again swamped the lifeboat the Chief and Third Officer were bailing. The ship then started to break up, and those in the boat called up to those still aboard, the Master, the Second Officer and the Wireless Officer, to jump over, but they disappeared aft, although throwing down some equipment such as the Master's sextant and some ship's papers and food as the lifeboat drifted aft. Then the remainder jumped over, just as the ship broke in two and sank, the stern section first, then the bow.

With no oars, the Third Officer's boat drifted astern, its crew still bailing out as quickly as possible, with a sea anchor rigged. The Chief Officer's boat which had jammed drifted clear when *Rothermere* sank, so men on one of the rafts, including the Fourth Officer, climbed into it, bailed it out, then rowed around to other rafts collecting food, supplies and men. They then came over to the Third Officer's boat and passed him some of their oars. By this time they realized that there was no sign of the Master, Captain Sime, or the Chief Officer, even after rowing through the debris of the sunken freighter. Night came on, and the two boats stuck together, riding to sea anchors, hoping for someone to rescue them the next day. Indeed during that day two destroyers and a merchantman appeared on the horizon, one destroyer passing within a couple of miles but failing to see the boats' flares in the bright sunlight. On the other hand the ship may have been otherwise engaged, as three more merchantmen were sunk from the convoy's numbers the same day. The survivors passed another night with no rescue in sight, so on the 23rd the two boats set sail for Iceland to the north. Then at 2300 that night lights of a small steamer were seen and all thirty-three survivors were picked up by the Icelandic *Brunafors* which had passed through their area by chance. The *Rothermere* survivors were landed in Reykjavik on the 27th. Sadly, one of those lost was a fifteen-year-old pantry boy, John Sandwell from Essex, England.

KK Robert Gysae was thirty years old when his attack on Convoy HX-126 took place. He had commanded torpedo-boats in the *Kriegsmarine* in the late 1930s and then transferred to U-boats. On his first war patrol in *U 98* he had sunk two ships, and on this his second patrol left Lorient on 1 May 1941. Joining a group of boats attacking Convoy SC-30 southeast of Greenland he succeeded in sinking the 10,500-ton armed merchant cruiser HMS *Salopian*, although it took five torpedoes to put her under. By 19 May *U 94*, KL Herbert Kuppisch, having wreaked havoc on *Esmond's* Convoy OB-318 had moved off and then sighted and reported Convoy HX-126. On BdU's instructions four boats attacked, including Gysae's *U 98* and Wohlfarth's *U 556*. Kuppisch sank two freighters, Wohlfarth two and damaged the large British freighter *San Felix*; KL Wilhelm Kleinschmidt in *U 111* sank another, all between 0300 and 1444 local time on 20 May. Then at 0530 Gysae torpedoed *Rothermere*, taking two torpedoes to ensure her destruction. Kuppisch and Kleinschmidt both had another success, as did two other boats. Gysae claimed another victim, reporting the ship sinking in thirty-three minutes, but it has not been possible to identify any other loss creditable to him. In all Convoy HX-126 lost nine ships, with another damaged but able to reach England, before the U-boats lost contact on 22 May.

U 98 was then sent south to provide a diversion for the breakout of the German battleship *Bismarck* and her attendant cruiser *Prinz Eugen*, and then to try and assist them when *Bismarck* was caught and attacked by British forces. The submarine did not make contact, and returned to St. Nazaire on 29 May. Gysae made several more patrols in this boat, sinking four more ships, his total reaching twenty-four ships in two boats. He was awarded the Knight's Cross with Oak Leaves and appointed ashore in December 1943. He commanded the 25th U-Flotille, and at the war's end was Commander of the 1st Naval Anti-Tank Regiment. He was retained in the Navy after the war by the Allies at Kiel to administer Baltic minesweeping operations until 1947.

U 98 herself was sunk off Gibraltar under another commander in November 1942 by HMS *Wrestler* while trying to disrupt Allied North African landings. There were no survivors.

Those lost:	George M. Sime, Master	Edward F Bissell	John Hector, MC
	Charles I Hinchliff	Thomas Holden	John E Horsley
	Frederick R Jenkins	John Keenan	Herbert Lowther
	Kenneth J MacAskill	Frederick McCallum	Victor D McDougall
	Archibald H McMillan	Werner Olsson	Alexander C Paton
	John B W Sandwell	Arthur B Utting	Thomas D Wallace
	Harry A E White		

Plus two DEMS ratings and one passenger also lost. (Note: In some records the Master's name is shown as George McCartny, but it was actually George McCartny Sime.)

Sources: Third Officer D.M. Kennedy's SCS Survivor Interview; *Lloyd's Register, 1939-1940*. Rohwer, *Axis Submarine Successes*; Wynn, *U-Boat Operations, Vol. 1*; Kurowski, *Knight's Cross Holders*; correspondence with Capt. Joe Prim; *Shipping—Today And Yesterday*, "U-boats target vital tankers," April 2000.

KITTY'S BROOK

SHIP: 4031 grt, 325 ft. two-deck freighter. Built in 1907 by Irvine's Shipbuilding & Drydock Company Ltd., West Hartlepool, England. was ex-*Abonema*, ex-*Sapele*, and ex-*San Jorge* of the Cia Argentina de Nav. Mihanovich Lda. until 1941. Then owned by Bowaters Paper Company of Corner Brook, Newfoundland, registered in St. John's.

FATE: Torpedoed by *U 588* on 9 May 1942 about eighty miles southeast of Lockeport, N.S., near Cape Sable. Nine lost.

This elderly freighter, indicated in tables in the 1939 Lloyd's Register as "no longer capable of 12 knots or more," was acquired in 1941 from her Buenos Aires owners to replace the *Humber Arm* sunk in 1940, as well as offsetting the losses of the Anglo-Newfoundland Steamships. Given her thirty-four years of age, frequent re-builds (her original tonnage was shown as 2881 grt.) and changes of ownership, it was obvious that Bowaters was picking up whatever ships they could locate in a market where demand seriously outstripped availability. New construction merchant ships had not yet even begun to replace the sinkings in the Atlantic battle so far. In 1941-42 *Kitty's Brook* was listed but not classified by Lloyd's, indicating some doubt as to her serviceability, although she was probably classed elsewhere. Most shippers, for easy insurability, had reliable ships classed by Lloyd's Register. But

Kitty's Brook alongside Bowaters' mill at Corner Brook to load rolls of newsprint for England.
(Memorial University)

in the bad days of early 1941, they took whatever was available. In the spring of 1942 *Kitty's Brook* had sailed from St. John's for New York under Captain Jack R. Morbey, late of the torpedoed *Humber Arm*. With a crew of thirty-two, she was loaded mostly with machinery and equipment for American bases in Newfoundland. On 7 May she set off from New York alone, keeping reasonably close to the coast, heading for Halifax and then Argentia on the southeast coast of the island. She was making 9 knots and was carrying out a zigzag from noon on the 9th.

But, on a cold, clear, utterly dark night, with little wind but spitting snow, when some fifty to eighty miles southeast of the tip of Nova Scotia, at about 2120 local time on 9 May (10 May on the U-boat's clocks) she was sighted by KL Viktor Vogel in the Type VIIC *U 588*. With no warning he was able to torpedo the elderly ship, just below and forward of the bridge on the starboard side at No.2 hold, which opened a large hole in her hull and set fire to the cargo. The ship sank quickly, the Captain reported, in less than ten minutes. There was time to lower two lifeboats, a small dinghy-sized "jolly boat" and some liferafts from *Kitty's Brook's* rigging. Most of the crew were, surprisingly, undressed and in bed, so were ill equipped to face the rigours of a small boat in the Atlantic in early May. Also life jackets were in a large storage box on the boat deck so many crew had to leap into the sea or slide into the boats or rafts without them. Captain Morbey ended up in the jolly boat. He was able to get into a lifeboat, as were the men in the jolly boat, but others on a raft simply floated away and were never seen again, including the Chief Officer, William West, an Englishman from London. In fact there were nine casualties. Twenty-three of the crew eventually survived.

These survivors gathered in the two larger lifeboats, let the jolly boat go, and broke out the oars and sails. There was little wind, so they commenced rowing towards Nova Scotia, about eighty-three miles away. They had some biscuits, a little water and some cans of condensed milk. These hardy crewmen were in the boats from Friday night to Sunday morning, when they approached land, having seen not a single or aircraft. They continued rowing right in under the Lockeport lighthouse where they encountered at last two little fishing boats hauling trawls. One boat rescued the men from one of the lifeboats, the other boat took the second one in tow and brought them up harbour to the fish packing plant. The survivors were given the opportunity to wash themselves down after their immersion in the oil from the sunken *Kitty's Brook*, given some fishermen's clothes and taken for a breakfast at a local restaurant. The next day they were on a bus for Halifax. Some had to go into hospital there for the five days, suffering from exposure, especially swollen feet. A few got tired of this attention and simply moved down to the Merchant Seamen's Club. Thence most went back to Newfoundland—and almost right away back to sea. Three of the crew had been on their first trip to sea, two of those lost being only seventeen years old. Only one survivor was seriously injured, from a heavy block falling on his foot.

U 588 was to be Vogel's only U-boat command. He had started in the *Kriegsmarine* in minesweepers and torpedo boats and then in 1941 transferred to the U-boat service. On this his third war patrol, he left St. Nazaire on 19 April 1942 for operations in North American waters where he had been on his previous patrol. He crossed to the Nova Scotia coast, searching off Halifax and encountering *Kitty's Brook* southeast of the province, and then the Norwegian *Skottland* which he also sank. Vogel then moved south along the American coastline where he had no further successes and returned to St. Nazaire on 7 June.

On his next patrol in *U 588*, with other boats, he tried to approach westbound Convoy ON-115 but was detected by HMCS *Skeena*, LCdr Ken Dyer, RCN and the Canadian corvette *Wetaskiwin*, LCdr Guy Windeyer, RCN in the early morning hours of 31 July 1942. In a carefully coordinated attack the two ships sank *U 588*, from which there were no survivors of the forty-six crew.

Those Lost: In an unusual assessment, all but W.J. West are omitted from the Merchant Navy Memorial at Tower Hill in the UK as being members of the "Canadian Merchant Navy," although all of them were from Newfoundland, not then part of Canada.

E L Anderson	William H Anderson	George W Carter
George C Crocker	W Osmond	William J West
Herbert W White	J Whiteway	I Woods

Sources: Parker, *Running The Gauntlet*; Hadley, *U-Boats Against Canada*; Wynn, *U-Boat Operations, Vol.2*; Rohwer, *Axis Submarine Successes*; *RCL Legion Magazine*; Busch & Röll, *German U-Boat Commanders*; Merchant Navy *Book of Remembrance*; D Hist ship's file, Form SA.

WATERTON

SHIP: 2115 grt, 253 ft. laker-style freighter. Built in 1928 by Armstrong Whitworth & Company, Newcastle, England. Owned by Bowaters Newfoundland Pulp & Paper Company of Corner Brook. Registered in St. John's.

FATE: Torpedoed by *U 106* on 11 Oct. 1942 in the Cabot Strait, in Convoy BS-31. None lost.

In 1939 this laker was owned by McKellar Steamships Ltd. with R. Scott Misener of Port Colborne as managers. But war losses of Bowaters Newfoundland led the firm to buy (or possibly long-term charter) the vessel and register her in St. John's, to haul newsprint and wood sulphate pulp between their mill at Corner Brook and other mills and their customers. *Waterton* was noted in Lloyd's as "For service on the Great Lakes & River St. Lawrence, also to St. John's Nfld. and Nova Scotia from 1st April to 30th November."

On Saturday 10 October 1942 she left Corner Brook at 12:30 under Captain William Lutjens and with a crew of twenty-four, plus two DEMS gunners for her 3-inch American-made gun on the after deckhouse. *Waterton* was loaded with a bulk cargo of 2000 tons of wood sulphite pulp and finished newsprint rolls, many of these carried on top of her hatches as deck cargo. She was bound up the St. Lawrence River for Cleveland, Ohio. The vessel joined the smaller Panamanian-flagged laker *Omaha* and their escort, the modern, 181-foot armed yacht HMCS *Vison*, LCdr W.E. Nicholson,

The little laker *Waterton* bought by Bowaters for local pulp and newsprint shipping; in June, 1939 when owned by McKellar Steamships of Port Colborne, Ontario.
(Skip Gillham)

RCNR (ex-RCMP Marine Division), forming Convoy BS-31. The ships were roughly in line abreast, with *Waterton* on the port wing of the group moving at 6 to 8 knots. They proceeded with no problems through the night. The next morning they were joined by a patrolling Canso aircraft, R of 117 Sqn., RCAF. The visibility was good but with some haze and there was a brisk breeze stirring up a considerable chop.

Then at 10:50, when about ten miles southeast of St. Paul's Island off Cape Breton and with no prior warning or sighting of a U-boat or even a torpedo track *Waterton* was hit by two torpedoes, the first just forward of the bulkhead between No.4 hold and the engine room, on the port side aft. There was little explosion to be seen, and the Captain reported looking aft, thinking it might just have been a heavy cross sea hitting them, worried about his deck load of newsprint rolls. Nothing was done at that moment, except the Master sent someone aft to see what had happened. Then a second torpedo hit in No.3 hold with a considerably more startling explosion, throwing up a huge column of water, blowing off hatch covers, throwing ton-weight rolls of newsprint into the sea and bringing down the ship's wireless aerial.

The ship immediately rolled thirty degrees to port and began sinking by the stern, although no-one had been killed. Those in the engine room were able to evacuate it in safety, reporting that the forward bulkhead was bulging. The ship continued to settle and roll slowly to port, so Captain Lutjens ordered her abandoned. The port lifeboat on the after deckhouse had been blown off into the sea, but with difficulty the crew lowered the starboard boat, and four men jumped overboard and climbed onto a liferaft that was dropped from the forward rigging. All this within three minutes of the second explosion.

The Master hurried to the forward wireless office to ensure the operator had got away, or if he had not, to signal to *Vison*. But on his way aft as the ship settled he was washed overboard and left struggling in the swirl and suction of the sinking *Waterton*, clinging to debris, fortunately wearing his life jacket. One of the DEMS gunners, F. Buxton was also in difficulty, maybe having been blown overboard in the explosion, and the Radio Officer dove from the lifeboat to rescue him and haul him to the boat. The Master later noted "This gallant action undoubtedly saved the gunner's life as he seemed on the point of exhaustion." There is no record that the Radio Officer, Mr. Paul, received any award. Two other swimmers reached the damaged and flooded port lifeboat, climbed aboard it and pulled Captain Lutjens in with them, then reached the four men on the liferaft and took them aboard as well. The balance of the crew, twenty men, were safely in the starboard boat.

In the meantime, the Canso, aware of the first torpedo hit from half a mile away at 750 feet, dove toward *Waterton* and was just passing over her when the second torpedo struck, enveloping the aircraft in water and debris thrown up by the explosion. The aircraft captain maintained control with considerable difficulty, circled around but saw nothing of the U-boat that had obviously attacked the little convoy. Nor did he pick up anything on his new ASV radar to indicate a surfaced boat.

A boatload of survivors from the *Waterton*, about to be rescued by the Armed Yacht HMCS *Vison* in the Cabot Strait.

(Fotheringham photo, author's collection)

Meanwhile *Vison* surged over from a mile away on the other wing of the group, and picked up a reasonable asdic contact. Nicholson made one quick attack by eye, dropping one depth charge to discourage any further action by the U-boat, then in very difficult and sporadic asdic conditions typical of the Gulf's mix of fresh and salt water, carried out two more attacks, dropping twelve charges, although one failed to detonate. With no sight or contact of the U-boat, Nicholson returned and picked up all the *Waterton* survivors, firstly from the starboard boat, then after another quick search about the area for their attacker, from the flooded port boat. A Sub Lieutenant in *Vison*, J.B. Fotheringham (later Captain, RCN) noted that the newsprint rolls blown or floated off "looked for all the world like large rolls of toilet paper unrolling across the sea", adding that "It was most frustrating to realize that despite ideal weather conditions, as well as the presence of an aircraft, we were unable to prevent such an event."

Vison then circled *Omaha*, which suddenly discovered she could make almost 9 knots, and they hastened toward Sydney, to be met by another escort ship. This allowed *Vison* to proceed ahead into Sydney with her survivors, arriving at 1800 that day. All were safe, but a well-escorted little convoy had lost fifty percent of its numbers.

Their attacker had been the Type IXB *U 106*, KL Herman Rasch in his last success against Allied shipping. In seven war patrols he sank twelve ships, including CNSS's *Lady Drake* when he was part of *Operation Paukenschlag*. He was unsuccessful after the *Waterton* sinking in any more attacks. In this patrol he had crossed the Grand Banks being continually forced under as his radar device (FuMB) warned him of approaching aircraft. The same had happened off the south Newfoundland coast, so he and OL Hans-Joachim Schwantke in *U 43*, a Type IX boat, had been allowed, at their suggestion to BdU, to enter the Gulf of St. Lawrence. Schwantke penetrated further upriver than any U-boat had done before, just east of Rimouski, but encountered no ships and left without success. *U 106* was not damaged in *Vison's* attacks, but left the Gulf, participated in attempts to attack a Mediterranean convoy without success, and returned to Lorient on 26 December 1942.

After one more unsuccessful patrol, Rasch was appointed to BdU staff, awarded an Iron Cross in December 1942, and at the war's end was commanding a flotilla of the *Kleinkampfverbände*, the midget two-man submarines. He was retained in the post-capitulation Navy for minesweeping duties and then on the staff of the Naval High Command East, being released only in July of 1946.

Those lost: None.

Sources: SCS interview, Captain Lutjens; USN Survivor Interview transcript; Hadley, *U-Boats Against Canada*; notes from Fr. van der Linden; How, *Night of the Caribou*; McKee, *Armed Yachts of Canada*; Lloyd's Register, *1939-40 and 1941-42*; Busch & Röll, *German U-Boat Commanders*; Wynn, *U-Boat Operations, Vol.1*.

CARIBOU

SHIP: 2222 grt, 266 ft 2-deck passenger ferry/freighter, strengthened for operation in ice. Accommodation for about 175 cabin passengers, although able to carry about 240 in cabins and lounge seating. Built 1925 by New Waterways Shipbuilding Company, Schiedam (Rotterdam) Netherlands. Built for and owned by Newfoundland government, Railway and Steamship Dept.

FATE: Torpedoed by *U 69* on 14 October 1942, fifteen miles east of Cape Breton Island, N.S. on normal ferry run between Sydney, Cape Breton and Port aux Basques, Newfoundland. Total of 137 casualties, 31 of them merchant seamen.

The sinking of the passenger ferry *Caribou* was the worst Canadian/Newfoundland merchant disaster of the war, surpassing even the losses from the much larger CNSS passenger freighter *Lady Hawkins* when 109 were lost, and only surpassed in naval losses by those of HMCS *St. Croix* at 146 killed, and *Margaree's* 142 killed. One hundred thirty-seven crew and passengers were drowned or died of exposure in the sinking of *Caribou* on a cold and black October night in the fall of 1942. Only 101 persons survived of the 238 that sailed in her on her normal ferry run between Sydney, Cape Breton and the railway terminus at Port aux Basques in the southwest corner of Newfoundland. It was probably the passenger losses that provoked the intense feeling of unfairness. Naval sailors are expected to go in harm's way, and if they are lost, it is a sad but possible event. Not so for civilians on the simple short passage by ship from one port to another.

Caribou, built at a cost of some $600,000, was an extension of the government-owned railway in Newfoundland that operated the much maligned "Newfy Bullet" from St. John's, 525 miles west and south to the little seaport of Port aux Basques.

The unfortunate ferry *Caribou* on some festive occasion, with flags flying.
(F.McBride/Shipsearch Marine)

A memorial paper produced in St. John's to commemorate
the 31 merchant seamen lost in *Caribou*'s sinking.
(Maritime Museum of the Atlantic)

There the ship and an alternate, the new but smaller ferry *Burgeo* provided a connection across the 90-mile wide Cabot Strait to the Canadian railway system in Nova Scotia. The Canadian Navy operated one of its major convoy escort commands out of St. John's, and flew its aircraft on patrols from Newfoundland airports. The Americans also had several naval and air bases on "The Rock." There was much traffic back and forth on the ferry, civilian Newfoundlanders or native Canadians going to and from duties at wartime bases. Servicemen, Canadians, Americans, Brits and Newfoundlanders moved on leave and duty back and forth. Almost every ferry trip was full to capacity.

The ferry always had a naval escort by 1942, after the depredations of U-boats in the Gulf and St. Lawrence River from May through to September, when a few U-boats managed to sink fifteen merchantmen and two warships in the Gulf. This was played down as much as possible to allay the fears of the civilian populace that the Germans would attack the mainland. The problems in the Gulf and its approaches were dealt with, but were not allowed to draw off vital escorts from the ocean war. The *Caribou* had passed her normal steamship inspection only two weeks before her loss.

On Tuesday 13 October shortly after 1900, 237 souls boarded *Caribou* at her dock at the North Sydney terminal for an overnight passage across to Port aux Basques. Including Captain Ben Taverner and his two sons Stanley and Harold as Mates, there were forty-six in the crew, largely Newfoundlanders, most of them from around Port aux Basques. Also aboard were 118 military personnel, including several American servicemen going on leave to Newfoundland or returning to duty there; and seventy-three civilians, men, women and children. Captain Taverner was about to retire after this voyage and hoped to turn the over to one of his sons. The ship had several cabins and, due to the crowd sailing, even those who had booked a single cabin were asked to share if there were extra bunks. Just as *Caribou's* lines were cast off a last minute passenger raced down the ferry terminal wharf and leapt aboard— Bob Newman, a businessman from Petites. Because the passenger list had already been left ashore, his last minute arrival on board later caused some confusion in numbers, and raised the total on board to 238, the civilian total to seventy-four.

Before sailing, all passengers were shown where emergency facilities such as life jackets and lifeboats were located, but the point was not stressed to avoid unnecessarily disturbing them, and some of the passengers "did not take very kindly to this order." Some knew that the paper-carrier *Waterton* had been sunk two days before not far away, but this too was played down. The ship's escort was to be the 800-ton Bangor minesweeper HMCS *Grandmère*, Lt James Cuthbert, RCNR. A standard escort, capable of anti-submarine attack, for a single on passage.

Grandmère slipped from the Sydney naval dockyard at 2000 local time, passed out through the protective gate half an hour later and at once started an asdic sweep of the wide bay off Sydney Mines in case there was a lurking U-boat. *Caribou* followed her shortly after and at 2130 the two set off to the north then northeast, working up to 12 knots. Observing convoy doctrine orders, *Grandmère* followed *Caribou*, weaving across her track about half a mile astern. The night was black, cold and clear, with visibility out to 2500 yards, about a mile and a half even on a dark night. Both ships could make little more than 14 knots at the most, so there was little speed in hand for emergencies. Ben Taverner didn't like sailing in these waters with reported U-boats about at night, but the Navy insisted it was safer to cross then than in daylight—witness the torpedoing of *Waterton*.

All went peacefully for just under seven hours, the ships about one third of the way across, when with no prior warning, a single torpedo struck *Caribou* amidships on her starboard side (although some of the survivors later thought it was on the port side). There is a few minutes' discrepancy between the three eventual reports, the U-boat's, *U 69*, *Caribou's* and *Grandmère's* but the disaster took place a minute or two after 3:30 a.m. All lighting failed, and the ship began to settle almost at once. The angle of her heel to starboard caused major problems in getting boats away. Nos. 1 and 3 boats, on the starboard side, had been swung out and were demolished by the explosion. Of the useable boats, one, her No.4 boat with a full load of possibly sixty people, capsized as soon as it hit the sea, and although later serving as an inverted raft, all but about five of its passengers were lost. Eventually it was righted, but with the breaking seas was continually filled with water.

No. 2 boat was launched with only a few crew in it, but they were able to man oars and rescued another forty floundering passengers and crew from the icy sea, at the same time having to bail continually. Rafts were promptly released, but with the ship's momentum causing her to still make way through the water, some of these were soon left astern. Aft, on the steerage deck, No. 5 and 6 boats were still swung in and on their chocks. They were quickly filled with terrified passengers and others, sitting in the boats hoping for rescue. The ship's Bosun, Elias Coffin, tried to persuade these people to get out and allow the boats to be launched and probably save them. But his exhortations were to no avail, and the death toll was no doubt higher thereby when the ship sank shortly after.

Some swimmers were able to scramble onto emergency rafts that floated free or hold onto wooden debris when *Caribou* sank in about four or five minutes. The night was black and these few rescue lifeboats and rafts could only search about in the utter dark guided by the cries for help which gradually faded away.

Aboard *Grandmère* the bridge watchkeepers could now see the faint outline of a surfaced submarine some 350 yards to starboard of the smoking and settling *Caribou*, almost a mile from the escort. Lt Cuthbert at once increased speed and attacked the U-boat, which turned away to the southeast and dived almost at once, her CO later recording he thought the shadowy Bangor escort was a destroyer. Cuthbert's action, chasing after the U-boat rather than rescuing survivors, was tactical doctrine, and not to be disobeyed, although this left those survivors from the ferry to fend for themselves. This was to greatly bother him and many of his crew for years afterwards. It was the mere appearance of abandoning those trying to launch the remaining boats and rafts or forced to just jump clear into the bitterly cold water that was to haunt him and others.

Lt. Cuthbert in *Grandmère* increased to 15 knots and when the submarine dived shortly after, dropped a six depth charge pattern by eye right over the swirl where the U-boat dived. He assessed this attack as very close, although as it turned out it did little damage. In fact it was over half a minute between the time the U-boat dived and when the first charges would have exploded, giving the U-boat quite enough time to turn and be 100 yards clear after diving, which was their operating tactic. Although no contact was ever made by the ship's asdic, *Grandmère* dropped two more patterns of three charges each in the general area in the hope of discouraging the U-boat from further attacks. At the same time Cuthbert messaged naval authorities in Sydney that *Caribou* had been sunk. After an hour and forty minutes and still no contact, Cuthbert presumed the U-boat had departed and turned to go back and rescue *Caribou's* survivors. However in the black of night and unable to use a searchlight because of the hazard to his own ship, it was almost three hours after the torpedo had struck that *Grandmère's* crew actually began hauling survivors out of the water. Only one lifeboat had been successfully launched, the others either destroyed in the torpedo's blast, left aboard with people already in them, and one overturned in launching. Several passengers were found clinging to a couple of rafts, others to various bits of wooden debris.

With no other help available, the little escort used her own boats and plucked 103 souls from the lifeboat and the water. Even then two died from exposure after arriving on board. Aircraft arrived after dawn, but no more survivors were ever found... 137 had been lost. Reporting by radio to his senior officer at Sydney and relieved in his searching through the debris for any one left alive by the two armed yachts HMCS *Elk* and *Reindeer*, Cuthbert was ordered back to port at 0920, arriving at the Sydney dockyard at 1540 that afternoon.

The tragedy took many families' lives as well as individuals: two mothers each with their two children were lost. The Master, Ben Taverner and both his sons did not survive. Lost in all were thirty-one crew members, forty-nine civilian men, women and including ten children, forty-nine Canadian and British service personnel including one Nursing Sister, and eight US Forces men. The count is nearly always out by the one civilian passenger who arrived aboard just as *Caribou* sailed and was not included in her sailing manifest. Many bodies, including Captain Taverner's, were recovered and buried in cemeteries near Port aux Basques.

The ship was sunk by the Type VIIC *U 69* on her second last patrol, under KL Ulrich Gräf. Gräf had served in the cruiser *Nüremburg* and destroyers before joining the U-boat service in 1940. He had commanded *U 23* and then *U 69* from March 1942. In his first patrol in this boat he had sunk four ships, including two Canadians, the schooner *James E. Newsom* and the Paterson laker *Torondoc* far to the south. This time, departing his base in St. Nazaire on 15 August 1942 for minelaying in Chesapeake Bay, after completing that task he then moved south to Hatteras, and finding no targets, went north, entering the Gulf of St. Lawrence on 30 September. He encountered Convoy NL-9 near Baie Comeau and sank the Canadian-registered but Finnish freighter *Carolus*, penetrating far upriver, although repeatedly harassed by aircraft patrols which failed to damage him. Gräf was on his way out into the Atlantic on the surface on 14 October when he sighted the shadow of *Caribou* and, stalking her from starboard, hit her amidships with a single torpedo. He thought *Grandmere* was a destroyer, but knowing of the difficulty in detecting him in the freshwater layering of the Gulf, elected to dive and escape. The escort's depth charges did not damage the U-boat which quietly slipped away into the Atlantic.

Off Newfoundland he encountered the Canadian collier *Rose Castle* and fired at her but his torpedo failed to explode. He arrived back in St. Nazaire on 5 November. On 2 January 1943 Gräf sailed on his next patrol for Atlantic operations. After several abortive searches for convoys, on 17 February the group he was assigned to intercepted and was setting up to attack Convoy ONS-165 southwest-bound for Canada. But *U 69* was detected by HMS *Fame* east of Newfoundland and sunk with no survivors of her crew of forty-six. In initial historical reports *U 69* was recorded as sunk by HMS *Viscount*, but in a search of German records it was shown that *Viscount* attacked *U 201* which she also sank. In any case, Gräf and *U 69* sank more Canadian ships than any other U-boat throughout the war, but paid the ultimate price as well.

Those Lost: The list includes merchant seamen and women only. In some lists Victor Lamend is shown, but this is a duplication for V.W. Lomond

Ben Taverner, Master	Israel Barrett	Lewis Carter
Elias G Coffin	James H Coffin	Howard Cutler
Richard Feltham	Bride Fitzpatrick	Charles Ford
Maywell French	George Gale	Jerome Gale
Clarence Hann	Harry G Hann	William P Hogan
Charles Humphries	Victor W Lomond	Thomas Moyst
Charles Pearcey	R T Pike	James L Prosper
Joseph Richards	William R Samms	Israel Sheaves
John W Skeard	Albert B Strickland	Garfield Strickland
Harold Taverner	Stanley Taverner	Arthur Thomas
George A Thomas		

Sources: Cuthbert, *Report of Proceedings*, 15 Oct.'42; How, *Night of the Caribou*; Yorke, *Nova Scotia Historical Review*, 1985; *Lloyd's Register, 1941-42*; Wynn, *U-Boat Operations, Vol.1*; Busch & Röll, *German U-Boat Commander*; Hadley, *U-Boats Against Canada*; D Hist files, Merchant Ships, General; Prim & McCarthy, *Those In Peril*; conversation with Captain John Smith, Ottawa.

LIVINGSTON

SHIP: 2115 grt 253 ft. lake freighter. Built in 1928 by Armstrong Whitworth & Company of Newcastle, England for Canadian Great Lakes shipping operators McKellar Steamships Ltd./R. Scott Misener Ltd of Port Colborne, Ont. as managers. She was owned or on long-term charter by Bowaters Newfoundland Pulp & Paper when sunk.

FATE: Torpedoed by *U 541* at the south end of the Cabot Strait between Cape Breton and Newfoundland on 3 Sept 1944. Twelve or thirteen crew lost, plus one DEMS.

    This is another late war loss for which there is only a very modest amount of information. With the war against the U-boats obviously being won the naval authorities no longer required extensive reports. The only detailed record in this narrative comes from secondary sources.

    Livingston had been acquired by Bowaters Newfoundland Pulp & Paper Mills Ltd. of St. John's to replace their lost ships *Humber Arm*, *Kitty's Brook* and *Waterton*, all sunk between 1940 and 1942. That company had also been assigned the ex-German freighter *Christenson Doreen*, seized on 3 September 1939 at Botwood when war was declared on Germany. Also she may have been registered in England at the time of her loss, but is included with the other Bowaters ships.

The laker *Livingston*, taken up by Bowaters from McKellar like their *Waterton* and lost in the Gulf.
(Pier Museum)

On *Livingston*'s last voyage, under Captain Reuben T. Robinson and with a crew of twenty-six, almost all from Newfoundland, and two RN DEMS gunners, she had been briefly in slow Convoy ONS-251 from the UK but left it outside Halifax, bound for St. John's with a general cargo of supplies, including cement for the American base at Fort Pepperrill. She was on charter to the US Army Newfoundland Command. Often she had brought supplies from the Great Lakes and St. Lawrence to Bowaters mills in Newfoundland and took newsprint to their customers. She was armed with a 3-inch 12-pounder gun. One Royal Navy DEMS rating from Ireland was killed in her sinking, another wounded and sent to hospital.

Well before dawn on 3 September, *Livingston* was sailing alone 110 miles east of Cape Breton when apparently KL Kurt Petersen in *U 541* was alerted by a briefly shown light from the steamer. He then tracked her for almost an hour in what Dr. Hadley in *U-Boats Against Canada* calls "a relentless game of cat-and-mouse," firing at least two torpedoes which the crew of the steamer saw and which proved faulty, one passing under the without exploding, the other, according to the ship's Chief Officer, hitting the forepeak but also not detonating. The Master steered evasive courses to try and avoid further attacks, but his ship was capable of only about 5 knots, one third of the U-boat's surfaced speed. Petersen eventually, at 0425 and just before dawn, hit her on the starboard side aft in the engine room with a successful shot from 350 yards. The ship settled quickly by the stern, broke up and sank rapidly in about two minutes, with thirteen casualties, six from the engine room crew alone.

Four crew had been blown over the side into the ocean by the explosion, along with one of the ship's lifeboats. Albert McKay clambered into that boat and was able to rescue the other three, all quite seriously injured, one being the DEMS rating. Forward, the Master and four more crew launched one of the two fishing dories the ship also carried, and they were able to rescue four of the crew holding onto hatch covers or emergency rafts. These then all climbed into the larger lifeboat, and set sail before the prevailing wind for St. Pierre, 110 miles away to the northeast. Since no emergency signal had been sent, no-one ashore was even aware that *Livingston* had been sunk. Survivors reported that the U-boat had surfaced and looked over the wreckage by searchlight without noticing their dory, and then later had followed them submerged as they saw its periscope on two occasions.

These survivors were rescued by chance around noon, about eight hours after taking to their boat, by the corvette HMCS *Barrie*, being protected by the Bangor escort HMCS *Shawinigan*. Fortunately the two warships had been escorting the troopship *Lady Rodney*, bound for St. John's. Lt Wilfred Stokvis stopped his *Barrie* to rescue the men in the lifeboat, and shortly after stopped again to lower her whaler to transfer the injured; this later was reported by one of *Barrie*'s officers, Lt Bill Waldron, that "it was a this point that my hair started to turn grey!" since the survivors reported seeing the periscope during the dawn hours. In fact, just after this an asdic contact was obtained and *Barrie* carried out a hedgehog attack without observable results. A doctor from *Lady Rodney* came over to *Barrie* and transferred the more severely injured seamen to the larger ship for treatment. *Barrie* on this occasion picked up one survivor who had also survived the sinking of the Newfoundland ferry *Caribou*, and Stokvis had been one of the officers in the Bangor escort *Grandmère* that rescued her pitifully few survivors. These *Livingston* crew were landed at St. John's on 5 September where the injured were taken to hospital. All of those rescued survived. *Shawinigan* herself was to be sunk with no survivors of her crew of ninety-one two and a half months later in the same area. *Barrie* survived the war.

Petersen was *U 541*'s only CO from her commissioning in March 1943. He made four war patrols and managed to sink only one ship, the unfortunate *Livingston*. This was his third patrol, on which he had left his base in Lorient, France on 6 August for operations in Canadian waters. Attacks in the Gulf of St. Lawrence by a predecessor boat, *U 802* had indicated to Canadian authorities that U-boats were again planning on entering the Gulf, renewing their 1942 series of attacks there. In fact shore authorities credited that boat with sinking *Livingston*, as they did not yet know about *U 541*. The U-boat commanders reported that anti-submarine measures, apart from overflights by hunting aircraft, were "extraordinarily light." *U 541*, apart from reporting *Barrie*'s unsuccessful attack, was sighted by aircraft on 28/29 August off Cape Sable Island but no serious attack developed. One report says Petersen was in fact searching for *Lady Rodney*'s convoy, directed to it by BdU code-breakers.

The series of misses on Petersen's boat is an example of the difficulty in effectively attacking a well-handled U-boat. After sinking *Livingston* Petersen hastened away, surfacing on 7 September to attack another ship. He was clearly sighted by HMCS *Norsyd* which attacked the surfaced boat by oerlikon gunfire without seriously damaging it. Petersen was hunted without success by C-6 Escort Group as well as by EG-16's seven ships, and by aircraft, which tried to prevent the U-boats from entering the Gulf, again without any success or even contact. *U 541* entered the Gulf of St. Lawrence anyway and joined *U 802*, with both operating off Anticosti Island and protected by the fresh water–salt water layering problems. They found no further targets and *U 541* exited by the Cabot Strait again and returned, part of the way under the edge of Arctic ice, via Norway to Flensburg in Germany by 11 November 1944. The boat made no more war patrols, and both the U-boat and Petersen survived the war. Other U-boats entered the Gulf that fall, but had only modest success, one damaging the RCN frigate *Magog* by a GNAT torpedo.

Those lost: Although this comprises the list of the twelve casualties in official records, Ronald O'Brien's name was found in NCSO St. John's message traffic as a casualty. No other trace of him is found elsewhere.

Lloyd J Bishop   Gordon K Carew   Michael Carew

Cecil G Clarke   H James Clarke   G Baden Cunning

Hubert Fry   Oscar Neilson   Charles R Pieroway

Samuel A Raike   Hubert Short   Arthur H Thomas

Plus one RN DEMS gunner, L.F. Shirley.

Sources: Hadley, *U-Boats Against Canada*; *Legion Magazine*, May/June 1998; Milner, *The U-Boat Hunters*; Lamb, *On The Triangle Run*; *Lloyd's Registers, 1939-40* and *1941-42*; Runyan & Copes, *To Die Gallantly*; Wynn, *U-Boat Operations, Vol.2*; D Hist files; Rohwer, *Axis Submarine Successes*; Prim, *Those In Peril*; USN Survivor Interview transcript; article by Bill Waldron, NOAC Windsor's *Voicepipe*, summer 2003.

CHAPTER 18

Some Ships Sunk "By Other Means" Three Not Canadian Registered

"God knows! I have, in my own person, done my full duty."
But when he had to stand at the bar of the House of Commons
and defend the conduct of the Navy Office ... he spoke confidently
and fluently.

—Geoffrey Trease, *Samuel Pepys And His World*

The preceding chapters are the stories of Canadian and Newfoundland registered ships sunk or seized by the enemy, German and Japanese. The following sections record some ships which were not Canadian registered, or were lost due to other causes, even if these were war-related. They quite often appear in lists of Canadian merchantmen sunk due to enemy action, but either they were sunk "by other means" or were not Canadian-registered.

NEREUS AND PROTEUS

These two mysterious ships have appeared on many lists of Canadian ships lost to the enemy. Canadian they certainly were, albeit only recently, and they sank with the loss of about 119 lives. But lost to the enemy? It does not appear so on careful and recent re-examination.

These two were elderly ex-US Navy colliers. *Nereus* and *Proteus* both commissioned into that Navy within a day of each other in September 1913 at Newport News Shipbuilding & Dry Dock, becoming their type and hull numbers AC 10 and AC 9, as auxiliary colliers. Each was of 6275 grt (10,650 dwt), 522 feet, and capable of carrying 11,800 tons of coal. By 1924 both were laid up as being less than modern and no longer required as the Navy converted largely to oil-fired engines. They are also sometimes confused with two other ships of the same names in Lloyd's Registers of 1939 to 1942 which were never Canadian owned, one being a German tanker, the other a much smaller Norwegian ship.

In a desperate search for additional shipping, both of these colliers were discovered idle, bought in February and March 1941 by the Canadian government and assigned to Saguenay Terminals Ltd. as managers for the Aluminum Company of Canada. They were at once put to hauling bauxite for the parent company's aluminum smelters from a transshipment point at St. Thomas in the American Virgin Islands to Portland, Maine.

Proteus, under Scottish Captain Walter H. Millar, sailed northbound for New England in late November 1941. Not a single word or artifact was ever had from her again—she utterly disappeared at sea about 23 November 1941. *Nereus* also sailed seventeen days later, at the beginning of December, and also completely disappeared by 10 December. No survivors were ever discovered of their total combined crews of between 115 and 119 souls, nor was any wreckage ever seen that was identifiable with the ships. The ships were not being escorted at the time of their loss. Initial Allied reports at the time put their loss down to U-boat torpedoes. However even Allied intelligence soon determined there were no U-boats operating along their paths at that time, nor, by radio intercepts, were there any claimed sinkings by any U-boat or German surface craft. Then it was thought maybe sabotage could have occurred, but there was nothing factual to support this. And so it has been recorded.

In the late 1960s Rear Admiral George van Deurs, USN (Ret'd) had been studying, with the availability of post war records, various ex-USN ships that had just disappeared. He located some, but not *Cyclops* or the Canadians *Nereus* and *Proteus*, all relatively sister-ships. He recalled that when he had served in the similar collier *Jason* that she tended to work badly, to twist, when in any kind of a following sea or especially in a heavy quartering sea. The ships were built without fore-and-aft bulkheads for stiffening, but did have heavy I beams, almost like railroad tracking, which ran the length of the ship just inside the skin. In *Jason* in 1932 a seaman's chipping hammer pierced the hull plating and dropped inside. On closer examination it was found that the sulphurous coal had not only eaten away several layers of hull plating but also most of the stiffening I beams. The three studied, all of similar age and design, had become quite unsafe, although this was unrecorded in official documents.

Although *Nereus* and *Proteus* had not encountered any severe storms on their last voyages, the US Navy Oceanographic Office noted that they had passed through a moderate cold front with winds of 30 to 40 knots, the front moving fast enough to outrun the waves the winds kicked up. Thus without warning the ships met head winds followed by relatively high seas. In each case the waves would have been roughly half a ship's length apart so that with the load of heavy bauxite concentrated fore and aft (the ships had mid-ships engine rooms), they were being supported by waves at each end, hence sagging in the centre and, no longer with the supporting I beams, breaking in half in moments. With a bulk cargo such as bauxite, there would have been no chance to launch boats and with the wind and sea, any modest debris would soon be dispersed.

With no German claims of their sinking and no evidence of sabotage, certainly not in their loading ports in the West Indies, but at a time when the world was stunned by the Japanese attack on Pearl Harbor it is likely that the reporting offices decided that sabotage was the most plausible cause and a convenient rationalization, and closed their files.

Source: Admiral van Deurs' articles appear in the US Naval Institute *Proceedings* of January 1970 and in the *Naval Engineers' Journal* for October 1974; Official *Dictionary of American Naval Fighting Ships*; and this is all summarized with similar losses in John Harris's book *Without Trace*. It would seem likely that corrosion was the cause of these ships' loss, and it is so accepted here.

CANADIAN PACIFIC SHIPS

Most CP ships were not Canadian registered but registered and even crewed in Great Britain, as this was where most of CPR's financing originated. Apart from the two ships covered in Chapter 10, *Empress of Asia* and *Princess Marguerite*, CP's other lost ships were either transferred outright to the Royal Navy (*Montcalm* and *Montclare*) and survived, or the ten ships listed below were lost as British ships, including the largest merchant sunk, the *Empress of Britain*. In all CP had twenty-two ships taken up for war service. The following were their losses:

Empress of Britain: lost 28 October 1940. Set afire by aircraft on 27 October, then torpedoed by *U 32* north of Ireland.

Empress of Canada: lost 14 March 1943. Torpedoed by *Leonardo da Vinci* in Gulf of Guinea, off Liberia.

Duchess of Atholl: lost 10 October 1942. Torpedoed by *U 178*, South Atlantic, near Ascension Isld.

Duchess of York: lost 11 July 1943. Sunk by aircraft off Moroccan coast.

Beaverburn: lost 5 February 1940. Torpedoed by *U 41* southwest of Ireland.

Beaverford: lost 5 November 1940. Sunk by *Admiral Scheer* in mid-Atlantic.

Beaverbrae: lost 25 March 1941. Sunk by aircraft northwest of Scotland.

Beaverdale: lost 1 April 1941.Torpedoed by *U 48* in Atlantic southwest of Iceland.

Niagara: lost 18 June 1940. Mined at Hauraki Gulf, New Zealand.

Montrose: lost 2 December 1940. Torpedoed by *U 99* when serving with RN as **HMS *Forfar***, an armed merchant cruiser. Had been requisitioned in September 1939. 184 men lost, 220 survivors.

OCEANS, FORTS AND PARKS

As described in Chapter 15, none of the Canadian-built Ocean or Fort ships remained under Canadian registry during the war. Their losses are given in other references. Two Parks, *Greenhill Park* and *Silver Star Park* were lost due to marine accident, albeit while on war service (see below), and while *Nipiwan Park* was only half lost, her story was included in Chapter 14 with the other fully lost Parks.

Other Park Ships

There were two Park ships that became constructive total losses attributable to their war services and its dangers, although not due to enemy action:

Greenhill Park, a Victory type 10,000-ton dry cargo freighter, was launched as the *Fort Simcoe* for the US Maritime Authority, but re-named before delivery and turned over to Park Steamships Ltd. On 6 March 1945 at Vancouver, while loading she caught fire in No.3 hold just aft of the bridge, which spread forward causing explosions on board. She was beached to prevent her sinking. Refloated and sold to Greek interests, she was rebuilt as *Phaeax II*. Two crew and six longshoremen lost their lives, and the tug Master who towed her clear from her downtown berth, Captain Harry Jones, received an MBE.

Silver Star Park, another 10,000-ton dry cargo freighter, was badly damaged in a collision with the US freighter *Mangore* and caught fire off New Bedford, Mass., on 12 April 1945. The unfortunate *Mangore* had already gone aground on April 5th at Barnegat, north of Atlantic City and required assistance. In the collision fifteen crew and one DEMS gunner lost their lives, including the Master, the Second Officer, a Wireless Officer, Bosun and Chief Engineer. There were twenty-nine survivors of the explosion and fire. *Silver Star Park* was repaired, rebuilt and sold to the Brazilian Navy as the supply *Santa Cecilia*.

Source: Heal, *Conceived in War, Born in Peace.*

Fort Ships

The following Fort ships were lost due to enemy action, all registered in Britain, with largely British crews, although most were still Canadian-owned:

Fort Athabaska was bombed and destroyed at Bari, Italy, 2 December 1943 when two other merchantmen of the thirteen alongside, both loaded with ammunition, exploded during an air raid. Of forty-six crew and ten Navy and Army DEMS, forty-six were killed. Of ships in port, seventeen were sunk, six damaged extensively in one of the War's most disastrous shipping calamities.

Fort Bellingham was torpedoed in Convoy JW-56A to Russia, 25 January 1944 by *U 360* and *U 957*. She was sunk next day by HMS *Offa*. Of the crew of forty-five, plus twenty-three Navy and Army DEMS and the Convoy Commodore and six staff, for a total of seventy-five, there were thirty-six survivors.

Fort Gloucester, although torpedoed while in Convoy FTM-70 from the Normandy beaches on 18 August 1944, bound for the Thames, was abandoned at first by her crew, but the was re-boarded, towed in and repaired. Thus she was not "lost."

Fort Missanabie was torpedoed in the Mediterranean on 19 May 1944 by *U 453* while in Convoy HA-43 of forty ships, with five Italian corvettes as escort. She was hit and her bridge demolished, No.2 hold flooded, at which point she broke up. Of her crew of forty-seven, plus seven Navy and seven Army DEMS, there were twelve men killed, forty-nine survivors. She had almost broken up before, at the same point in her hull, from stress of weather during a Russian convoy, so there was criticism by her officers of her construction.

Fort Norfolk was sunk by a mine off the Normandy beaches, 24 June 1944. The bottom-laid mine exploded under her engine room and stokehold while she was under way, following another ship. Of her crew of fifty-two plus the unusually large number of twenty-one DEMS, seven crew and one DEMS gunner were lost. The survivors were rescued by US Navy motor launches.

Fort Maisonneuve was mined and sunk in the Scheldt estuary 15 December 1944. No record seen of casualties.

Fort Qu'Appelle was torpedoed by *U 135* halfway between Bermuda and Nova Scotia on 17 May 1942.

Fort St. Nicholas was torpedoed right aft in No.5 hold, in the Mediterranean off western Italy on 15 February 1944 by *U 410*. She was sailing independently from Naples to Salerno with 4000 tons of military supplies. Of her crew of forty-nine plus six Naval and eight Army DEMS, there were no casualties.

FORT LOST DUE TO WAR SERVICE, BUT NOT FROM ENEMY ACTION

Fort Stikine was loaded with munitions, she caught fire in No. 2 hold and exploded at Victoria Dock, Bombay on 14 April 1944, destroying five other ships and setting eleven afire in a blast as powerful as the December 1917 Halifax Explosion, destroying much of the Bombay waterfront. Similar to the Bari incident involving *Fort Athabaska* above.

Source: D Hist files, and USN OPNAV Survivor Interview records.

REGISTERED ELSEWHERE OR LOST "BY OTHER MEANS"

For various reasons, mostly financial and tax reasons, many Canadian-owned ships were registered offshore. CP registered most of theirs in Britain; Imperial Oil Ltd. registered most of the tankers assigned to that company by the Canadian government in Panama, thus making their crewing easier and less costly, as well as providing tax advantages.

Many ships later sunk during the war do not appear in the foregoing chapters for reasons of space. Some of those ships appear on memorials, on lists of "Canadian" ships sunk, or in the Merchant Navy *Book of Remembrance*, and below are a few examples of these.

Western Head was an elderly (1919) 2599 grt, 251 ft. oil-fired freighter, ex-*Bartholomew* and ex-*Cumberland* until 1939, owned under *Cumberland* and her later name by the Maritime Navigation Company of Liverpool, N.S., but registered in Nassau, Bahamas. Sunk by *U 107*, KL Harald Gelaus on his third patrol on 28 May 1942, in the Windward Passage between the east end of Cuba and Haiti with heavy loss of life. This U-boat had already sunk the Canadian *Maplecourt*.

Nerissa was owned and registered in Bermuda, a passenger liner of some 5583 grt. While not Canadian, when sunk she was carrying a large contingent of Canadian soldiers and with several Canadians in her crew. Her name figures distressingly frequently in lists of Canadians lost at sea. Sunk by *U 552*, KK Erich Topp (one of the U-boat arm's leading aces) on 30 April 1941 northeast of Rockall, 300 miles west of Scotland.

The following examples are schooners lost due to convoy collisions. This is probably a partial list, as others may have been lost but not identified as due to collisions:

Flora Alberta was a Smith & Ruhland-built auxiliary-powered schooner out of Lunenburg, 93 grt, 133 ft., built in 1940 for Captain Guy Tanner on sixty-four shares. Twenty-one lives were lost of twenty-eight on board in a collision with the Belfast based Ulster Steamship Company's (the "Head Line") SS *Fanad Head* in Convoy HX- 235 on 21 April 1943. The *Flora Alberta* had sailed for fishing on the Grand Banks on the evening of Saturday 17 April. Arriving ninety miles south-southeast of Sambro lightship, she stopped and her twelve two-man dories commenced long line fishing. For three days they took aboard 90,000 lbs of fish, and on the evening of Tuesday 20 April after a modest haul, helm was put hard up and the schooner drifted for the night. On Wednesday there was dense fog and a rising sea, but Capt. Tanner headed westerly to another fishing location. At just before 0500 a.m. they were hit by *Fanad Head* with only about thirty seconds' warning, the steamer cutting the schooner in half at the fore rigging. Both were sounding fog horns or whistles, although the frequency was argued later in court hearings. Eight men escaped the shattered halves of the schooner by leaping into the frigid sea and seizing debris or dories that had floated free. One survivor, James Malloy, was to die later in the rescuing lifeboat from the *Fanad Head*. Twenty had died on board the schooner, mostly in their bunks below although one watchman, Henry Best, who got away into the ocean was never seen again. The steamer dropped a lifeboat which rescued seven men within the hour and one man, John Reinhart, was hauled aboard with a rope tied to a life ring.

The *Eva U. Colp*, a 92-ton Newfoundland coastal trading schooner, was also run down by a convoy ship, in the black of night at 2 a.m. on 13 June 1942. She was coasting eight miles southeast of Flint Island, near Sydney, Cape Breton, when she found herself in the path of a small convoy. Although she turned on lights and sounded a hand-operated fog horn, the small Norwegian freighter *Aun* struck her aft on the port side. Three of the crew were able to scramble to safety up ropes and cargo straps hanging down the freighter's side. The Master, Captain Will Thornhill, and the mate stayed aboard the now sinking schooner to rescue the ship's papers and log, and were able to take to a dory as their schooner foundered ten minutes after the collision. They too were taken aboard the *Aun* and into Sydney the next morning.

The barquentine **Mariana**, taken from the Vichy French at sea and then commanded by Captain Isaac Thornhill of Newfoundland, was carrying a cargo of fluorspar from the St. Lawrence to Sydney when she was run down by an inbound convoy in dense fog and sunk in 1942, fortunately with no loss of life.

The large schooner **Lillian E. Kerr** (521 grt), owned by J.L. Publicover and registered in La Have, Nova Scotia, with W.J. Publicover as her Master, was run down about 2330 on 12 November 1942 by the American 4869-ton steamer *Alcoa Pilot* of convoy HF-13, Halifax to St. John, N.B., southwest of Nova Scotia in the Gulf of Maine. One crewman, the mate John Parker Richards was picked up but died without regaining consciousness. All the rest of her crew of eight or nine perished. The *Alcoa Pilot* was port leading ship in an eight ship convoy, with three RCN corvette escorts, none of which detected the schooner before she was hit and cut in half.

Sources: Dr. the Rev. Gregory P. Pritchard, *Collision At Sea*; Garfield Fizzard, *Unto The Sea*; Parsons, *Lost At Sea, Vol.2*; correspondence with Rob Fisher.

St. Lindsay: This appears on some "Canadian" lists, but she was owned by St. Quentin Shipping Company of Cardiff, Wales and managed by a Cardiff shipping company when sunk on 13 June 1941 by *U 751* in mid-Atlantic. The U-boat reported her as exploding, but without identifying the ship, which also went missing on that date. She had been built in 1921 at Wallace Shipbuilding and Dry Dock, North Vancouver as *Canadian Highlander*, which is probably what causes the confusion.

The ex-French 2594 grt. lumber carrier **Lisieux**, (ex-*Murnami*) is another ship sometimes appearing in Canadian war losses. Although seized from the Vichy French like the *Angelus* (see Chapter 13), she foundered in heavy weather off Newfoundland on 27 September 1940. Of her crew of twenty-nine, only nineteen survived after twenty hours in a lifeboat, rescued by the Norwegian freighter *Bernard*. Two had died in the lifeboat.

Reine Marie Stewart is a 1087-ton schooner with a Canadian connection, owned by R.A. McLean and originally registered in Yarmouth, N.S., but whose registry was changed to Panamanian in 1941. She was sunk by gunfire from the Italian submarine *Da Vinci*, Captain Luigi Longanesi-Cattani, on 2 June 1942 just off Freetown, Sierra Leone. There is nothing in the records about any casualties.

Source: Correspondence with C.B. Ellwood, Australia; Rohwer, *Axis Submarine Successes*.

FOREIGN-OWNED

In some records (Rohwer, *Axis Submarine Successes* and Wynn, *U-Boat Operations*) the ex-Danish little 1555 grt freighter *Randa* is shown as "Canadian." But in Lloyd's for 1942 she is still recorded as owned by J. Lauritzen of Esbjerg, Denmark. Since that country was by then long overrun by Germany, it is possible that *Randa* was, like *Carolus*, *Europa* and others, assigned to Canadian management. But she appears on no official lists seen of lost "Canadian" ships.

She was sunk by *U 207*, OL Fritz Meyer, when in Convoy SC-42 on 11 September 1941 just after midnight when southeast of the Greenland ice barrier. Although her position in this substantial convoy was 113 (third in the 11th column) it seems she had dropped back to rescue survivors of other sunken ships when attacked herself. The convoy had already been under serious attack since 8 September by some eight U-boats which had sunk thirteen ships and damaged another three before *Randa* was hit. The submarines went on, over the next eight days, to sink another five ships including one of those damaged earlier.

Randa's attacker, after sinking three ships, surfaced astern of the convoy, was sighted by the British destroyers HMS *Leamington* and *Veteran* and herself sunk with no survivors of her crew of forty-one.

The mystery deepens when it is noted that Dr. Rohwer in his reference places only a question mark after *Randa*'s name, not a "sunk" or "damaged" although the Senior Officer of the escort force noted her as sunk, and Wynn and Rohwer both presume it must have been by Meyer's *U 207* as that was the only boat that didn't have the chance to report her sinkings. In addition, the Canadian Veterans Affairs website shows one *Randa* fatality, Bertram Berkoid, but on 20 July 1942, almost a year later. The Commonwealth War Graves Commission records show no names for *Randa*.

IMPERIAL OIL'S PANAMANIAN-FLAGGED SHIPS

Like Canadian Pacific, Imperial Oil Ltd. operated tankers under non-Canadian registry, in its case Panamanian, at the behest of the Canadian Government Merchant Marine. Two of these ships were lost, oddly enough both due to mines:

Joseph Seep was mined in the approaches to Le Havre on 24 May 1940 while anchored, awaiting instructions to depart during the evacuation of France. Mines had been dropped by German aircraft three days before.

James McGee was mined in the Bristol Channel off Wales, in convoy going up to discharge her oil cargo, on 20 June 1940. Also sunk by aircraft-laid mines.

N.M. PATERSON'S OTHER LOST SHIPS

Hamildoc foundered in heavy weather off Trinidad, loaded with 3300 tons of bauxite on 1 January1943. Because of boiler tube problems, the ship anchored about halfway between British Guyana and Trinidad on 28 December 1942. Water leaked into her ballast tanks, and just as the American freighter *Freeman* arrived alongside she broke in two and sank. Although there was considerable confusion in abandoning her, there were no casualties. It is interesting, and probably typical, that although her normal draft was fourteen feet, in this bauxite trade she was loaded deeper, to sixteen feet.

Mondoc was grounded and a constructive total loss after striking a submerged object, possibly Darien Rock, off the coast of Trinidad on 5 October 1941.

Soreldoc was sold outright to the USA, registered by US Maritime Commission in Panama and employed as a US Army stores transport for American forces in France. She was torpedoed and sunk by the Type VIIC *U 1302*, KL Wolfgang Herwatz, on 28 February 1945 in lower St. George's Channel off southwest Wales. There were fifteen casualties, including the Master; twenty-one survivors, all Americans. *U 1302* was then sunk herself on 7 March by three frigates of the Canadian 25th Escort Group (A/S.O. LCdr H.L. Quinn, RCNVR), with no survivors. There is some doubt about this case, as Wynn's record of *U 1302*'s patrols doesn't record the sinking of *Soreldoc* at all, and John Paterson (the Senator's son) flying a Spitfire off the French coast reported a Paterson ship run aground over there, which he presumed could only have been *Soreldoc*.

CANADIAN NATIONAL STEAMSHIPS' OTHER LOSSES

Lady Somers was sold outright for war service to the British Admiralty, and served as an armed ocean boarding vessel, her Royal Navy crew containing many Newfoundlanders. *Lady Somers* was sunk on 15 July 1941 by the Italian submarine *Morosini* operating out of German-occupied French bases, just north of the Azores.

Lady Nelson was hit by a torpedo, flooded and settled in relatively shallow water in the harbour at Port Castries, St. Lucia, on 10 March 1942, with four casualties. It was fired by KL Albrecht Achilles in *U 161* who hit another British merchant at the same time. *Lady Nelson* was patched, raised, repaired and became a hospital ship.

WRECKED ASHORE, NOT LOST TO THE ENEMY

R.J. Cullen. This ship of 6973 grt. owned by Atlantic Transportation Ltd. of Montreal, was driven ashore on 15 January 1942 on Barra Island in the Outer Hebrides in a tremendous gale when outbound from the UK with Convoy ON-57. The fifteen ships had left Liverpool on 13 January and the gale lasted for several days, from at least the 15th to the 21st of January. The ships were light, in ballast, and *R.J. Cullen* which simply lost her propellor, and four others all were wrecked ashore off the Hebrides. The next convoy, ON-58 is noteworthy as having returned to harbour because of the weather, one of the very few of the thousands of convoys to which that precaution was applied. (Hague, *Allied Convoy System*, p. 156.)

Watkins F. Nisbet. See Chapter 11 on St. Lawrence and Upper Lakes Shipping losses for the brief story on this ship's loss at South Wales on 6 December 1940.

> Our revels now are ended...
> These our actors, as I foretold you,
> Were all spirits, and
> Are melted into air, into thin air.
>
> —Shakespeare, *The Tempest*

Appendix

TABLE 1

A Summary of Canadian and Newfoundland Ships Lost

Ship's Name, Owner & Registry	Type	Date Lost	Location	Sunk By	Crew Lost
A.D. Huff Atlantic Transportation Canadian	freighter 6219 grt built 1920	22 Feb 41	Mid Atlantic 47° 12'N 40° 13'W	Armed ship *Gneisenau* by gunnery	2
Albert C. Field UL & St. Lawrence Shipg Canadian	laker 1764 grt built 1923	18 Jun 44	Eng. Channel SW of Isle of Wight	German acoustic torpedo	4
Angelus Govt. of Canada ex-French (seized)	barquentine 338 grt built 1921	19 May 43	Western Atlantic 38° 40'N 64° 00'W	U-boat *U 161* by gunnery	8
Avondale Park Park SS (Govt.) Canadian	freighter 2878 grt built 1944	7 May 45	North Sea Firth of Forth	U-boat *U 2336* by torpedo	2
Bic Island Govt. of Canada ex-Italian *Capo Noli* (captured)	freighter 4000 grt built 1917	28 Oct 42	Mid Atlantic 55° 05'N 23° 27'W	U-boat *U 224* by torpedo	36 (all)
Calgarolite Imperial Oil Ltd. Canadian	tanker 11,941 grt built 1929	9 May 42	NW Caribbean West of Caymans	U-boat *U 125* by torpedo	(nil)
Canadian Cruiser Montreal/Aust/NZ Line Canadian	freighter 7178 grt built 1921	21 Feb 41	W Indian Ocean West of Seychelles	Armed ship *Admiral Scheer* by gunnery	(nil)
Canadolite Imperial Oil Ltd. Canadian	tanker 11,309 grt built 1926	25 Mar 41	Central E Atlantic 03° 30'N 23° 48'W	Raider *Kormoran*	(nil)
Caribou Nfld. Govt. Newfoundland	ferry 2222 grt built 1925	14 Oct 42	Cabot Strait SW of Port aux Basques	U-boat *U 69* by torpedo	31 (+ 106 passengers)
Carolus Govt. of Canada/CNSS ex-Finnish	freighter 2245 grt built 1919	9 Oct 42	St. Lawrence River between Matane & Rimouski	U-boat *U 69*	11

Ship's Name, Owner & Registry	Type	Date Lost	Location	Sunk By	Crew Lost
Chr. J. Kampmann Govt. of Canada ex-Danish	freighter 2281 grt built 1924	3 Nov 42	E Caribbean West of Grenadines	U-boat *U 160* by torpedo	19
Collingdoc Paterson SS Co. Canadian	laker 1788 grt built 1925	13 Jul 40	Thames at Southend	Mined (salvaged, expended)	2
Cornwallis CNSS Canadian	freighter 5458 grt built 1921	3 Dec 44	Gulf of Maine 20 miles S of Bar Harbour	U-boat *U 1230* by torpedo	37 (+ 6 DEMS gunners)
Donald Stewart CSL Canadian	laker 1781 grt built 1923	3 Sep 42	Strait of Belle Isle Newfld	U-boat *U 517* by torpedo	3
Empress of Asia CPSS Canadian	liner 16,909 grt built 1913	5 Feb 42	Singapore channel	Japanese acoustic bombs	1 (+ 1 as POW, & c.15 soldiers)
Erik Boye Govt. of Canada ex-Danish	freighter 2010 grt built 1924	15 Jun 40	135 miles NW of Land's End	U-boat *U 38* by torpedo	(nil)
Esmond Anglo-Nfld SS Co. Newfoundland	freighter 4975 grt built 1930	9 May 41	Mid Atlantic 60° 45'N 33° 02'W	U-boat *U 110* by torpedo	(nil)
Europa Govt. of Canada ex-Danish	passenger- freighter 10,224 grt built 1931	4 May 41	Liverpool docks	German acoustic bombs *Luftfl.* 3	(nil)
Frank B. Baird UL & St. Lawrence Shipg Canadian	laker 1748 grt built 1923	22 May 42	Mid Atlantic 28° 03'N 58° 50'W	U-boat *U 158* by gunnery	(nil)
Geraldine Mary Anglo-Nfld SS Co. Newfoundland	freighter 7244 grt built 1924	4 Aug 40	Atlantic, S of Rockall 56° 46'N 15° 48'W	U-boat *U 52* by torpedo	2 (+ 1 passenger)
George L. Torian UL & St.Lawrence Shipg Canadian	laker 1754 grt built 1926	22 Feb 42	Off British Guyana	U-boat *U 129* by torpedo	13
Helen Forsey William Forsey Newfoundland	schooner 167 grt built 1929	6 Sep 42 SE of	Mid Atlantic *U 514* Bermuda	U-boat by gunnery	2
Humber Arm Bowaters Nfld. Newfoundland	freighter 5758 grt built 1925	8 Jul 40	St. George's Channel 90mi. S of Ireland	U-boat *U 99* by torpedo	(nil)
James E. Newsom Capt Dawson Gelert and Zwicker & Co. Canadian	schooner 671 grt built 1919	1 May 42	Mid Atlantic 35° 50'N 59° 40'W	U-boat *U 69* by gunnery	(nil)
Jasper Park Park SS (Govt.) Canadian	freighter 7130 grt built 1942	6 Jul 43	Indian Ocean South of Madagascar	U-boat *U 177* by torpedo	4

Ship's Name, Owner & Registry	Type	Date Lost	Location	Sunk By	Crew Lost
J.B. White Atlantic Transportation Canadian	freighter 6869 grt built 1919	17 Mar 41	E Atlantic 60° 57'N 12° 27'W	U-Boat *U 99* by torpedo	2
John A. Holloway UL & St. Lawrence Shipg Canadian	laker 1745 grt built 1925	6 Sep 42	E.Caribbean South of Haiti	U-boat *U 164* by torpedo	1
Kenordoc Paterson SS Co. Canadian	laker 1780 grt built 1926	15 Sep 40	Atlantic near Rockall 57° 42'N 15° 02'W	U-boat *U 48* by gunnery	7
Kitty's Brook Bowaters Nfld. Newfoundland	freighter 4031 grt built 1907	10 May 42	SE of Cape Sable Nova Scotia	U-boat *U 558* by torpedo	9
Lady Drake CN(WI)SS Canadian	passenger -freighter 7831 grt built 1928	5 May 42	Mid Atlantic 35° 43'N 64° 43'W	U-boat *U 106* by torpedo	6 (+ 6 passengers)
Lady Hawkins CN(WI)SS Canadian	passenger -freighter 7831 grt built 1928	19 Jan 42	W Atlantic 35° 00'N 72° 30'W	U-boat *U 66* by torpedo	88 (+ c. 4 DEMS & c. 158 passengers)
Lennox CSL Canadian	laker 1904 grt built 1923	23 Feb 42	Off British Guyana	U-boat *U 129* by torpedo	2
Liverpool Packet Markland SS Canadian	freighter 1188 grt built 1926	30 May 42	Off Nova Scotia 35 mi. S of Yarmouth	U-boat *U 432* by torpedo	2
Livingston Bowaters Nfld. Newfoundland	laker 2115 grt built 1928	3 Sep 44	S. Cabot Strait E of Cape Breton	U-boat *U 541* by torpedo	13 (+ 1 DEMS gunner)
Lord Strathcona Dominion Shipg Co. Canadian	freighter 7335 grt built 1915	5 Sep 42	Bell Island Newfoundland	U-boat *U 513* by torpedo	(nil)
Lucille M. Frederic Sutherland Canadian	schooner 54 grt built 1918	25 Jul 42	100 mi. S of Cape Sable NS	U-boat *U 89* by gunnery	(nil)
Magog CSL Canadian	laker 2053 grt built 1923	5 Jul 40	SE of Ireland 50° 31'N 11° 05'W	U-boat *U 99* by gunnery & torpedo	(nil)
Maplecourt United Towing & Salv. Canadian	freighter 3388 grt built 1893	6 Feb 41	Mid Atlantic 55° 39'N 15° 56'W	U-boat *U 107* by torpedo	35 (all) (+ 1 or 2 DEMS)
Mildred Pauline A.G. Thornhill Canadian	schooner 245 grt built 1919	7 May 42	About 600 mi. SE of Nova Scotia	U-boat *U 136* by gunnery	7 (all)

Ship's Name, Owner & Registry	Type	Date Lost	Location	Sunk By	Crew Lost
Mona Marie L. Ritsey Canadian	schooner 126 grt built 1920	28 Jun 42	E Caribbean off the Grenadines	U-boat *U 126* by gunnery	(nil)
Mont Louis Hall Shipping Canadian	laker 1905 grt built 1927	8 May 42	NW of Georgetown British Guyana	U-boat *U 162* by torpedo	13
Montrolite Imperial Oil Ltd. Canadian	tanker 11,309 grt built 1926	4 Feb 42	Mid Atlantic 35° 14'N 60° 05'W	U-boat *U 109* by torpedo	27 (+ 1 DEMS)
Nipiwan Park Park SS/Imperial Oil Canadian	tanker 2400 grt built 1943	4 Jan 45	Off Halifax Nova Scotia	U-boat *U 1232* by torpedo	2
Norfolk CSL Canadian	laker 1901 grt built 1923	18 Sep 42	Off NW British Guyana	U-boat *U 175* by torpedo	6
Oakton Gulf & Lake Navigation Canadian	laker 1727 grt built 1923	7 Sep 42	Gulf of St. Lawrence 25 mi. SE of Gaspé	U-boat *U 517* by torpedo	(nil)
Point Pleasant Park Park SS (Govt.) Canadian	freighter 7130 grt built 1943	23 Feb 45	S Atlantic off Africa 29° 42'S 09° 58'E	U-boat *U 510* by torpedo	9
Portadoc Paterson SS Co. Canadian	laker 1740 grt built 1924	7 Apr 41	Atlantic W of Sierra Leone	U-boat *U 124* by torpedo	1 (as POW)
Prescodoc Paterson SS Co. Canadian	laker 1938 grt built 1929	29 Jul 42	Off NW British Guyana	U-boat *U 160* by torpedo	16
Princess Marguerite CPSS Canadian	passenger 5875 grt built 1924	17 Aug 42	East Mediterranean N of Port Said	U-boat *U 83* by torpedo	(nil) (+ c. 55 troops)
Robert Max Grand Bank Fisheries Newfoundland	schooner 172 grt built 1920	4 Aug 41	SE of Azores	U-boat *U 126* by gunnery	(nil)
Robert W. Pomeroy UL & St.Lawrence Shipg Canadian	laker 1724 grt built 1923	1 Apr 42	North Sea off Norfolk	Mined	(nil) (+1 DEMS)
Rose Castle Dom. Steel & Coal Canadian	freighter 7803 grt built 1915	2 Nov 42	Bell Island Newfoundland	U-boat *U 518* by torpedo	35 (?)
Rothermere Anglo-Nfld. SS Co. Newfoundland	freighter 5356 grt built 1938	20 May 41	Mid Atlantic 57° 48'N 41° 36'N	U-boat *U 98* by torpedo	19 (+ 2 DEMS & 1 passenger)
St. Malo Govt. of Canada/ CNSS, ex-French	freighter 5779 grt built 1917	12 Oct 40	Atlantic off Rockall 57° 58'N 16° 32'W	U-boat *U 101* by torpedo	28

Ship's Name, Owner & Registry	Type	Date Lost	Location	Sunk By	Crew Lost
Sarniadoc Paterson SS Co. Canadian	laker 1940 grt built 1929	14 Mar 42	Central Caribbean S. of Puerto Rico	U-boat *U 161* by torpedo	21 (all)
Shinai G.L. Shaw (Foochow) Canadian	freighter 2410 grt built 1920	24 Dec 41	NW Borneo at Kuching	Japanese forces - seized	1 (as POW)
Taber Park Park SS (Govt.) Canadian	freighter 2875 grt built 1944	13 Mar 45	North Sea off Lowestoft	Midget submarine torpedo	24 (+ 4 DEMS)
Thorold Q & O Transportation Canadian	laker 1689 grt built 1922	22 Aug 40	S. Irish Sea off Milford Haven	German acoustic bombs *KG 2*	11
Torondoc Paterson SS Co. Canadian	laker 1927 grt built 1927	21 May 42	E Caribbean W of Martinique	U-boat *U 69* by torpedo	23 (all)
Trevisa Cdn. Lake Carriers Canadian	laker 1813 grt built 1915	16 Oct 40	Mid Atlantic 57° 28'N 20° 30'W	U-boat *U 124* by torpedo	7
Troisdoc Paterson SS Co. Canadian	laker 1925 grt built 1925	21 May 42	Caribbean SW of Jamaica	U-boat *U 558* by gunnery	(nil)
Vancouver Island Govt. (captured) ex-German *Weser*	passenger -freighter 9472 grt built 1929	15 Oct 41	Mid Atlantic 53° 37'N 25° 37'W	U-boat *U 558* by torpedo	64 or 65 (all) (+32 passengers & 6 DEMS)
Victolite Imperial Oil Ltd. Canadian	tanker 11,410 grt built 1928	10 Feb 42	Mid Atlantic 36° 12'N 67° 14'W	U-boat *U 564* by gunnery & torpedo	45 (all) (+ 2 DEMS)
Vineland Markland Shipping Canadian	freighter 5587 grt built 1919	20 Apr 42	Atlantic off Caicos Islands	U-boat *U 154* by torpedo	1
Waterloo CSL Canadian	laker 1905 grt built 1923	10 Jul 40	North Sea off Yorkshire	German acoustic bombs *KG 2*	(nil)
Waterton Bowaters Nfld. Newfoundland	laker 2115 grt built 1928	11 Oct 42	Cabot Strait off Cape Breton	U-boat *U 106* by torpedo	(nil)
Watuka NS Steel & Coal Canadian	freighter 1621 grt built 1918	22 Mar 44	SW of Halifax	U-boat *U 802* by torpedo	1

Ships lost to other than enemy action, or not Canadian/Newfoundland-registered. A partial list.

A. Canadian-registered, lost to marine hazards:

- *Canatco*, 2415 grt freighter; ran ashore, Labrador coast, 24 Oct 42.
- *Flora Alberta*, schooner, run down in fog by convoy *Fanad Head* 21 Apr 1942.
  Also ex-French barquentine *Mariana*, run down during 1942.
- *Greenhill Park*, 7168 grt freighter; caught fire on 6 Mar. 1945, run aground off Vancouver;
  salvaged, rebuilt & sold, 3 May 45.
- *Hamildoc*, 1926 grt laker; foundered off British Guyana, 1 Jan 43. None lost.
- *Lisieux*, ex-French schooner; foundered, Atlantic, 27 Nov 40.
- *Mondoc*, 1926 grt laker; struck submerged object, Caribbean, written off, 5 Oct 41.
  None lost.
- *Nereus*, 10,650 grt freighter; broke up in heavy weather, 12 Dec 41. 61 lost, including
  some passengers.
- *Proteus*, 10,650 grt freighter; broke up in heavy weather, 25 Nov 41. 58 lost.
- *R.J. Cullen*, 6973 grt freighter; wrecked, Outer Hebrides, Scotland, 15 Jan 42.
- *Silver Star Park*, 7243 freighter; collision & fire off Portland, ME; salvaged, rebuilt & sold;
  12 Apr 45. 16 lost.
- *Watkins F. Nisbet*, 1,747 grt laker; ran ashore, English Channel, 6 Dec 40. None lost.

B. Sunk in harbour by enemy, but salvaged and repaired for use:

- *Lady Nelson*, 7970 grt passenger freighter; torpedoed in Castries harbour; salvaged,
  repaired, became a hospital ship.

C. Not Canadian-registered at time of loss to enemy action:

- *Lady Somers*, 8194 grt passenger freighter; requisitioned and sold to Admiralty, as an ocean
  boarding vessel; sunk by Italian submarine *Morosini* on 15 Jul 41.
- Most CP liners and freighters were British-registered, including these later sunk: *Empress of
  Britain, Empress of Canada, Duchess of Atholl, Duchess of York, Beaverbrae, Beaverburn,
  Beaverdale, Beaverford, Niagara.*
- CPSS's *Montrose*, 16,402 grt, requisitioned by the Admiralty, became the British AMC HMS
  Forfar, sunk by U 99 on 2 Dec 1940.
- Paterson's *Soreldoc*, 1926 grt was sold, Panamanian-registered and US chartered, for a US
  Army stores carrier when lost to *U 1302* on 28 Feb 45.
- All Canadian-built Fort ships lost (29 ships) were British-registered when lost: 7 owned by
  Canada, registered in Britain (Forts *Athabaskan, Bellingham, Crevier, Maisoneuve, Missanabi,
  Norfolk* and *St. Nicholas*); and 22 owned by the US Maritime Commission but loaned to
  Britain under "lend-lease": Forts *Corne, Babine, Battle River, Buckingham, Cedar Lake,
  Chilcotin, Concord, Fitzgerald, Franklin, Good Hope, Halkett, Howe, Jemseg, la Maune, la Reine,
  Longeueil, McLeod, Mumford, Pelly, Qu'Appelle, Rampart* and *Fort Yale.*
- Imperial Oil Company's Panamanian-registered tankers *Joseph Seep*, mined in the La Havre
  approaches on 24 May 40, and *James McGee*, also mined, in the Bristol Channel on 20 Jun 40.
- *Western Head*, a 2599 grt passenger freighter, sunk with heavy loss of Canadian military
  lives on 28 May 42 in the Caribbean, was owned in Liverpool, NS, but registered in
  Nassau, Bahamas.

D. Not Canadian-registered and lost to marine hazard:

- CPSS's *Beaverhill*, 10,041 grt, stranded 24 Nov 44.
- *Fort Confidence, Fort Montee* and *Fort Stikine*.

The Ships

From this list, there were 67 Canadian and Newfoundland registered ships sunk due to enemy
action in the Second World War. Even this figure may be at variance by one or two ships: one
Newfoundland freighter (*Livingston*) may have been registered in England when sunk, although

owned by a Newfoundland-based company; one schooner's registry was changed from Lunenburg to Barbados while on the voyage in which she was lost (*James E. Newsom*).

Thus lost were:

- 5 passenger liners/ferries: *Empress of Asia, Princess Marguerite,* two CNSS Lady boats and the ferry *Caribou.*
- 20 lakers/canallers from the Great Lakes (30 percent of the losses, 33 percent of merchant losses))
- 24 standard freighters
- 4 tankers (all Imperial Oil Company)
- 2 captured ships (*Bic Island* and *Vancouver Island*)
- 4 Allied freighters then registered in Canada (2 Danish, 1 Finnish and 1 French)
- 1 Allied passenger freighter registered in Canada (the Danish *Europa*)
- 7 fishing and trading schooners

Of these, 9 were Newfoundland ships; 5 were Allied ships temporarily "Canadian;" 53 were Canadian, although 1, *Shinai* was owned by a China-based operator.

Of the 53 Canadian ships, 9 were owned and operated by the Canadian government-controlled companies Park Steamships and CNSS.

The Men and Women

The number of merchant seamen lost in all these ships is considerably harder to determine with absolute accuracy:

- Some memorials also include men and women who died in the ships before they were sunk, due to illness or accident;
- Others omit names of those whose bodies were recovered and buried in marked graves ashore.
- DEMS gunners are particularly hard to identify; they were "Navy," not Merchant Navy. But because they usually "signed articles" when joining the merchant ship, they are sometimes included with "crew" lost.
- Some Merchant Navy and naval personnel taking passage were included with crew.
- Some non-Canadian merchant seamen, such as from Britain, Barbados and British Guyana, from Denmark and Finland, are recorded on the Canadian memorials, but not all, nor even consistently.
- Names of those lost in Allied merchant ships registered in Canada indicate many were natives of the ship's home country.

The names given at the end of each ship's story are those found on Canadian memorials and on the Merchant Navy Memorial on the bank of the Thames in London. Without a major search in records to ensure absolute accuracy, many of which would be missing anyway, the listings will at least give a close indication of the cost in human lives that the Merchant Navy paid - the "Price of Admiralty."

The total number of merchant seamen and women lost in the ships whose stories are told here would appear to be between 708 and 710 (not including DEMS gunners), of a total crew at risk in these ships alone of between 2881 and 2888, excluding *Europa* (not manned for sea when lost) and *Shinai* (abandoned by crew before seizure). This is a rate of about 24.5 percent loss. Not all were naturalised "Canadians." This total does not include either the DEMS or passengers lost, nor any merchant seamen rescued from other sunken ships and then lost when their rescuer was in turn sunk.

TABLE 2

Means of Destruction – Merchant Ships and Sailing Vessels

Sunk By		Ship's Name	How sunk	Date Lost
Aircraft		*Waterloo*	bombed	10 Jul 1940
		Thorold	bombed	22 Aug 1940
		Europa	bombed in dock	3 May 1940
		Empress of Asia	bombed	3 Feb 1942
		Albert C. Field	torpedoed	18 Jun 1944
Surface		*Canadian Cruiser*	by Admiral Scheer	21 Feb 1941
		A.D. Huff	by Gneisenau	22 Feb 1941
Capture or Seizure		*Canadolite*	by Kormoran	25 Mar 1941
		Shinai	by Japanese Forces	24 Dec 1941
Mined		*Collingdoc*	13 Jul 1941	
		Robert W. Pomeroy		1 Apr 1942
U-Boats:	U 38	*Erik Boye*	torpedoed	15 Jun 1940
	U 48	*Kenordoc*	shelled	15 Sep 1940
	U 52	*Geraldine Mary*	torpedoed	4 Aug 1940
	U 66	*Lady Hawkins*	torpedoed	19 Jan 1942
	U 69	*James E. Newsom*	shelled	1 May 1942
	U 69	*Torondoc*	torpedoed	12 May 1942
	U 69	*Carolus*	torpedoed	9 Oct 1942
	U 69	*Caribou*	torpedoed	14 Oct 1942
	U 83	*Princess Marguerite*	torpedoed	17 Aug 1942
	U 89	*Lucille M.*	shelled	25 Jul 1942
	U 98	*Rothermere*	torpedoed	20 May 1941
	U 99	*Magog*	torpedoed & shelled	5 Jul 1940
	U 99	*Humber Arm*	torpedoed	8 Jul 1940
	U 99	*J.B. White*	torpedoed	17 Mar 1941
	U 101	*St. Malo*	torpedoed	12 Oct 1940
	U 106	*Lady Drake*	torpedoed	5 May 1942
	U 106	*Waterton*	torpedoed	11 Oct 1942
	U 107	*Maplecourt*	torpedoed	6 Feb 1941
	U 109	*Montrolite*	torpedoed	4 Feb 1941
	U 110	*Esmond*	torpedoed	9 May 1941
	U 124	*Trevisa*	torpedoed	16 Oct 1940
	U 124	*Portadoc*	torpedoed	7 Apr 1940
	U 125	*Calgarolite*	torpedoed & shelled	9 May 1942
	U 126	*Mona Marie*	shelled	28 Jun 1942
	U 126	*Robert Max*	shelled	4 Aug 1941
	U 129	*George L. Torian*	torpedoed	22 Feb 1942
	U 129	*Lennox*	torpedoed	23 Feb 1942
	U 136	*Mildred Pauline*	shelled	7 May 1942
	U 154	*Vineland*	torpedoed	20 Apr 1942
	U 158	*Frank B. Baird*	shelled	22 May 1942
	U 160	*Prescodoc*	torpedoed	15 Mar 1942
	U 160	*Chr. J. Kampmann*	torpedoed	3 Nov 1942
	U 161	*Sarniadoc*	torpedoed	15 Mar 1942
	U 161	*Angelus*	shelled	19 May 1943

Sunk By	Ship's Name	How sunk	Date Lost
U 162	*Mont Louis*	torpedoed	8 May 1942
U 164	*John A. Holloway*	torpedoed	6 Sep 1942
U 175	*Norfolk*	torpedoed	18 Sep 1942
U 177	*Jasper Park*	torpedoed	6 Jul 1943
U 432	*Liverpool Packet*	torpedoed	30 May 1942
U 510	*Point Pleasant Park*	torpedoed	23 Feb 1945
U 513	*Lord Strathcona*	torpedoed	5 Sep 1942
U 514	*Helen Forsey*	shelled	6 Sep 1942
U 517	*Donald Stewart*	torpedoed	3 Sep 1942
U 517	*Oakton*	torpedoed	7 Sep 1942
U 518	*Rose Castle*	torpedoed	2 Nov 1942
U 541	*Livingston*	torpedoed	3 Sep 1944
U 558	*Vancouver Island*	torpedoed	15 Oct 1941
U 558	*Troisdoc*	torpedoed	21 May 1942
U 564	*Victolite*	torpedoed	10 Feb 1942
U 588	*Kitty's Brook*	torpedoed	10 May 1942
U 624	*Bic Island*	torpedoed	29 Oct 1942
U 802	*Watuka*	torpedoed	22 Mar 1944
U 1230	*Cornwallis*	torpedoed	3 Dec 1944
U 1232	*Nipiwan Park*	torpedoed, part	4 Jan 1945
U 2336	*Avondale Park*	torpedoed	7 May 1945
Kleinkp v.Bd.	*Taber Park*	torpedoed	13 Mar 1945

Thus of 67 Canadian and Newfoundland registered and flagged merchant ships and fishing vessels lost to enemy action during the war:

- 5 were lost to aircraft = 7.5 percent
- 2 were lost to surface warships
- 2 were captured
- 2 were mined
- 56 were lost to U-Boats = 84 percent

This was offset in part by the capture of two enemy merchantmen, ex-German *Weser* and ex-Italian *Capo Noli* that were later lost as *Vancouver Island* and *Bic Island*.

In addition there were many Canadian owned vessels lost during the war due to marine hazards connected with war service, but not directly due to enemy action – ammunition explosions, running ashore while with a convoy but straggling, rammed by other convoy ships, etc. There were 6 Canadian government owned Fort ships and 10 CPR ships registered in Britain and lost, and two ships ex-Canadian but sold and registered in Britain or the US and then lost.

TABLE 3

Losses in Convoy

Convoy/Destination	Date Sailed	Involved	Date Lost	Comments
BM-12, Far East Bombay to Singapore	23 Jan 42	*Empress of Asia*	5 Feb 42	Aerial bombs
BS-3, St. Lawrence coastal Corner Brook to Sydney		*Waterton*	11 Oct 42	
EBC-14, UK coastal Bristol Channel		*Albert C. Field*	18 Jun 44	Aerial torpedo
EN-91, North Sea coastal Methil to Oban		*Avondale Park*	7 May 45	
FN-40, North Sea coastal Thames to Firth of Forth		*Robert W. Pomeroy*	1 Apr 42	Mined
FS-1753, North Sea coastal Firth of Forth to the Thames	12 Mar 45	*Taber Park*	13 Mar 45	Kleinkampfverbände
HX-47, North Atlantic Halifax to U.K.	2 Jun 40	*Erik Boye*	15 Jun 40	
HX-52, North Atlantic	21 Jun 40	*Magog*	5 Jul 40	Straggler
HX-53, North Atlantic	25 Jun 40	*Humber Arm*	8 Jul 40	
HX-60, North Atlantic	23 Jul 40	*Geraldine Mary*	4 Aug 40	
HX-77, North Atlantic	30 Sep 40	*St. Malo*	12 Oct 40	Straggler
HX-112, North Atlantic	1 Mar 41	*J.B. White*	17 Mar 41	
HX-126, North Atlantic	10 May 41	*Rothermere*	20 May 41	
HX-212, North Atlantic	18 Oct 42	*Bic Island*	29 Oct 42	
LN-7, St. Lawrence coastal St. Lawrence to Labrador		*Donald Stewart*	3 Sep 42	
NL-7, St. Lawrence coastal Labrador to St. Lawrence		*Carolus*	9 Oct 42	
OB-318, North Atlantic outbound, Liverpool to N. America	2 May 41	*Esmond*	9 May 41	
ONS-251, North Atlantic (coastal) outbound, slow, Liverpool to N. America	1 Sep 44	*Livingston*	3 Sep 44	

Convoy/Destination	Date Sailed	Involved	Date Lost	Comments
S-33, St. Lawrence coastal Quebec City to Sydney, Cape Breton		*Oakton*	7 Sep 42	
SC-3, North Atlantic Sydney to U.K.	2 Sep 40	*Kenordoc*	15 Sep 40	Straggler
SC-7, North Atlantic	5 Oct 40	*Trevisa*	16 Oct 40	Straggler
SC-20, North Atlantic	22 Jan 41	*Maplecourt*	6 Feb 41	Straggler
SH-125, Nova Scotia coastal Sydney to Halifax	21 Mar 44	*Watuka*	22 Mar 44	
TAG-18, Caribbean Trinidad-Aruba-Guantanamo	2 Nov 42	*Chr. J. Kampmann*	3 Nov 42	Straggler

From this list of 23 ships out of 67 lost in total (34 percent), one can deduce:

i. Being in convoy did not necessarily guarantee safety, from U-boats, aircraft attack or mines.
ii. However, if *Shinai* (seized), *Rose Castle* and *Lord Strathcona* (sunk at anchor) and all seven sailing vessels are deducted from the total, then of the 54 ships, 23 were lost in convoy, or 40 percent
iii. All the rest, 60 percent, were lost when sailing independently or straggling from convoys.

This supports the contention of Naval Control of Shipping authorities that merchantmen were always safer to be with or remain with convoys; and that "romping" or "straggling" significantly increased one's chances of being torpedoed.

However, most of the ships sunk as "independents" in these stories (29 ships) were not necessarily convoy stragglers (only six were), but had been sailed by the authorities independently and without escorts despite their slow speeds in all but three cases. Those three, *Lady Drake*, *Lady Hawkins* and *Vancouver Island* had enough speed to be sailed as true independents. All the rest, 26 ships, including 13 little lakers, should have had escorts based on their slow speeds and the dangers of attack in their areas of operations, of which authorities were quite well aware in at least general terms. It is a measure of the severe lack of escort vessels that none could be provided. A problem of government unpreparedness, not of naval neglect.

TABLE 4

All Merchant Ships Lost, By Owner

Company*	Lost	Date Lost	Chapter Ref.
ANGLO-NEWFOUNDLAND STEAMSHIP COMPANY	*Geraldine Mary*	4 Aug 40	CH 17
	Esmond	9 May 41	CH 17
	Rothermere	20 May 41	CH 17
ATLANTIC TRANSPORTATION LTD	*A.D. Huff*	22 Feb 41	CH 6
	J.B. White	17 Mar 41	CH 2
BOWATER NEWFOUNDLAND PULP & PAPER MILLS LTD	*Humber Arm*	8 Jul 40	CH 17
	Kitty's Brook	10 May 42	CH 17
	Waterton	11 Oct 42	CH 17
	Livingston	3 Sep 44	CH 17
CANADA STEAMSHIP LINES	*Magog*	5 Jul 40	CH 1
	Waterloo	10 Jul 40	CH 1
	Lennox	23 Feb 42	CH 1
	Donald Stewart	3 Sep 42	CH 1
	Norfolk	18 Sep 42	CH 1
CANADIAN GOVERNMENT MERCHANT MARINE	*Angelus*	14 May 43	CH13
CANADIAN LAKE CARRIERS LTD	*Trevisa*	16 Oct 40	CH 2
CANADIAN NATIONAL STEAMSHIPS	*Lady Hawkins*	19 Jan 42	CH 9
	Lady Drake	5 May 42	CH 9
	Cornwallis	3 Dec 44	CH 9
CANADIAN PACIFIC STEAMSHIPS	*Empress of Asia*	5 Feb 42	CH 10
	Princess Marguerite	17 Aug 42	CH 10
DOMINION SHIPPING CO	*Lord Strathcona*	5 Sep 42	CH 4
DOMINION STEEL & COAL CO	*Rose Castle*	2 Nov 42	CH 4
H.O. EMPTAGE & CO and ZWICKER & CO	*James E. Newsom*	1 May 42	CH 13
WILLIAM FORSEY	*Helen Forsey*	6 Sep 42	CH 13
GRAND BANK FISHERIES LTD	*Robert Max*	4 Aug 41	CH 13
GULF & LAKES NAVIGATION LTD	*Oakton*	7 Sep 42	CH 3
HALL CORPORATION	*Mont Louis*	8 May 42	CH 3
IMPERIAL OIL LTD	*Canadolite*	25 Mar 41	CH 8
	Montrolite	4 Feb 42	CH 8
	Victolite	10 Feb 42	CH 8
	Calgarolite	9 May 42	CH 8
MARKLAND SHIPPING LTD	*Vineland*	20 Apr 42	CH 12
	Liverpool Packet	30 May 42	CH 12

Company*	Lost	Date Lost	Chapter Ref.
MONTREAL-AUSTRALIA-NEW ZEALAND LINE	*Canadian Cruiser*	21 Feb 41	CH 6
NEWFOUNDLAND GOVERNMENT, RAILWAYS DEPT	*Caribou*	14 Oct 42	CH 17
NOVA SCOTIA STEEL & COAL	*Watuka*	22 Mar 44	CH 3
PARK STEAMSHIP CO	*Jasper Park*	6 Jul 43	CH 14
	Nipiwan Park	1 Jan 45 in part	CH 14
	Point Pleasant Park	23 Feb 45	CH 14
	Taber Park	13 Mar 45	CH 14
	Avondale Park	7 May 45	CH 14
N.M.PATERSON STEAMSHIPS LTD	*Kenordoc*	15 Sep 40	CH 7
	Portadoc	7 Apr 41	CH 7
	Collingdoc	13 Jul 41	CH 7
	Sarniadoc	15 Mar 42	CH 7
	Torondoc	21 May 42	CH 7
	Troisdoc	21 May 42	CH 7
	Prescodoc	29 Jul 42	CH 7
QUEBEC & ONTARIO TRANSPORTATION CO	*Thorold*	22 Aug 40	CH 2
L.RITCEY	*Mona Marie*	28 Jun 42	CH 13
G.L. SHAW	*Shinai*	24 Dec 41	CH 5
FRED SUTHERLAND	*Lucille M.*	25 Jul 42	CH 13
A.G. THORNHILL	*Mildred Pauline*	7 May 42	CH 13
UNITED TOWING & SALVAGE CO	*Maplecourt*	6 Feb 41	CH 2
UPPER LAKES & ST. LAWRENCE SHIPPING	*George L. Torian*	22 Feb 42	CH 11
	Robert W. Pomeroy	1 Apr 42	CH 11
	Frank B. Baird	22 May 42	CH 11
	John A. Holloway	6 Sep 42	CH 11
	Albert C. Field	18 Jun 44	CH 11
NON-CANADIAN OWNED SHIPS	*Erik Boye*	15 Jun 40	CH 16
	St Malo	12 Oct 40	CH 16
	Europa	3 May 41	CH 16
	Vancouver Isld	15 Oct 41	captured ship
	Carolus	9 Oct 42	CH 16
	Bic Island	29 Oct 42	captured ship
	Chr.J.Kampmann	3 Nov 42	CH 16

* Names are those of the parent company or sub-company. Some ships, such as *Rose Castle*, were "owned" by a company set up to manage them as a business entity, in her case The Rose Castle SS Co. for instance. The two CNSS Lady boats were owned by CN(WI)SS Co., a subsidiary of CNSS, itself a subsidiary of the CNR, in turn owned by the Canadian Government.

TABLE 5

Casualty Rates: Merchant Navy & RCN

MERCHANT NAVY LOSSES

- In a study of 27,000 merchant seamen in ships sunk by 1944, the chances of survival were 68 percent, losses 32 percent, of which 6 percent were lost while in lifeboats or on rafts. There is no reason to suppose these figures would vary much by the war's end, except for a slight improvement as a result of better equipment, more available escorts for rescue, and the oldest and most infirm ships being already sunk or withdrawn. But then fewer ships were sunk, proportionately, to affect the statistic.

- From the Canadian/Newfoundland ships sunk, only excluding *Europa* and *Shinai* (see notes at end of Table 1), the loss rate for the Canadian ships in these stories was between 24.5 per cent and 24.6 percent, despite the use of the little lakers.

- If the two ships with large crews, *Empress of Asia* and *Princess Marguerite* are deducted from these totals because they tend to distort them, making up about 28 percent of total crews of all ships, then: there were about 2,068 crew at hazard, about 706 lost (taking mean figures— a 34.1 percent loss, very close to the Allied average. A very risky occupation indeed.

(Source: R.A. McCance The Hazards To Men Lost At Sea, MRC, London, 1956)

RCN LOSSES

- The RCN lost 28 vessels, excluding the MTBs lost by fire at Ostende, but including losses due to collisions and groundings.

- In these ships there were 2,552 crew at hazard (including RN crew), and there were 1,258 crew lost—a 49.3 percent loss.

- If we exclude those warships lost to other than enemy action, there were 1,802 crew at hazard, 987 lost—a 54.8 percent loss.

- In both cases, of course, if one includes the crews of ships not lost or not even damaged by the enemy, the rate drops to less than 10 percent. But if a was lost, the chances of survival were poor.

(Source: Darlington & McKee, The Canadian Naval Chronicle, Vanwell, St. Catharines, 1996)

TABLE 6

Convoy Statistics and Other Losses

SUMMARY

This is a study of convoys in the North Atlantic in the 3rd quarter of 1942, 1 July to 30 September, a period of 3 months, or 13 weeks and 92 days. This was a time of maximum danger.

1. **North Atlantic Convoys which sailed in this time period (excluding those to Gibraltar, Freetown and southeast):**

   A. Eastbound:
   - i. HX Convoys 197 (on 6.07.42) to 209 (on 24.09), a total of 13 convoys, 502 ships; 1 lost, on 4 October
   - ii. SC Convoys 90 (on 3.07.42) to 103 (on 26.09), a total of 14 convoys, 568 ships; 17 ships lost, and 1 by collision

   B. Westbound:
   - i. ON Convoys 109 (on 3.07.42) to 134 (on 26.09), a total of 26 convoys, 905 ships; 15 lost, and 1 by collision

   C. Also at sea in the period, sailing before 1 July:
   - i. HX: 2 convoys, 72 ships, no losses
   - ii. SC: 2 convoys, 74 ships, no losses
   - iii. ON: 3 convoys, 99 ships, no losses

   D. Totals, convoys in the North Atlantic in the quarter:
   - i. 60 convoys, 2,220 ships
   - ii. Averages: 37 ships per convoy; if in columns of 4.5 ships, there were 8 columns. Spacing at night (in 1942): 2 cables (400 yds.) between ships in column; 5 cables (1,000 yds) between columns. (The spacing was increased due to inexperienced Masters arriving in 1943, and the column spacing was made 5 cables by day as well).
   - iii. Thus the area occupied by the average 1942 convoy was 4.1 miles across its front, by 1.2 miles deep. The area taken up by the close escorts was about double.

   E. Losses, convoy ships:
   - i. 33 ships lost to U-boats, plus 2 by collision, total 35 ships lost; a 1.6 percent loss rate of ships in convoy.
   - ii. Tonnage of ships lost: 201,747 grt., plus cargoes lost (partial list only):

Fuel oils: 150,000 bbl	General cargo: 31,275 tons
Pulp: 3,200 tons	Ammunitions: 2,530 tons
Lumber: 3,979 tons	Food stores: 3,000 tons
Iron/steel: 11,040 tons	Molasses: 13,000 tons
Grain: 10,362 tons	

   F. Merchant seamen lost in the 35 ships in the quarter:
   - i. 246 people in 24 ships (i.e., in 69 percent of the ships sunk) ranging from 1 lost to 50
   - ii. no losses in 11 ships that were sunk
   - G. nationalities of the ships sunk (including collisions):

British: 22	Greek: 2
Norwegian: 4	Dutch: 1
American: 3	Panamanian: 1
Belgian: 2	

2. Ships lost while not in convoy, or in other than North Atlantic convoys, such as TAW/TAG convoys in the Caribbean and in the Gulf of Mexico; QS & SG convoys in the Gulf of St. Lawrence, SL & LS convoys to and from Freetown. Only the ships sunk in the Atlantic as far out as the Canary Islands, and North of 10 N and West of 15 W. That is, in the general North Atlantic theatre:

A Ships sunk in the 3rd quarter, 1942, excluding those in convoy as above and fishing vessels, and any lost by sea hazard, such as collisions and groundings:
   i.   152 merchant ships lost to U-boats. There were no losses in this period in this area to German raiders or aircraft.
   ii. by location: North Atlantic: 55 vessels
                      Caribbean & Gulf of Mexico: 85 vessels
                      Gulf & River St. Lawrence: 12 vessels
        (The latter two indicate the changed efforts of the Kriegsmarine southward as the USN became more efficient along the eastern seaboard, after Operation Paukenschlag.)
   iii. tonnage lost: 824,002; an average size of 5,421 grt/ship.
   iv. there is no reliable record of number of persons lost in these independents or other convoys. If the rate is taken as the same as the Atlantic convoy losses in personnel, i.e. from 69 percent of the ships and an average of 10.25 persons lost per ship: .69 x 152 x 10.25 = 1,075 persons lost.

3. Nationalities of all ships sunk in the 3rd quarter:

CONVOY SHIPS (FROM 1.G. ABOVE)	NON-CONVOY & OTHER (FROM 2.A.I. ABOVE)	TOTALS NO.	%
British: 22	British: 48	70	37%
American: 3	American: 33	36	19
Norwegian: 4	Norwegian: 17	21	11
Dutch: 1	Dutch: 12	13	7
Greek: 2	Greek: 7	9	5
Panama: 1	Panama: 7	8	4
	Brazil: 6	6	3
	Canada: 5	5	3
Belgium: 2	Belgium: 2	4	2
	Cuba: 2	2	1
	Honduras: 2	2	1
	Mexico: 2	2	1
	Sweden: 2	2	1
	Egypt: 1	1	fi
	Latvia: 1	1	fi
	Nicaragua: 1	1	fi
	Spain: 1	1	fi
	Uruguay: 1	1	fi
	U.S.S.R: 1	1	fi
	Yugoslavia: 1	1	fi

4. Total losses in 3rd quarter:

   A. Convoy losses: 35 ships — 201,747 grt
   B. Other losses to enemy: 152 — 824,002 grt
   C. Totals: 187 vessels of 1,025,749 grt
   D. This equals 2 ships sunk every day, 14 ships a week; 342,000 grt a month, on the average, in this period.

(Sources: Arnold Hague, The Allied Convoy System 1939-1945, Vanwell,
St. Catharines, 2000; Jürgen Rohwer, Axis Submarine Successes 1939-1945,
Patrick Stephens Ltd., Cambridge, (& USNI) 1983)

Glossary

AMC	Armed Merchant Cruiser: a civilian liner taken into the Navy and armed to combat surface warships
A/S	Anti-submarine; equipment, men, tactics or ships
ASV	Air-to-surface vessel radar carried in aircraft
Asdic	The equipment used to track submerged submarines by sound waves, called sonar by the USN. Invented during the First World War, and only fitted in warships
BEM	The British Empire Medal, an award for unusually valiant service
BdU	*Befehlshaber der Unterseeboote*: U-boat headquarters, in Paris, then Lorient, then near Berlin
Bos'n	Short for boatswain, the senior seaman in a merchantman
Cable	Apart from the anchor cable chain, a unit of distance measure, one tenth of a nautical mile, or about 200 yards
Canallers	Small merchantmen, almost identical with lakers, designed to pass through the pre-war upper St. Lawrence canal between Montreal and Kingston, and the Welland Canal at Port Colborne
Cbs	Confidential Books (and papers) issued to each ship, regarding radio codes and signals, routes for the convoy and alternates, location of coastal minefields. To be thrown overboard in a lead-weighted bag or box if the was sinking or likely to be boarded
Chief Officer	In larger ships, the next senior to the master
CNSS	Canadian National Steamships, the government's Canadian National Railway Steamship Services
Corvette	A small 950-ton, 250-foot warwith a crew of 60 to 90, speed 16 kts. Designed strictly for anti-submarine work just before the war Cutter USCG escort ships of various sizes, from the size of corvettes to almost destroyer size
DEMS	Defensively Equipped Merchant Ships and ratings
Depth Charge	A 350-pound canister with a depth-influenced firing mechanism in a 5-inch diameter central tube, dropped from warships and aircraft on suspected U-boats
D/F	Radio direction finding of U-boats' radio transmissions. Thus HF/DF is High Frequency Direction Finding
Enigma	A complicated and very secret coding and cyphering machine used by the German Navy
Falls	The ropes by which a lifeboat is lowered, one set at each end of the boat
Fathom	Six feet; a measurement of depth. Thus 50 fathoms = 300 feet depth
First Officer	In smaller freighters, the deck officer next in rank to the master. In larger ships, second in line, after the chief officer. German ranks (in U-boats) and their abbreviations:

Fregattenkapitän (FK) - equivalent to junior Captain
Korvettenkapitän (KK) - Commander
Kapitänleutnant (KL) - Lieutenant Commander
Oberleutnant zur See (OL) - Lieutenant
Leutnant zur See (LzS) - Junior Lieutenant or Sub Lieutenant

grt	Gross Registered Tonnage of a merchantman. The official weight measurement of the plus normal stores, but not cargo. Other measurements are net and gross tonnage
Hatches	The large wood or metal covers over the tops of the merchant ships' holds, usually covered with canvas and wedged in place
Holds	The large spaces below decks in freighters in which their cargo was stored
Kriegsmarine	The German Navy of 1933 to 1945 (before that it had been the *Kaiserlichtmarine* and the *Reichsmarine*; post-war it was the *Bundesmarine*, and now is the *Deutschesmarine*).
Lakers	Merchant ships designed for the Great Lakes and St. Lawrence. Flat bottomed, with a small bridge right forward and engines right aft
Master	The traditional title for the captain of a merchantman
MBE	An award of Member of the Order of the British Empire, like the BEM, but for officers
MWT	The British Ministry of War Transport; successor to the Board of Trade, which became the Ministry of Shipping, then became the MWT
NOIC	Naval Officer In Charge of merchant routing and reporting in all sea ports
NSHQ	Naval Service Headquarters in Ottawa
Oerlikon	A Swiss-developed anti-aircraft heavy machine gun firing a 20mm explosive shell, useful in fending off surfaced U-boats, which were often supplied with the same guns themselves
Plimsoll Marks	The painted indication on a merchantman's side indicating the depth to which she can be safely loaded
Rafts	In addition to lifeboats, most merchantmen were eventually supplied with quick-release wooden three-foot thick rafts. Some were even provided with emergency food and supply lockers. Early ones were simply wooden frameworks over half a dozen empty barrels
RCNR	The Royal Canadian Naval Reserve, those officers and seamen with merchant or fishing schooner experience who joined the wartime Canadian Navy. The permanent force personnel were RCN, the inexperienced volunteers the RCNVR
Schnorkel	A U-boat's folding mast allowing it to draw air from the surface and expel exhaust while the boat itself remained submerged, permitting use of its diesel engines rather than battery power
Sonar	American term for British asdic anti-submarine detection equipment
Standing rigging	The permanent heavy wire stays supporting the ships' masts and funnels
ULTRA	The top secret name given to decoded German messages generated by the supposedly unbreakable Enigma cyphering machines
Wolf Pack	A group of U-boats operating together under direction from BdU
USCG	United States Coast Guard - ships, men or aircraft
USN, USS	United States Navy, United States
Western Approaches	The area to the west of the United Kingdom and Ireland, out to some 250 miles and more as the war progressed, controlled from Liverpool

Bibliography

Published Sources

Attiwill, Kenneth. *The Singapore Story*. London: Frederick Muller, 1959.

Barry, James P. *Ships of the Great Lakes*. Berkeley, CA: Howell-North Books, 1974.

Bekker, C.D. *K-Men*, London: William Kimber Pocket Books, 1961.

Bekker, Cajus *The Luftwaffe Diaries*. New York: Ballantine Books, (pocket book edition), 1969.

Bennett, G.H. & R. Bennett. *Survivors: British Merchant Seamen in the Second World War*. London: The Hambledon Press, 1999.

Blair, Clay. *Hitler's U-boat War; The Hunters, 1939-1942*. Wiedenfeld & Nicolson, 1997.

Borrett, William. *Down To the Sea Again*. Halifax: Imperial Publishing Co., 1847.

Boutillier. James A., ed. *The RCN In Retrospect, 1910-1968*. Vancouver: University of British Columbia Press, 1982.

Bowen, Dana T. *Lore of the Lakes*. Cleveland: Freshwater Press, 1973.

Stephens, Patrick. *British Vessels Lost at Sea, 1939-45*. Cambridge: HMSO, 1976.

Brown, David. *WarLosses of World War Two*. Revised ed. Annapolis: Naval Institute Press, 1995.

Burrow, Len, and Emile Beaudoin. *Unlucky Lady: The Life & Death of HMCS Athabaskan*. Stittsville: Canada's Wings Inc., 1982.

Busch, Rainer and Hans-Joachim Röll. *German U-boat Commanders of World War II*. London: Greenhill Books, 1999.

Cameron, James M. *Ships And Seamen Of New Glasgow*. New Glasgow: Hector Publishing, 1959.

Canadian Fisherman, Dartmouth, N.S. Aug. 1942.

Caplan, Ronald (ed). *Cape Breton Shipwreck Stories*. Wreck Cove, Cape Breton: Breton Books, 1999.

Dickson, W.W.F. ("Seedie") Chatterton. *Seedie's List of Merchant Navy Awards for World War II*. Tisbury: Ripley Registers, 1990.

Collard, Edgar Andrew. *Passage To The Sea: The Story of Canada Steamship Lines*. Toronto: Doubleday Canada Ltd., 1991.

Commonwealth War Graves Commission. *The War Dead of the Commonwealth & Empire*. Halifax Memorial. Register No. 23, Parts 1 (1955) and 2 (1990). Maidenhead, Berks.

Darlington, R.A. and F.M. McKee. *The Canadian Naval Chronicle*. St. Catharines: Vanwell Publishing, 1998.

Dull, Paul S. *A Battle History of the Imperial Japanese Navy (1941-1945)*. Annapolis: Naval Institute Press, 1978.

Dunmore, Spencer. *In Great Waters*. Toronto: McClelland & Stewart Inc., 1999.

Edwards, Bernard. *Dönitz and the Wolf Packs*. London: Cassell Military Classics, 1999.

Essex, James W. *Victory in the St. Lawrence*. Erin: The Boston Mills Press, 1984.

Ferguson, David M. *The Wrecks of Scapa Flow*. The Orkney Press, 1985.

Fizzard, Garfield. *Unto the Sea: A History of Grand Bank*. St. John's: Dicks & Co., 1987.

Foo, Vincent H.K. and Chai Foh Chin. *Story of the Sarawak Steamship Company*. Kuching: Sarawak Steamship Co., 2001.

Gannon, Michael. *Operation Drumbeat*. New York: Harper & Row Publishing, 1990.

Gentile, Gary. *Track of the Grey Wolf*. New York: Avon Books, 1989.

German, Tony. *The Sea Is At Our Gates*. Toronto: McClelland & Stewart, 1990.

Greenwood, John O. *Namesakes*. Vols II-IX. Cleveland: Freshwater Press, var. dates.

Gröner, Erich. Revised by Dieter Jung & Martin Maass. *German Warships, 1815-1945*. Vols. 1 and 2. Annapolis: Naval Institute Press, 1990.

Hacking, Norman R. And W. Kaye Lamb. *The Princess Story*. Vancouver: Mitchell Press, 1974.

Hadley, Dr. M.L. *U-boats Against Canada*. Kingston: McGill Queen's Press,1985.

Hague, Arnold. *The Allied Convoy System 1939-1945, Its Organization, Defence and Operation*. St. Catharines: Vanwell Publishing, 2000.

Halford, Robert G. *The Unknown Navy: Canada's World War II Merchant Navy*. St. Catharines: Vanwell Publishing, 1995.

Halifax Herald. 1 June 1943.

Hannington, Felicity. *The Lady Boats. Halifax: Canadian Marine Transportation Centre,* Dalhousie University, 1980.

Harris, John. *Without Trace.* N.p. British Columbia, 1982.

Hay, Doddy. *War Under the Red Ensign, The Merchant Navy.* London: Jane's Publishing, 1982.

Heal, S.C. *Conceived In War, Born In Peace.* Vancouver: Cordillera Books, 1992.

Hickam, Homer H. Jr. *Torpedo Junction.* Annapolis: Naval Institute Press, 1996.

Hogan, Margaret. *Esso Mariners, a History of Imperial Oil's Fleet Operations.* Toronto: Imperial Oil Ltd., 1980.

Holman, Gordon. *The King's Cruisers.* London: Hodder and Stoughton, 1947.

How, Douglas. *Night Of The Caribou.* Hantsport, N.S.: Lancelot Press, 1988.

Howarth, Stephen, and Derek Law. *The Battle of the Atlantic 1939-1945.* London: Greenhill Books, 1994. Papers given at a 1993 conference, Liverpool.

Hughes, John. *Port in a Storm.* Liverpool: Merseyside Port Folios, 1993.

Hughes, Terry, and John Costello. *The Battle of the Atlantic.* New York: Dial Press/John Wade, 1977.

Imperial Oil Review. Toronto: Imperial Oil Ltd., various dates, 1941 to 1994.

Infield, Glenn B. *Disaster At Bari.* New York: Ace Books, 1971.

Joubert de la Ferté, Sir Philip. *The Third Service.* London: Thames & Hudson, 1955.

Kaplan, Philip & Jack Currie. *Convoy: Merchant Sailors at War 1939-1945.* Annapolis: Naval Institute Press, 1998.

———Wolf Pack, *U-Boats at War 1939-1945.* London: Arum Press Ltd., 1997.

Kemp, Paul. *Underwater Warriors.* England: Brockhampton Press, 1999.

Kemp, Peter. *Escape Of The Scharnhorst and Gneisenau.* Shepperton: Ian Allan, 1975.

Koop, Gerhard and Klaus-Peter Schmolke. *Pocket Battleships of the Deutschland Class.* London: Greenhill Books, 2000.

Krammer, Arnold. *Nazi Prisoners of War in America.* Lanham, MD: Scarborough House, 1992.

Kranke, Theodore and H.J. Brennecke. *Pocket Battleship.* New York: Berkley Publishing Corp., 1958.

Kurowski, Franz. *Knight's Cross Holders Of The U-boat Service.* Atglen, PA: Schiffer Publishing Ltd., 1995.

Lamb, James B. *On The Triangle Run.* Toronto: Macmillan of Canada, 1986.

Lamb, W. Kaye. *Empress to the Orient.* Vancouver: Vancouver Maritime Museum, 1991.

Legion Magazine. Various issues, 1992-2001. Ottawa: Royal Canadian Legion.

Lenton, H.T. *German Surface Vessels. Vol.1.* London: Macdonald & Co., 1966.

———*American Gunboats & Minesweepers.* London: MacDonald & Co. and Jane's Fact Files, 1974.

Lloyd's Register of Merchant Shipping. London: various editions from 1900 to 1942,.

London Gazette. 19 Nov. 1940.

Lund, Paul and Harry Ludlam. *Night of the U-boats.* London: New English Libray, Nel Paperback, 1974.

The Lunenburg Times. Halifax: Effective Publishing Ltd., 2001.

Macht, Wally. *The First 50 Years; A History of Upper Lakes Shipping Ltd.* Toronto: Virgo Press, 1981.

Macintyre, Donald. *The Battle of the Atlantic.* London: B.T. Batsford Ltd., 1961.

MacKay, Donald. *The People's Railway.* Vancouver: Douglas & McIntyre, 1993.

Macpherson, Kenneth R. and Ron Barrie. *The Ships of Canada's Naval Forces 1910-2002.* 3rd edition. St. Catharines: Vanwell Publishing, 2002.

Mann, Alan. *The Wallaceburg News.* Var. articles. Wallaceburg, Ont., 1996.

McCormick, Daniel C. *The Wishbone Fleet.* Massena, NY: Daniel C. McCormick, 1972.

McKee, Fraser M. *The Armed Yachts Of Canada.* Erin: The Boston Mills Press, 1983

———"Princes Three." War International. March, 1970.

McLean, David and Antony Preston. *Warship, 1997-1998.* London: Conway Maritime Press, 1997.

Milner, Marc. *North Atlantic Run.* Toronto: University of Toronto Press, 1985.

———*The U-Boat Hunters.* Toronto: University of Toronto Press, 1994.

Mitchell, W.H. and L.A. Sawyer. *The Oceans, The Forts And The Parks.* Liverpool: Sea Breezes, n.d.

Muggenthaler, August K. *German Raiders of World War II.* London: Robert Hale, 1977.

Musk, George. *Canadian Pacific Afloat, 1883-1968.* Montreal: Canadian Pacific, 1968.

———*Canadian Pacific, The Story.* Newton Abbott: David & Charles, 1981.

Neary, Steve. *The Enemy on Our Doorstep: Bell Island.* St. John's: Jesperson Publishing Ltd., 1994.

Newbolt, Henry. *A Naval History of the War, 1914-1918*. London: Hodder and Stoughton. 2nd edition, n.d.

HMSO. *British Vessels Lost at Sea 1939-45*. 1947. Reprint. Cambridge: Patrick Stephens, 1976.

Onchulenko, Gene and Skip Gillham. *The Ships Of The Paterson Fleet*. St. Catharines: Riverbank Traders, n.d.

Paquette, Edward R. and Charles G. Bainbridge. *Honours and Awards: Canadian Naval Forces World War II*. Vancouver: E.W. Bickle Ltd., n.d.

Parker, Mike. *Running the Gauntlet: An oral history*. Halifax: Nimbus Publishing, 1994.

Parsons, Robert C. *Lost At Sea. Vol. 2*. Grand Bank, NFLD: Parsons, 1992.

———*Wake Of The Schooners*. Grand Bank, NFLD: Parsons, 1993.

———*Toll Of The Sea*. Grand Bank, NFLD: Parsons, 1995.

Pratt E.J. *Behind The Log*. Toronto: MacMillan & Co., 1947.

Prim, Joseph and Mike McCarthy. *Those In Peril*. St. John's: Jesperson Publishing Ltd., 1945.

Raddall, Thomas H. *The Mersey Story*. Liverpool, N.S. privately pub., n.d.

Readers' Digest. *The Canadians At War 1939-45. Vols. 1 & 2*. Montreal: Readers' Digest Assn., 1969.

Reid, Max. *DEMS At War! Defensively Equipped Merchant Ships and the Battle of the Atlantic 1939-1945*. Ottawa: Commoners Publishing Society, 1990.

Richardson, Evelyn. B. *Was For Butter and Enemy Craft*. Halifax: Pentheric Press Ltd., 1976.

Robertson, Terence. *Night Raider of the Atlantic*. New York: Ballantine Books, 1974. (Also in the original *The Golden Horseshoe*. London: Evans Bros., 1955.)

Rohwer, Jürgen. *Axis Submarine Successes 1939-1945*. Cambridge: Patrick Stephens, 1983.

Roscoe, Theodore. *United States Destroyer Operations in World War II*. Annapolis: Naval Institute Press, 1953.

Runyan, Timothy J. and Jan M. Copes. *To Die Gallantly: The Battle of the Atlantic*. Oxford: Westview Press, 1994.

Roskill, Stephen W. *The War At Sea*. 3 vols. London: HMSO, 1950-59.

———*The Secret Capture*. London: Collins Publishing, 1959.

Ruge, Friedrich. *Der Seekrieg*. Annapolis: Naval Institute Press, 1957.

Schmalenback, Paul. *German Raiders*. Cambridge: Patrick Stephens, 1979.

Schull, Joseph. *Far Distant Ships*. Ottawa: King's Printer, 1950.

Shipping Today And Yesterday. April 2000.

Stanton, Samuel W. *Great Lakes Steam Vessels*. Meriden, CT: Meriden Gravure Co., 1962.

Syrett, David. *The Battle of the Atlantic And Signals Intelligence: U-Boat Situations And Trends, 1941-1945*. Aldershot: Navy Records Society/Ashgate Publishing, 1998.

Tarrant, V.E. *The Last Year of the Kriegsmarine, May 1944 - May 1945*. London: Arms & Armour Press, 1996.

Torzen, Christian. *Soefolk og Skibe 1939-1945*. Copenhagen: Grafisk Forlag, c. 1985.

Trembley, David. *How Great the Harvest Is*. Thunder Bay: Paterson SS Co., 1984.

Trident. Various editions.

Tucker, Gilbert N. *The Naval Service of Canda. Vol. II*. Ottawa: King's Printer, 1952.

US Naval Historical Center. *Dictionary of American Fighting Ships*. Washington, 1959-1991. Also DANFS website reference.

van der Vat, Dan. *The Atlantic Campaign*. New York: Harper & Row, 1988.

van Deurs, George. *Proceedings*. Annapolis: USNI, January 1970.

———*Naval Engineers' Journal*. Washington, October 1974.

von der Porten, Edward P. Pictorial *History of the German Navy In World War II*. New York: Thomas Y. Crowell & Co., 1976.

Wallaceburg News. Wallaceburg, Aug. 1996.

Whitley, M.J. *German Coastal Forces of World War Two*. London: Arms & Armour Press, 1992.

Wilcox, Garnet and Skip Gillham. *The Ships of Upper Lakes Shipping*. St. Catharines: Riverbank Traders, 1994.

Winton, John. *Convoy: The Defence of Sea Trade 1890-1990*. London: Michael Joseph, 1983.

Woodward, David. *The Secret Raiders*. London: William Kimber, 1955.

Wynn, Kenneth. *U-Boat Operations Of the Second World War. Vols. 1 & 2*. Annapolis: Naval Institute Press, 1997.

Unpublished Sources

Canada. National Archives. Requisition notes, RG 12: Upper Lakes & St. Lawrence Shipping; RG 95.

Canada. Veterans Affairs web site. Merchant Navy Book of Remembrance and Newfoundland Book of Remembrance.

Canada. Transport Canada. [Ottawa]: Marine Services Records Section for Masters' details. Charlottetown, PEI.

Canada. Directorate of History and Heritage. [Ottawa]: Department of National Defence. Vertical files, Merchant Shipping General, and Ships A-Z; WIR's, 1942.

Canada. Commonwealth War Graves Commission website for Register details, plus some crew personal detail.

Fisher, Robert C. *Directorate of History and Heritage.* [Ottawa]: Department of National Defence. Reference notes on losses. (Version 5.0)

Fisheries Museum of the Atlantic, Lunenburg, Nova Scotia. Vertical ships' files.

Helsingor, Denmark. Danish Maritime Museum. Reports on ex-Danish ships. Translated by Knud Jensen, Markdale.

Kew, England. Public Record Office (PRO). Survivor interviews, ADM116 & 199. Shipping Casualty Section, Trade Division records. Cited as SCS interviews.

Mackenzie, Dr. K.S. Paper on the Canadian Merchant Marine. Prepared for Directorate of History and Heritage, Ottawa, 1988.

Marine-Rail Museum, Owen Sound, Ontario. Vertical files, ships & companies.

van der Linden, Father Peter. Notes. Detroit.

Various web sites re convoys, USN, RCN ships; Veterans Affairs Canada (VAC); <U-boat.net>; Cabinet documents, 1956, Vols. 22-747; USN's Armed Guard - <armed-guard.com>

Washington D.C. Naval Historical Section, Washington Navy Yard. USN OPNAV files (Chief of Naval Operations) Op-16-B-5, Survivor Interviews.

Correspondence

Doug Adams (*Vancouver Island*); Air Cmdre Leonard Birchall (*Capo Noli*); Mrs. Walter Bowen (*Mont Louis*); Richard Breeze (*Mildred Pauline*); Bill Butland (*Albert C. Field*); LCdr J. Butterfield (*Jasper Park*); Mike Cooper, Merseyside; CDR C.W. Copelin (Markland ships): Zoe Cuthbertson (*Collingdoc*); Bernard de Neumann (*Portadoc*): Floyd Domina (*Canadian Cruiser*); Cmdre J.J. Drent (CP ships); Robert Dundas (*Vancouver Island*); C.B. Ellwood (*Reine Marie Stewart*); V.H.K. Foo (*Shinai*); Ralph Getson (Imperial Oil ships); John Henderson; Masahiro Kawai, JNIDS (*Shinai*); Jack Keeping (*Helen Forsey*); Ole Kolborg, Denmark (*Europa*); Lloyd's Register (*J.B. White*); Ken MacAskill; Alan Mann (*Sarniadoc*); Mrs. Johanne McKee (N.S. schooners); Captain Joseph Prim (Newfoundland ships & schooners); Dr. Achille Rastelli, Italy (*Capo Noli*); Captain Cecil Ritcey (*Mona Marie*); George Shaker (*A.D. Huff*); Captain John Smith (*Caribou*); Geoff Tozer (*Empress of Asia*); Captain Earle Wagner; Dr. Robert Wright (*Shinai*).

Index

INDEX OF U-BOATS